Study Guide
for use with

Understanding
CANADIAN BUSINESS
fourth edition

William G. Nickels
University of Maryland

James M. McHugh
St. Louis Community College at Forest Park

Susan M. McHugh
Applied Learning Systems

Paul D. Berman
Retired Chartered Accountant and Professor of Business

Rita Cossa
McMaster University

PREPARED BY

Raymond Klapstein
Dalhousie University

**McGraw-Hill
Ryerson**

Toronto   Montréal   Boston   Burr Ridge, IL   Dubuque, IA   Madison, WI   New York   San Francisco   St. Louis
Bangkok   Bogotá   Caracas   Kuala Lumpur   Lisbon   London   Madrid   Mexico City   Milan   New Delhi
Santiago   Seoul   Singapore   Sydney   Taipei

McGraw-Hill
Ryerson Limited
A Subsidiary of The McGraw·Hill Companies

Study Guide for use with
Understanding Canadian Business
Fourth Edition

ISBN: 0-07-089806-5

1 2 3 4 5 6 7 8 9 10 CP 0 9 8 7 6 5 4 3

Printed and bound in Canada

Vice President and Editorial Director: Pat Ferrier
Sponsoring Editor: Lenore Gray Spence
Managing Editor, Development: Kim Brewster
Director of Marketing: Jeff MacLean
Supervising Editor: Anne Macdonald
Production Coordinator: Paula Brown
Cover Design: Sharon Lucas
Cover Image Credits: Stephen Simpson/FPG—Canada Inc.
Printer: Canadian Printco

Table of Contents

CHAPTER 1

Major Trends Affecting Canadian Business

Learning Goals

After you have read and studied this chapter, you should be able to
1. Explain the importance and impact of technological developments.
2. Describe what is meant by the *information age* and what its implications are.
3. Discuss the globalization of business and why it is important for Canadian companies.
4. Identify how big business is becoming more competitive and the pressures to do so.
5. Explain why small and home-based businesses have become so popular.
6. Show how the service sector has replaced manufacturing as the principal provider of jobs but manufacturing remains vital for Canada.
7. Explain current population trends and their major impact on business.
8. Describe how environmental and other ethical issues play a major role in all business planning and actions.
9. Show how jobs and careers are affected by the trends discussed in the chapter.

Key Terms and Definitions

Listed here are important terms found in this chapter. Choose the correct term for each definition and write it in the space provided.

business   globalization   restructuring
customer-driven   goods-producing sector   service sector
decentralized   information age   sustainable development
empowerment   joint ventures or strategic alliances

1. _____*globalization*_____ A globally integrated system of production, marketing, finance, and management.

2. _____*customer-driven*_____ Customer satisfaction becomes the driving force that permeates the company.

3. _____*goods-producing sector*_____ The sector of society that produces tangible products, things that can be seen or touched.

4. _____*empowerment*_____ The leaders of organizations give their workers the freedom, incentives, and the training to be decision makers and creative contributors to the organization.

5. _____*sustainable dev't*_____ Economic development that meets the needs of the present without endangering the external environment of future generations.

6. _____*business*_____ An organization that manufactures or sells goods or services in the attempt to generate a profit.

7. _____*joint ventures*_____ Arrangements whereby two or more companies cooperate for a special or limited purpose.

8. _Restructuring_ — The process of reorganizing the structure of companies to make them more efficient.

9. _Service Sector_ — The sector of society that provides intangible products such as financial, information, marketing, health, recreational, and repair services.

10. _Information Age_ — An era in which information is a crucial factor in the operation of organizations.

11. _Decentralized_ — Decision making is spread downward from the top of an organization.

Trends

Describe the two most important universal trends affecting the nature of the business world today.

Technology — technology has radically altered the way we produce and what we produce, the way we communicate, the way we buy & sell etc.

Globalization — advances in comm. & transportation have made the planet into a very small place and have made it possible for business' to operate globally.

The Technological Revolution

Identify the three major effects on business of electronic marvels like computers, faxes, communication satellites, and fibre optics.

- Rate of technological change continues to accelerate
- Information age has arrived
- Distance is shrinking due to better trans. & communication
- Business operations are changing more rapidly than ever before

The Information Age

The 19th century and early 20th century were the era of production. We are now in the information age. Explain why information is a key to competitiveness at the beginning of the 21st century.

Because now companies are able to track shipments, guarantee to customers that they will receive their product within the given times.
• Enhanced competition means shorter response times are necessary
• Communication is easier & faster
and due to information

The Globalization of Business

Explain why British Columbia leads the country in trade and investment with the Pacific Rim.

Because BC is the closest by trader for these countries ie. China, Japan South Korea, Indonesia etc.
→ Free trade

Big Business Sharpens Its Competitive Position

1. Describe how computers have contributed to the restructuring of companies, including cutbacks in staffing.

   - Managers use computers instead of middle managers to get info and keep on top of operations
   - Use computers to become more efficient, more organized.

2. How has the increased delegation of power associated with restructuring benefited companies?

   decision making is decentralized

   - aid to greater effectiveness is a more rapid response to the demands of the market and to challenges from competitors.
   - faster reaction time to demands and challenges → improves companies ability to compete
   - lower level man. feel greater responsibility → feel more fulfilling → increase performance

3. How did the "throw-away philosophy" of the 1960s, which emphasized the volume of products produced rather than their quality, harm Canadian and American business?

4. In the book *Workplace 2000* some of the trends discussed include the following:
   As businesses strive to become more effective and efficient in serving people, several trends are surfacing.
   - ☐ restructuring organizations
   - ☐ empowering employees
   - ☐ emphasizing leadership versus management

   Listed below are several situations which reflect these trends. Read the situation and describe which trend has caused the situation to occur.

   a. Dave Robinson was sent to Banff for a week-long seminar on self-directed work teams. Afterward, Dave will be responsible for organizing his work area into these types of teams, as well as be a part of a team.

   b. In describing his role when he was CEO of NeXt Computers, Steven Jobs said that part of his job was to be the keeper and reiterator of the vision.

   c. Ford reduced the number of layers of management in a typical assembly plant from 15 to 10.

3

Small Business: A Growing Impact on the Canadian Economy

1. List the three criteria used to determine whether a business falls into the category of being a small business.

   - is it independently operated
   - is not dominant in its field
   - meets certain size limits in terms of number of employees and annual sales   Emp. from 0-100, sales up to 10 million, profit $200 000.00

   ★ small bus. are 60% of our GDP

2. It is estimated that as much as 53% of self-employed Canadians are home-based. List as many reasons for this development as you can think of.   *9% of our workforce*

   - flexible work hours
   - quality lifestyle
   - doing the work of your choice
   - self-motivation
   - opportunity to expand using technology

The Service Sector   *78% of workers (2000)*

Describe three factors that have contributed to the increase in employment in the service sector of the Canadian economy in recent years, and are expected to continue to cause growth in this sector to outpace growth in goods-producing areas for the remainder of this century.

• Technological improvements - helps business to reduce payroll while increasing output
• Other service firms - led to the proliferation of service specialists
*   - traditional services that used to be done by women at home have created many more service jobs such as food prep., child care, household maintenance etc.*
• Gov't - Education, health care, public admin.

How Important Is Manufacturing to Canada?

1. State the main arguments in favour of and against continuation of the significance of the Canadian manufacturing industry in the future.

   FOR - service & manufacture sectors feed each other
   *   - companies can't make products if they can't get the raw materials from the manufacturing industry*

2. How is it misleading to say that there will be almost no growth in goods-producing industries in the future?

3. The text indicates that the trends to watch for in the next decade include: genetic engineering, multi-sensory robotics, high-tech ceramics, fibre-reinforced composites, and super-conductors. What kinds of jobs may be created in these industries? What do these businesses have in common? What should that tell you about the kind of preparation you will need to get ahead for a career in the future?

_____
_____
_____
_____
_____

Population Trends

1. List the major demographic or population trends that will affect Canadian business over the next few decades.
   - Baby boom era will retire within next 10 years
   - declining birthrate due to "the pill" touched everyone - schools, real estate etc.
   - population continues to age
   - caring for the aged is a growth sector in our economy - really big soon

2. Trends in the population, in society, and in the way we live have had a major impact on Canadian business during the last decade. Briefly, the major trends or changes include

   A. Demographic trends
      1. An increase in the older adult population over 65
      2. Increase in middle-aged adults between 35 and 65
      3. Fewer younger workers in the labour pool
      4. The aging of the baby boom generation
      5. Higher incomes for people aged 55 and over

   B. Social trends
      1. More women in the workplace
      2. Increase in women's pay
      3. Increase in two-income families
      4. Fewer children, later in life
      5. Demand for a better, more comfortable life

   C. International trade and investment, globalization
   D. Concern for ethics in management
   E. Growth of environmentalism
   F. Emphasis on quality

   Listed below are several situations which are reflective of these trends and changes. Read the situations and describe what trend or trends have caused each situation to occur. There could be several trends happening concurrently.

   a. McDonnell Douglas publishes a written code of ethics for its employees.
      Ethics in management

   b. Mail Boxes Etc. and five pellet manufacturers devise a method to recycle nonbiodegradable plastic pellets used in packaging.
      Growth of environmentalism

   c. An advertisement depicts a man using a hair care product to enhance the colour of his already gray hair.
      increase in middle-aged & older adults

d. A day care centre that takes infants from six weeks of age has a waiting list. The centre charges $155/week for infant care.

increase for women in workforce

e. McDonald's runs television advertisements showing a retiree starting his first day behind the counter.

f. Ben (age 60) and Shirley (age 57) Summers build a $250,000 lake-front home in suburban Edmonton.

g. Theresa Cox graduates from law school and takes her first job as a lawyer at a salary of $45,000 a year.

h. Charlie Berkmeyer continues to teach accounting at the local community college three years after he retires. Charlie is 73.

i. In 1999 Tony Miller turned 40 and left his job as a successful lawyer to work in a provincial agency.

j. In a large metropolitan area in the Midwest, nearly 50% of the small retailers and fast food restaurants have Help Wanted signs in their windows.

k. General Electric invests $90 million in the stock of foreign firms listed on overseas stock exchanges.

l. Diamond Star Motors, a Mitsubishi Motors and Chrysler Corp. joint venture, rapidly expands production at its Bloomington-Normal, Illinois plant in 1989.

m. Used Rubber, Canada, is a fashion firm that collects inner tubes from roadsides and a curbside recycling program to use in making belts, wallets, and handbags.

n. Colleges experiencing declining enrolment in the 1980s are facing continued problems in the 1990s, as their market shrinks.

o. The Ford Probe is a combination of Mazda engine technology and Ford sheet metal.

Environmental and Other Ethical Issues

Describe how the public concern about threats to the physical environment, caused by rapid expansion of populations and industrial activities, affects Canadian business.

- companies expanding - concern to forests, wildlife etc. or Home building
- factories giving off major amounts of or
- more concern for environment → less combustion engine automobiles & more electric ones.

Careers and Jobs for the Future

1. a. What do you want to do as a career?

    _____

    _____

    _____

    b. What kinds of jobs have you had up to this point in your life?

    — grocery store _____

    _____

    _____

    c. How can you translate those jobs into a career? (What is the common theme with your previous jobs? What kinds of companies might need the skills you have developed?)

    goods-sector _____

    _____

    _____

2. a. Look in the classified ads and on the Internet for job opportunities in your area. What types of jobs can you identify? What industries are they in? How do the opportunities you found correspond to the information in the text regarding these areas?

    _____

    _____

    _____

    b. How can you take advantage of these opportunities?

    1. training _____ 3. stay flexable _____

    2. follow technological advancements 4. " current _____

CHAPTER CHECK

1. As of the year 2000, what percentage of British Columbia's foreign trade was with the U.S.? Pacific Rim?

    US — 67.2 %   P.Rim — 20.6 _____

    P.m — _____

2. What is Edwards Deming known for?

    teaching Japanese kids importance of quality _____

    _____

3. How many new businesses are being established annually in Canada?

    150,000 _____

    _____

4. Describe the difference between the goods-producing and the service-producing sectors.

    _____

    _____

    _____

_____

5. Why is information becoming such a critical resource today?

_____

_____

_____

6. What are four ways the labour market of today is different from that of the past?
   a. _Unions_____
   b. _imigrants make up a larger population of workers_
   c. _____
   d. _____

7. Where will the job opportunities of today and beyond be for workers in Canada?

_____

_____

8. Identify six major trends or changes in business, other than the shift to small business and the service sector.

   a.   d.
   b.   e.
   c.   f.

9. What are four demographic trends occurring in Canada?
   a. _____
   b. _____
   c. _____
   d. _____
   e. _____

10. What are five social trends affecting businesses in Canada?
   a. _____
   b. _____
   c. _____
   d. _____
   e. _____

PRACTICE TEST

Multiple Choice: Circle the best answer.

1. The major effects of computerization and other electronic innovations in our era include
   a. operations have been revolutionized
   b. the information age has been ushered in
   c. our large planet has been made into a small globe
   d. all of the above

2. A computer or other sophisticated piece of technological equipment may include components from a dozen different countries. Companies with their head offices in Canada may do more business in foreign lands than at home. Cars may be designed, engineered, and tested in various countries. These are examples of
   a. the information age
   b. eutelsat
   c. globalization
   d. the technological age
3. British Columbia leads Canadian provinces in trade with
   a. the U.S.
   b. the Pacific Rim
   c. other Canadian provinces
   d. Latin America
4. Directly, manufacturing output contributes 18% of the Canadian economy. However, it indirectly creates an additional _37_ % of economic activity.
   a. 7%
   b. 18%
   c. 37%
   d. 82%
5. In the year 1971, 8% of the Canadian population was 65 years old and over. It is expected that in the year 2011, _14_ % of the Canadian population will be in this age group.
   a. 4%
   b. 8%
   c. 14%
   d. 31%
6. In the period from 1990 to 1998, the only developed country that was able to decrease its unemployment rate to below 5% was
   a. Canada
   b. the United States
   c. Germany
   d. the United Kingdom
7. There are many large and small software companies scattered across Canada. The software industry is growing at a remarkable 25%–30% annual rate, generating large numbers of new jobs. Many of these new jobs have not been filled! By 1996, the number of job vacancies in Canada in this field was approximately
   a. 1,000
   b. 20,000
   c. 150,000
   d. 1,000,000
8. The *Asian flu* of mid-1998 was an example of
   a. the spread of an influenza virus that the world's best medical researchers were unable to find a cure for
   b. the spread of an influenza virus that the world's best medical researchers were able to find a cure for
   c. the virtual collapse of several Asian economies
   d. a disease contracted by members of the Canadian trade mission to East-Asian countries

9. The quality focus of Edwards Deming's approach to business management was first adopted in
   a. Canada
   b. the United States
   c. Germany
   d. Japan

10. The small business sector in Canada contributes 60 % of the Gross Domestic Product and 66 % of employment in the private sector
    a. 60%; 30%
    b. 25%; 33%
    c. 60%; 66%
    d. 50%; 80%

11. *Downsizing* refers to
    a. going after a smaller share of a particular market
    b. building smaller factories
    c. lowering profit expectations
    d. eliminating workers or managers to become more efficient

12. Information management today is
    a. becoming less important as computers manage information for us
    b. only important for large companies such as Bombardier or Chrysler
    c. done primarily by colleges and universities
    d. becoming increasingly important for businesses and individuals

13. The most important driver of businesses today is
    a. the expectations of the owners of the business
    b. the wants and needs of customers
    c. the demands of employees
    d. management

14. In today's environment, businesses have found that they must do all BUT which of the following in order to be competitive?
    a. meet the needs of all stakeholders
    b. supervise employees more closely
    c. delight customers by exceeding their expectations
    d. be aware of potential damage and hazards to the environment

15. As businesses increasingly serve global markets and exports continue to increase, it is likely that
    a. fewer jobs will be created in Canada
    b. students who expect to prosper will have to compete in a changing environment, and continually update their skills
    c. international trade agreements will lose their importance
    d. cooperation among firms will become less important

True/False

1. _T_ Business skills are useful in non-profit institutions.
2. _T_ Electronic data interchange has allowed for a smoother flow of information and goods between manufacturers and retailers.
3. _T_ Telecommuting has increased opportunities for men and women to raise families and increase their standard of living.
4. _F_ The more that companies decentralize their decision-making processes, the more difficult it becomes to respond quickly to market demands.
5. _T_ Participation in decision-making makes work more meaningful and fulfilling for employees.

6. __T__ About 150,000 new businesses are started annually in Canada.
7. __T__ In recent years, the small business sector has been responsible for almost all net job creation in Canada.
8. __F__ By the year 2000, the service sector accounted for 50% of all jobs in Canada.
9. __F__ Canadian demographic trends do not have a significant impact on the level of demand for goods and services.
10. __T__ The concept of *sustainable development* suggests that continuous growth is essential for a business to be profitable in the long term.
11. ____ *Jobless recovery* refers to economic recovery and growth without new job creation.
12. ____ The late 19th century and early 20th century were an era of production, focused on trying to produce enough of everything to meet people's needs.
13. __F__ Only 10% of all new companies survive their first year of operation.
14. __T__ Every dollar of manufacturing output adds three dollars of value to the Canadian economy.
15. ____ In Canada, there is an inverse relationship between unemployment and years of education.

ANSWERS

Key Terms and Definitions

1. globalization
2. customer-driven
3. goods-producing sector
4. empowerment
5. sustainable development
6. business
7. Joint ventures or strategic alliances
8. Restructuring
9. Service sector
10. Information age
11. Decentralized

Trends

The two most significant trends are **the technological revolution** (e.g., development and use of computers, robots, lasers, fibre optics, satellites) and **the globalization of business**, which makes it possible for businesses to operate on a global basis by applying recent advances in communication and transportation technology.

The Technological Revolution

The three major effects on business are
1. Operations have been revolutionized
2. The information age has been ushered in
3. Our large planet has been made into a small globe

The Information Age

Access to information about your own operations and those of your competitors, your markets, government activities, and technological developments that may affect your business is crucial. Computers and information systems are critical to competitiveness for corporations that have operations and facilities around the world. For example, Federal Express is able to promise next-day delivery to any major city in the world and know exactly where every parcel is, only because it has a computer that enables it to know where every truck and plane in its system is at all times.

The Globalization of Business

British Columbia leads because it is situated on the Pacific Ocean, and because of the substantial level of Asian capital investment and large population of Asian immigrants.

Big Business Sharpens Its Competitive Position

1. Computers are used instead of middle managers to get information to senior managers. Computers are also used to perform many of the tasks traditionally performed by factory workers, secretaries, and assistants.
2. ! More rapid response to the demands of the market and challenges from competitors.
   ! Employees and lower-level managers feel a greater sense of participation in important decisions, making their work more meaningful and fulfilling.
   ! Employees who are involved in making decisions carry them out more enthusiastically.
   ! A more satisfied workforce means fewer accidents, less absenteeism, and a lower turnover of personnel.
3. The throw-away philosophy is not customer-driven; it disregards the importance of customer satisfaction. It also fails to focus on the need to ensure that quality is as high as possible.
4. a. This reflects both restructuring and empowering. Under restructuring middle managers are often eliminated and work groups become more responsible for self-management. With the increased need for team building, problem solving, and facilitation, workers will need to have much more training in decision making and skills needed for effective teamwork.
   b. Leadership begins with a vision, a comprehensive picture of what needs to be done and how to do it. Leaders must express that vision to workers.
   c. Restructuring and elimination of middle management positions is important for survival. In a time-competitive world quick decision making is vital. Decision making can no longer filter through several layers of management before workers know what to do.

Small Business: A Growing Impact on the Canadian Economy

1. a. Independently operated
   b. Not dominant in its field
   c. Falls below certain size limits in terms of number of employees and annual sales.
2. Reasons given should include
   ] A job that the person does not like, finds unfulfilling, or provides no opportunity for advancement
   ] No other job, either because of being laid off or being unable to find one
   ] A desire to be self-employed
   ] A desire for a change in lifestyle
   ] A blocked career path, particularly for women
   ] A way to earn a livelihood while being at home to look after children

The Service Sector

1. Technological improvements have enabled businesses to reduce the number of employees while increasing output, limiting the rate of growth of employment in manufacturing. At the same time, these companies have become more specialized, relying more heavily on outside service firms.

2. As increasing numbers of women have entered the workforce, the demand for services formerly provided by women who stayed at home has grown sharply (e.g., food preparation, child care, and household maintenance).

3. The demand for government and quasi-government services has grown rapidly as a result of developments like the post-war baby boom, installation of Medicare, and increased levels of immigration.

How Important Is Manufacturing to Canada?

1. Continued importance:
   ] Canada has a large deficit in trade and investment with other countries, and exports of manufactured goods can play a significant role in reducing it.
   ] Manufacturing exports helped to lead the economy out of the deep recession of the early 1990s, and contributed to Canada's achievement of 15 consecutive quarters of growth up to March 31, 1999.
   ] Stimulating the goods sector helps the entire economy; stimulating the service sector has a much less significant payoff.
   ] The performance of the Japanese economy since the Second World War suggests a direct relationship between manufacturing and general economic success.

   Reduced importance:
   ] Some experts (e.g., Michael Walker of the Fraser Institute) say that the service sector could account for 99.9% of economic output without damaging the economy.
   ] "Knowledge workers" now make up 30% of the North American workforce, while only 10% are actually involved in production.
2. The statement is misleading because of where the changes in the manufacturing sector will occur. Major manufacturers such as GM, IBM, Ford, and others may indeed experience no growth. But there are many mid-size, innovative companies that could grow relatively rapidly. We may not know their names and, in fact, some of those companies do not yet exist.
3. The jobs that will be created include: predicting and correcting for inherited diseases, robot programming and repair, manufacturing high ceramics, and fibre-reinforced composites and superconductors, as well as marketing, accounting, finance, and research in companies specializing in these areas.

   What these new areas have in common is that they are innovative, new concepts, and they all stem from high-tech applications of scientific knowledge. To prepare for a career in the 21st century, we will need to keep current on the kinds of new, small business start-ups and get an education in areas which will provide the correct high-tech training.

Population Trends

1. ! More people are living longer. By 2011, the proportion of the population over 65 and 75 will be almost twice what it was in 1971.
   ] The proportion of the population that is very young will continue to decrease.
   ] Steady immigration will continue to speed population growth.
2. a. Concern for ethics
   b. Concern for the environment
   c. Increase in the number of middle-aged and older adults. New products meeting their needs
   d. Increase in women in the workforce and two-income families with more money to spend on family-related items. Could also represent the increase in women's pay
   e. Increases in older adults. Fewer younger workers in labour pool
   f. Wealth of the middle-aged to older adult
   g. More women in the workplace and the increase in women's pay
   h. Older adults working longer

i. Change in lifestyle
j. Fewer teenagers are available to fill low-pay service jobs
k. International investments are becoming an important part of business investment
l. Joint ventures with foreign firms have become a major element in business involvement in international trade and investment
m. Concern for the environment
n. Fewer teenagers mean fewer customers or students for colleges across the country
o. International investment through joint ventures is expected to continue

Environmental and Other Ethical Issues

] Companies can no longer make decisions based only on immediate economic interests.

] New laws impose higher standards against pollution, with the effect of increasing costs for the producer and raising prices to the consumer.

] New industries and professions are being created (e.g., recycling and waste management companies).

] Businesses are discovering new ways to reduce costs and become more competitive.

Careers and Jobs for the Future

1. Answers will vary from individual to individual.
2. a. Answers will vary
   b. (1) get trained
      (2) followed technological developments
      (3) stay flexible
      (4) stay current

CHAPTER CHECK ANSWERS

1. 67.2%; 20.6%
2. Teaching Japanese industry the importance of quality
3. 150,000
4. The goods-producing sector produces tangible items which can be touched, seen, and inspected, such as furniture and clothing. The service-producing sector provides products which are intangible, or in other words cannot be inspected before consumption. Examples would be financial and medical services.
5. In order to become more responsive to global clients and consumers, organizations will have to become better listeners, and better at giving the information to workers to do a better job designing goods and services.
6. a. The population and the number of qualified workers are growing more slowly.
   b. The pool of young workers entering the workforce is declining as the average age of the population rises.
   c. More women are entering the workforce.
   d. Immigrants make up a larger percentage of new workers.
7. Most job opportunities will be in services, but job prospects are expected to occur in every part of the economy.
8. a. Demographic trends
   b. Social trends
   c. International trade and investments, globalization
   d. Concern for ethics

e. Growth of environmentalism

f. Emphasis on quality

9. a. Increase in the adult population over 65

   b. Increase in the middle-aged adults 35–65

   c. Fewer younger workers in the labour pool

   d. The aging of the baby boom generation

   e. Higher incomes for people aged 55 and over

10. a. More women entering the workforce

    b. Increase in women's pay, especially for women with higher levels of education

    c. Dramatic growth in two-income families resulting in programs to assist two-income families

    d. Trend toward fewer children, later in life

    e. Demand for a better, more comfortable life

PRACTICE TEST

Multiple Choice		**True/False**	
1.	d	1.	T ✓
2.	c	2.	T ✓
3.	b	3.	T ✓
4.	c	4.	F ✓
5.	c	5.	T ✓
6.	b	6.	T ✓
7.	b	7.	T ✓
8.	c	8.	F ✓
9.	d ✓	9.	F ✓
10.	c ✓	10.	F ✗
11.	d ✓	11.	T
12.	d ✓	12.	T
13.	b ✓	13.	F ✗
14.	b ✓	14.	T ✓
15.	b ✓	15.	T

CHAPTER 2

How Economic Issues Affect Business

Learning Goals

After you have read and studied this chapter, you should be able to

1. Describe how free markets work, using the terms *supply*, *demand*, and *prices*.
2. Discuss some limitations of the free market system and what countries are doing to offset those limitations.
3. Understand the mixed economy of Canada.
4. Explain how inflation, recession, and other economic developments affect business.
5. Discuss the issues surrounding the National Debt and its effect on business.

Keys Terms and Definitions

Listed here are important terms found in this chapter. Choose the correct term for each definition and write it in the space provided.

capitalism	demand	national debt
consumer price index (CPI)	economics	productivity
cyclical unemployment	gross domestic product (GDP)	seasonal unemployment
deficit	inflation	structural unemployment
	mixed economy	supply

1. _____Deficit_____ An excess of expenditures over revenue.

2. _____Demand_____ The quantity of particular products or services that buyers are willing to buy at certain prices at certain locations.

3. _____GDP_____ The total value of a country's output of goods and services in a given year.

4. _____Seasonal Unemployment_____ Unemployment that occurs where the demand for labour varies over the year.

5. _____Capitalism_____ Economic system with free markets and private ownership of companies operating for profit.

6. _____Consumer Price Index_____ Monthly statistics that measure changes in the prices of a basket of goods and services that an average family would buy.

7. _____Economics_____ The study of how society chooses to employ resources to produce goods and services and distribute them for consumption among various competing groups and individuals.

8. _____Supply_____ The quantity of particular products or services that manufacturers or owners are willing to sell at certain prices at certain locations.

9. _____Structural Unemployment_____ Unemployment that results from changes in the structure of the economy that phase out certain industries or jobs.

10. _Inflation_ A general rise in the prices of goods and services over time.

11. _Productivity_ The total output of goods and services in a given period of time divided by the total hours of labour required to provide them.

12. _Cyclical Unemployment_ Unemployment caused by a recession or similar downturn in the business cycle.

13. _Mixed Economy_ An economy that includes free markets and some degree of state ownership or control of the means of production or both.

14. _National Debt_ The accumulated amount owed by the Canadian government from its past borrowings.

The Economic and Political Basis of Business Operations

1. Who is known as the *"father of economics"*?

   Adam Smith
   - wrote book "An Inquiry into the Nature and Causes of the Wealth of Nations" (1776)
   - his ideas have stuck for 150 years
   - developed theory of Capitalism → economic system with free markets...

2. In a capitalist system, who/what owns the businesses and decides what to produce, how much to produce, how much to pay workers and how much to charge for goods?

   Business people decide for their own businesses what to produce, how much to ... etc

3. What is the foundation of capitalism?
   - system of Rights & freedoms
     - right to make a profit
     - right to private property
     - right to buy or sell
     - freedom to compete
     - freedom from Gov't interference

   X How a free market works

   How prices are determined

4. What did Adam Smith believe was vital to the survival of any economy?

17

5. How does the economy benefit if workers can keep the profits they earn by working?

_____
_____
_____
_____
_____
_____

6. What is Adam Smith's theory of the invisible hand?

_____
_____
_____
_____
_____
_____

7. They're everywhere! McDonald's hamburgers can be purchased in cities and suburbs, on riverfronts, and in football stadiums. Families with sick children can stay in Ronald McDonald Houses located close to the hospital where the children are receiving treatment. Ray Kroc, the founder, started with one restaurant in 1955, and had 2500 more by 1960. How does the story of the founding and growth of McDonald's illustrate Adam Smith's invisible hand theory?

_____
_____
_____
_____
_____
_____
_____
_____

8. Why does free market capitalism lead to inequality of wealth?

_____
_____
_____
_____
_____

9. Who is known as the *"father of communism"*?

___Karl Marx_____
_____
_____
_____
_____

10. In a communist system, who/what make economic decisions?

Gov't / State

11. Why have communist systems had a problem, and what has been the result?

Because the people had very little or no control over the gov't - So the gov't could do whatever they please

Gov't doesn't know how much to produce → shortages ie food.

12. What is the basic premise of a socialist system?

13. In a socialist system, what is the government expected to provide?

jobs for everyone
-education
-healthcare
-retirement & unemployment benefits

14. Experience has shown that neither capitalism nor socialism has had optimal results in terms of the economy. What are the problems with
    a. A free market system?

    not responsive to the needs of the old, disabled, and environment

    b. Socialism and communism?

    haven't created enough jobs or wealth to keep economy growing

c. What political trends have resulted from these problems?

_____
_____
_____

15. The success of the Canadian system is based largely on an economic and political climate that allows business to operate freely.

Read the following situations and match the correct term to what is being described.

Economics; Socialist system; Communist system; Capitalist system

a. _____Communist_____ Mary Conaty often finds shortages of products she needs, because she lives in a country where the government determines the quantities of each product produced.

b. _____Economics_____ A question constantly facing those in government is how to use the limited resources available to them, and how to ensure equal distribution among competing groups and individuals.

c. _____Socialist_____ Bonnie Jergensen works for a large corporation, but lives in a country where the government owns many large businesses, and provides her with free or low-cost medical care. Her biggest problem is the high tax rate to which she is subject.

d. _____Capitalism_____ When the Andersons had their third child, they needed a bigger car. They went to several dealerships, found the car they wanted, and bargained for a price they could afford.

How Free Markets Work

1. In general, how do consumers in Canada and other free market systems send signals to producers—in others words, what tells producers what and how much to produce?

   We tell producers what and how much to make by buying them at the stores. We buy more TV's, they make more TV's.

   _____
   _____
   _____
   _____

2. What is "supply"?

   refers to quantity that manufactures are willing to (sell) at different prices

   _____
   _____
   _____
   _____

3. What happens to quantity supplied as price goes up?

    P↑ S↑

4. What is "demand"?

    Same as 'supply' but (buy)

5. What happens to demand as price goes up?

    P↑ D↓

6. Shown below is a supply schedule illustrating the relationship between price per unit and the number of units a supplier will offer.

Unit Price (dollars)	Amount Supplied (units)
125	500
100	400
75	300
50	200
25	100

    Plot a supply curve using the information listed above.

7. Shown below is a demand schedule illustrating the relationship between price per unit and the number of units demanded.

Unit Price (dollars)	Amount Demanded (units)
125	100
100	200
75	300
50	400
25	500

    a. Plot a demand curve using the information listed above.
    b. Plot the corresponding supply curve from the previous page.
    c. What is the equilibrium price? $75
    d. At this price, how many units will be produced and purchased?

        300 units

8. Indicate whether the price of a product will most likely go up or down in the following situations:
   a. U   There is a drought in Saskatchewan. What happens to the price of a bushel of wheat?
   b. D   Strawberries are in season. What happens to their price?
   c. U   It's the ski season in the Rockies. What happens to the price of motel rooms?
   d. D   A nutrition study indicates that red meat should be eaten only in moderation, if at all.
             What happens to the price of red meat?
   e. D   A major corporation announces that is has to borrow money in order to stay in business.
             What happens to the price of its stock?

9. *The haves and the have-nots.*
    Joe and Jeanne Contino, typical baby boomers, are a recently married couple in their thirties. Their combined income is around $50,000 per year. They had each been living in apartments for several years, and were interested in buying a house in a nice neighbourhood. They were surprised to find that they were unable to find a house they could afford, as housing prices in their town, in nice neighbourhoods, had skyrocketed. They resigned themselves to staying in an apartment for a while longer.

    How does this situation reflect what you know about supply, demand, and the limitations of capitalism?

    _____
    _____
    _____
    _____
    _____

10. In Winnipeg, John Starr disappears, along with several million dollars of his company's money. In Toronto an unemployed single mother with three children can barely make ends meet, and is arrested for prostitution. In Vancouver, drug dealers drive expensive imported cars. The government extends unemployment benefits for the unemployed.

    Can you draw on your own knowledge to describe similar situations? How has the free market system helped to create these and similar scenarios? What is the economic question here in terms of creating and allocating resources, and freedom versus equality.

    _____
    _____
    _____
    _____
    _____

11. What is the goal of the economic system in socialist countries, such as Sweden? What problems are inherent in this?

    _____
    _____
    _____
    _____
    _____

12 a. Julie Marshall, a recent business school graduate, got a lot of first-hand experience with socialism while working in Sweden for two years. She has been tapped by an international group of business people to act as a consultant to the emerging states of the Independent Commonwealth (formerly the Soviet Union), who are moving toward a free market system. What issues will she be dealing with?

_____

_____

_____

_____

_____

b. What form is the new capitalism likely to take in the East and other parts of the world?

_____

_____

_____

_____

_____

Mixed Economies

1. Listed below are statements that describe different aspects of the economic systems we have studied. Decide which system is being described in each statement.

   Capitalism
   Mixed economy
   Socialism
   Communism

a. _____Communism_____ Abolition of private property and of all right to inheritance.

b. _____Mixed_____ Government control of some areas, such as postal service, but most industries privately owned.

c. _____Socialism_____ A system depending upon private enterprise to create wealth, and the government to create even distribution of wealth.

d. _____Comm_____ Organizations owned by the state, with profits going to the state.

e. _____Cap_____ An economic system built upon the foundations of freedom and incentives.

f. _____Mixed_____ Scarcity and oversupply controlled by government.

g. _____Social_____ An economic system that tries to meet the needs of all its people by allowing private enterprise, but that maintains government control of such areas as health and dental care, among others.

h. _____Communish_____ An economic system in which resource allocation is almost exclusively government controlled.

i. _____mixed Cap_____ Resource allocation depends on bargaining and trading goods and services between individual consumers and organizations.

j. _____Cap_____ A system built upon basic rights for its citizens, including the right to private property.

k. _____ You have a guaranteed job, but it might not be what you want to do.

l. _____ You have no guarantee, or right, to a job; you could end up on the streets as a result of long-term unemployment, but hard workers are rewarded for high productivity.

m. _____ A system based on a blend of private enterprise and government control.

n. _____ Government regulation to assure fair trade among nations.

Economics and Business

1. What was the annual growth rate of Canada's GDP in the 1960s? 1970s? 1980s? 1990s?

   1960 - 5.2   1970 - 4.3   1980 - 3.2

   1990 - 3.7

2. Bob Sloan is concerned. He is up for promotion at General Dynamo where he has worked for several years, the last three of which were spent as general manager of the G.D. Service division. His counterpart, Gerry Franz, is also in line for the job Bob wants. Gerry is general manager of a manufacturing division. Bob's concern is that while he has completely automated his division and has received recognition for high-quality work, productivity in his division is only up by 1%. Gerry's division through automation has increased productivity by over 6%. Bob is afraid he won't look as good as Gerry in performance reviews. What's the problem?

   _____

   _____

   _____

3. What is "productivity"?

   G&S   the output of goods & services in a given period divided by the
   labour   total hours of labour

4. What is the benefit of an increase in productivity?

   You produce more products in less time → more $

   _____

5. What is the difficulty in measuring productivity in the service sector?

   _____

   _____

   _____

6. Discuss the relationship between productivity and price levels. What is the relationship between productivity and Gross Domestic Product?

   _____

   _____

   _____

The Issue of Unemployment

1. There are three categories of unemployment: structural, seasonal, and cyclical. Match the situations being described below and the category of unemployment each demonstrates.

   a. _____ As foreign imports increase their market share, Canadian auto makers lay off thousands of workers.

   b. _____ A migrant worker, finished with his job in the orchards of the Okanagan, travels to Alberta to look for a job harvesting grain.

   c. _____ A clerical worker is laid off because her job has been eliminated with the installation of updated word-processing equipment.

2. Governments have often applied the basic principles of Keynesian economics in attempts to slow inflation or grapple with high unemployment. Explain how Keynes believed that fiscal policy can be used to achieve these goals.

   _____

   _____

   _____

   _____

   _____

Inflation and the Consumer Price Index

1. What is the difference between inflation and deflation?

   inflation - consumer prices go up
   deflation - consumer prices go down

2. Why is the CPI an important figure? What does it measure?

   measures monthly changes in price
   - important because gov't benefits, wages, salaries, interest rates are
     dependent on it

3. How much is the national debt? What is the daily interest on this amount of national debt?

   $600 billion / $100 million

CHAPTER CHECK

1. What is the "equilibrium point" on a graph of supply and demand?

   where supply & demand meet or intersect.

   _____

   _____

   _____

2. What are the basic rights of individuals living in a capitalist system?

   _____

   _____

   _____

3. Why did the Canadian economy develop with a greater degree of government involvement than the U.S. economy?

_____

_____

_____

_____

4. Approximately, what was Canada's inflation rate in 2001? What was the range of unemployment rates from 1989 to 1998?

_____

_____

5. What do most experts predict will happen with inflation, interest rates, and unemployment levels in Canada over the next few years?

_____

_____

_____

_____

6. What important factor do the experts say has led them to their predictions about future unemployment levels in Canada?

_____

_____

_____

_____

7. What are the implications of these expert predictions about future levels of unemployment in Canada for people like you who will be seeking jobs?

_____

_____

_____

_____

PRACTICE TEST

Multiple Choice: Circle the best answer.

1. Bill Ding started his own construction company to support his family. The going was slow at first, but after some time Bill got so busy he had to hire three workers. Bill and his workers do high quality work, and now there is quite a demand for their services. Bill is considering hiring two more people. He also has an exclusive deal with a local lumber yard. Because of Bill's business, the yard has added another employee. This is an example of the _____ in action.
   a. marketing concept   c. benefits of communism
   b. invisible hand   d. resources development theory

2. One of the problems with _____ is that it naturally leads to unequal distribution of wealth.
   a. communism   c. a command economy
   b. socialism   d. capitalism

3. Karl Marx believed that
   a. businesses should be owned by workers and decisions should be made by the government.
   b. business and government should not mix, and so all businesses should be privately owned by stockholders.
   c. capitalism was not the kind of system where wealth could be created.
   d. eventually all of the countries in the world would operate under capitalist beliefs.
4. Citizens of socialist nations can rely on the government to provide all of the following EXCEPT
   a. education
   b. health care
   c. unemployment and retirement benefits
   d. money to start a business
5. What kind of a system exists when the marketplace largely determines what goods and services get produced, who gets them, and how the economy grows?
   a. command economy   c. free market economy
   b. socialist economy   d. communist economy
6. Most countries in the world have a _____ economy.
   a. capitalist   c. mixed
   b. socialist   d. communist
7. Which of the following is NOT one of the four basic rights of a capitalist system?
   a. The right to have a job
   b. The right to private property
   c. The right to compete
   d. The right to freedom of choice
8. Typically, the quantity of products that manufacturers are willing to supply will _____ when prices _____ .
   a. increase/increase   c. stay the same/increase
   b. decrease/increase   d. increase/stay the same
9. A(n) _____ shows the amount people are willing to buy at the prices at which sellers are willing to sell.
   a. supply curve   c. marginal revenue point
   b. demand curve   d. equilibrium point
10. One holiday season a few years ago, there was a toy called Tickle My Elbow that was all the rage. Demand for this toy was so high that stores couldn't keep them on the shelves! There was quite a shortage of Tickle My Elbow that year. When a shortage such as this exists, what generally happens?
    a. The price goes up.
    b. The price stays the same, and mothers everywhere fight for the last toy.
    c. The government intervenes, and forces the manufacturer to make more of the toy.
    d. When customers realize they can't get the toy, they give up, and the price goes down.

11. Which of the following would NOT be considered a key economic indicator?
    a. GDP
    c. the tax rate
    b. the unemployment rate
    d. the price indexes
12. Juan Valdez was laid off from his job at the coffee factory because the demand for coffee weakened. The kind of unemployment Juan is experiencing would be
    a. frictional
    c. structural
    b. seasonal
    d. cyclical
13. Measures to increase productivity
    a. are failing in manufacturing, as productivity is slowly decreasing
    b. can improve quality of service providers, but not always improve worker output
    c. are always successful in manufacturing and services industries
    d. are becoming unimportant in today's competitive market
14. Which of the following probably won't occur during a recession?
    a. high unemployment
    c. drop in the standard of living
    b. increase in business failures
    d. increase in interest rates
15. The sum of all the federal deficits over time is known as the
    a. fiscal policy
    c. national debt
    b. gross national debt
    d. aggregate demand for money

True/False

1. _____ Adam Smith believed that as long as workers, or entrepreneurs, had the freedom to own property (or business), and could see economic reward for their efforts, they would work long hours.
2. _____ One of the consequences of a socialist system is a high tax rate on those who do work, in order to pay for services for those who don't, or can't work.
3. _F_ Canada has a purely free market economy.
4. _____ In a free market system, price is determined through negotiation between buyers and sellers.
5. _____ When there is a surplus of products, manufacturers will tend to raise the price so that they will make a profit from those products they are able to sell.
6. _____ As capitalist systems evolved in Canada and other parts of the world, wealth became more equally distributed.
7. _____ A communist system is based upon the premise that all economic decisions are made by the state, and the state owns all major forms of production.
8. _____ Socialism and communism are popular terms used to describe free market economies.
9 _____ Mixed economies exist where some allocation of resources is made by the marketplace, and some by the government.
10. _____ Betty Bixler worked for Chrysler for 20 years before being laid off when her job was eliminated because updated technology made it obsolete. Betty is structurally unemployed.
11. _____ The CPI is important because some government benefits, wages and salaries, rent and leases, tax brackets and interest rates are all based upon this figure.
12. _____ Part of the income from producing goods and services goes to the government in the form of taxes.
13. _____ An increase in productivity means the same worker produces more in the same amount of time.
14. _____ During a recession, we could experience an overall drop in our standard of living, high unemployment, and increased business failures.
15. _____ Discussions regarding reduction of the national debt must include a discussion of what our national priorities should be.

ANSWERS

Key Terms and Definitions

1. deficit
2. demand
3. gross domestic product
4. seasonal unemployment
5. capitalism
6. consumer price index
7. economics
8. supply
9. structural unemployment
10. inflation
11. productivity
12. cyclical unemployment
13. mixed economy
14. national debt

The Economic and Political Basis of Business Operations

1. Adam Smith is known as the *father of economics*.
2. Business people decide for their own businesses what to produce, how much to produce, and how much to charge in capital systems.
3. Competition is the foundation of capitalism.
4. Adam Smith believed that the freedom to own your own property and to keep the profits from your work were vital to the survival of any economy.
5. Smith believed that people will work hard if they know they will be rewarded for work. As a result, the economy will prosper with plenty of food and available goods.
6. The "invisible hand" is what Smith believed is the mechanism for creating wealth. The idea is that people working for their own benefit will provide goods and services that are needed by others. As a business grows and prospers, jobs are created and people are hired to work for the business. As a consequence, people will have food and goods available, and many people will have jobs. So, anyone who is willing and able to work will have a job and access to homes and so forth.
7. *Capitalist Economics*
   Adam Smith believed that an economy would prosper when people were allowed to produce needed goods and services and keep the profit in an attempt to improve their own standard of living. The invisible hand turns self-directed gain into social and economic benefits. Ray Kroc saw a need for fast food in the marketplace. He took an idea and developed it into a multimillion-dollar corporation; he became the quintessential self-made millionaire.

   Along the way he provided jobs for hundreds of thousands of people from high school kids who work at the counter after school to the franchisee who owns 20 restaurants. McDonald's provides a service consumers need and want, makes a profit providing the service, and gives people jobs. McDonald's also goes beyond jobs and other economic benefits with Ronald McDonald Houses, a social benefit beyond economic measure.
8. A free market economy leads to inequality of wealth because business owners and managers will make more money and have more wealth than workers. Further, there will be people who are unable or unwilling to work.
9. The *father of communism* is Karl Marx.
10. In a communist system, all economic decisions are made by the state and the state owns all the major forms of production.
11. The problem with a communist system is that a government doesn't always know what is the right amount to produce. As a result, there can be shortages of many goods, even basics such as food.
12. The basic premise of a socialist system is that some business should be owned by the government and that the government should decide what gets produced, how much workers should be paid, and how much trade should take place between nations.

13. In a socialist system, the government is expected to provide education, health care, retirement benefits, unemployment benefits, and care for everyone not able to work.

14. a. Many believe that a free market system is not responsive enough to the needs of the old, the disabled, the elderly, and the environment.
    b. Socialism and communism have not created enough jobs or wealth to keep economies growing fast enough.
    c. Voters in free market countries have elected officials who adopt the social programs needed to solve the problems created by a free market system. Communist governments are disappearing and socialist governments have been cutting back on social programs and lowering taxes. The result has been a trend for "capitalist" countries, such as the United States, to move toward more socialism, and for "socialist" countries to move toward capitalism.

15. a. Communist system
    b. Economics
    c. Socialism
    d. Capitalism

How Free Markets Work

1. The consumers in a free market economy send signals to producers which tell them what and how much to make. We do so by buying products and services at the price we are charged in the store. As long as we are willing to pay the price, the supplier will continue to make that supply available.

2. Supply refers to the quantity of products that manufacturers or owners are willing to sell at different prices at a specific time.

3. As price goes up, the quantity supplied will go up.

4. Demand refers to the quantity of products that people are willing to buy at different prices at a specific time.

5. In general, as price goes up, quantity demanded will go down.

6.

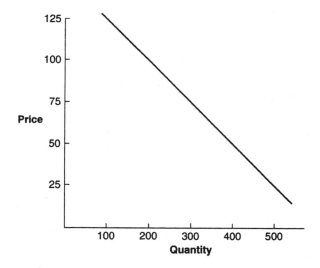

7. a.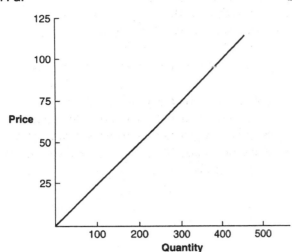

b.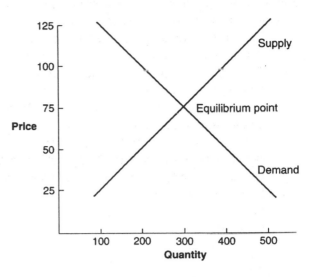

c. Equilibrium is $75/per unit
d. 300

8. a.   Go up   d.   Go down
   b.   Go down   e.   Go down
   c.   Go up

9. *Possible Answer*
   Because of a rapidly rising population in the Continos' age group, there is a great demand for housing. Because the supply of housing in nice neighbourhoods is not meeting the demand, prices have gone up. The Continos can't afford the prices that result from the free market system and the forces of supply and demand, so they become the have-nots.

10. Many answers possible. The free market system can help to foster white collar crimes such as Starr's by idealizing continually increasing standards of living. Other kinds of crime often can be attributed to individuals unable to support themselves and unable to receive adequate government support. The hunger for economic freedom and expectations of an increasingly higher standard of living can lead to an increased tolerance for negative social behaviours.

    The economic question becomes how much money to allocate to provide for social welfare, and how much to leave to free market forces to provide incentives for more output.

11. The goal is to provide enough freedom to stimulate initiative and still provide social benefits that are more generous than in capitalist countries. The problem is to find the right balance between government and private industry. Socialist countries are finding it more difficult to compete in the global economy because the costs of their social programs make their costs higher than those of capitalist economies.

12. a. In her job as a consultant, Julie will have a number of serious issues to deal with. There will be a great deal of unemployment and a high rate of inflation. As a result standards of living will fall.

    In order to adapt to a free market economy, the former Soviet Union will have to begin selling government-owned businesses to private investors. To encourage business growth, taxes will have to be cut. In addition, if businesses are going to survive and grow, new laws and regulations will have to be passed to make sure people and other businesses will do as promised. Further, rules and procedures that hinder entrepreneurship will have to be minimized. Governments will have to rid themselves of the corruption that makes it difficult to get building permits, vendor permits, and other business permits.

    A market economy means a new network of private wholesalers and retailers will have to be established, as well as a means to transport goods.

Aside from strictly business needs, a new currency system will have to be established, one that will be exchangeable with currency from other countries in order to enable free trade to take place.

b. The new form of capitalism in the East may actually be a blend of capitalist freedom with socialist security. Free markets will be combined with some central government control. The strong socialist support for social programs to help the sick, the poor, and the unemployed will remain in some form.

New forms of capitalism will combine more social programs than what is currently found in capitalist countries. National health care insurance programs are likely to appear. There are trends indicating that more attention will be paid to the environment, the homeless, education, childcare, and unemployment, as well as social problems such as crime.

Mixed Economies

1. a. Communism
   b. Mixed economy
   c. Socialism
   d. Communism
   e. Capitalism
   f. Mixed economy
   g. Socialism
   h. Communism
   i. Capitalism
   j. Capitalism
   k. Communism
   l. Capitalism
   m. Socialism
   n. Mixed economy

Economics and Business

1. 5.2%; 4.3%; 3.2%; 3.1%
2. *Possible Answer*
   Bob's concern stems from how productivity gains are measured. Productivity increases measure the increasing output using the same amount of labour, thus reducing costs. Service productivity, which is the area Bob is concerned with, is difficult to measure because services are labour-intensive. Automation may increase the quantity of the output but not the quality. This type of measurement will favour Bob's friend Gerry, who works in manufacturing.
3. Productivity is the total volume of goods and services one worker produces in a given period of time.
4. An increase in productivity means that a worker can produce more goods and services than before. Higher productivity means lower costs in producing goods and services, and lower prices. This can help to make a firm more competitive.
5. Productivity is an issue in the service industry because service firms are labour intensive. In manufacturing, machines can increase labour productivity, but in the service area, machines may add to the quality of the service provided, but not to the output per worker.
6. Increases in productivity mean that the same amount of labour is able to produce a greater output. Costs are thus lower in producing goods and services, so prices can be lower. So, efficiency in both manufacturing and the service sector can help to hold down inflation. If productivity slows, GDP growth could also slow. This would have a negative effect on the economy.

The Issue of Unemployment

1. a. cyclical
   b. seasonal
   c. structural

2. Keynes believed that inflation could be slowed by increasing taxes and reducing government spending, and that unemployment could be reduced by cutting taxes and increasing government spending.

Inflation and the Consumer Price Index

1. *Inflation* means that consumer prices are going up and *deflation* means that consumer prices are going down.
2. The CPI is an important figure because some government benefits, wages and salaries, rents and leases, tax brackets and interest rates are all based on the CPI.
3. $600 billion; $100 million.

CHAPTER CHECK ANSWERS

1. It is the point at which the two lines (supply and demand) cross. At the equilibrium point, supply and demand are equal.
2. The right to private property; the right to make and keep all profits (after taxes); the right to freedom of competition; the right to freedom of choice.
3. Canada has a very low population density, making provision of transportation and communication services relatively costly and making it more difficult to achieve economies of scale. Perhaps more significant, political considerations have led Canadian governments to pass laws and become involved in order to protect Canadian institutions, industries, and culture from being taken over by Americans.
4. 3%; 7.5% to 11.3%
5. Most predict that interest rates and inflation will remain relatively low, and that unemployment levels will remain relatively high.
6. Continued high unemployment will be largely due to the continuing need for Canadian business to be competitive, keeping payroll costs down. They can do this because they have learned to operate with fewer people by reducing the number of levels of management, etc., through using computers and other up-to-date technological developments.
7. Getting a job will require skills in information and technology, in science, engineering, and math. Computer literacy will be essential. Marketing will continue to be a major area of employment.

PRACTICE TEST

Multiple Choice		True/False	
1.	b	1.	T
2.	d	2.	T
3.	a	3.	F
4.	d	4.	T
5.	c	5.	F
6.	c	6.	F
7.	a	7.	T
8.	a	8.	F
9.	d	9.	T
10.	a	10.	T
11.	c	11.	T
12.	d	12.	T
13.	b	13.	T
14.	d	14.	T
15.	c	15.	T

CHAPTER 3

Competing in Global Environments

Learning Goals

After you have read and studied this chapter, you should be able to

1. Discuss the critical importance of the international market and the role of comparative advantage in international trade.
2. Understand the status of Canada in international business.
3. Illustrate the strategies used in reaching global markets.
4. Discuss the hurdles of trading in world markets.
5. Review what trade protectionism is and how and why it is practised.
6. Discuss the future of international trade and investment.

Key Terms and Definitions

Listed here are important terms found in this chapter. Choose the correct term for each definition and write it in the space provided.

balance of trade
bartering
common market
comparative advantage theory
consortium
countertrading
embargo
exchange rate
foreign subsidiary

General Agreement on Tariffs
    and Trade (GATT)
import quota
international joint venture (JV)
International Monetary Fund
    (IMF)
licensing
mercantilism

multinational corporation (MNC)
    or transnational corporation
    (TNC)
producers' cartels
trade deficit
trade protectionism
World Bank

1. _Trade protectionism_ The use of government regulations to limit the import of goods and services, based on the theory that domestic producers should be protected from competition so that they can survive and grow, producing more jobs.

2. _Comparative Advantage_ Theory that a country should produce and sell to other countries those products that it produces most efficiently and effectively and should buy from other countries those products it cannot produce as effectively or efficiently.

3. _IMF_ An international bank that makes short-term loans to countries experiencing problems with their balance of trade.

4. _mercantilism_ Economic principle advocating the selling of more to other nations than was bought from them.

5. _Int. Joint Venture_ A partnership in which companies from two or more countries join to undertake a major project or to form a new company.

6. _Countertrading_ Bartering among several countries.

7. _MNC or TNC_ An organization that has investments, plants, and sales in many different countries; it has international stock ownership

8. _~~producers' cartels~~_ *exchange rate*
The value of one currency relative to currencies of other countries.

9. _~~comparative adv. theory~~_ *producers cartels*
Organizations of commodity-producing countries that are formed to stabilize or increase prices to optimize overall profits in the long run. (An example is OPEC, the Organization of Petroleum-Exporting Countries.)

10. _World Bank_
An autonomous United Nations agency that borrows money from the more prosperous countries and lends it at favourable rates to less-developed countries to develop their infrastructure.

11. _bartering_
The exchange of goods or services for goods or services.

12. _balance of trade_
The relationship of the amount of exports to the amount of imports.

13. _Common market_
A regional group of countries that aims to remove all internal tariff and nontariff barriers to trade, investment, and employment. (An example is the European Union.)

14. _embargo_
A complete ban on all trade with or investment in a country.

15. _licensing_
Agreement in which a producer allows a foreign company to manufacture its products or use its trademark in exchange for royalties.

16. _GATT_
Agreement among trading countries that provides a forum for negotiating mutual reductions in trade restrictions.

17. _foreign subsidary_
A company owned by another company (parent company) in a foreign country.

18. _import quota_
A limit on the number or value of products in certain categories that can be imported.

19. _consortium_
A temporary association of two or more companies to bid jointly on a large project.

20. _trade deficit_
Occurs when the value of imports exceeds the value of exports.

The Globalization of Business

An MNC is an organization that does manufacturing and marketing in many different countries, and has international stock ownership and multinational management.

Name five Canadian-based MNCs. *(transnational company)*

Nortel, Nova, Alcan, Bombardier, INCO

Why Countries Trade with Each Other

1. Give three reasons why a country would engage in trade with others.

   - to get products that another country has such as oil, lumber, seafood etc.
   - we dont produce citrus fruits, so we export for them

2. Describe the basic theory of comparative advantage.

   • countries export goods that they produce efficiently & effectively
   •   "   import goods/services where they dont have comparative adv.

3. Figure 3.1 in your text shows the level of Canadian imports and exports in (among other things) forest products, energy products, and agricultural and fish products. Using the theory of comparative advantage, briefly explain why Canada's exports are considerably higher than its imports in these industries.

4. What's the difference between comparative advantage and absolute advantage?

   Absolute - a country that has a monopoly of one product and they can produce it very cheaply. i.e. Japan's electronics.

5. What is a favourable balance of trade?

   exists when the value of exports exceeds the value of imports

6. Why do countries prefer to have a favourable balance of trade?

   Because they are producing more money for themselves so they can buy more products from other countries

7. Three methods business people have used to get involved in international business are
   - ☐ Taking a typical "Canadian" good or service and selling it abroad (i.e., exporting)
   - ☐ Importing a foreign good to Canada
   - ☐ "Find a need and fill it" while living overseas

   Without travelling to another country and learning its culture, it is difficult to "find a need and fill it" with a Canadian product. Take an inventory of the goods and services *you* own and use. How many of them are "foreign"? (For example, do you ever go to a Mexican restaurant? Eat Baskin-Robbins ice cream? Do you own a Sony, Panasonic, or Canon?)

   _____
   _____
   _____
   _____

Terminology of International Trade

Some terms to be familiar with in international business are
   - ☑ Trade protectionism
   - ☐ Exchange rate
   - ☑ Import quota
   - ☐ Balance of trade (favourable; unfavourable)

Read the following statements and determine which term is being referred to:

1. _Import quota_ — Canada convinced Japanese auto manufacturers to voluntarily limit the number of Japanese cars sold here.

2. _trade protectionism_ — The Canadian auto industry lobbied for import tariffs on Japanese-made autos in an effort to protect Canadian manufacturers.

3. _unfavourable Balance Trade_ — The U.S. imported $70 billion worth of goods from Japan, but exported only $40 billion.

4. _Exchange Rate_ — When the value of the dollar is lowered, foreign goods become more expensive.

Trading in World Markets: The Canadian Experience

Foreign investment in Canada is a trend that is expected to continue throughout the years to come as we become a more global economy. Explain the "good news" of this trend.

- large % of our economy relies on the ability to export
our goods
_____
_____

Strategies for Reaching Global Markets

There are several ways to become involved in world trade. Among them are
   - ☐ Consortium –
   - ☐ Licensing
   - ☐ Joint ventures
   - ☑ Creating subsidiaries
   - ☐ Countertrading

☑ Franchising

1. Identify which form of trade is being described or illustrated below:

a. _Subsidaries_ The primary advantage of this form is that the company maintains control over any technology or expertise it possesses.

b. _Franchising_ McDonald's, Ramada, and Kentucky Fried Chicken have used this form of operating in foreign markets. They were successful after altering their product to meet the different needs of the host countries.

c. _joint venture_ Journey's End of Belleville entered an arrangement with Choice Hotels International Inc., giving it 50 more hotels to manage in Canada and access to Choice's reservation system.

d. _Countertrading_ Chrysler traded its vehicles in Jamaica for bauxite in this form of international trade.

e. _licensing_ In this form of global marketing, a firm sends representatives to a foreign producer to help set up the production process.

f. _Consortium_ Bombardier teamed up with Alsthom of France to bid for a New York City subway car contract.

2. What are some advantages and disadvantages of each form?

a. Licensing

Advantage _____

Disadvantage _____

b. Creating subsidiaries

Advantage _____

Disadvantage _____

c. Franchising

Advantage _____

Disadvantage _____

d. Joint ventures

Advantage _____

Disadvantage _____

f. Consortium

Advantage _____

Disadvantage _____

Hurdles of Doing Business in World Markets

1. What are ~~four~~ three forces affecting trading in global markets?

• cultural differences
• societal & economic differences
• legal & regulatory differences
_____

2. What are some of the sociocultural elements of which it is important to be aware in working with individuals from other cultures? How do economic forces relate to this?

_____
_____
_____
_____

3. What is *global marketing*? What is a sound philosophy to adopt with regard to global marketing?

Selling the same product the same way in every country

→ never assume what works in one country will work in another

4. How is trade conducted in many developing nations?

bartering or countertrading — don't have the $ to buy goods, so they trade product for product

_____
_____

5. Understanding what three things is vital to a company's success in the global market?
a. economic conditions
b. currency fluctuations
c. countertrade opportunities

6. How can businesses increase their chances of success in foreign markets with regard to legal and regulatory forces?

contact local businesspeople and gain their cooperation & support

_____

7. The difficulties of doing business are compounded by a variety of differences between Canadian markets and foreign markets. Differences stem from cultural, social, economic differences, legal and political regulations, and problems with currencies.
You are interested in opening an ice cream/frozen yogurt store in Saudi Arabia. What are some of the problems you could encounter?

_____
_____
_____
_____
_____
_____
_____
_____
_____

Trade Protectionism

1. Governments have developed a variety of methods to protect their domestic industries from the

potential negative impact of foreign trade:
- ☐ Protective tariffs
- ☐ Revenue tariffs
- ☐ Import quotas ✓
- ☐ Embargoes ✓
- ☐ Non-tariff barriers

Match the correct type of trade protection method to each of the following statements:

a. _Import quotas_ In an effort to protect the Canadian auto industry, the Canadian government persuaded Japanese auto manufacturers to voluntarily limit the number of Japanese cars sold here.

b. _Revenue tariff_ This is a type of tax on imports designed to raise money for the government.

c. _Protective tariff_ Because domestically made products are often more expensive than similar products made in countries with lower labour costs, the government may levy a type of tax on the import designed to raise its retail price.

d. _Embargo_ Because of this policy, Cuban cigars cannot legally be sold in the United States.

e. _Non-tariff barrier_ Belgium requires margarine to be sold in cubes, cutting off those companies which manufacture margarine in tubs.

2. One of the underlying principles for imposing tariffs on imports is the economic principle of mercantilism, which is an effort to create a favourable balance of trade — in other words, export more than you import.

What are the arguments for imposing tariffs?
a. _Gov't revenue_
b. _Protect Canadian jobs_
c. _protects industries vital_
d. _____

3. What are the arguments against imposing tariffs?
a. _reduce competition_
b. _Can lead to foreign retalliation_
c. _____
d. _____

4. What do advocates believe is the benefit of trade protectionism?
_____
_____
_____

5. What is the difference between a *revenue tariff* and a *protective tariff*?
protective - to protect domestic goods because imported ones are cheaper - labour
revenue - raise $ for gov't
_____
_____

6. What is the difference between an *import quota* and an *embargo*?

quota – limit on importing of certain goods

certain
embargo – ban of an imported goods

7. What are *nontariff barriers?* What are some examples of nontariff barriers?

International Trade Organizations

1. "... some nations have joined together to form trading partnerships and to write up trade agreements that facilitate open trade."
   Match the correct trade organization to each of the descriptions below.

   International Monetary Fund (IMF)
   The World Bank
   General Agreement on Tariffs and Trade (GATT)

   a. _____IMF_____ Its basic objectives are to promote exchange stability and deal with other problems regarding the exchange of currency between countries.

   b. _____World Bank_____ An autonomous United Nations agency concerned with the development of the infrastructure of less developed countries.

   c. _____GATT_____ An agreement among 23 countries that provides a forum for negotiating mutual reductions in trade restrictions.

2. What organization replaced the GATT in 1995?
   World Trade organization (WTO)

3. Two other, more detailed, types of trade agreement are
   ☐ Producer cartels
   ☐ Common markets
   These agreements are made between countries within the same region.
   a. What is the primary focus of each group?
      i. Producer Cartels _stabilize commodities produced by member nations_

      ii. Common markets _promote trade among regional group of countries_

   b. Give two examples of each type of agreement.

Producer Cartels	i.	
	ii.	
Common Markets	i.	
	ii.	

Common Markets

1. a. What percentage of Canada's foreign trade is with the U.S.?

   _85%_

   b. What was the formal purpose of the Canada–U.S. Free Trade Agreement, entered into on January 1, 1989?

   NAFTA, to phase out tariffs on imported goods

2. a. When did NAFTA come into effect?

   Jan 1 1993

   b. What three countries are NAFTA members?

   CANADA, US, MEXICO

   c. Why is there a continuing concern in Canada that manufacturing jobs may be lost to Mexico because of NAFTA?

   because of the very low labour costs, products are very cheap and they can't put a tax on them, so ppl buy the Mexican goods more

3. a. What five countries belong to the Mercosur common market?

   Brazil, Argentina, Uruguay, Paraguay, Chile

4. What resulted from the formation of the European Union in 1992?

   It became one big market of 320 million ppl

How Does Canada Shape Up as an International Competitor?

1. Summarize Michael Porter's explanation for his conclusion that drastic and immediate action must be taken if Canada is to compete in future world markets.

_____

_____

_____

_____

2. Joseph Fletcher, who conducted a study of Canadian attitudes to capitalistic and entrepreneurial ideologies (for the Department of Industry, Science and Technology), reached conclusions very different from Porter's. What did Fletcher conclude?

_____

_____

_____

_____

CHAPTER CHECK

1. How do governments prevent comparative advantage theory from having its natural effect?

_____

_____

_____

_____

2. What are three ways for an individual to get involved in international business?
   a. _____
   b. _____
   c. _____

3. During the latter half of the 1980s, Canada had an unfavourable balance of payments. What does this mean?

_____

_____

_____

_____

4. List six ways for business to become involved in world markets.
   a. _____
   b. _____
   c. _____
   d. _____
   e. _____
   f. _____

5. What are four hurdles to trading in world markets?

    a. _____

    b. _____

    c. _____

    d. _____

6. What proportion of Canada's total exporting and importing activity is with the U.S.?

_____

7. Name two specific cultural and three social differences that could be encountered in global markets.

              Cultural   *Social*

    a. _____   a. _____

    b. _____   b. _____

                                         c. _____

8. List five forms of trade protectionism.

    a. _____

    b. _____

    c. _____

    d. _____

    e. _____

9. What are the characteristics of an MNC?

    a. _____

    b. _____

    c. _____

10. What were the three major goals of the Canadian negotiating team in the Canada–U.S. Free Trade Agreement negotiations?

    a. _____

    b. _____

    c. _____

11. What are the 15 countries which are in the European trade community?

    a. _____   g. _____

    b. _____   h. _____

    c. _____   i _____

    d. _____   j _____

    e. _____   k _____

    f. _____   l _____

PRACTICE TEST

Multiple Choice: Circle the best answer.

1. Selling products to another country is known as

    a. importing

    b. trade protectionism

    c. comparative advantage

    d. exporting

2. All of the following are reasons for countries to participate in foreign trade EXCEPT

a. countries need to make a profit from foreign trade, because the market in the U.S. has slowed.
b. no nation can produce all of the product its people want and need.
c. even if a country were self-sufficient, other nations would demand to trade with that country.
d. some nations have resources, but not technological know-how, others have know-how, but lack resources.

3. Producing and selling goods that we produce most effectively and efficiently, and buying goods that other countries produce most effectively and efficiently is known as
   a. absolute advantage
   b. free trade
   c. international marketing
   d. comparative advantage

4. When the value of exports from a country exceeds the value of imports into that country there is a

   _____ .

   a. trade deficit
   b. balance of payments
   c. unfavourable balance of trade
   d. favourable balance of trade

5. The difference between money coming into a country from exports and money leaving a country due to imports, plus money flows from other factors, is known as the
   a. balance of trade
   b. dumping effect
   c. balance of payments
   d. trade deficit

6. A basic formula for success in exporting to the global marketplace would be
   a. buy here, sell there
   b. find a need and fill it
   c. always sell a product for less than what you charge at home
   d. focus only on countries where incomes are the highest

7. Coke and Pepsi often enter foreign markets by allowing a foreign manufacturer to use their trademark and pay them (Coke or Pepsi) a royalty for that right. This is an example of
   a. joint venture
   b. exporting
   c. licensing
   d. creating a subsidiary

8. Nike uses this type of global strategy when Nike distributes products which have been manufactured by a foreign company, but which have the Nike brand name.
   a. international joint venture
   b. franchising
   c. exporting
   d. contract manufacturing

9. In franchising to foreign markets, companies such as McDonald's and KFC have had to
   a. be careful to adapt to the countries they are attempting to enter
   b. find franchisees with money they can afford to lose if the franchise fails
   c. be sure not to alter their products for foreign markets, so that consumers know exactly what they are getting
   d. find opportunities for joint ventures, as franchising doesn't seem to work in foreign markets

10. Guillermo Martinez was concerned that his new boss, Donald Darr, didn't know his job very well. Donald is continually asking Guillermo and the other workers in this plant in Mexico City to give him

their opinions before he makes a final decision. Guillermo's concern stems from _____ differences between him and Donald.

    a. economic
    b. cultural
    c. language
    d. regulatory

11. The makers of Whirlpool washers and other electrical appliance manufacturers need to be concerned about the kind and availability of electricity in the global marketplace. If there were a compatibility problem, it would be the result of a _____ difference.

    a. cultural
    b. technological
    c. economic
    d. societal

12. When Mexico devalued the peso, the peso became _____ valuable relative to other currencies.

    a. more
    b. less
    c. equally
    d. significantly more

13. Using government regulations to limit the import of goods and services in order to protect domestic industries against dumping and foreign competition is called

    a. mercantilism
    b. regulating the balance of trade
    c. global marketing
    d. trade protectionism

14. Which of the following would NOT be considered a non-tariff barrier?

    a. A requirement that all products sold in a country be packaged in a certain way
    b. A tradition of semipermanent ties between domestic firms, which have the effect of shutting out foreign manufacturers
    c. Signing a trade agreement such as the GATT
    d. A set of quality standards that must be met by all companies wishing to do business within a country

15. This agreement was established in 1948, and is designed to facilitate the exchange of goods, services, ideas, and cultural programs.

    a. General Agreement on Tariffs and Trade (GATT)
    b. World Trade Organization (WTO)
    c. North American Free Trade Agreement (NAFTA)
    d. The European Union (EU)

16. The _____ took over supervision of the _____ in 1995, and is assigned the task of mediating trade disputes.

    a. NAFTA; WTO
    b. GATT; EU
    c. WTO; GATT
    d. GATT; NAFTA

17. An organization that does manufacturing and marketing in many different countries and has multinational stock ownership and multinational management is considered a

    a. common market
    b. free trade area

c. global marketer
d. multinational corporation

True/False

1. It is expected that the amount of international trade will level off or decline in the next millennium.

2. Trade relations enable a nation to produce what it's most capable of and to buy what it needs but cannot produce.

3. An example of exporting is the Meridian Group, based in the United States, selling sand to customers in the Middle East.

4. When the country of Monrovia is buying more from Canada than it is selling to Canada, a favourable balance of trade exists for Monrovia.

5. The goal of global trade is always to have more money flowing into the country than flowing out of the country.

6. One disadvantage of licensing is the cost to the company licensing its product or trademark (the licensor) to the foreign firm (the licensee).

7. An international joint venture is helpful to companies wishing to enter countries with planned economies, such as China, or markets which for some reason are difficult to enter.

8. Countertrading, or bartering, is not a particularly important part of international trade, and few countries participate.

9. Religion is an important element of a society's culture, and should be considered in making many business decisions.

10. Economic differences between countries can affect purchasing patterns, such as quantity purchased at a given time.

11. A sound global philosophy is "always assume that what works in one country will work in another."

12. Trade protectionism is based upon the idea that barriers will help domestic producers grow, and create more jobs.

13. Non-tariff barriers can be just as detrimental to free trade as tariffs.

14. The World Trade Organization was replaced by the GATT.

15. It is possible that there will be a new currency in the European Union, called the "euro."

ANSWERS

Key Terms and Definitions

1.	trade protectionism	11.	Bartering
2.	Comparative advantage theory	12.	Balance of trade
3.	International Monetary Fund	13.	Common market
4.	Mercantilism	14.	Embargo
5.	International joint venture	15.	Licensing
6.	Countertrading	16.	General Agreement on Tariffs and Trade (GATT)
7.	Multinational corporation (MNC)	17.	foreign subsidiary
8.	Exchange rate	18.	import quota
9.	Producers' cartels	19.	Consortium
10.	World Bank	20.	trade deficit

The Globalization of Business

Canadian-based MNCs include Nortel, Alcan, Seagrams, INCO, MacMillan Bloedel, Bombardier, Hees International, and Nova.

Why Do Countries Trade with Each Other?

1. ! No country can produce all the products that its people want and need.
   - ☐ Even if a country was self-sufficient, others would seek to trade with it to meet their population's wants and needs.
   - ☐ Some countries have a surplus of resources and a shortage of technical skills; other countries have the opposite situation.
2. The theory of comparative advantage states that a country should produce and sell to other countries those products that it produces most effectively and efficiently, and should buy from other countries those products it cannot produce as effectively or efficiently.
3. These are resource-based industries in which Canada has a relative abundance of supply while many other countries have shortages of these resources. Some products can be produced more cheaply in other countries than in Canada. Both trading partners benefit when Canada trades its resource-based products for those produced more cheaply by the trading partner.
4. Comparative advantage states that a country should produce and sell products it produces most effectively and efficiently, and should buy those products other countries are better at producing and selling. A country has an absolute advantage when it has a monopoly on production of a good, or can produce it more cheaply that any other country.
5. A favourable balance of trade exists when the value of exports exceeds the value of imports.
6. Countries prefer to export more than they import, or have a favourable balance of trade, because the country will retain more of its money to buy other goods and services. As the example in the text illustrates, if I sell you $200 worth of goods, and only buy $100, I have an extra $100 available to buy other things.
7. This question will yield a wide variety of responses.

Terminology of International Trade

1. Import quota
2. Trade protectionism
3. Unfavourable balance of trade
4. Exchange rate

Trading in World Markets: The Canadian Experience

A large percentage of our standard of living depends on our ability to export.

Strategies for Reaching Global Markets

1. a. Creating subsidiaries
   b. Franchising
   c. Joint venture
   d. Countertrading
   e. Licensing
   f. Consortium

2. a. Licensing

   Advantage: Additional revenue that wouldn't be generated domestically. Foreign licensees purchase start-up supplies.
   Disadvantage: Licensing agreements are for extended time, bulk of revenues go to licensee. Foreign licensee may break agreement.

   b. Creating

   Advantage: Company maintains subsidiary's control over any technology or expertise it possesses.
   Disadvantage: Company commits large amounts of funds and technology within foreign boundaries, assets could be taken over by foreign government.

   c. Franchising

   Advantage: Tested management systems.
   Disadvantage: Problems arise when product isn't adapted to local markets.

   d. Joint venture

   Advantage: Shared technology, shared marketing expertise, entry into previously unattainable markets, shared risk.
   Disadvantage: Partners can take technology and go off on their own, technology can become obsolete, partnership can become too large.

   e. Counter trading

   Advantage: Helps avoid problems and hurdles experienced in global markets.
   Disadvantage: Limited usefulness.

   f. Consortium

   Advantage: Same as joint venture.
   Disadvantage: Same as joint venture.

Hurdles of Doing Business in World Markets

1. a. sociocultural
   b. economic and financial
   c. legal and regulatory
   d. physical and environmental
2. Some of the sociocultural elements of which it is important to be aware are religious customs, cultural perspectives an time, human resources management, change, competition, natural resources and even work itself. For example, in India the average person consumes only three soft drinks annually, compared to fifty gallons per year per person in the U.S. The potential soft drink market in India would appear to be huge if only this fact is considered. However, the level of consumption relates to cultural differences and to per capita income levels. Tea is considerably less expensive than a soft drink in India.
3. Global marketing is selling the same product in essentially the same way everywhere in the world. A sound philosophy to adopt in global markets is to never assume that what works in one country will work in another!
4. In poorer, or developing nations trade is largely conducted through bartering, the exchange of merchandise for merchandise or service for service with no money involved. Countertrading is a

complex form of bartering in which several countries may be involved, each trading goods for goods or services for service. It has been estimated that countertrading accounts for 25% of all international exchanges.

5. To be successful in global markets it is important to understand:
   a. economic conditions
   b. currency fluctuations
   c. countertrade opportunities

6. To be successful, it is often important to contact local businesspeople and gain their cooperation and sponsorship. Local contacts can help a company penetrate the market and deal with bureaucratic barriers.

7. *Possible Answer*

   One of the first things that needs to be considered is how the Saudis feel about ice cream/frozen yogurt as a product. How it's eaten, their view on dairy products (some religions have different views on dairy products and how they should be handled), where it can be marketed (do they have the same kind of grocery stores? do you open a free-standing store?) are all questions that will need to be answered. There is a possibility that this may be a totally new concept and you as a seller of the product will need to be aware of how to convince the Saudi Arabian people that these are viable and acceptable products.

   Social and economic differences from the Canadian market must also be considered. In Canada, frozen yogurt and ice cream may be bought on a trip to the grocery store, and then stored at home in the refrigerator. Is that a similar lifestyle to the Saudis? Is there the type of equipment available which is needed to store the product before it is purchased? Does a typical Saudi home have the type of storage needed (i.e., a freezer)? Canadian families may go to a typical ice cream store as a family outing. Would that be true of a typical Saudi family? We eat ice cream or frozen yogurt as a dessert or some-times as a snack. How would the Saudi population view the product? When might they choose to eat it? Although Saudi Arabia as a nation may be wealthy, does the average Saudi have the money to buy a non-essential item like this?

   Further questions to be answered revolve around legal and regulatory differences. The way of doing business in Middle Eastern countries is different from in Canada. Laws and regulations will vary, and practices will be different there than at home.

Trade Protectionism

1. a. Import quotas
   b. Revenue tariffs
   c. Protective tariffs
   d. Embargo
   e. Non-tariff barriers
2. a. Tariffs save jobs.
   b. Tariffs are imposed on Canada by its competitors.
   c. Tariffs protect industries vital to Canadian security.
   d. Tariffs are needed to protect new domestic industries from established foreign competitors.
3. a. Tariffs reduce competition.
   b. Tariffs tend to increase inflationary pressure.
   c. Tariffs tend to support special interest groups.
   d. Tariffs can lead to foreign retaliation and subsequently to trade wars.
4. Advocates of trade protectionism believe it allows domestic producers to survive and grow, producing

more jobs. Countries often use protectionist measures to guard against such practices as dumping.

5. A protective tariff is designed to raise the retail price of an imported good so the domestic product will be more competitive. A revenue tariff is designed to raise money for the government.

6. An import quota limits the number of products in certain categories that can be imported into a nation. An embargo is a complete ban on the import or export of certain products.

7. Nontariff barriers take a variety of forms. They are not as specific as embargoes but can be as detrimental to free trade. Japan has created relationships through keiretsu, which are close-knit groups of Japanese companies within an industry. Outsiders, such as foreign companies, cannot belong to such groups. Other countries have imposed restrictive standards that detail exactly how a product must be sold in a country.

International Trade Organizations

1. a. International Monetary Fund
    b. The World Bank
    c. General Agreement on Tariffs and Trade
2. The World Trade Organization
    3. a. i. Producer Cartels — the focus is to stabilize or increase prices of commodities produced by member nations.
        ii. Common markets — the focus is to promote trade among a regional group of countries. There are no internal tariffs, and they have a common external tariff.
    b.   Producer Cartels
    i. OPEC
    ii. Council of Copper Exporting Countries
    Common Markets
    i. European Economic Community (EEC)
    ii. Central America's Common Market (CACM)

Common Markets

1. a. More than 80%
    b. To phase out most tariffs and other restrictions to free trade between the two countries over a period of 10 years.
2. a. January 1, 1993
    b. Canada, the United States, and Mexico
    c. Wages and general conditions are much poorer in Mexico. Also, it has a poor policy on environment problems, etc.
3   Brazil, Argentina, Uruguay, Paraguay, and Chile.
4. Europe became one market of approximately 320 million people. There will be free movement of labour, shared social programs, new tax systems, and shared professional standards. An advantage to Canada is that English will be Europe's common language.

How Does Canada Shape Up as an International Competitor?

1. Michael Porter concluded that the biggest barriers to improving Canada's competitiveness are attitudinal. He criticized government, business, and labour for refusing to adopt a new view in which all

three work together as partners to improve education, transform foreign subsidiaries into home-based companies, and adopt advanced technologies.

2. Fletcher found that Canadians are even more committed to the free enterprise system and the need for competitiveness than are Americans.

CHAPTER CHECK ANSWERS

1. By restricting imports and subsidizing non-competitive domestic producers.
2. a. Set up to sell overseas
   b. Import
   c. "Find a need" which is not being met and sell while living in the foreign country
3. More money leaving the country to pay for imports than is coming in from purchasers of exports.
4. a. Exporting
   b. Licensing
   c. Creating subsidiaries
   d. Franchising
   e. Joint venture
   f. Counter trading
5. a. Cultural differences
   b. Social/economic differences
   c. Legal/political restrictions
   d. Problems with currency shifts
6. 75%–80%
7. *Cultural*
   a. Religious differences
   b. Differences in attitudes about management, time, work itself
   Social
   a. Economic differences in disposable and discretionary income
   b. Different technology
   c. Primitive transportation and storage
8. a. Protective tariffs
   b. Revenue tariffs
   c. Import quotas
   d. Embargoes
   e. Non-tariff barriers
9. a. A multinational company is constantly checking opportunities for expansion all over the world
   b. Aggressively markets its products, capitalizing on its technological and management expertise
   c. Has manufacturing capacity or other physical presence in various nations
10. a. Relief from unilateral U.S. protectionist moves
    b. Expose Canadian companies to tougher competition, forcing them to become more competitive
    c. Provide better access to the American market for Canadian companies
11. a. Germany
    b. France
    c. Portugal
    d. Greece
    e. United Kingdom
    f. Ireland
    g. Spain
    h. The Netherlands
    i. Italy
    j. Denmark
    k. Belgium
    l. Luxembourg

m. Austria
o. Sweden

n. Finland

PRACTICE TEST

Multiple Choice		True/False	
1.	d	1.	F
2.	a	2.	T
3.	d	3.	T
4.	d	4.	F
5.	c	5.	T
6.	b	6.	F
7.	c	7.	T
8.	d	8.	F
9.	a	9.	T
10.	b	10.	T
11.	b	11.	F
12.	b	12.	T
13.	d	13.	T
14.	c	14.	F
15.	a	15.	T
16.	c		
17.	d		

CHAPTER 4

The Role of Government in Business

Learning Goals

After you have read and studied this chapter, you should be able to

1. Explain the historical role of government in the Canadian economy.
2. List some of the major crown corporations in Canada and understand their role in the economy.
3. Understand how the start-up and operations of companies take place within a framework of government laws and regulations.
4. Identify some major legislation affecting competition in Canada.
5. Discuss the role of government in stimulating or restraining the economy.
6. Understand the role of government in consumer and investor protection.
7. Understand the controversy about a government industrial policy.

Key Terms and Definitions

Listed here are important terms found in this chapter. Choose the correct term for each definition and write it in the space provided.

articles of incorporation   industrial policy   privatization
crown corporation   marketing boards   prospectus
economies of scale   monetary policy   securities commission
fiscal policy   National Policy

1. _Privitization_ — The process of governments selling crown corporations.

2. _Crown corporation_ — A company owned by the federal or a provincial government.

3. _industrial policy_ — A comprehensive coordinated government plan to guide and revitalize the economy.

4. _Securities commission_ — The official body set up by a province to regulate the stock exchange and to approve all new issues of securities in that province.

5. _Marketing Boards_ — Organizations that control the supply or pricing of certain agricultural products in Canada.

6. _Prospectus_ — A document, which must be prepared by every public company seeking financing through issue of shares or bonds, that gives the public certain information about the company. It must be approved by the securities commission of the province where these securities will be offered for sale.

7. _Fiscal Policy_ — The use of taxation to stimulate or restrain various aspects of the economy or the economy as a whole.

8. _Articles of Incorporation_ — The legal documents, obtained from the federal or provincial governments, authorizing a company to operate as a corporation.

9. _National Policy_ — Federal government policy that imposed high tariffs on

imports from the United States to protect Canadian manufacturing.

10. _Economies of Scale_   The cost savings that result from large-scale production.

11. _Monetary Policy_   The Bank of Canada's exercise of control over the supply of money and the level of interest rates in the country.

How Government Affects Business

1. List and describe the seven categories of government activities affecting business.

   Crown Corporations - gov't owned business

   Laws & Regulations - cover wide range; taxation, working conditions etc.

   (policy) Taxation & financial - all levels of gov't collect taxes (Fiscal Policy)

   Financial Aid - levels of gov't provide aid packages; tax reductions, tariffs, loans etc.

   Services - direct & indirect activities ie. help industries go international, bring comp. to Canada

   Purchasing Policies - Federal Gov't is single largest purchaser in Canada; supplies, services etc.

   Other Expenditures - Gov't pay out billions to unemployed, elderly, disabled etc

2. Explain the purpose of John A. MacDonald's National Policy. What effect has it had on the cost of goods for Canadian consumers?

   it imposes high tariffs on imports from the US to protect Canadian manufacturing. Higher cost for Canadian consumers

3. What is "privatization"? Give three examples of privatization by the federal government.

   It is the process in which the gov't sells the crown corporations

   → Canadian National Railway

   → Air Canada

   → Petro Can

4. What is a "crown corporation"? Name 10 crown corporations. company owned by gov't

   a. Canada Post

   b. CBC

   c. EDC (Export Develp. Corp.)

   d. Bank of Canada

   e. Atomic Energy of Canada Ltd.

   f. Canadian Wheat Board

   g.

   h.

   i.

   j.

5. What reasons do governments have for establishing crown corporations?

   • Gov't uses them to provide goods/services that no other company does

   • Help bail out a failing industry

   • Special services (ie. Bank of Canada)

Laws and Regulations

1. What reasons do governments have for requiring all businesses to register with them in order to be allowed to do business?

   So the gov't knows everything that is being imported/exported
   ensure taxes are being paid

2. Do you agree that the reasons given actually do entitle governments to require all businesses to be registered? Can you think of any situations in which this requirement should not be imposed? Explain.

Taxation of Companies

1. Explain how governments can use adjustments in taxation levels to heat up or cool down the economy.

2. How do governments use fiscal policy to stimulate economic activity in geographic regions where there is chronically high unemployment?

   Reduced taxes or tax credits → lowers costs

How Governments Spend Tax Dollars to Help Business

1. How much do interprovincial trade barriers cost the Canadian economy each year? Why hasn't action been taken to eliminate these barriers?

   $6 billion annually

2. What do Canadian governments frequently do to help Canadian businesses when contracts are made with foreign companies for sophisticated equipment (e.g., modern military ships and aircraft)?

3. Why do governments often provide direct financial assistance to large established companies (e.g., Chrysler Corp.) that are in danger of going bankrupt?

_____

_____

_____

_____

4. a. Why were Ontario and Quebec the first provinces to develop economically?

   Much larger populations, similar to US, abundance of natural resources.

   b. What is the purpose of the Canadian system of regional transfer payments?

   Payments are transferred from the richer ones to the poorer ones.
   → Designed to adjust for regional economic differences.

The Effect of Other Departments and Regulations on Business

1. Two ways in which the government manages the economy are
   ] Fiscal policy *— tax to stimulate/restrain aspect of economy*
   ] Monetary policy *— B of C control over supply of money*

Match the situations below to the type of policy being implemented or discussed.

a. *Fiscal* — Parliament debates a major income tax revision.

b. *Monetary* — The Bank of Canada raises interest rates to its member banks.

c. *Fiscal* — A candidate for major political office promises to cut government spending in an effort to reduce the national debt.

d. *Fiscal* — Major government programs lose federal funding.

e. *Monetary* — In an attempt to ease unemployment, the Bank of Canada encourages borrowing by reducing the cost of money.

f. *Monetary* — The money supply is reduced to combat a high rate of inflation.

g. *Fiscal* — A proposal is made to cut defence spending, but to raise taxes to fund government social programs.

h. *Fiscal* — Canadian taxpayers express concern over tax loopholes for "rich people."

i. *Fiscal* — A debate centres around whether to lower the national debt through more taxes or less spending.

Fiscal policy — how the gov't collects & spends tax $

2. What is the role of the *Competition Act* and the federal Bureau of Competition Policy regarding corporate mergers?

_____

_____

_____

_____

Protecting Consumers

1. What does the Canadian Deposit Insurance Corporation do? How is it funded?

CDIC insures individual deposits in banks against these institutions' failure or collapse. Up to $60,000
Funded by annual premium payments from all banks & trust companies
→ Reports to the chair of the Treasury Board

_____

2. What do *securities commissions* do?

Set up by a province to regulate its stock exchange and to approve all new issues of securities in that province

_____

_____

3. Which level of government establishes zoning regulations? What do these regulations do?

Municipal gov't - restricts areas for residential, commercial building etc.
Also limits the height of buildings

_____

_____

Labour Standards and Working Conditions

List as many matters as you can in the area of labour standards and working conditions that are regulated by legislation.

Minimum wage, overtime, holiday/vacation pay, maternity, compensation etc.

_____

_____

Environmental Regulations

Identify at least three of the negative consequences to the environment that have resulted from uncontrolled industrial activity. How do you think governments should deal with this problem?

_____

_____

_____

_____

Employment and Immigration in Canada

What criteria would you set for deciding whether or not to accept an application from someone wishing to immigrate to Canada? Explain.

_____

_____

_____

_____

National Research Council *(1916) Employs over 3000 Scientists & technicians*

Funding to the NRC has been severely cut over the past few years, along with many other government operations, in the continuing struggle to deal with the national deficit. If you were in government, would you have made an exception for the NRC? Explain.

→ Promotes Research Development

→ Helps Canadian industry to innovate & remain competitive

_____

_____

Government Impact on Farming Business

What do marketing boards do? What is the reason for having them?

_____

_____

_____

_____

Role of the Canadian Government Domestically and Globally

If the federal government decided to develop a long-term industrial policy for Canada, with whom would it need to consult? Explain why.

_____

_____

_____

_____

CHAPTER CHECK

1. Canada has a mixed economy. Explain what this means.

    Not just capitalism, but a bit of socialism also

    _____

2. What is *Caisse de depot et placement du Quebec?* When and why was it established? How is it used by the government of Quebec?

    _____

    _____

    _____

    _____

    _____

3. What is *EDC?* What does it do to assist Canadian businesses?

    _____

_____
_____
_____
_____

4. What is *BDC?* What does it do to assist Canadian businesses?

    _Business Development Bank_____
_____
_____
_____
_____

5. Identify the single largest source of revenue for
    a. Municipal governments   _____
    b. Provincial governments   _____
    c. Federal government   _____

6. Developments such as the Canada–U.S. Free Trade Agreement and NAFTA show that the federal
    government is concerned about the need for Canadian businesses to be internationally competitive,
    and this necessitates reduction and removal of tariff barriers. Provincial governments, though, have
    maintained walls against businesses from other provinces. How do these barriers make costs higher
    for Canadians?

    _____
    _____
    _____
    _____
    _____
    _____

7. In recent years, the federal government has reduced the relative size of the Canadian system of
    transfer payments. What does this transfer payment system do?

    _____
    _____
    _____
    _____

8. What kind of *policy,* in economic terms, includes the establishment or change of interest rates by the
    Bank of Canada? What does the Bank hope to achieve when it raises the short-term lending rate to
    banks? When it lowers it?

    _____
    _____
    _____
    _____
    _____

9. What is a prospectus? Why are companies required to issue one when they intend to raise money

through the issue of stocks or bonds?

_____

_____

_____

_____

10. Why was the Canadian system of marketing boards considered unacceptable by so many countries in the GATT negotiations?

_____

_____

_____

_____

11. Name three of the countries pointed to as examples by those who argue that in Canada, too, government should have an industrial strategy to improve Canada's competitive position in the global marketplace.

_____

_____

_____

_____

PRACTICE TEST

Multiple Choice: Circle the best answer.

1. The fact that the Canadian dollar is worth considerably less than the U.S. dollar has the effect of
   a. making Canadian products relatively less expensive in the U.S.
   b. making U.S. products relatively more expensive in Canada.
   c. attracting tourists to Canada because things are relatively less expensive here than in the U.S.
   d. all of the above.

2. Which of the following is NOT a crown corporation?
   a. Air Canada
   b. Canada Post Corporation
   c. Canada Mortgage and Housing Corporation
   d. CBC

3. The National Policy under Prime Minister John A. Macdonald
   a. was Canada's first free-trade agreement
   b. placed high tariffs on imports from the U.S.
   c. required that all government publications be printed in both French and English
   d. established an elaborate federal form of government

4. The National Research Council
   a. maintains records on the level of compliance with the *Income Tax Act*
   b. helps Canadian industry to remain competitive and innovative
   c. monitors the impact of NAFTA on the Canadian economy and the level of unemployment in the different regions of the country
   d. is the Canadian counterpart of the F.B.I.

5. The Bank of Canada
   a. acts as a lender of last resort, loaning money to small businesses when other banks will not
   b. oversees the operations of all of Canada's chartered banks

    c.   is prevented by law from setting monetary policy

    d.   has more branches than any other bank in Canada

6.   Governments in Canada provide assistance to businesses in the form of

    a.   grants

    b.   loan guarantees

    c.   consulting advice

    d.   all of the above

7.   The power to regulate "trade and commerce" is given to this arm of government under the Canadian constitution:

    a.   provincial government

    b.   municipal government

    c.   central (federal) government

    d.   Supreme Court of Canada

8.   The amount of money disbursed annually by Canadian governments under social programs is

    a.   none

    b.   thousands of dollars

    c.   millions of dollars

    d.   billions of dollars

9.   The term "economies of scale" refers to

    a.   the number of national economies that have adopted the capitalist system

    b.   the cost of weighing Canada's wheat production each year

    c.   the cost savings that result from large-scale production

    d.   the additional costs associated with exporting products to other countries

10. The level of equalization transfer payments to poorer provinces from richer ones under the Canadian federal system has _____ in recent years.

    a.   been reduced

    b.   been eliminated

    c.   been increased

    d.   remained constant

11. The CRTC does NOT

    a.   hold public hearings before granting or renewing radio station licences

    b.   regulate the use of satellite dishes

    c.   deal with disputes between cable and telephone companies regarding distribution of television signals

    d.   classify movies that are shown in theatres

12. Insider trading regulations are designed to prevent

    a.   trading of stocks and bonds by individuals who are not licensed as brokers

    b.   "over the counter" trading of stocks and bonds

    c.   taking advantage of private information not available to the public by individuals who have *inside* information

    d.   takeover of Canadian companies by foreign companies

13. The number of jobs lost in Canada during the recession of 1990–1992 was

    a.   10,000

    b.   400,000

    c.   1,000,000

    d.   none

14. Canadian government cutbacks in the last decade have had the direct effect of reducing

    a.   the number of government employees

b. the level of immigration

c. the national debt

d. cooperation between the federal and provincial governments

15. The National Transportation Agency

a. subsidizes the trucking industry

b. investigates train and plane accidents

c. ensures that all provinces have the same safety regulations

d. regulates the price of gasoline

True/False

1. Canada has a system of marketing boards that are designed to stabilize the supply of agricultural products and their prices.

2. Canadian-based companies are exempt from federal income tax.

3. Canada is a member of the Group of Seven (eight, including Russia) leading industrial countries.

4. Municipalities do not play a role in consumer protection.

5. The Canadian government has sold off all its crown corporations.

6. Alberta is the only province that does not have a sales tax other than GST.

7. The "four tigers" of Southeast Asia are South Korea, Taiwan, Hong Kong, and Singapore.

8. The Bank of Canada sets the interest rate charged by Canadian banks for loans to their customers.

9. One of the direct results of free trade with the U.S. has been the elimination of provincial policies that discriminate against companies from other provinces.

10. Fiscal policy is often used to stimulate economic activity in specific regions of the country.

11. In 1998, the Competition Bureau recommended that the Bank of Montreal and the Royal Bank of Canada be allowed to merge.

12. The Bank of Canada is prohibited from setting monetary policy.

13. The Department of Citizenship and Immigration tries to ensure that immigrants have the proper skills or finances to fit the needs of the Canadian economy.

14. Canada has a mixed economy, the U.S. does not.

15. The lowering of taxes to stimulate activity when the economy is weak is an example of the use of fiscal policy.

ANSWERS

Key Terms and Definitions

1.	Privatization	7.	fiscal policy
2.	crown corporation	8.	articles of incorporation
3.	industrial policy	9.	National Policy
4.	securities commission	10.	economies of scale
5.	marketing boards	11.	monetary policy
6.	Prospectus		

Government Involvement in the Economy

1. The seven categories are

] Laws and regulations, covering a wide range including taxation, consumer protection, labour-management relations, etc.

] Crown corporations, engaging in a wide range of activities, sometimes in competition with private companies
] Taxation and financial policies
] Financial aid, including tax reductions, tariffs and quotas, grants, loan guarantees, etc.
] Services, including direct and indirect activities such as information for new businesses, workforce training, etc.
] Purchasing policies regarding acquisition of supplies, equipment, and services used by governments themselves
] Other expenditures

2. The National Policy was designed to protect Canadian manufacturers against competition from imports from the U.S. by imposing tariffs on them. Its effect has been to raise the prices paid by Canadians.

3. Privatization is the sale to private owners of crown corporations. Examples given will vary, but include PetroCanada, Air Canada, and CN Rail.

4. A crown corporation is a company owned by government. The examples given will vary, but some of the larger ones are Canada Post, AECL, CMHC, CNR, CBC, Alberta Heritage Trust Fund, and a host of utility companies.

5. Crown corporations are used to provide services not being provided by independent business (e.g., Air Canada's predecessor, TCA, in the 1930s), bail out an industry that is in trouble (e.g., the CNR), or provide special services that would not otherwise be available (e.g., Atomic Energy of Canada).

Laws and Regulations

1. Reasons given include
   ] ensure compliance with laws or regulations
   ] no duplication of business names
   ] ensure taxes are being paid

2. Answer will vary

The Taxation of Companies

1. If taxes are lowered, costs are effectively reduced for both producers and consumers, and economic activity is stimulated. Raising taxes has an inflationary effect. Costs are effectively raised for everyone, and economic activity is slowed.

3. Reduced taxes or tax credits are used to encourage potential employers to establish operations in the depressed region. This lowers their costs, offsetting some of the additional costs associated with operating in this location.

How Governments Spend Tax Dollars to Help Business

1. The annual cost is estimated to be up to $6 billion annually. The reason is that removal of barriers would mean a difficult period of readjustment as each province loses jobs due to the closing of uncompetitive operations.

2. By imposing requirements that specified minimum portions of the finished product must be produced by Canadian companies or, at least, in Canada.

3. If a large company goes bankrupt, many thousands of jobs are lost. People working for the company's suppliers, and other creditors, as well as people whose jobs depend on spending by all of these employees, all lose their jobs, as do the employees of the company itself.

4. a. They had much larger populations, proximity to the U.S., an abundance of natural resources, and a developed transportation infrastructure.
   b. It is designed to adjust for regional economic differences. Payments are transferred from wealthy provinces to poorer ones.

The Effect of Other Departments and Regulations on Business

1. a. fiscal
   b. monetary
   c. fiscal
   d. fiscal
   e. monetary
   f. monetary
   g. fiscal
   h. fiscal
   i. fiscal

2. They examine proposed mergers to ensure that the mergers will not have the effect of unduly restricting competition. The ultimate purpose is to protect consumers from the negative effects of market dominance by very large corporations with virtually monopolistic power.

Protecting Consumers

1. The CDIC insures individual deposits in Canadian banks and trust companies. If a member bank or trust company fails, depositors are insured against losses up to $60,000. It is funded by annual insurance premiums, paid by the member banks and trust companies.

2. They regulate stock exchanges and must approve all new issues of securities in their province.

3. Municipal/local governments.
   Zoning regulations control how landowners use their property, and what they do or allow on their property, to protect the interests of the general public.

Labour Standards and Working Conditions

The lists will vary, but major topics include: minimum wage, overtime pay rates, entitlement to holiday pay and vacation pay, compensation for unjust dismissal, maternity and paternity leave, bars against discrimination or harassment, UI arrangements, CPP arrangements, workers' compensation.

Environmental Regulations

Answers will vary.

Employment and Immigration in Canada

Answers will vary.

National Research Council

Answers will vary. One argument for not cutting the NRC's budget (or even substantially increasing it) is its great contribution to the development of technological know-how. Research and development spending in Canada is, relatively, lower than in other industrialized countries, making it very difficult for Canada to compete with countries that are developing cutting-edge technology.

Government Impact on Farming Business

Marketing boards act to control the supply, and price, of products. The intention is to stabilize the industry being regulated, protecting both producers and consumers from dramatic swings in supply, and price, levels.

Role of the Canadian Government Domestically and Globally

Business and labour. Probably the academic community, too.

CHAPTER CHECK ANSWERS

1. A capitalist economy where government plays an important role, including provision of a wide range of services.
2. It is a large pool of investment funds. It was set up in 1966, to hold the funds held as a result of Quebec's operation of its own plan in parallel with the Canada Pension Plan. The Quebec government uses it as a powerful investment vehicle to guide economic development in the Province.
3. The Export Development Corporation. It provides trade financing for Canadian exporters.
4. The Business Development Bank of Canada. It acts as a lender of last resort for businesses that cannot get loans from other banks, and invests in enterprises that are starting up or expanding.
5. Municipal: property taxes
   Provincial: income taxes
   Federal: income taxes
6. The provinces have clung to the logic that says when provincial government money is being spent it should be spent within the province, paid to local contractors rather than contractors from out-of-province. However, the result is frequently that costs are higher than they otherwise would be, because economies of scale cannot be achieved.
7. Under the transfer payment system, some of the monies collected from the wealthier provinces are redistributed to poorer provinces, reducing the difference in wealth between them.
8. Monetary policy. Higher interest rates tend to discourage business activity and purchasing, to slow the economy down. Lower rates have the exact opposite effect.
9. A prospectus is a document, which must be approved by the securities commission, which provides all of the relevant information about the company and its plans. It is required in order to make sure that potential investors are aware of these matters.
10. The system of supply management reflected by marketing boards does not permit normal competitive forces to operate. Its opponents argue that it artificially inflates prices by protecting producers against

development of lower-priced competing suppliers.
11. Japan, Germany, South Korea, Taiwan, Singapore, Hong Kong.

PRACTICE TEST

Multiple Choice		True/False	
1.	d	1.	T
2.	a	2.	F
3.	b	3.	T
4.	b	4.	F
5.	b	5.	F
6.	d	6.	T
7.	c	7.	T
8.	d	8.	F
9.	c	9.	F
10.	a	10.	T
11.	d	11.	F
12.	c	12.	F
13.	b	13.	T
14.	a	14.	F
15.	b	15.	T

CHAPTER 5

Ethical Behaviour, the Environment, and Social Responsibility

Learning Goals

After you have read and studied this chapter, you should be able to

1. Discuss how business, in the early capitalist period, ignored ethical standards of behaviour.
2. Describe the modern beginnings of business ethics and understand why ethical issues are so important now.
3. Define management's role in setting ethical standards and list the six-step approach to ethical decisions.
4. Identify what first led to concern about the environment and list some of the major environmental problems.
5. Understand why business tends to see a conflict between a clean environment and competitive ability.
6. Describe the Rule of 72 and explain its relationship to growth.
7. Explain how sustainable development has become the major international goal for reconciling growth with environmental constraints.

Key Terms and Definitions

Listed here are important terms found in this chapter. Choose the correct term for each definition and write it in the space provided.

bid rigging   NIMBY   social audit
corporate social responsibility organic farming   stakeholders
exponential function   robber barons   white-collar crime
laissez-faire capitalism   Rule of 72

1. _white-collar crime_ Crime, usually theft, committed by an executive or other white-collar office worker.

2. _organic farming_ Farming that is done without chemicals.

3. _Rule of 72_ Divide the rate of increase of any activity into 72 to get the number of years it takes for the result of that activity to double.

4. _Robber barons_ Capitalists of the 19th century whose wealth came in part through shady if not criminal acts.

5. _NIMBY_ Not in my backyard; people don't want waste disposal facilities in their towns, though they agree that such facilities are needed somewhere.

6. _Corporate social responsibility_ The recognition by corporations that their actions must take into account the needs and ethical standards of society.

7. _exponential function_ The mathematical description of anything that changes steadily in one direction over a given period of time.

8. _____Stakeholders_____ Those people who can affect or are affected by the achievement of an organization's objectives.

9. _____Social adult_____ A systematic evaluation of an organization's progress toward implementing programs that are socially responsible and responsive.

10. _____bid rigging_____ Secret agreement among competitors to make artificially high bids.

11 __laissez-faire capitalism__ Theory that if left alone, unhindered by government, the free market in pursuit of economic efficiency would provide an abundance of goods at the lowest prices, improving everyone's life.

11 ~~_____~~ Theory that if left alone, unhindered by government, the free market in pursuit of economic efficiency would provide an abundance of goods at the lowest prices, improving everyone's life.

A Brief History of Ethics in Business

1. What event in the 1960's, attributable largely to Ralph Nader's efforts, has been called "the first important signal of a move toward corporate social responsibility?"

   Ralph Nader wrote "unsafe at any speed" questioning GM's ethics

   → first recall in the history of automobile making

   _→_

2. a. Describe the relationship between Adam Smith's economic philosophy and laissez-faire capitalism.

   laissez-faire is a laid-back theory — let things work themselves out, and like Adam Smith's philosophy, let the gov't take care of it.

   → INVISIBLE HAND ←

   b. What led to the twentieth century move away from laissez-faire capitalism?

   _____

   _____

   _____

   _____

A New Emphasis on Corporate Social Responsibility

1. What is the distinction between acting legally and acting ethically?

    _____
    _____
    _____
    _____

2. Where does a sense of personal ethics begin?

    _____
    _____
    _____

3. How *socially minded* are Canadians in general? Explain your reasoning.

    _____
    _____
    _____

4. What is an *ethical dilemma*?

    _____
    _____
    _____

5. What are three questions to ask yourself when faced with an ethical dilemma?
    a. _____
    b. _____
    c. _____

6. Where does a sense of organizational ethics begin?

    _____
    _____
    _____

7. How do people learn standards and values?

    _____
    _____
    _____

8. What is *corporate social responsibility*?

    _____
    _____
    _____

9. Describe three dimensions of corporate social responsibility.
    a. _____
    b. _____
    c. _____

10. What is the responsibility of business to customers? What is the surest way of failing to please customers?

_____
_____
_____

11. What could be the payoff for socially conscious behaviour for a business?

_____
_____
_____

12. How does socially responsible behaviour affect shareholders and potential investors?

_____
_____
_____

13. What responsibilities do businesses have toward employees?

_____
_____
_____

14. Daryl, the general supervisor of a marketing department, is an ambitious young man. He is writing a book that he hopes will make a name for him in the business community. Because the word processing for the actual text is very time-consuming, Daryl is using the secretary he shares with two other managers, as well as some of his market research interns to type the book while they're at work. Because they are often busy doing his book, people from the other departments are finding they can't get their work-related business done. The secretary and interns feel they have to do what Daryl says because he is their direct supervisor.

You are Daryl's peer in another department, and you also have some outside work you need to have typed. You're annoyed at Daryl's actions, but would rather not inform your boss (who is also Daryl's boss) about what's going on because you want to maintain a friendly working relationship with Daryl, and besides, you never know how "the boss" is going to react. Sometimes you begin to think that if Daryl can get away with using company equipment, personnel, and time for his personal projects, why can't you?

What would you do?

_____
_____
_____
_____

15. You work for a major car manufacturer as a district manager, calling on car dealerships as a representative of the manufacturer. It is three days before the end of a sales incentive contest, and one of your dealers is close to winning a trip to Hawaii. If your dealer wins the contest for your area, you get a lot of recognition and a good chance for a promotion, which will enable you to stop travelling so much during the week. The dealer wants you to report as sold eight cars that he has not yet sold but will have deals on next week. Those eight cars will put him over the top and enable him to win the contest. You just received a directive from the corporate headquarters on this practice of pre-reporting

sales, indicating that the company would take strong action against anyone discovered doing so. But your boss and his boss have taken you aside and encouraged you to take whatever action is necessary to win the contest. You think you could get by with it and not get caught. An added problem is that the customer warranty starts the day the car is reported sold, so whoever purchases the car would lose several days of warranty service.

What is the "ethical" thing for you to do? What would you do?

_____
_____
_____
_____
_____

16. How would you answer the following questions? Did you act in an ethical manner?
    Have you ever
    a. taken paper, pens, paper clips, staplers, etc. from your employer?
    b. let a friend borrow a term paper you have written to hand in for another class?
    c. been undercharged in a store and failed to tell the cashier?
    d. failed to inform a competitor (in a class or a game or in a job) about something important to both of you?
    e. taken a gift from a supplier or salesman trying to sell you something even though you had no intention of buying?

17. Given your responses in question 4, what is meant by "Ethical behaviour begins at home"?

_____
_____
_____
_____
_____

Some Questionable Practices

1. a. How would you respond to the R.J. Reynolds company's argument that "no linkage has been made between advertising and the consumption of cigarette products," in answer to the criticism it faced regarding the use of the cartoon character Joe Camel (who is readily identified by young children throughout the U.S.) in its advertising?

    _____
    _____
    _____
    _____
    _____

    b. Is your response to Part A influenced by the fact that you are a smoker or non-smoker? Explain why or why not.

    _____
    _____

_____
_____
_____

Progress in Corporate Social Responsibility

What are the six steps to follow for a long-term improvement of business ethics?

a. _____

b. _____

c. _____

d. _____

e. _____

f. _____

Corporate Responsibility in the 21st Century

1. Read the situation described below and answer the questions that follow.

   Dan Furlong, president of a successful medium-sized firm that supplies parts for electric motors, was being interviewed by the business features writer of the local newspaper. The reporter asked Dan his views on social responsibility, and how his firm reflected a socially responsible position. Dan replied that although he had never done a so-called social audit ("as the textbooks call it"), he did figure that he was a good corporate citizen. He said, "I pay our employees a good salary, and the guys in the shop are getting paid above average hourly for this area. I make a profit, and give everyone a bonus at the holidays. We take a lot of precautions in the shop, and no one's had an accident in several years. Whenever we have customer complaints, I make sure someone handles them right away. I charge what I think is a fair price for our product, which is of a higher quality than most. I pay my bills on time and don't cheat on my taxes."

   a. Keeping the idea of social audits and socially responsible business activities in mind, is Mr. Furlong running his business in a socially responsible manner?

   _____
   _____
   _____
   _____
   _____

   b. What suggestions would you make to improve Mr. Furlong's position, if any?

   _____
   _____
   _____
   _____
   _____

2. Identify seven classes of stakeholders who are affected by a company's actions.

   _____
   _____
   _____

_____

_____

3. a. Describe the two different views of corporate responsibility to stakeholders.

_____

_____

_____

_____

_____

b. Which view do you consider to be more appropriate? Why?

_____

_____

_____

_____

_____

The Impact of Environmental Issues on Business

1. In your text, there is a discussion of the UN Conferences on the Environment and Development, held in Rio de Janeiro in 1992, Geneva in 1996, Bonn in 1997, and Kyoto in 19989. It says that the conference goal is "to find a way to bridge that divide between wealth and nature, growth and conservation, developed and developing." Go to the library and do some research on the conferences. What countries have taken what positions? What resolutions have been passed and what decisions have been taken? Why do you think the conferences have achieved the things they have, and failed to achieve the things they have not? How do you think the results could be improved?

_____

_____

_____

_____

_____

2. The harvesting of B.C.'s first-growth forests has been a major political issue for years. Environmentalists and aboriginal peoples demand new laws to protect the trees, while those in the lumber industries argue against them. What are the main arguments on both sides? What is *your* position on the issue? Describe your reasoning.

_____

_____

_____

_____

_____

_____

_____

_____

_____

3. Your text described the environmental problems associated with the sinking of the tanker *Irving Whale*. Who do you think should pay for raising the *Irving Whale* and related clean-up costs? Explain.

_____

_____

_____

_____

_____

4. What are four types of "watch-dog" groups that monitor how well companies enforce ethical and social responsibility policies?

a. _____

b. _____

c. _____

d. _____

The Problem of Endless Growth

1. Various scientists, including David Suzuki, have argued that the rapid rates of population growth and resource consumption cannot be sustained indefinitely. If new attitudes and policies are not in place within 20 years, it will be too late to avoid an eventual collapse. Others argue that mankind has always managed to develop solutions to such problems before disaster strikes. What is your view?

_____

_____

_____

_____

_____

What is the Answer?

1. "Enviropig" is the name of the genetically engineered pig developed at the University of Guelph. Its great benefit is that its manure is much more environmentally friendly than that of other pigs.
   a. Discuss the pros and cons of this sort of genetic engineering.

_____

_____

_____

_____

_____

   b. Do you feel that there are ethical issues involved in genetic engineering intended to reshape the characteristics of various forms of animal life? Discuss.

_____

_____
_____
_____
_____

A Radically Different Answer

1. How does Paul Hawken, author of *The Ecology of Commerce*, suggest the philosophy of taxation must be revised in order to facilitate long-term economic and ecological sustainability?

_____
_____
_____
_____
_____

CHAPTER CHECK

1. What does the term "corporate social responsibility" mean?

_____
_____
_____
_____
_____

2. Describe Adam Smith's notion of the "invisible hand," and how it led to strong support for laissez-faire capitalism.

_____
_____
_____
_____
_____

3. Identify and describe at least four of the "questionable practices" discussed in your text.

    a. _____

    b. _____

    c. _____

    d. _____

4. Identify and describe at least two "questionable practices" not discussed in your text.

a. _____

_____

_____

b. _____

_____

_____

_____

5. What does "NIMBY" mean? Do you have any suggestions for dealing with the NIMBY mentality?

_____

_____

_____

_____

_____

6. What is "sustainable development"?

_____

_____

_____

_____

_____

7. What is the Rule of 72?

_____

_____

_____

_____

_____

8. Describe the six-step approach to long-term improvement of business ethics.

_____

_____

_____

_____

_____

PRACTICE TEST

Multiple Choice: Circle the best answer.

1. The difference between ethics and legality is that
   a. Legality reflects how people should treat each other, while ethics is more limiting.
   b. Ethics refers to ways available to us to protect ourselves from theft, violence, and fraud.
   c. Legality is more limiting than ethics and applies to written laws.
   d. Ethics refers to a narrower range of behaviour than legality.

2. _____ is behaviour that is accepted by society as morally right.
   a. Ethics
   b. Legality
   c. Integrity
   d. Social responsibility

3. Sometimes an obvious choice from an ethical standpoint has personal or professional drawbacks. An example might be when a supervisor asks you to do something unethical, and you face negative consequences if you refuse. When you are in such a situation you are faced with
   a. two lousy choices
   b. an ethical dilemma
   c. deciding the legality of your choice
   d. a social responsibility issue

4. An ethics-based manager has all of the following in mind when attempting to make an ethical decision EXCEPT
   a. creating a win-win situation for all parties
   b. avoiding major imbalances whenever possible
   c. making sure his/her department wins over another department
   d. making a decision that benefits all parties involved

5. Many people now believe that ethics has _____ to do with management.
   a. little
   b. nothing
   c. something
   d. everything

6. Organizational ethics begin
   a. at the top levels of management
   b. only with employees
   c. with the unions
   d. with mid-level managers

7. People learn standards from
   a. observing what others do
   b. listening to what people say
   c. making their own decisions
   d. following corporate goals and standards

8. The first step to improving business ethics is the following:
   a. Managers must be trained to consider ethical implications of decisions.
   b. An ethics office should be set up.
   c. Outsiders should be told about the ethics program.
   d. Top management must adopt a code of conduct.

9. Which of the following would NOT be considered as a dimension of the social performance of a corporation?
   a. corporate philanthropy
   b. corporate legal standards
   c. corporate policy
   d. corporate responsibility

10. Being energy conscious, ensuring that employees have a safe working environment, and monitoring corporate hiring policies to prevent discrimination is part of
    a. corporate philanthropy
    b. corporate responsibility
    c. corporate policy
    d. corporate legal standards

11. Who are the stakeholders to whom a business is responsible?
    a. employees
    b. customers
    c. investors
    d. all of the above

12. In terms of social responsibility, many people believe that
    a. it makes good financial sense when companies are not "up front" about potential product problems.
    b. it makes financial and moral sense to invest in companies whose goods and services benefit the community and the environment.
    c. businesses have no responsibility to create jobs.
    d. businesses have no responsibility to social causes.

13. Which of the following would NOT be included in a social audit?
    a. Support for higher education, the arts, and nonprofit social agencies
    b. Community-related activities such as fund-raising
    c. Employee-related activities
    d. Ability to compete with other major firms

14. Government and business leaders are being held to
    a. lower ethical standards than in the past.
    b. ethical standards in Canada, but foreign leaders are not being subjected to ethical scrutiny.
    c. higher ethical standards than in the past.
    d. ethical standards that cannot be met by most leaders.

15. Canadian businesses are
    a. demanding socially responsible behaviour from international suppliers, particularly in the areas of environmental standards and human rights issues.
    b. holding international suppliers to different standards than Canadian companies must adhere to at home.
    c. not concerned with the ethical or socially responsible behaviour of their international suppliers.
    d. are demanding that international suppliers adhere to higher standards than their Canadian counterparts.

True/False

1.	The first step in ethical behaviour is following the law.
2.	According to the text, ethical behaviour begins with observing religious leaders.
3.	An ethics-based manager will always try to do whatever will benefit his or her department over all others.
4.	There are usually easy solutions to ethical problems.
5.	With strong ethical leadership, employees feel part of a corporate mission that is socially beneficial.
6.	The first step to improving business ethics is for top management to adopt and unconditionally support explicit codes of conduct.
7.	The best way to communicate to all employees that an ethics code is serious and cannot be broken is to back the program with timely action if rules are broken.
8.	Corporate social responsibility is the concern businesses have for their profitability.
9.	In reality, it appears that people want to be socially responsible, but they can't define what being socially responsible means.
10.	One of the best ways to please customers is to hide product defects from them.

11.   Businesses have a responsibility to employees to create jobs.
12.   Businesses owe it to employees to maintain job security, or warn employees if layoffs are inevitable.
13.   One of businesses' major responsibilities to the environment is not to pollute.
14.   One element of a business's social responsibility programs includes such activities as local fund-raising campaigns and donating executive time to nonprofit organizations.
15.   Ethical problems and issues of social responsibility are unique to Canada and the United States.

ANSWERS

Key Terms and Definitions

1.   white-collar crime
2.   Organic farming
3.   Rule of 72
4.   Robber barons
5.   NIMBY
6.   Corporate social responsibility

7.   exponential function
8.   stakeholders
9.   social audit
10.   bid rigging
11.   laissez-faire capitalism

A Brief History of Ethics in Business

1. The first recall of cars in the history of automobile manufacturing. It was GM's recall of defective Corvairs.

2. a. Adam Smith believed in the operation of the "invisible hand," that would provide an abundance of goods at the lowest price, improving everyone's life. Laissez-faire capitalism adopted this approach; governments did not intervene, but relied on the invisible hand to guide economic activity.

   b. The invisible hand wasn't working as well as expected. It failed to prevent arbitrary discrimination, high unemployment, severe cyclical changes causing booms and busts, etc.

A New Emphasis on Corporate Social Responsibility

1. Many immoral and unethical acts are legal. Being legal means following the laws written to protect ourselves from fraud, theft, and violent acts. Ethical behaviour requires more than simply following the law, and looks at behaviour in terms of people's relations with one another.
2. A sense of personal ethics begins at home!
3. It appears we are not as socially minded as we could be. Many Canadians do not give any volunteer service time to the community, many do not support charities. Many students confess to cheating on exams. Maybe times are changing though?
4. An ethical dilemma is a situation in which there may be no desirable alternative. You must choose between equally unsatisfactory alternatives when making a decision.

5. Three questions to ask are:
   a.   Is it legal?
   b.   Is it balanced ("Am I acting fairly?")
   c.   How will it make me feel about myself?
6. A sense of organizational ethics is instilled by the leadership and example of strong top managers.
7. People learn their standards and values from observing what others do.
8. Corporate social responsibility is the concern businesses have for the welfare of society.
9. a.   corporate philanthropy – charitable donations
   b.   corporate responsibility – in all business decisions, such as hiring, pollution control and product decisions
   c.   corporate policy – the position taken on social and political issues
10. One responsibility of business is to satisfy customers by offering them goods and services that have a real value to the customer. One of the surest ways of failing to please customers is not being totally honest with them.
11. The payoff for socially conscious behaviour could be new business as customers switch from rival companies simply because they admire a company's social efforts. This can become a powerful competitive edge.
12. Ethical and socially responsible behaviour is good for shareholder wealth and adds to the bottom line. In fact, many people believe it makes financial, as well as moral, sense to invest in companies that are planning ahead to create a better environment. By choosing to put their money into companies whose goods and services benefit the community and the environment, investors can improve their own financial health while improving society's health.
13. The responsibilities of businesses to employees include:
   a.   a responsibility to create jobs
   b.   an obligation to fairly reward hard work and talent
   c.   a responsibility to maintain job security, or if layoffs are impossible to avoid, businesses have a responsibility to give employees warning.
14. This is a difficult problem, but ethically it's not really too hard to figure out what to do. The decision about going to the boss is an individual one, but using the secretary and the interns for personal business, particularly to the extent that Daryl is doing, is unethical.
15. There is no "correct" answer!
16. Answers will vary.
17. The phrase "ethical behaviour begins at home" means that we cannot expect "society" to become more moral and ethical unless we as individuals commit to becoming more moral and ethical ourselves.

Some Questionable Practices

1. a. & b. Answers will vary widely. What is important is that you think seriously about the issues and reach your own well thought-out conclusions.

Progress in Corporate Social Responsibility

The six steps are
a.   Top management must adopt and support an explicit code of conduct.

b. Employees must understand that top management expects ethical behaviour.
c. Managers and employees must be trained to consider ethical implications of business decisions.
d. Companies must set up an ethics office for employees to inquire about ethical matters.
e. Outsiders must be told about the ethics program.
f. The ethics code must be enforced.

Corporate Responsibility in the 21st Century

1. Answers will vary. Some will include
    a. Social responsibility includes providing a safer work environment, good benefits, product safety, prompt complaint handling, and honest pricing policies. The result of a social audit would indicate that Mr. Furlong is running his business in a socially responsible manner, as far as he goes.
    b. Although he would get fairly high scores from his employees in social responsibility, Mr. Furlong doesn't appear to have any involvement with the community in which he operates. Of the three dimensions of corporate social performance, he addresses only the corporate responsibility issue; those of corporate philanthropy and corporate policy appear to be ignored. He could improve community relations (and even increase his customer base) by encouraging his employees to get involved in community-related projects, donating time and/or money to local charities, developing a stand on local issues important to the community, and improving employee-related benefits with job enrichment and employee development programs.
2. Shareholders, employees, customers, suppliers, distributors, competitors, and the public.
3. a. The strategic approach requires that management's primary orientation be toward the economic interests of shareholders. The pluralist approach recognizes the responsibility of management to optimize profits, but not at the expense of employees, suppliers, customers, and community at large.
    b. Answers will vary.

The Impact of Environmental Issues on Business

1. Answers will vary. There should be some understanding of the differences in problems and issues faced by developed and developing countries.
2. Answers will vary, but should include some discussion of the role of government in protecting society from the ill effects of business activities and in creating an environment that encourages businesses to create jobs, etc.
3. Answers will vary.
4. a. socially conscious investors, who insist that companies extend the company's high standards to all their suppliers
    b. environmentalists, who apply pressure by naming companies that don't abide by environmentalists' standards
    c. union officials, who force companies to comply with standards to avoid negative publicity
    d. customers who take their business elsewhere if a company demonstrates unethical and socially irresponsible practices.

The Problem of Endless Growth

1. Answers will vary. Attention should be paid to the exponential rate of growth in consumption and the fact that it cannot be sustained without a dramatic increase in the resources available. Either growth must be curtailed or more resources must be "created" for sustainability to be achieved.

What is the Answer?

1. Answers will vary considerably!

A Radically Different Answer

1. Instead of taxing jobs, payrolls, creativity, and real income, what must be taxed are degradation, pollution, and depletion of resources.

CHAPTER CHECK ANSWERS

1. The recognition by corporations that their actions must take into account the needs and ethical standards of society.
2. If left alone and unhindered by government, the free market in pursuit of economic efficiency will provide an abundance of goods at the lowest prices, improving everyone's life, including rewards for the capitalist (for work and taking on financial risk) and the population in general (by creating employment and improving living standards).
3. a. Weapons sales to governments such as Saddam Hussein's in Iraq.
   b. Sale of nuclear reactors to governments such as Nicolae Ceausescu's in Romania.
   c. The proliferation of land mines that kill innocent victims in many African and Asian nations.
   d. Inadequate testing that allowed HIV infected blood to enter the Canadian blood supply.
   e. Pay discrimination against women.
      Etc.
4. a. & b. Answers will vary.
5. "Not in my backyard!" Suggestions for how to deal with the NIMBY mentality will vary.
6. Economic and industrial development that can be sustained over time without damaging the environment.
7. Dividing the rate of increase of any activity into 72 will give the number of years it takes for the result of the activity to double.
8. a. Top management must adopt and support an explicit corporate code of conduct.
   b. Employees must understand that expectations for ethical behaviour begin at the top and senior management expects all employees to act accordingly.
   c. Managers and others must be trained to consider the ethical implications of all business decisions.
   d. An ethics office must be established, and employees must be able to call it anonymously.
   e. Outsiders must be told about the ethics program.
   f. The ethics code must be enforced.

PRACTICE TEST

Multiple Choice		**True/False**	
1.	c	1.	T
2.	a	2.	F
3.	b	3.	F
4.	c	4.	F
5.	d	5.	T
6.	a	6.	T
7.	a	7.	T
8.	d	8.	F
9.	b	9.	T
10.	c	10.	F
11.	d	11.	T
12.	b	12.	T
13.	d	13.	T
14.	c	14.	T
15.	a	15.	F

CHAPTER 6

Forms of Business Organization

Learning Goals

After you have read and studied this chapter, you should be able to

1. List the three basic forms of business ownership and compare the advantages and disadvantages of each.
2. Explain the differences between limited and general partnerships.
3. Summarize the important clauses of a partnership agreement.
4. Define public and private corporations.
5. Compare the advantages and disadvantages of private and public corporations.
6. Define franchising and compare its advantages and disadvantages.
7. Outline the areas you need to analyze when evaluating a franchise.

Key Terms and Definitions

Listed here are important terms found in this chapter. Choose the correct term for each definition and write it in the space provided.

acquisition ✓	franchisor ✓	partnership agreement ✓
cooperative ✓	general partner	private corporation ✓
corporation ✓	horizontal merger ✓	public corporation ✓
franchise ✓	limited liability ✓	sole proprietorship ✓
franchise agreement ✓	limited partner ✓	unlimited liability ✓
franchisee ✓	merger ✓	vertical merger ✓
franchising ✓	partnership ✓	

1. ___unlimited liability___ The responsibility of a business owner for all of the debts of the business, making the personal assets of the owners vulnerable to claims against the business.

2. ___partnership agreement___ Legal document that specifies the rights and responsibilities of the members of a partnership.

3. ___public corporation___ A corporation that has the right to issue shares to the public; its shares may be listed on stock exchanges.

4. ___horizontal merger___ The joining of two firms in the same industry, to allow them to diversify or expand.

5. ___limited partner___ Owner who invests money in the business, but does not have any management responsibility or liability for losses beyond the investment.

6. ___cooperative___ An organization that is owned by members who pay an annual membership fee and share in any profits.

7. ___sole proprietorship___ A business that is owned directly, and usually managed, by one person.

8. ___franchisor___ A company that develops a product concept and sells others

the right to make and sell the products.

9. _Franchise agreement_ An arrangement whereby someone with a good idea for a business sells the rights to use the business name and sell its products or services in a given territory.

10. _Franchise_ The right to use a specific business's name and sell its products or services in a given territory.

11. _vertical merger_ The joining of two firms involved in different stages of related businesses.

12. _limited liability_ The responsibility of a business's owners for losses only up to the amount they invest.

13. _acquisition_ One company buys another company.

14. _corporation_ A legal entity with an existence separate from its owners.

15. _general partner_ One of two or more owners who has unlimited liability and is active in managing the firm.

16. _private corporation_ Corporation that is not allowed to issue stock to the public; its shares are not listed on stock exchanges and the number of shareholders is limited to an established maximum.

17. _franchisee_ A person who buys a franchise.

18. _merger_ The result of two firms uniting to form one company.

19. _partnership_ A legal form of business with two or more owners.

20. _franchising_ A method of distributing a product or service, or both, to achieve a maximum market impact with a minimum investment.

Forms of Business Ownership

1. What are the three major forms of business ownership?
   - Sole proprietorship
   - partnership
   - corporation

2. What percentage of all sales in Canada are made by corporations? By sole proprietorships? By partnerships?
   87% corporations
   9% proprietorship
   4% partnership

Sole Proprietorships

1. What are the advantages of a sole proprietorship?
   a. ease of starting & ending the business
   b. being your own boss
   c. pride of ownership
   d. retention of profit
   e.

2. What are the disadvantages of sole proprietorships?
   a. *unlimited liability — risks of losses*
   b. *limited financial resources*
   c. *overwhelming time commitment*
   d. *few fringe benefits*
   e. *limited growth*
   f. *limited lifespan*
   g. _____

3. Jeff Baker has his own business as the owner of a tanning salon in his home town. Bill Jacobs is interested in going into business for himself and has come to Jeff for advice and information.

   The following statements are from Jeff's conversation with Bill. Read each statement and decide whether Jeff is referring to (i) an advantage or a disadvantage of having a sole proprietorship, and (ii) what that advantage or disadvantage is.

   a. i. *Adv.*

   ii. *ease of starting*

   "After I had purchased the necessary equipment, all I had to do was open my doors; it was as easy as that."

   b. i. *Disadv.*

   ii. *time commitment*

   "I get here at 8 a.m., two hours before we open, and I don't usually leave until 10 or 11 p.m."

   c. i. _____

   ii. _____

   "I owe a lot of money for this tanning equipment. I'll be in pretty bad shape if we go under."

   d. i. *dis*

   ii. *few fringe benefits*

   "When I worked for AMF, I had company-paid life and health insurance. I don't have those anymore."

   e. i. _____

   ii. _____

   "The fun thing about owning this business is how creative I can be. I can try things I couldn't try in my old job."

   f. i. *adv*

   ii. *Retention of profit*

   "We made a profit for the first six months of the year. We bought a new car."

   g. i. _____

   ii. _____

   "I need to find a good bookkeeper. I'm a salesman, not an accountant."

   h. i. _____

   ii. _____

   "I'd like to open another facility on the other side of town, but we don't have the money, and I'm at my limit with the bank."

   i. i. _____

   ii. _____

   "My accountant needed a lot of forms, but I shouldn't have to pay anything extra this year."

   j. i. _____

   ii. _____

   "I need to talk to my lawyer about making a will. I'd like to make sure my kids will get the business if something happens to me."

   k. i. *dis*
   ii. *few fringe benefits*

   "I can't be sick!"

   l. i. _____

   "Hey man, I did a good job on this!"

ii. _____

Partnerships

1. What are two forms of partnerships under the law?
   a. limited _____ b. general _____

2. What is the difference between a limited partner and a general partner?
   limited partner is one who invests money in a company but has no management responsibilities of loss
   _____
   _____
   _____

3. What are the advantages of a partnership?
   a. more financial resources _____
   b. shared management _____
   c. _____

4. What are the disadvantages of a partnership?
   a. unlimited liability _____
   b. division of profits _____
   c. disagreements among partners _____
   d. difficult to terminate _____

5. a. Joe Langston and Randy Allen want to work together as partners in a consulting business. Joe is an engineer, Randy an architect, and they have already started doing some business. Joe and Randy have come to you, their good friend and business school graduate, for information on what they should do to get the partnership started. What will you tell them?

   b. Joe and Randy have considered that sometime in the future they may want to expand their partnership in some way. The various categories of partners are

] Silent partners	] Dormant partners
] Secret partners	] Senior partners
] Nominal partners	] Junior partners

   Read the following situations and match to the correct category of partner:

   i. _____ Randy's younger sister Linda is in architecture school and would eventually like to assume a limited role in managing the partnership.

   ii. _____ H.O. Kyota, an experienced architect, is actively helping Joe and Randy with the management, but prefers to remain anonymous as he has his own large firm.

   iii. _____ Chuck Vaaler is a prominent engineer in town who is lending his name to Randy and Joe for promotional purposes only. He is not actually involved in management and is not an investor.

   iv. _____ Joe has a friend, Sam, who has bought into the partnership. Sam wants no role in management, but is proud of his investment and has told all his friends.

   v. _____ There are several individuals who worked with Randy and Joe at their former employer, who would like to invest. However these people are still employed at the old firm, don't want to be identified as investors, and don't have time to be involved in management.

vi. _____ As their partnership grows, Randy and Joe expect to continue to be the major decision makers, and to take the lion's share of the profits.

Corporations

To avoid the disadvantages of sole proprietorships and partnerships, business owners may choose to incorporate.   *public or private*

1. What are the advantages of incorporation?

a. *More money for investment*
b. *size*
c. *separation of ownership from management*
d. *limited liability*
e. *perpetual life*
f. *ease of ownership change*

2. What are the disadvantages of incorporation?

a. *more paperwork*
b. *less flexability*
c. *initial cost*

3. Read the following statements. Which advantage is being described in each one?

a. _____ The initial sale of stock to anyone who is interested.
b. _____ The ability to diversify the risk of doing business.
c. _____ The opportunity to bring in different owners at any time.
d. *limited liability* The owners of the company don't have to be involved in running the business.
e. _____ In case of failure, a stockholder can lose only the amount he or she has invested, and cannot be sued.
f. *perpetual life* If an owner dies, the company does not necessarily go out of business.

Corporate Expansion: Mergers and Acquisitions

1. What is a merger?
   Merger is when two companies unite to make one company

2. What is the difference between a merger and an acquisition?

89

acquisition is when one company buys the other one to unite.

3. a. What are the two major types of corporate mergers?

    i. _____

    ii. _____

    b. Which type of merger is demonstrated by the following examples?

    i. _____ In the past, Holiday Inns, Inc. has purchased carpet mills and furniture manufacturers to supply its hotels in a more cost-efficient manner.

    ii. _____ The Toronto-Dominion Bank acquired Central Guaranty Trust.

Franchising

to other stores/companies

1. What is the difference between a franchisor and a franchisee?

    – *franchisor sells the right to sell their product*

    – *franchisee buys a franchise*

2. List four advantages of owning a franchise.

    a. *training & management assistance*

    b. *personal ownership*

    c. *nationally recognised name*

    d. *franchise advice & assistance*

3. Why does a franchisee have a greater chance of succeeding in business?

    a. *large start-up costs*

    b. *shared profit*

    c. *management regulation*

    d. *coattail effects – success is tied to franchisors success*

4. List four disadvantages of owning a franchise.

    a. _____
    b. _____
    c. _____
    d. _____
    e. _____
    f. _____

5. Kentucky Fried Chicken (KFC) is an international fast-food franchise. All prospective KFC franchise owners must go through an evaluation process, during which they must submit an application and site proposal for approval and submit to a personal interview in Louisville, Ky., KFC's headquarters. Upon approval, KFC offers the franchisee a training program covering management functions such as accounting, sales, advertising, and purchasing. KFC pays a portion of this training program. KFC

makes available to the franchisee an advertising and promotion kit, opening assistance, equipment layout plans, and a choice of interior decor from a list they provide. In addition to standard menu items, a franchisee may offer other items upon approval from KFC management. KFC outlines the estimated cash requirements for opening for such things as equipment, insurance payments, utility down payments, as well as for the facility itself to give franchisees an idea of their cash needs. The franchise fee and the costs of the building and land are the responsibility of the franchisee. There is a royalty rate based on a percentage of gross sales which is paid on a regular basis to KFC for continuing franchises.

KFC advertises on nationwide television on behalf of its franchisees, so local owners do not have to develop their own television advertising. The local owners do pay a percentage of their gross sales to KFC as a national advertising fee, and each franchisee is required to spend an additional percentage for local advertising.

Based on this description, identify some of the benefits and drawbacks of owning a franchise.

_____
_____
_____
_____
_____
_____
_____
_____
_____
_____
_____
_____
_____
_____
_____
_____
_____
_____
_____

Cooperatives

1. What are two kinds of cooperatives?
   a. producer
   b. consumer

2. What is the members' benefit in a *producer* co-op?
   Combined purchasing power is used to buy equipment, seeds etc.
   et

3. What is the members' benefit in a *consumer* co-op?
   _____
   _____
   _____
   _____

4. What kind of involvement do members of cooperatives have?

_____

_____

_____

_____

Which Form Is for You?

1. There are many choices for business ownership. What would be the best choice for these types of businesses? Why?

   a. Landscape/lawn care service

   _partnership on sole proprietorship_____

   _____

   _____

   _____

   b. Small manufacturer of component parts for automobiles

   _partnership corporation_____

   _____

   _____

   _____

   c. Fast-food restaurant

   _franchise_____

   _____

   _____

   _____

   d. Construction/remodeling firm

   _partnership or proprietorship_____

   _____

   _____

   _____

2. Read the following description and determine which form of ownership you think would be most appropriate.

   Julie Anderson wants to start her own business as a financial consultant. As in many service-type businesses, there won't be a substantial capital investment: Julie already has the computer she thinks she'll need, and she plans to start out working from her home, opening up an office later. Julie anticipates the major start-up costs to be the initial office supplies, some advertising, and the costs associated with a seminar she would like to sponsor to introduce her service to prospective clients. Julie likes the idea of being her own boss, and she wants control of the business, but she doesn't have the money to cover these initial expenses. As with most small businesses, it is unlikely that Julie could obtain a bank loan for the money she needs.

   a. Which form of ownership would you recommend?

   _____

b. What are the advantages and disadvantages of your suggestion?

Advantages	Disadvantages

CHAPTER CHECK

1. List four common forms of business ownership in Canada.

   —Sole proprietorship
   — panthership
   — corporation
   — cooperative

2. What proportion of Canadian businesses are sole proprietorships? Corporations? Partnerships?

   ~~corporations — 87%~~   corporation — 17%
   ~~partnership — 69%~~   partnership — 9%
   ~~proprietorship — 74%~~   proprietorship — 74%

3. What are the two types of partners in Canadian partnerships? What is the difference between them?

   limited partner

   general partner

4. What 16 items should be included in a partnership agreement?

   a. name of business
   b. names of all partners
   c. purpose, nature, location of business
   d. date it will start and for how long
   e. contributions of all partners
   f. management responsibilities
   g. provision of losses & profits
   h. " for accounting procedures
   i. requirements for new partners
   j. special restrictions
   k. provision for retiring partner
   l. salaries for each partner
   m. provision for share of deceased partners $
   n. " for grievances
   o. " how to dissolve partnership & distribute assets

5. Distinguish between a public corporation and a private corporation

   public — has right to sell stocks
   private — does not have right to sell stocks (also limited for # of shareholders)

93

6. Describe how ownership is transferred in
   a. sole proprietorships
   b. general partnerships
   c. limited partnerships
   d. public corporations
   e. private corporations

   a. _Sales terminates S.p._
   b. _requires partners agreement_
   c. _partnership agreement_
   d. _easy - sell shares_
   e. _"   "   "_

7. List five Canadian non-financial cooperatives and five Canadian financial cooperatives.

   Non-financial   Financial
   _____   _____
   _____   _____
   _____   _____
   _____   _____
   _____   _____

8. List four advantages and four disadvantages of working for a corporation rather than starting your own business.

   Advantages   Disadvantages
   _____   _____
   _____   _____
   _____   _____
   _____   _____

PRACTICE TEST

Multiple Choice: Circle the best answer.
1. Which of the following is NOT considered to be an advantage of sole proprietorships?
   a. It's easy to start and end.
   b. You don't have to share the profits with anyone.
   c. You get to be your own boss.
   d. You have limited liability for debts and damages.
2. One of the problems with a _____ is that there is no one to share the burden of management with.
   a. sole proprietorship
   b. limited partnership
   c. S corporation
   d. limited liability company
3. If you are interested in starting your own business, you want to minimize the hassle, and you don't want to have anyone tell you what to do, you should organize your business as a(n)
   a. S corporation
   b. limited partnership
   c. sole proprietorship
   d. closed corporation

4. When going into a partnership, you should always
   a. put all terms of the partnership into writing, in a partnership agreement
   b. make sure that you have limited liability while you are in charge
   c. make sure all the profits are reinvested into the company
   d. divide the profits equally
5. One of the benefits a general partnership has over a sole proprietorship is
   a. limited liability
   b. more financial resources
   c. easy to start
   d. a board of directors to help with decisions
6. The owners of a corporation are called
   a. general partners
   b. stockholders
   c. limited partners
   d. proprietors
7. A_____is one whose stock is not available to the public through a stock exchange.
   a. alien corporation
   b. domestic corporation
   c. public corporation
   d. private corporation
8. All of the following are advantages of a corporation EXCEPT
   a. unlimited liability
   b. the amount of money for investment
   c. the ease of changing ownership
   d. ability to raise money from investors without getting them involved in management
9. Which of the following is NOT considered an advantage of a limited liability company?
   a. limited number of shareholders
   b. personal asset protection
   c. choice of how to be taxed
   d. flexible ownership rules
10. When the May Company, which owns several department store chains, bought Lord & Taylor, another department store chain, so May could expand their product offerings, it was a
    a. vertical merger
    b. horizontal merger
    c. conglomerate merger
    d. cooperative merger
11. When a major national bakery bought out a smaller more regional bakery in the east, it took over all their assets and their debt. This is an example of a(n)
    a. acquisition
    b. merger
    c. nationalization
    d. appropriation
12. When Pat Sloane bought a Tidy Maid franchise, she became a
    a. franchisor
    b. stockholder
    c. venture capitalist
    d. franchisee

13. One of the advantages of a franchise is
   a. receiving management and marketing expertise from the franchisor
   b. fewer restrictions on selling than in other forms of businesses
   c. lower start-up costs than other businesses
   d. you get to keep all the profits after taxes
14. International franchising is
   a. a successful area for both small and large franchises
   b. costs about the same as domestic franchising
   c. becoming increasingly difficult, and so is not growing
   d. easy, because you really do not have to adapt your product at all
15. In a _____, members democratically control the business by electing a board of directors that hires professional management.
   a. corporation
   b. cooperative
   c. franchise
   d. master limited partnership

True/False

1. One of the benefits of a sole proprietorship is that you have easy availability of funds from a variety of sources.
2. It is relatively easy to get in and out of business when you are a sole proprietor.
3. A common complaint among sole proprietors is that good people to work for you are hard to find.
4. It is best to form a limited partnership, because then there is no one individual who takes on the unlimited liability.
5. In a partnership, one of the major disadvantages is the potential for conflict.
6. The owner of a corporation is called a director.
7. One advantage of a corporation is easy withdrawal of profits by owners
8. An individual may not incorporate.
9. A limited liability company can choose to be taxed either as a corporation or as a partnership.
10. An example of a vertical merger is MCI Communications and WorldCom, another communications company.
11. A franchise can be formed as a sole proprietorship, a partnership or a corporation.
12. As a franchisee, you are normally entitled to financial advice and assistance from the franchisor.
13. One of the disadvantages of a franchise is that if you want to sell, the franchisor must approve of the new owner.
14. One of the advantages that a home-based franchisee has over a business owner based at home is that the franchisee feels less isolated.
15. One element of some cooperatives is for members to work a few hours a month as part of their duties.

ANSWERS

Key Terms and Definitions

1.	unlimited liability	11.	vertical merger
2.	partnership agreement	12.	limited liability

3.	public corporation	13.	acquisition
4.	horizontal merger	14.	corporation
5.	limited partner	15.	general partner
6.	Cooperative	16.	private corporation
7.	sole proprietorship	17.	franchisee
8.	Franchisor	18.	merger
9.	franchise agreement	19.	partnership
10.	Franchise	20.	franchising

Forms of Business Ownership

1. sole proprietorship, partnership, corporation
2. 87%; 9%; 4%

Sole Proprietorships

1. a. Ease of starting and ending business
   b. Being your own boss
   c. Pride of ownership
   d. No special taxes
2. a. Unlimited liability and the risk of losses
   b. Limited financial resources
   c. Difficulty in management
   d. Overwhelming time commitment
   e. Limited growth
   g. Limited life span
3. a. i. Advantage
      ii. Easy to open
   b. i. Disadvantage
      ii. time commitment
   c. i. Disadvantage
      ii. Unlimited liability
   d. i. Disadvantage
      ii. few fringe benefits
   e. i. Advantage
      ii. you are your own boss
   f. i. Advantage
      ii. Retention of profits
   g. i. disadvantage
      ii. difficulty in management
   h. i. disadvantage
      ii. limited financial resources
   i. i. advantage
      ii. no special taxes
   j. i. disadvantage
      ii. limited life span
   k. i. disadvantage
      ii. limited growth
   l. i. advantage
      ii. pride of ownership

Partnerships

1. The two legal forms of partnership agreements are
   a. general partnership   b. limited partnership
2. In a general partnership agreement, the partners agree to share in the operation of the business and assume unlimited liability for the company's debts. In a limited partnership, the limited partners do not have an active role in managing the business, and have liability only up to the amount invested in the firm.
3. a. More financial resources
   b. Shared management/pooled knowledge
   c. Longer survival
4. a. Division of profits
   b. Disagreements between partners

    c. Difficult to terminate
    d. Unlimited liability
5. a. *Possible Answer*

    I would suggest to Joe and Randy that they draw up a partnership agreement, in writing. They need to include the name of the business and their names, and what kind of business they will be in, and where the company will be located. Since this is a service business, there may not be any significant capital investment from each partner, but both Randy and Joe need to determine how much and what each is going to contribute at the beginning of the partnership, and what proportion of profits or losses will be distributed to each partner. Although they have different backgrounds, they need to state in the agreement that Joe will handle the engineering contracts, Randy the architectural contracts. Finally, their agreement should include a description of what will happen when or if either Randy or Joe want to leave the partnership or if one of them should die, and how to take in new partners.

    b. i.   junior   iv. silent
        ii. silent   v.   dormant
        iii. nominal   vi. senior

Corporations

1. Advantages:
    -   more money for investment
    -   size
    -   separation of ownership from management
    -   limited liability
    -   perpetual life
    -   ease of ownership change

2. Disadvantages:
    -   more paperwork
    -   less flexibility
    -   legal procedures required for starting and winding-up

3. a. more money for investment
    b. size
    c. ease of ownership change
    d. separation of ownership from management
    e. limited liability
    f. perpetual life

Corporate Expansion: Mergers and Acquisitions

1. A merger is the result of two companies forming one company.
2. An acquisition is one company buying the property and obligations of another company, while a merger is when two companies join and create one company. It's like the difference between a marriage (merger) and buying a house (acquisition).
3. a. i. vertical mergers
          ii. horizontal mergers
    b. i. vertical merger
          ii. horizontal merger

Franchising

1. A franchisor is someone with a good idea for a business who sells the right to use the business name to someone else, the franchisee.
2. The advantages of a franchise are
   a. training and management assistance
   b. personal ownership
   c. nationally recognized name
   d. financial advice and assistance

3. A franchisee has a greater chance of succeeding because franchises generally
   a. have an established product
   b. help with choosing a location
   c. help with promotion
   d. assist in all phases of operation

4. The disadvantages of franchising are
   a. large start-up cost
   b. shared profit
   c. management regulation
   d. coattail effects

5. This description identifies several of the benefits of owning a franchise. One of the first in this case is the fact that KFC is a nationally recognized name, which almost guarantees an established customer base. That helps to reduce the risk of failing. KFC provides management training and pays for part of it. They offer advice with opening the store, for such things as advertising, layout, and interior decor. They offer financial advice also and give the franchisee a feel for what the initial costs are going to be. The franchisee can take advantage of a national advertising campaign, while still advertising on a local basis so they are able to meet local needs.

   The drawbacks stem from the franchise fee, which could be relatively high for a nationally recognized franchise, and so adds to the initial cost of opening. Further, a royalty rate must be paid on a regular basis to KFC, which takes away part of your profits, and the franchisee must contribute to a national advertising fund. Your menu items are limited to what the franchisor tells you, and you must get permission to offer anything different, so you are closely regulated in terms of the menu, as well as interior decor.

Cooperatives

1. Producer cooperatives and consumer cooperatives.
2. Combined purchasing power is used to buy equipment, seeds, and other items at reduced prices.
3. Members may work in the store and make their purchases there, and share any profits as a reduction in the cost of these purchases.

Which Form Is for You?

1. a. The landscape/lawn care firm could start out as a sole proprietorship or partnership. There may be no great need for capital to start out with, so there would be no need to incorporate. A partnership may be an advantage because of the amount of labour involved to build the business, and do more than one job in a day. Another possibility would be to be a sole proprietor and hire workers to help.

b. A small manufacturer of component parts would likely do best as a corporation, primarily due to the capital investment required and the need for a variety of skills such as marketing, manufacturing, engineering and so on. There is also the potential for liability in a manufacturing setting, and a corporate structure would protect the owners.

c. If you want to get into the fast-food business, one of the easiest ways would be to investigate owning a franchise. Some fast-food franchises are among the fastest growing franchises in the country, and the industry is very competitive. A "guaranteed" market would be a definite plus! The drawback, of course, is the initial expense, but if you can come up with the money a franchise may be the best way to go.

d. The construction/remodeling business again could be a sole proprietorship or partnership. There is a definite need for several people to be working, so you could either hire workers to work for you, or find a partner who can help in the business. The investment in tools may be substantial which may be another indication of the need for a partner.

2. Answers to this question will vary. However, there are some considerations. For example, (1) where to get the money for start-up costs; can it be borrowed from friends or family? If so, she could set up a limited partnership with herself as general partner, since she wants control; or she could incorporate. (2) With limited funds, the cost of incorporation may be prohibitive. (3) Since there is limited capital investment, and the risk of loss is not substantial, Julie may prefer to choose a sole proprietorship, if she can borrow the money she needs without selling a portion of the business. (4) However, at some point the issue of unlimited liability may be a concern should Julie be sued by a disgruntled client.

CHAPTER CHECK ANSWERS

1. Sole proprietorship, partnership, corporation, cooperative.
2. 74%; 17%; 9%
3. General partners and limited partners. General partners are allowed to be actively involved in the partnership business and have unlimited liability. Limited partners are not allowed to be actively involved in the business and their liability is limited to the amount of their investment.
4. The name of the business; the names and addresses of all partners; the purpose, nature, and location of the business; the date the partnership will start and how long it will last; the contributions made by each partner; the management responsibilities: the duties of each partner; the salaries and drawing accounts of each partner; provision for sharing profits and losses; provision for accounting procedures; requirements for taking in new partners; special restrictions, right or duties of any partner; provision for a retiring partner; provision for the purchase of a deceased or retiring partner's share; provision for how grievances will be handled; provision for how to dissolve the partnership and distribute the assets.
5. A public corporation has the right to issue shares to the public and can be listed on stock exchanges. A private corporation cannot issue shares to the public and generally is limited in the number of shareholders it can have.
6. a.   sale terminates a sole proprietorship
   b.   requires partners' agreement
   c.   partnership agreement usually allows for transfers
   d.   easy- just sell the shares
   e.   easy – just sell the shares
7. Answers will vary. Non-financials include Federated Co-operatives, Saskatchewan Wheat Pool, Alberta Wheat Pool, Co-op Atlantic, Manitoba Pool Elevators, United Farmers of Alberta Co-op. Financials include Co-operators Group, Co-operators General Insurance, Desjardins Life Assurance Co., Caisse Centrale Desjardins, Vancouver City Savings C.U., Credit Union Central (Saskatchewan).

8. Answers will vary.

Advantages: fixed salary, paid vacations, health coverage, job security, limited risk, promotion possibilities, etc.

Disadvantages: limited income potential, fixed hours, repetitive work, close supervision, limited freedom, etc.

PRACTICE TEST

Multiple Choice		True/False	
1.	d	1.	F
2.	a	2.	T
3.	c	3.	T
4.	a	4.	F
5.	b	5.	T
6.	b	6.	F
7.	d	7.	F
8.	a	8.	F
9.	a	9.	T
10.	b	10.	F
11.	a	11.	T
12.	d	12.	T
13.	a	13.	T
14.	a	14.	T
15.	b	15.	T

CHAPTER 7

Small Business and Entrepreneurship

Learning Goals

After you have read and studied this chapter, you should be able to

1. Define small business and discuss its importance to the Canadian economy.
2. Summarize the major causes of small business failures.
3. Explain why people are willing to take the risks of entrepreneurship.
4. Describe the attributes needed to be a successful entrepreneur and explain why women have a higher success rate than men.
5. Identify ways you can learn about small businesses.
6. Explain what a business plan is and outline the general areas of information it should include.
7. Explain what a market is and why it is important for a business person to know the market.
8. List the requirements to operate a small business successfully.

Key Terms and Definitions

Listed here are important terms found in this chapter. Choose the correct term for each definition and write it in the space provided.

business plan ✓   intrapreneur ✓   venture capitalist ✓
entrepreneur ✓   skunkworks ✓
entrepreneurship ✓   small business ✓

1. _____Skunkworks_____ Highly innovative, fast-moving entrepreneurial units operating at the fringes of a corporation.

2. _____business plan_____ A detailed written statement that describes the nature of the business, the target market, the advantages the business will have over competitors, the resources and qualifications of the owners, and much more.

3. _____entrepreneur_____ A person who organizes, manages, and assumes the risks of starting and operating a business to make a profit.

4. _____venture capitalist_____ An individual or organization that invests in new businesses in exchange for partial ownership.

5. _____entrepreneurship_____ Having the skills and determination to start and operate a business and to accept the calculated risks that are part of such an undertaking.

6. _____intrapreneur_____ (~~venture capitalist~~) A person with entrepreneurial skills who is employed in a corporation to launch new products and who takes hands-on responsibility for innovation in an organization.

7. _____small business_____ Business that is independently owned and operated, not dominant in its field, and meets certain standards of size in terms of number of employees or annual revenue.

The Entrepreneurial Challenge

1. Identify six of the reasons people become entrepreneurs.

   a. new ideas, process or product

   b. independence

   c. challenge

   d. family pattern

   e. profit

   f. ~~job security~~ job insecurity

2. List six qualities that will increase a person's chances of success as an entrepreneur, and explain how each one contributes to success.

   - Self direction
   - determination
   - high energy level : put in long hours, take hard work - physically/mentally
   - risk orientation : live with uncertainty
   - vision
   - ability to learn quickly

3. What "pearls of wisdom" would you offer to a new entrepreneur who is seeking advice?

   - research your market
   - start out slowly
   - set specific objectives
   - dont be afraid to fail

4. Why is the rate of increase in the number of self-employed females so much greater than it is for males?

   financial need - feminism
                  - part time occupation
                  - spousal partnership

5. a. What is an entrepreneurial team?

   a group of experienced people who join together to form a managerial team to develop, make, and market a new product (people from different areas of business)

   b. What does the term "skunkworks" refer to?

   a highly-innovative, fast-moving entrepreneurial units operating at the fringes of a corporation

6. A recent trend is to develop entrepreneurial teams, which combine individuals from different business areas to take advantage of their expertise in those areas.
   List two advantages that an entrepreneurial team has over the individual entrepreneur.

   a. combines skills from different areas. Helps prevent poor decision _making_

b. _more coordination among areas_

7. a. Suggest some advantages to "intrapreneuring" in a big business in comparison to being an independent entrepreneur.

i. _____
ii. _____
iii. _____
iv. _____
v. _____
vi. _____

b. What are the disadvantages for the individual?

i. _____
ii. _____

What Is Small Business?

1. What are three criteria used to classify a business as "small"?

a. _Small number of employees_
b. _small level of sales_
c. _not dominant in its field_

2. Name six Canadian industries in which there are a lot of small businesses.

- _Service_   • _wholesale_
- _retail_   • _manufacturing_
- _Construction_   • _farming_

3. Why do small businesses have an advantage over big businesses?

a. _more personal customer relations_
b. _quickly can respond to opportunities_
c. _provide employment opportunities ie: for students etc._

4. Artur Miscovenski is a government official in a country struggling to create a free market economy for the first time in decades. Artur has turned to you, a Canadian student of business, to help. Artur knows that there is plenty of land and labour available, and that an influx of capital from more developed countries will be forthcoming. Yet, Artur is concerned. What advice can you give Artur about creating a free market economy in his country?

_____
_____
_____
_____
_____

Starting a Small Business

1. Only a small percentage of small businesses are likely to survive their first few years. However, as you have read throughout the chapter, owners of small businesses can take many steps to increase their chances of being successful, including
    - ☐ knowing your customers
    - ☐ managing employees
    - ☐ keeping efficient records
    - ☐ looking for help

    Read the following situation carefully, keeping in mind what you have learned about successful small businesses. Determine whether the owners of the company followed the suggestions listed above, whether you think this company will "beat the odds," and why or why not.

    Dave and Kevin are two men in their mid-30s who worked together as sales representatives for a clothing manufacturer in Quebec. They were both successful at their jobs but also were interested in what they could do working on their own. They began to develop a plan for starting a partnership as manufacturer's representatives, selling clothing and hats to their current customers (if possible) through a network of suppliers they would develop. During a six-month period, while they were working full-time for their employer, Dave and Kevin spent time finding backers (companies to lend them money), lining up suppliers for the products they intended to sell, consulting casually with a lawyer and an accountant, and getting a feel for who they could count on as customers, now and in the future.

    The day came when they decided they were ready to start doing business as manufacturer's reps under the name of Premium Incentives, Inc. Here is the situation as of that day.

    1. To save money, they both chose to work at home, and to use home addresses and phones for company business.

    2. They had promises (no written contracts) from two supplier companies to lend them a total of $100,000 over a one-year period in return for all their business. They had no business plan, and did not approach any other financing sources.

    3. They hired a lawyer and an accountant to help incorporate their company.

    4. Dave's wife agreed to do the bookkeeping for the firm, as she has a degree in business (marketing) and they couldn't afford to hire someone to do the books. However, she had a full-time job and a three-year-old child and was expecting a second child in five months.

    5. Dave and Kevin had a list of companies willing to supply them with their products.

    6. They set up a price schedule designed to undercut their competitors, one of whom was their former employer, by a significant amount.

    7. They made Kevin president, Dave vice president, and split the stock 50–50.

    8. They decided to hire some other sales representatives to help with sales outside the province, and pay them on commission.

    After two months in business Dave and Kevin were still hopeful, but disappointed in the way things had turned out. They had made $5,000 in sales which they were happy with. However, after covering phone expenses and other start-up costs (such as company stationery and office supplies) they were left with only $3,000 between them. This had to be used to cover the lawyer's and accountant's fees of approximately $2,000, leaving them each with a gross take-home pay of $500 for two months assuming they have been paid for the product they had sold. They hadn't yet received any payment from any customer. This would not have posed a problem, as they had been promised start-up money from two of their suppliers. However, one supplier, after reconsidering, decided not to lend them any money. The second dropped his offer down to $5,000 a month for six months, with repayment beginning as soon as the payments had stopped. Since Premium Incentives, Inc. had made no contract with those suppliers, the company had no legal recourse. Dave and Kevin didn't worry too much about repayment. They figured they still had four months to build up their business. Dave's wife was having problems keeping up with doing the books, so they began spending several days a month working on that. She suggested they develop some way of re-billing if a customer hadn't paid within 15 days. They didn't do that, but they did hire a bookkeeper after about six months of keeping the books themselves. Otherwise, Dave and Kevin had no idea when a customer was going to pay, and they had no idea how much income they were going to have each month.

Your comments:

_____
_____
_____
_____
_____
_____
_____
_____
_____
_____
_____
_____
_____
_____
_____
_____
_____
_____
_____
_____

2. a. Eric is a young man with a vision. He sees himself as heading up a large corporation someday, that he has started and helped to grow. He has basically supported himself since he was 15, and has, at the age of 20, already started and sold two successful small businesses. Right now he is going to college full time because he feels that getting an education will be beneficial to him in the long run. He is supporting himself partially with the money he received from the sale of his last business. He intends to start yet another business as soon as he graduates.

   Eric's most recent business was in a fairly competitive market in the area in which he lives, Edmonton. He says that while he received some encouragement from a few friends, for the most part they all said he was crazy to work as hard as he was working. But Eric says he just felt that he "had to do things my own way." He built his business into the second largest of its type in the Edmonton area.

   How does Eric portray the entrepreneurial attributes your text identifies?

_____
_____
_____
_____

b. Eric seems to have beaten the odds already. What do you think Eric would tell you about success (or failure) and how to learn to be a successful small business owner?

_____
_____
_____
_____

c. Eric has graduated from school, and is ready to start his new business. He has never applied for a bank loan, and has come to you for advice on how to get the loan. What will you tell him?

_____
_____
_____
_____

Funding a Small Business

1. What are six financial reasons for small business failures?
   a. too little capital
   b. too much capital but careless in its use
   c. borrowing money without repayment plan
   d. too much business with very little capital
   e. not allowing for setbacks & unexpected expenses
   f. extending credit too freely

2. What tips would you give to small business owners who want to borrow money?
   a. pick bank that services small businesses
   b. have good accountant to prepare financial statements etc.
   c. go to bank with accountant
   d. borrow from a Commercial Bank
   e. _____
   f. _____
   g. _____

3. Other than personal savings, what is the primary source of capital for entrepreneurs?
   individual investors

4. What is an *angel investor*?
   An angel investor are individuals who invest their own money in potentially hot companies before they go public.

5. What is one potential drawback with using venture capitalists?

_____
_____
_____
_____

Causes of Small Business Failure

1. In what area do most small business owners feel they need assistance the most?

   accounting
   _____
   _____

2. How can an accountant help in managing a small business?

   prepare financial reports, help set up software to handle inventory, customer records, payroll etc.
   Also, give advice on purchasing equipment, rent/own building etc.

3. In what ways can a lawyer help?

   help in areas of leasing, contracts, protection against liabilities etc.
   _____
   _____

4. How can marketing research help?

   help determine where to locate, whom to select as your target customers, and an effective strategy in reaching them.
   _____

5. What are the five signs of poor management that lead to most small business failures?

   - lack of finances
   - lack of experience
   - poor allocation of time
   - weak or no professional guidance
   - lack of necessary personal qualities

6. a. Your friend Isabella wants to open her own veterinary clinic. Another friend, Frank, is planning on going into business for himself to manufacture "jams" (flowered beach attire) for overseas markets. At a party Isabella and Frank each enthuse about their prospective projects and dreams of making "big bucks." You think they may be overlooking some information about small business success and failure. What do you tell them?

   _____
   _____
   _____
   _____
   _____
   _____
   _____
   _____
   _____
   _____
   _____

_____
_____

b.   What are some non-financial reasons for the failure of small businesses?

—Managerial incompetence
~poor planning

Operating a Small Business

(i)

1.   Tony R. owns his own beauty salon, Russo's, in a wealthy area of suburban Montreal. Before opening his own salon, Tony worked for another salon, owned by his boss, Brenda, a woman in her 50s. While at Brenda's, Tony built up his clientele to the point where he worked about 50 hours a week, and had been named manager by the time he left. Tony has a number of friends in the industry and before opening Russo's he spent a great deal of time talking with them about how they ran their own salons *(ii)*

  a.   Of the steps outlined in your book, which two has Tony taken to ensure his success as a small business owner?

   i.   *Get experience,*
   _____

   ii.   *learn from others*
   _____

  b.   As an alternative to starting his own salon, what choice could Tony have made in going into business for himself?

      take over an established Salon
      _____
      _____
      _____

International Aspects of Entrepreneurship

1.   What are four hurdles small businesses face in the international market?
  a.   *financing is too difficult*
  b.   *would-be exporters don't know how to get started*
  c.   *global business don't know cultural differences*
  d.   *overwhelming beauracratic paperwork*

2.   Identify five reasons for going international.
  a.   *market is outside Canada*
  b.   *exporting expands absorbs excess inventory*
  c.   *"   extends product lives*
  d.   *"   spices up dull routine*
  e.   _____

3.   List the advantages small businesses have over large business in the international market.
  a.   *begin shipping faster*

b. <u>provide wide variety of suppliers</u>
c. <u>give more personal service</u>
d. _____

4. Imagine that you have established a successful small business in Canada. After five years of serving the Canadian market, you are ready to consider expanding into other countries. Suggest at least four different approaches you might use.
   a. _____
   b. _____
   c. _____
   d. _____

CHAPTER CHECK

1. List eight of the reasons for the marked increase in the number of women who start their own businesses.
   - $ need
   - lack of promotion oppor.
   - return to workforce
   - feminism
   - family responsibility
   - part time
   - spousal partnerships
   - $ rate of success

2. How many businesses are there in Canada? How many of these have less than 50 employees?
   <u>900,000 , 97%</u>

3. What three things should you always do before getting started in a business, whether you are starting a new one, buying an old one, or buying a franchise?
   - gather info
   - obtain prof. advice
   - prepare business plan

4. What are the five most common "internal" reasons for the fact that most new businesses fail in the first two years?
   - poor finances
   - lack of experience
   - poor allocation of time
   - no prof. guidance
   - lack of personal necessary qualities

5. Identify the seven things it is important to include in a business plan.
   a. <u>cover letter</u>   e. <u>operating plan</u>
   b. <u>description of industry</u>   f. <u>capitalization plan</u>
   c. <u>marketing plan</u>   g. _____

d. _Market analysis_

6. Give two examples of Canadian small businesses that are competing successfully in foreign markets.
   - _Thinkway Toys of Toronto_
   -

PRACTICE TEST

Multiple Choice: Circle the best answer.

1. Entrepreneurs take the risk of starting a business for all of the following reasons EXCEPT
   a. they want independence
   b. they like the challenge
   c. they want to make money for themselves
   d. they want to work less

2. An entrepreneurial team is
   a. a group of people who work within a corporation to expand the market for the company's products
   b. a group of experienced people who join together to develop and market a new product
   c. a group from the Small Business Administration which consults with small business owners
   d. a group of managers who get together to find creative solutions to problems

3. Which of the following is a false statement about small business?
   a. The number of women owning small businesses is increasing
   b. The vast majority of businesses in Canada are considered small
   c. The first job for most Americans will probably not be in a small business
   d. The majority of the country's new jobs are in small business

4. A small business
   a. must have fewer than 100 employees to be considered small
   b. is considered small relative to other businesses in its industry
   c. cannot be a corporation
   d. should be a sole proprietorship

5. In general
   a. the easier to start the business, the more likely it is to succeed
   b. businesses that are more difficult to start are most likely to fail
   c. the easier a business is to start, the higher the growth rate
   d. businesses that are difficult to start are the easiest ones to keep going

6. Miriam Njunge wants to start a small business importing some products from her native Kenya. Before she starts, some good advice to Miriam would be
   a. talk to others who have been or are in the import business
   b. get a loan right away
   c. find a business to buy as soon as possible
   d. incorporate immediately

7. In measuring the value of a small firm, which of the following would NOT be included?
   a. What the business owns
   b. What the business earns
   c. What makes the business unique
   d. What products the business makes

8. The primary concerns when first starting your business are

a. marketing and accounting
b. planning and human resources
c. financing and planning
d. financing and marketing

9. A business plan for a new business does not need to include
   a. a marketing plan
   b. a discussion of the purpose of the business
   c. a description of the company background
   d. the name of the lending bank

10. What are the primary sources of funding for entrepreneurs?
    a. personal savings and individual investors
    b. finance companies and banks
    c. the Small Business Administration and banks
    d. former employers and the Economic Development Authority

11. For a market to exist, there must be potential buyers
    a. and a product that is safe and inexpensive
    b. who have a willingness and the resources to buy
    c. and stores which are willing to carry the product
    d. who are looking for a bargain

12. Employees in small businesses generally
    a. are more satisfied with their jobs than counterparts in big business
    b. are less satisfied with their jobs because there is less room for advancement
    c. are generally only using the job as a springboard to get into a larger company
    d. are most likely going to quit to find a company that accepts their ideas

13. Small business owners say that the most important assistance they need is in
    a. marketing   c. planning
    b. accounting   d. manufacturing

14. There are many reasons why small business owners don't go international. Which is NOT considered to be one of the reasons?
    a. They don't know how to get started.
    b. Financing is often difficult to find.
    c. Paperwork is often overwhelming.
    d. The market doesn't have great potential.

15. Small business owners who want to explore the opportunities in international business will find that
    a. there is not much information about exporting
    b. most small businesses still don't think internationally
    c. there is usually no need to adapt products to foreign markets
    d. it is more difficult for small businesses to enter international markets than for large businesses

True/False

1. It is important for an entrepreneur to be self-directed and self-nurturing.
2. An intrapreneur is an individual who is a member of an entrepreneurial team.
3. The majority of new jobs in the private sector are created by small business.
4. Many of the businesses with the lowest failure rates require advanced training to start.
5. One of the ways to get information about starting a small business is by attending classes at a local college.
6. A substantial percentage of small business owners got the idea for their businesses from their prior jobs.

7. An effective business plan should catch the reader's interest right away.
8. The most important source of funds for a small business owner is bank loans.
9. Governments have not been especially supportive of small business in Canada.
10. Finding funding for a small business is probably the easiest thing about starting a small business.
11. A market is basically anyone who wants to buy your product.
12. Employees of small businesses are often more satisfied with their jobs than counterparts in big business.
13. Most small businesses can't afford to hire experts as employees, so they need to turn to outside assistance.
14. It is best to stay away from other small business owners for counsel, as they are likely to use your ideas before you can get started.
15. Approximately 95% of all banks' borrowing customers are small and medium-sized entrepreneurs.

ANSWERS

Key Terms and Definitions

1. skunkworks
2. business plan
3. entrepreneur
4. venture capitalist
5. entrepreneurship
6. intrapreneur
7. small business

The Entrepreneurial Challenge

1. Reasons people become entrepreneurs are
   a. new idea, process, or product
   b. profit
   c. independence
   d. challenge
   e. family pattern
   f. job insecurity or joblessness
   g. immigrants
2. ! Self-direction; need to be a self-starter, with lots of self-confidence
   ☐ Determination; need to keep going when others would give up, get through obstacles and difficulties
   ☐ High energy level; need to put in long hours and give up weekends
   ☐ Risk orientation; must be able to live with a high risk of failure
   ☐ Vision; must have a dream you are impelled to realize
   ☐ Ability to learn quickly; must be able to learn from inevitable mistakes
3. Advice for "would-be" entrepreneurs:
   ☐ Research your market, but do not take too long to act.
   ☐ Work for other people first and learn on their money.
   ☐ Start out slowly. Start your business when you have a customer. Maybe try your venture as a sideline first.
   ☐ Set specific objectives, but don't set your goals too high.
   ☐ Plan your objectives within specific time frames.
   ☐ Surround yourself with people who have knowledge or expertise that you don't.
   ☐ Do not be afraid to fail.

4. Financial need
   - ☐ Lack of promotion opportunities
   - ☐ Return to workforce after child-rearing, with outdated skills
   - ☐ Feminism
   - ☐ Family and personal responsibility
   - ☐ Part-time occupation
   - ☐ Partnership with spouse
5. a. An entrepreneurial team is a group of experienced people from different areas of business who join together to form a managerial team with the skills needed to develop, make, and market a new product.
   b. A highly innovative, fast-moving entrepreneurial unit operating at the fringes of a corporation.
6. Entrepreneurial team
   a. It combines the skills of many business areas. This helps to prevent poor decisions in an area in which an individual entrepreneur may be weak.
   b. Because managers work as a team, there is more coordination among all the areas.
7. Intrapreneuring
   a. Answers will vary. Some factors to be considered are:
      - ☐ More marketing clout
      - ☐ Larger technology base
      - ☐ Better access to financial backing
      - ☐ More and better people to look to for help
      - ☐ Access to information resources
   b. ! Less glory
      - ☐ Profits go to the company

What Is Small Business?

1. A small business is one that is
   a. independently owned and operated
   b. not dominant in its field of operation
   c. meets certain standards of size in terms of employees or annual receipts
2. Services, retail, construction, wholesale, manufacturing, farming
3. Small business advantages over large businesses are
   a. providing employment opportunities
   b. more personal customer service
   c. their ability to respond quickly to opportunities
4. The first step in the process of establishing a free market economy is to allow people to own their own property. The process of privatization is a term used to describe the sale of government-owned businesses to private individuals. Unfortunately, many of these businesses are inefficient, have old equipment, and have a very weak financial base. Additionally, it is very difficult to find and train managers to run these businesses in the "new" way. Therefore, it is better to allow new businesses to form. With the freedom to operate, entrepreneurs can do what is necessary to develop a free market economy, including building a needed infrastructure. The process will go much faster if developed countries help entrepreneurs by providing needed capital.

Starting a Small Business

1. Dave and Kevin did know their customers, as they were already selling to them in their old jobs. They

followed one of the suggestions in the text for successfully starting a business, as they worked for someone else before going out on their own. By all indications the market was there, with the resources to buy what Kevin and Dave were selling. Although they had funding, it appears to have been very "casual"; and not very well thought out. Since they didn't develop a business plan, and from other information, you can assume they didn't develop a marketing plan or a financial plan. They didn't have any other employees to manage, since they were using independent sales representatives, and the company paid them commission, which encourages the salespeople to be productive.

Keeping efficient records seems to be a real weakness in the company. Dave's wife didn't really have the skill, time (or probably the energy) to do the books. Since Dave and Kevin are in sales, it's probably safe to assume they aren't strong in bookkeeping either. Hiring a bookkeeper was a good idea. Perhaps the bookkeeper can suggest an effective billing method to help ensure proper payment on accounts.

2. a. The text mentions that desirable entrepreneurial attributes include being self-directed, self-nurturing, action-oriented, highly energetic, and tolerant of uncertainty. Eric demonstrates these characteristics in several ways. He is self-directed in that he had the discipline not only to build two businesses, but to leave those businesses when he decided that he wanted to go on to college. He has been self-supporting for a number of years, and most likely is quite tolerant of uncertainty, and probably felt quite comfortable with that element of risk in starting his own businesses. He continued to work while his friends told him he was "crazy for working that hard," so it seems that he doesn't depend on other people's approval, i.e., he's self-nurturing, and appears to be pretty energetic. He must be action-oriented, able to build his "dream into a reality" by taking an idea and creating a successful business.

    b. Eric seems to lend validity to the questionable failure statistics the text refers to. He has beaten the odds twice, and it would seem that the odds of failure may have been lower than traditionally reported.

    Eric may tell you that you need to talk to people who have already started their own businesses and get their advice. They can give you valuable information about the importance of location, finding good workers, and having enough capital to keep you going.

    He may also suggest that you work for a successful entrepreneur and get some experience in the fields in which you're interested.

    Another idea is to take over a firm that has already been successful. (That's what the *buyers* of Eric's most recent firm decided to do!) A strategy may be to work for the owner for a few years, then offer to buy the business through profit sharing, or an outright purchase.

    c. Tell Eric to be prepared. First have a business plan already prepared. Pick a bank that serves small businesses, have an accountant prepare complete financial statements, including a personal balance sheet, and take all the financial information with you to the bank, along with the business plan. Make an appointment with the loan officer, and ask for exactly what you need. Be prepared to personally guarantee the loan.

Funding a Small Business

1. a. starting with too little capital
    b. starting with too much capital and being careless
    c. borrowing money without planning payback
    d. trying to do too much business with not enough capital
    e. not allowing for setbacks and unexpected expenses
    f. extending credit too freely

2. Answers will vary, but might include the following
   a. Pick a bank that serves small businesses.
   b. Have a good accountant prepare a complete set of financial statements and personal balance sheet.
   c. Go to the bank with an accountant and all the necessary financial information.
   d. Make an appointment before going to the bank.
   e. Demonstrate good character.
   f. Ask for all the money you need.
   g. Be prepared to personally guarantee the loan.
3. Other than personal savings, individual investors are the primary source of capital for most entrepreneurs.
4. Angel investors are individuals who invest their own money in potentially hot companies before they go public.
5. The potential drawback with venture capitalists is that they will often ask for as much as 60% ownership of the business.

Causes of Small Business Failure

1. Most small business owners say they need the most assistance in accounting.
2. A good accountant can help in setting up computer systems for record keeping such as inventory control, customer records, and payroll. He/she can also help make decisions such as whether to buy or lease equipment and whether to own or rent a building. Further, an accountant can help with tax planning, financial forecasting, choosing sources of financing, and writing requests for funds.
3. Lawyers can help with such areas as leases, contracts and protection against liabilities.
4. Marketing research can help you determine where to locate, whom to select as your target market, and what would be an effective strategy for reaching those people.
5.
   a. lack of finances
   b. lack of experience
   c. poor allocation of time
   d. weak or no professional guidance
   e. lack of necessary personal qualities
6.
   a. One thing to remind Frank and Isabella of is the failure rate of small businesses; 20% in the first year, increasing to 66% by the end of the fifth year. Choosing the right business is critical. Isabella has chosen a field that may have one of the lowest failure rates. However, her dreams of "big bucks" will probably have to be put aside. Training and degrees may buy security, but growth possibilities are limited, and growth is what will produce wealth. Frank, in manufacturing, is in an area with the highest odds of growth, but manufacturing businesses are difficult both to start up and to keep going. Frank's dreams of "big bucks" may have to be put off until he is able to build a market.
   b. Many small businesses fail because of
      i. managerial incompetence
      ii. inadequate planning

Operating a Small Business

1. a. i. Get some experience. Tony worked for several years learning the business before starting out on his own.
   ii. Learn from others. Tony spent a lot of time with people who already owned their own salons

before actually going out on his own.

    b. An alternative would have been to take over an established salon. Brenda, for example, may have wanted to retire in the near future, and Tony already knew her business and had his own clientele. Or he may have been able to work out a profit-sharing deal with Brenda.

International Aspects of Entrepreneurship

1. Answers will vary, but might include the following
   a. Financing is difficult to find.
   b. Many would-be exporters don't know how to get started.
   c. Potential global business people do not understand cultural differences.
   d. The bureaucratic paperwork can be overwhelming.
2. Answers will vary, but might include the following
   a. Most of the world's markets lie outside of Canada
   b. Exporting can absorb excess inventory.
   c. Exporting softens downturns in the domestic market.
   d. Exporting extends product lives.
   e. Exporting can spice up dull routines.
3. Small businesses have advantages over big businesses in the international market in these ways:
   a. overseas buyers enjoy dealing with individuals rather than lare corporate bureaucracies
   b. small companies can begin shipping faster
   c. small companies provide a wide variety of suppliers
   d. small companies can give more personal service and more undivided attention.
4. Answers will vary. Possibilities include establishing your own branches, sales offices, or manufacturing facilities in the other country, or licensing a foreign company to use your patents, selling a franchise to someone in the foreign country, or entering a joint venture with a foreign company.

CHAPTER CHECK ANSWERS

1. a. financial need
   b. lack of promotion opportunities
   c. returning to the workforce
   d. feminism
   e. family and personal responsibility
   f. public awareness of women in business
   g. part-time occupations
   h. couples in partnership
   i. higher rate of success for women

2. Approximately 900,000; approximately 97%
3. Gather information, obtain professional advice, and prepare a business plan.
4. Lack of finances, lack of experience, poor allocation of time, weak or no professional guidance, lack of necessary personal qualities.

5. a. A cover letter summarizing the major facets of your proposed business
    b. A brief description of the industry and a detailed explanation of the products or services to be offered
    c. A thorough market analysis that discusses the size of the market, the need for the new product, and the nature of the competition
    d. A marketing plan that includes location, signs, advertising, and display
    e. An operating plan that includes a sales forecast, financial projections, accounting procedures, and human resource requirements
    f. A comprehensive capitalization plan describing how much money the owner is committing
    g. A description of the experience and expertise of the owner
6. Answers will vary. One example given in the text is Thinkway Toys of Toronto.

PRACTICE TEST

Multiple Choice		True/False	
1.	d	1.	T
2.	b	2.	F
3.	c	3.	T
4.	b	4.	T
5.	d	5.	T
6.	a	6.	T
7.	d	7.	T
8.	c	8.	F
9.	d	9.	F
10.	a	10.	F
11.	b	11.	F
12.	a	12.	T
13.	b	13.	T
14.	d	14.	F
15.	b	15.	T

CHAPTER 8

Leadership and Management

Learning Goals

After you have read and studied this chapter, you should be able to

1. Enumerate the four functions of management and reasons why the role of managers is changing.
2. Relate the planning process to the accomplishment of company goals.
3. Describe the organizing function of management, including staffing and diversity management.
4. Explain the differences between leaders and managers, and describe the various leadership styles.
5. Summarize the five steps of the control function of management.
6. Illustrate the skills needed at each level of management.

Key Terms and Definitions

Listed here are important terms found in this chapter. Choose the correct term for each definition and write it in the space provided.

autocratic leadership	Human relations skills	planning ✓
baby boomer ✓	Knowledge management	strategic (long-range)
conceptual skills	Internal customers	planning ✓
contingency planning ✓	Laissez-faire (free rein)	supervisory (first-line)
controlling	leadership	management ✓
decision making	Leading ✓	SWOT analysis
democratic (participative)	Management ✓	tactical planning ✓
leadership	Managing diversity	technical skills
empowerment	middle management ✓	top management ✓
enabling	mission statement	vision ✓
external customers	objectives ✓	
goals ✓	operational planning ✓	
	organizing ✓	

1. ___leading___ Creating a vision for the organization and guiding, training, coaching and motivating others to work effectively to achieve the organization's goals and objectives.

2. ___baby boomer___ A member of the group of people who were born between 1947 and 1966 and are now living in Canada

3. ___Management___ The process used to accomplish organizational goals through planning, organizing, leading, and controlling people and other organizational resources.

4. ___Contingency planning___ The process of preparing alternative courses of action that may be used if the primary plans do not achieve the objectives of the organization.

5. _____ Choosing among two or more alternatives.

6. ___planning___ Management function that involves anticipating trends and

determining the best strategies and tactics to achieve organizational goals and objectives.

7. _____ Management function that involves determining whether or not an organization is progressing towards its goals and objectives, and taking corrective action if it is not.

8. _____ Skills that involve the ability to picture the organization as a whole and the relationship among its various parts.

9. _organizing_____ Management function that involves designing the structure of the organization and creating conditions and systems in which everyone and everything works together to achieve the organization's goals and objectives.

10. _top management_____ Highest level of management, consisting of the president and other key company executives who develop strategic plans.

11. _Strategic planning____ Process of determining the major goals of the organization and the policies and strategies for obtaining and using resources to achieve those goals.

12. _tactical planning_____ Process of developing detailed, short-term decisions about what is to be done, who is to do it, and how it is to be done.

13. _Supervisory management_ Managers who are directly responsible for supervising workers and evaluating their daily performance.

14. _____ Giving workers the education and tools they need to assume their new decision-making powers.

15. _middle management____ The level of management that includes general managers, division managers, and branch and plant managers who are responsible for tactical planing and controlling.

16. _objectives_____ Specific, short-term statements detailing how to achieve the goals.

17. _____ Finding the right information, keeping the information in a readily accessible place, and making the information known to everyone in the firm.

18. _goals_____ Broad, long-term accomplishments an organization wishes to attain.

19. _____ Skills that involve the ability to perform tasks in a specific discipline or department.

20. _____ Skills that involve ommunication and motivation; they enable managers to work through and with people.

21. _democratic leadership__ Leadership style that consists of managers and employees working together to make decisions.

22. _vision_____ A sense of why the organization exists and where it's heading.

23. _____ Giving employees the authority and responsibility to respond quickly to customer requests.

24. _____ Units within the firm that receive services from other units.

(free-rein)

25. _laissez-faire leadership_ — Leadership style that involves managers setting objectives and employees being relatively free to do whatever it takes to accomplish those objectives.

26. _managing diversity_ — Building systems and a culture that unite different people in a common pursuit without undermining their individual strengths.

27. _autocratic leadership_ — Leadership style that involves making decisions without consulting others and implies power over others.

28. _mission statement_ — An outline of the fundamental purposes of an organization.

29. _operational planning_ — The process of setting work standards and schedules necessary to implement the tactical objectives.

30. _SWOT analysis_ — An analysis of an organization's strengths, weaknesses, opportunities, and threats

31. _____ — Dealers who buy products to sell to others, and ultimate customers who buy products for their own personal use.

The Changing Role of Managers

1. To meet the challenges of today's business, managers have begun to change their styles. Identify four ways today's managers have responded to the challenges found in Canadian corporations.
   - educated to guide /coach employees
   - emphasized teamwork & cooperation
   - more friendly
   - treat employees as partners

2. What does Peter Drucker say are the three things managers do?
   - give directions
   - provide leadership
   - decide how to use organizational resources to accomplish goals

Planning: Creating a Vision for the Organization

1. Distinguish between a *vision* an a *goal.*
   vision - greater than goal, larger explanation of why corp. exists

   goal - broad, long-term accomplishment

2. How does a *mission statement* relate to the *goals* of an organization?
   foundation for setting goals and selecting & motivating employees

3. Goals are broadly based long-term statements. Objectives are more specific short-term statements. (In other words, you can't "do" a goal.) Correctly identify whether each of the following is a goal statement or an objective statement.

a. _____ goal _____ I want to be rich!

b. _____ goal _____ Mrs. Field's Cookies states in 1989 that it wants to reduce the decline in its profits.

c. _____ objective _____ To broaden its market appeal, Mrs. Field's Cookies acquires La Boulangerie, a French-type bakery.

d. _____ goal _____ Procter and Gamble wants to avoid losing market share to Kimberly-Clark.

e. _____ objective _____ Weyerhauser, Inc. develops a disposable diaper to compete directly against Procter and Gamble and Kimberly-Clark.

f. _____ ~~goal~~ objective _____ In the quest to become an accountant, Judy Oswalt enrolls in her first accounting class.

4. The planning process involves setting objectives and making decisions within two time frames.

    Strategic planning has a long-range time frame, and considers the broad, overall perspective of the firm, i.e., "which customers to serve, what products or services to sell, and the geographic areas in which the firm will compete, and the best way to obtain and use resources."

    Tactical planning is the process of developing short-term decisions about what is to be done, who is to do it, and how it is to be done. In other words, tactical planning involves "deciding on the details of how to meet the strategic plan."

    Determine whether strategic or tactical planning is taking place in the following situations.

a. _____ In the early 1980s BIC Corporation discovered an opportunity to market disposable safety razors.

b. _____ Managers at Ford routinely move their zone sales managers to different territories to identify top performers.

c. _____ tactical _____ The life insurance industry decides to attempt to market life insurance policies to working women.

d. _____ Monsanto develops a policy of monitoring potential problems in the disposal of hazardous waste.

e. _____ tactical _____ To increase enrolment, a college offers classes on Saturdays and Sundays.

f. _____ tactical _____ A grocery store offers samples to attract customers to its deli section.

5. (a) Determine a personal strategic plan, tactical plan, and contingency plan.

Strategic plan _____

_____

Tactical plan _____

_____

Contingency plan _____

_____

b. How can you incorporate the need for "opportunism" and flexibility into your own plans?

_____

_____

_____

_____

6. Where does a SWOT analysis fit into the planning process?

deals with questions asked in the initial planning stage

— strength
— weakness
— opportunities
— threats

7. What is decided at the strategic planning stage? What is making strategic planning more difficult? What level of management is involved in strategic planning?

— what customers to serve, what products etc
— Top management

8. Describe tactical planning. At what level is tactical planning usually done?

— short term planning strategies
— managers / teams

9. What is operational planning? At what level is operational planning usually done?

setting work standards necessary to implement tactical objectives
— department management

10. Why is contingency planning important?

— back up — incase original plans don't meet their goals

11. *Strategic* and *Tactical* planning provide the framework for the planning process. *Contingency* planning provides alternative plans of action.
Look back to Chapter 7, where we introduced Eric, the young man who wants to start his own business. Eric has decided to start a small manufacturing business, making a product he invented for the automotive industry. It's a component part, designed as a "built-in" carrier for tapes and CDs that can be removed and taken with you when you get out of the car. The product is called "Music-stor." He wants to sell it to both auto manufacturers and auto parts stores. Can you outline a strategic plan, tactical plan, and contingency plan for Eric?
Strategic plan_____

_____

Tactical plan _____

_____

Contingency plan_____

_____

Organizing: Creating a Unified System

1. "Basically, organizing means allocating resources, assigning tasks, and establishing procedures for accomplishing the organization objectives." Match the organizing task being performed to the following statements.

   a. _allocate resources_ A hospital allocates an entire floor to pediatric medicine.

   b. _establish procedures_ A college develops a step-by-step process to follow for students applying for financial aid.

   c. _assign tasks_ To alleviate the problem of boredom, a production foreman gives assembly line workers a chance to perform a variety of jobs.

2. What positions will be found in top management?
   president / CEO / CIO / COO / CFO

3. What are the primary responsibilities of a:

   CEO _introducing change into organization_

   COO _putting changes into effect_

   CFO _obtains funds, budgeting, collecting funds_

   CIO / CKO _right info to other managers_

4. List some positions found in middle management.
   GM, division managers, branch managers, plant manager, deans

5. What is supervisory managment?
   involves people directly responsible for supervising workers & evaluating their performance

6. What has been the dominating question regarding organizing? Who are stakeholders?
   how to organize the firm to respond to the needs of customers

7. According to the text, what stakeholders have most influenced how companies are organized?

_____

_____

_____

_____

8. What has made the organizing task more complex today?

_____

_____

_____

_____

9. What is staffing, and what makes it so critical today?

_____

_____

_____

_____

10. Why is managing diversity important for businesss today?

_____

_____

_____

_____

11. An organization chart pictures who reports to whom, and who is responsible for each task. Identify two individuals at each level of management at your college or university, and draw a simple organization chart.

Top Managers	*Middle Managers*	*Supervisory Managers*
a. _____	a. _____	a. _____
b. _____	b. _____	b. _____

12. We have read in previous chapters about changes occurring in business and in the marketplace. In this chapter we read about the changes in the *structure* of business, which is becoming customer-oriented and is taking on the perspective of a "system" of interim relationships. Given what you know from previous chapters, why do you think this type of organizational structure began to evolve?

_____

_____

_____

_____

Leading: Vision and Values

1.   When is autocratic leadership effective?

_____
_____
_____
_____

2.   What is the benefit of participative leadership and when is it successful?

_____
_____
_____
_____

3.   When is laissez-faire leadership the most effective? What traits do managers need in organizations with laissez-faire leadership?

_____
_____
_____
_____

4.   What leadership style is best?

_____
_____
_____
_____

5.   How do traditional leaders differ from progressive leaders? How is a manager's role changing as a result?

_____
_____
_____
_____

6.   What are the steps in developing a knowledge management system? What is the key to a successful knowledge management system?

_____
_____
_____
_____

7.   You have just been promoted to first-line supervisor, after working at your company for five years. You're young and a manager of today. How has the concept of *leading* changed? In other words, as a first-line manager, how are you going to take your department and your employees into the 21st century?

_____
_____
_____
_____

8. Eric has hired you to be the supervisor in the "Music-stor" plant where they are going to make the tape/CD storage cases. Your workers are well educated and highly skilled. How do you intend to *lead* and organize these employees of today?

_____
_____
_____
_____

9. How will your approach differ from Eric's, the top manager?

_____
_____
_____
_____

10. You have been in your supervisory position for several months, and have found your boss to be a great person to work with. She speaks often about the kind of division she wants to create, one where all the employees feel a sense of loyalty to a team. She stresses customer service, high product quality, and fair treatment of her employees. If she makes a mistake, she is always up front about it. She insists on honesty from her employees, but you notice that everyone seems to be treated fairly. She expects a lot from her subordinates, but is sure to let them make their own decisions (as well as their own mistakes!). She encourages employee problem solving and is quick to implement changes which will make the division more effective and efficient. How does your boss differ from a "manager" and demonstrate the leadership of the 1990s?

_____
_____
_____
_____

11. "Leadership involves creating a vision for others to follow." Effective leadership styles range along a continuum, based upon the amount of employee involvement in setting objectives and making decisions. The terms to describe leadership styles along the continuum are
   ☐ Autocratic
   ☐ Democratic (participative)
   ☐ Laissez-faire (free rein)
   Read the following situations, and indicate which leadership style is being illustrated:
   a. Production workers complain about having to punch a time clock each day.
      i. _____ "Too bad. I'm not getting rid of it."
      ii. _____ "Let's get a committee together, and see if we can come up with some alternatives to using the time clock."
   b. A university sees a need for some action to be taken to reverse declining enrolment trends.
      i. _____ "Let's form a committee of faculty and administrators to give recommendations on how to solve the problem."

  ii. _____ "The objective for each division is to increase enrolment by 10% for the next school year. Each division is free to take whatever action is needed to reach that objective."

 c. A manager notices that an employee consistently turns work in past the deadline.

  i. _____ "Bob, this is a problem. How can we work together to solve it?"

  ii. _____ "Bob, your work has been late three times this month. One more time and you will be disciplined. Two times and you're fired. Got it?"

 d. What is meant by the statement "There is no one leadership style."

_____
_____
_____
_____

12. "Music-stor" has been in business for several months, and you have just been assigned to reorganize the production department. Eric knows that he will need inventory if things go as planned, production is very slow right now and there are already some orders to fill. Money, however, is tight. All the production workers are peers (none are supervisors), but there is one member of the group who appears to be the informal leader. The workers are paid by the hour, and they are well paid by normal standards.

You have some ideas about how to increase production without increasing costs. One idea, for example, is to change the method of paying workers from hourly to by how much they produce. The way you have figured, the workers would have to produce more to make the same income. Another way is to set up individual workstations to cut down on the amount of socializing you have seen going on. While you are confident these ideas, and others you have thought of, are the best solutions, you aren't sure how to implement the changes. You do know that this will be a test of your management and leadership skills.

 a. How would you go about developing alternatives and implementing changes you believe are necessary to increase productivity and save money?

_____
_____
_____
_____

 b. What leadership style do you think you used in developing your solution? Why?

_____
_____
_____
_____

13. Why is it important that a manager delegate effectively in today's new workplace with today's new workers?

_____
_____
_____

Controlling

1. What are the criteria for measuring success in a customer-oriented firm?

    _____

    _____

    _____

    _____

2. What is a corporate scorecard?

    _____

    _____

    _____

    _____

3. The control function of management provides feedback for managers to determine if the organization is progressing toward its objectives. The five steps are
    - ☐ Setting clear standards
    - ☐ Monitoring and recording results
    - ☐ Comparing results to standards
    - ☐ Communicating results and deviations to employees
    - ☐ Taking corrective action when needed

    Match the following statements to the correct step in the controlling function.

    a. _____ "Looks like sales are down this quarter. Our objective was 12,000 units; we're at 8,000."

    b. _____ "I need the sales figures for last month. The quarterly report is due next week and those figures have to be included."

    c. _____ "Our sales objective for the next quarter is 12,000 units. That's a 10% increase over the same period last year."

    d. _____ "Let's call the sales force in next week. I'll give them each a copy of my quarterly sales report. I'd like to know their ideas on what the problem is."

    e. _____ "The biggest problem the sales force has appears to stem from slow delivery problems. I'm going to call the distribution manager and see if we can work out a solution."

4. "The control system's weakest link seems to be the setting of standards." Characteristics of good standards are that they must be
    - ☐ Specific
    - ☐ Attainable
    - ☐ Subject to measurement
    - ☐ Set a time period

    Read the following objectives, and improve them:

    a. Increase sales_____

    _____

b. Improve quality control _____
_____

c. Get a degree _____
_____

d. Study harder _____
_____

e. Be a better manager _____
_____
_____

Tasks and Skills at Different Levels of Management

1. Describe *technical* skills.

_____
_____
_____
_____

2. What are *human relations* skills?

_____
_____
_____
_____

3. Describe *conceptual* skills.

_____
_____
_____
_____

4. How do the various levels of management differ in the skills needed?

_____
_____
_____
_____

5. There are five basic categories of skills that managers must have
   ☐ Technical skills (computer and other skills)
   ☐ Conceptual skills
   ☐ Human relations skills
   ☐ Communication skills (including verbal, writing, and listening skills)
   ☐ Time management skills
   These skills are used in varying degrees by managers, depending upon whether the manager is at the

supervisor, middle, or top management level.

For each of the following situations, indicate the management level, and the skills being used or described.

Alice Burling is concerned about Bob Maling's sales performance. In their meeting, Alice and Bob agree there's a problem, and Alice shows Bob how to improve. After the meeting Alice completes a schedule assigning new accounts to various salesmen.

Management Level   **Skills**

a. _____   _____
                                                        _____
                                                        _____

In a typical week in her office, Ann Doty composes a newsletter to be distributed to all employees, works on a long-range forecast for a new product the company is considering, and decides to implement a new program to encourage communication and idea exchange between division heads. She appoints several division heads to formulate a plan for implementation. While she can schedule most meetings, she leaves time open for interruptions and unplanned meetings with subordinates.

b. _____   _____
                                                        _____
                                                        _____

In reviewing weekly production reports, Joel Hodes notices a drop in overall production from last month. He works for a week on an incentive plan he thinks will push production back up to the company's objectives and still maintain high morale. He then calls a meeting with the line supervisors. After getting their responses and suggestions, Joel revises and implements the plan in his plant.

c. _____   _____
                                                        _____
                                                        _____

Don Schuler is a supervisor at a silicon growing plant. He has four first-line supervisors reporting to him, and there are 100 employees in his department. Don spends much of his time solving problems with the employees and developing software programs for the production line.

d. _____   _____
                                                        _____
                                                        _____

Stephen Lui begins each day writing a "to do" list of what he wants to accomplish, then makes sure to prioritize the list according to importance. He then generally looks through his electronic mailbox and responds to those memos needing immediate response.

e. _____   _____
                                                        _____
                                                        _____

6. "The most difficult task for most managers to learn is delegating." How is being a good leader related to delegating?

_____

_____

_____

_____

7. "The rational decision-making model is a series of steps ... to make logical ... decisions."
   The steps are as follows:
   1. Define the situation
   2. Describe and collect needed information
   3. Develop alternatives
   4. Develop agreement among those involved
   5. Decide which alternative is best
   6. Do what is indicated (implement the best alternative)
   7. Determine whether the decision was a good one and follow up (evaluate)

   Read the following statements and match to the correct stage in the decision-making process.
   a. _____   "From our research, it looks like we need to either redesign the package, reformulate the flavour, find new target markets, or lower the price."

   b. _____   "Sales are really picking up for the new improved version. Looks like we made the right decision."

   c. _____   "Sales for one of our most popular products are declining. Let's find out what's causing the decline and develop some ideas about reversing it."

   d. _____   "The new version will hit the shelves in a few weeks. I'm anxious to get consumer reactions."

   e. _____   "The consensus of the product development team seems to be to reformulate the flavour and redesign the package. Let's go for it."

   f. _____   "I need sales reports from the last two years, competitive sales reports, Census data, and demographic reports.

CHAPTER CHECK

1. a. What are "the four functions of management"?
      - planning organizing
      - organizing
      - leading
      - controlling

   b. Identify four activities performed within each of the four functions.
      i. _____planning_____   a. set goals
                                     b. develop strategies
                                     c. determine required resources

ii.	_organizing_	d.	
		a.	_allocate resources/assign tasks_
		b.	_develop structure_
		c.	_recruit, train etc._
		d.	_place employees_
iii.	_leading_	a.	_give assignments_
		b.	_guide/motivate empl._
		c.	_explain routines_
		d.	
iv.	_controlling_	a.	_monitor ~~progress~~ performance_
		b.	_reward outstanding " "_
		c.	
		d.	

2. What types of skills are required for tomorrow's managers?
   - _Skilled communicator, planner, leader, organizer, coordinator_

3. What are the three fundamental questions answered by planning?
   - _what is the situation now?_
   - _where do we want to go?_
   - _how can we get there?_

4. What are the three forms of planning?
   - _strategic_
   - _tactical_
   - _contingency_

5. Identify the three levels of management and describe their roles in performing the organization function.
   - _top: develop strategic plan_
   - _middle: responsible for plan_
   - _supervisory: assign people to that plan_

6. Identify four things that are involved when leading workers engaged in activities to meet the goals and objectives of the organization.
   - _give assignments   - explain routines   - clarify policies_

7. a. Identify the five steps in performing the control function.

b. What are three criteria that should be satisfied when setting standards?

_____

_____

_____

8. a. Summarize the difference between a "leader" and a "manager."

_____

_____

_____

_____

b. Name three different leadership styles.

_____

_____

_____

_____

9. List the six types of skills required to develop your managerial potential.

a. _____   d. _____

b. _____   e. _____

c. _____   f. _____

10. What other skills do the new global managers require, in addition to the six types of skills listed in Question 9?

_____

_____

_____

_____

PRACTICE TEST

Multiple choice: Circle the best answer.

1. Workers in the future
   a. will be more closely supervised and highly skilled
   b. will require managers that will give them direction and give precise orders
   c. will be more educated, highly skilled, and self-directed
   d. will work more individually rather than in teams

2. Which of the following would NOT be included in a discussion of the four functions of management?
   a. producing   c. leading
   b. organizing   d. controlling

3. Managers of the future
   a. will closely supervise highly skilled workers who would like to "do their own thing"
   b. will emphasize teamwork and cooperation, and will act as coaches, rather than "bosses"
   c. will have to become specialists in one or two functional areas
   d. will have to function as intermediaries between workers and unions

4. A(n) _____ is a specific short-term statement detailing how to achieve
    a. mission statement/goals
    b. goal/objectives
    c. goal/the mission statement
    d. objective/goals
5. Which of the following employees of the local hardware store, Hammerhead, would most likely be involved in strategic planning?
    a. Joe Hartley – department head
    b. Annelise Oswalt – advertising manager
    c. Elliot Nessy – President and CEO
    d. Manny Martinez — chief accountant
6. General Managers, division managers, plant managers, and college deans are all a part of
    a. supervisory management
    b. middle management
    c. top management
    d. first-line management
7. Which of the following is a false statement?
    a. Companies are looking at the best way to organize to respond to the needs of customers.
    b. Consensus is that larger companies are more responsive to customer needs than smaller companies.
    c. Most large firms are being restructured into smaller, customer-focused units.
    d. Companies are organizing so that customers have more influence, not managers.
8. In the future
    a. workers are more likely to be empowered to make decisions on their own
    b. firms will be less likely to establish close relationships with suppliers
    c. top managers will be allocating more of their time to giving more detailed instructions to workers
    d. small firms will stay away from each other as competition gets fierce
9. Measuring performance relative to objectives and standards is part of
    a. planning   c. directing
    b. organizing   d. controlling
10. Which step in the control process is considered to be the weakest?
    a. setting clear standards
    b. monitoring and recording results
    c. communicating results to employees
    d. taking corrective action
11. Which of the following statements is stated most effectively as a control standard?
    a. Cut the number of finished product rejects
    b. Empower employees to make more decisions next year
    c. Praise employees more often this month
    d. Increase sales of our top end product from 2,000 in the first quarter to 3,000 during the same period
12. Which of the following is NOT characteristic of a leader?
    a. A leader has a vision and rallies others around the vision.
    b. A leader will establish corporate values.
    c. A leader will emphasize corporate ethics.
    d. A leader will always attempt to keep things from changing.
13. When a manager uses democratic leadership, he or she will
    a. make managerial decisions without consulting employees.
    b. set objectives and allow employees to be relatively free to do what it takes to accomplish them.

c. give employees direction, and be sure that they are doing their job the way the manager wants them to.

d. work with employees to make decisions together.

14. As the trend toward self-managed teams continues, managers will
    a. find their jobs will remain essentially the same.
    b. delegate more planning, organizing, and controlling to lower levels.
    c. use more autocratic styles of leadership.
    d. be empowering more individuals than teams.

15. The basic categories of skills managers must have include all EXCEPT
    a. technical skills
    b. mechanical skills
    c. human relations skills
    d. conceptual skills

16. The level of management most likely to need conceptual skills is
    a. supervisory management
    b. first-line management
    c. middle management
    d. top management

17. The bulk of the duties of a manager will involve
    a. writing clearly.
    b. communicating with others through such things as meetings and presentations.
    c. using computers to send e-mail and surf the Internet.
    d. helping team members to learn how to work with people from different cultures.

True/False

1. _____ Accelerating change in business has increased the need for workers who are more highly educated and have higher skill levels.

2. _____ Today progressive managers are being educated to tell people what to do and to watch over these new type of workers.

3. _____ Organizing involves determining the best strategies and tactics to achieve the organization's objectives.

4. _____ A mission statement outlines a company's fundamental purpose.

5. _____ Planning answers the questions "What is the situation now?" and "Where do we want to go?"

6. _____ The consensus is that smaller organizations are more responsive to stakeholder needs than larger organizations.

7. _____ In today's organizations it is necessary to establish close relationships with suppliers and with retailers who sell our products.

8. _____ The planning function of management is the heart of the management system because it provides the feedback that enables managers and workers to make adjustments.

9. _____ The criteria for measuring success in a customer-oriented firm is customer satisfaction of both internal and external customers.

10. _____ The difference between managers and leaders is that a leader creates the vision, the manager carries it out.

11. _____ Generally, there is one best leadership style to which all leaders should adhere.

12. _____ Autocratic leadership will be effective in emergencies or when absolute followship is needed.

13. _____ The skills needed by managers are different at different levels.

14. _____ To delegate effectively a manager must make the people to whom a task has been assigned responsible for getting it completed on time.

15. _____ Most progressive managers of the 21st century will be team leaders.

16. _____ Managers of the future will not need to be computer literate, as their workers will be

empowered and will have decision-making responsibility anyway.

ANSWERS

Key Terms and Definitions

1. leading
2. baby boomer
3. management
4. contingency planning
5. decision making
6. planning
7. controlling
8. conceptual skills
9. organizing
10. top management
11. strategic planning
12. tactical planning
13. supervisory (first-line) management
14. enabling
15. middle management

16. objectives
17. knowledge management
18. goals
19. technical skills
20. human relations skills
21. democratic (participative) leadership
22. vision
23. empowerment
24. internal customers
25. laissez-faire leadership
26. managing diversity
27. autocratic leadership
28. mission statement
29. operational planning
30. SWOT analysis
31. external customers

The Changing Role of Managers

1.   a. Managers are being educated to guide and coach employees
       b. They emphasize teamwork and cooperation
       c. They are more friendly
       d. Managers treat employees as partners
2. Drucker says managers:
    a. give direction to their organizations
    b. provide leadership
    c. decide how to use organizational resources to accomplish goals.

Planning: Creating a Vision for the Organization

1.   Goals are broad, long-term accomplishments that an organization wants to reach. A vision is greater than a goal; it is the larger explanation of why the organization exists and where it is trying to head.
2.   A mission statement is the foundation for setting goals and selecting and motivating employees.
3.   a. Goal
       b. Goal
       c. Objective
       d. Goal
       e. Objective
       f. Objective
4.   a. Strategic
       b. Tactical
       c. Strategic
       d. Strategic
       e. Tactical

    f.   Tactical

5. a.   Answers will vary.
    b.   Answers will vary.

6. SWOT deals with the questions asked in the initial planning stage, such as: "What is the situation now? What is the state of the economy and other environments? What opportunities exist for meeting needs? What products are most profitable?" and so forth, form part of the SWOT analysis. This analysis begins with an analysis of the business environment in general. The internal strengths and weaknesses are identified. Lastly, external opportunities and threats are identified.

7. At the strategic planning stage, the company decides which customers to serve, what products or services to sell, and the geographic areas in which the firm will compete. Strategic planning is becoming more difficult because changes are occurring so fast that plans set for even months in the future may quickly become obsolete. Top management is involved in the strategic planning process.

    8. Tactical planning is the process of developing detailed, short-term strategies about what has to be done, who will do it and how it is to be done. Managers or teams of managers at lower levels of the organization do this type of planning.

    9. Operational planning is the setting of work standards and schedules necessary to implement the tactical objectives. Operational planning focuses on specific supervisors, department managers, and individual employees. The operational plan is the department manager's tool for daily and weekly operations.

    10. Contingency planning is important to do in the event that the primary plans do not achieve the organization's goals. The environment changes so rapidly that contingency plans are needed in anticipation of those changes. The idea is to stay flexible and to take opportunities when they present themselves, whether they were planned or not.

11. Eric has a big job ahead of him. There are many possible responses to this question, but some suggestions are
    a.   Strategic plan — Become the major supplier of tape and CD storage cases for automobiles within the next five years.
    b.   Tactical — Contact the production and/or engineering managers of the major automobile manufacturers and sell them on the product within the next 12 months. Continue to look for other markets.
    c.   Contingency plan — If the auto makers are not interested right now, begin focusing on the automotive after-market, to sell products as an add-on.

Organizing: Creating a Unified System

1. a.   Allocating resources
    b.   Establishing procedures
    c.   Assigning tasks
2. Top management consists of the president and other key executives who develop straetgic plans, such as the CEO (chief executive officer), COO (chief operating officer), and CF) (chief financial officer).

3. CEOs are responsible for introducing change into an organization. The COO is responsible for putting

those changes into effect. His or her tasks include structuring, controlling, and rewarding to ensure that people carry out the leader's vision. The CFO is responsible for obtaining funds, budgeting, collecting funds, and other financial matters. The CKO or CIO is responsible for getting the right information to other managers.

4. Middle management positions include general managers, divisional managers, branch managers, plant managers, and college deans.
5. Supervisory or first-line management includes people directly responsible for supervising workers and evaluating their daily performance.
6. The dominating question of organizing in recent years has been how to best organize the firm to respond to the needs of customers and other stakeholders. Stakeholders include anyone who is affected by the organization and its policies and products. That includes employees, customers, suppliers, dealers, environmental groups, and the surrounding communities.
7. Companies today are organizing so that customers have influence. Most large firms are being restructured into smaller, more customer-focused units.
8. Today the organizing task is more complex because firms are forming partnerships and joint ventures, so the job becomes an effort to organize the whole system, not just one firm.
9. Staffing involves recruiting, hiring, and retaining the best people available to accomplish the company's objectives. Today recruiting good employees is critical, especially in the Internet and high-tech areas. Firms with the most innovative and creative workers can go from start-up to major competitor with leading companies in a very short time.
10. Diversity includes people from a wide variety of backgrounds. If people are to work on teams, they have to learn to work together with people who have different personalities, different priorities, and different lifestyles. Research has shown that mixed groups are more productive than similar groups in the workplace. It is often quite profitable to have employees who match the diversity of customers so that cultural differences are understood and matched.
11. Answers will vary.

12. In earlier chapters we have learned about the changing nature of business, increasing global competition, and the continuing push for quality, and increased productivity. These new structures are reflective of the need to focus on productivity, quality, and the needs of the consumer in an increasingly competitive marketplace. For example, to be more productive we must cut costs, which interfirm relationships help to make possible. Further, to be more competitive, we must respond to customer demands by creating a "customer-oriented organization" with smaller, more customer-focused units.

Leading: Vision and Values

1. Autocratic leadership is effective when absolute followership is needed, and with new, unskilled workers who need more direction and guidance.
2. Employee participation in decisions usually increases job satisfaction. Progressive organizations are highly successful at using a democratic style of leadership where traits such as flexibility, good listening skills, and empathy are dominant.
3. Laissez-faire leadership is effective in professional organizations, where managers deal with doctors, engineers or other professionals. The traits needed by managers in laissez-faire organizations include, warmth, friendliness, and understanding.
4. Research indicates that successful leadership depends on who is being led and in what situation.

Different leadership styles, ranging from autocratic to laissez-faire, may be successfully depending on the people and the situation.

5. Traditional leaders give explicit instructions to workers, telling them what to do to meet the goals and objectives of the organization. This is called "directing." Progressive leaders are less likely than traditional leaders to give specific instructions to employees. They are more likely to empower employees than make decisions on their own. In cooperation with employees, these managers will set up teams that will work together to accomplish goals.

6. The steps to developing knowledge management include determining what knowledge is most important, and then setting out to find answers to those questions. The key to success is learning how to process information effectively and turn it into knowledge that everyone can use to improve processes and procedures.

7. As a manager of today, you are less likely to be giving specific instructions to your employees, and more likely to work closely with them in helping the employees to understand the objectives of the firm. You will probably set up teams, whose members will work together to accomplish those goals. Your role as a manager will be less that of a "boss" and more that of a coach, assistant, counsellor, and team member. These changes allow more employee participation in decision making, and more flexibility in how to get a job done.

8. As a manager of the new "breed" of workers, you are less likely to be giving specific instructions to your employees. Instead, you may give them the authority to make decisions which will allow them to respond quickly to any customer requests. In all likelihood, you will set up a team approach for the plant, using self-managed work teams if possible. Your job will be more that of a coach and team member, allowing for more participation in decision making and more flexibility for the workers.

9. Eric, as the top manager of the company, will be concerned with a broader view of where he wants the company to go. As a first-line manager, your job will be more specific, and your goals and objectives more specific than those Eric has outlined for the entire company. So your directions to subordinates, to the extent you will give them direction, will be more specific.

10. Leaders differ from managers in a number of ways. Effective leaders look at the four functions of management (planning, organizing, directing, and controlling) from a broader perspective than that of a "manager."

    Your boss has the qualities described as important to leaders. She has a vision of how she wants the division to operate. She trusts employees to make their own decision, thus "empowering" them with control over their jobs. Her sense of corporate values is demonstrated by her concern for quality, customer service, and in fair treatment of her employees, as well as by her concern for ethics.

11. a. i. Autocratic
    ii. Democratic
    b. i. Democratic
    ii. Laissez-faire
    c. i. Democratic
    ii. Autocratic
    d. It is generally believed that there is no one leadership style that is best in all situations. Which style is best depends upon the situation. A successful leader has the ability to use the leadership style most appropriate to the employee and the situation.

12. Your answers will vary, as each of you will have your individual style. However, review the material in this section of the chapter. Is there any opportunity to organize a self-managed team? Earlier in the study guide, the workers were described as the "new breed" of worker. Would a team-based approach be appropriate for this group? Could you use a participative management style? Did you consider getting opinions from the workers about what they see as a method to increase production without raising costs? In terms of the "Rules" and "Sins" of leadership, review them. Did you ask for advice? Did your solution inform them of the need for changing? Did you ask for new ideas?

13. As is noted throughout this chapter, the leaders and managers of the next century will be team leaders who are empowering their workers, giving them the freedom to decide how and when specific tasks will be done, as long as the goals of the company are accomplished. That is, by definition, delegating. Today's new breed of workers are more educated and trained, and will have the ability to work more within a team structure and with less direction from their manager. The manager will minimize the tendency to look over the team's shoulder to make sure things are being done correctly.

Controlling

1. The criteria for measuring success in customer-oriented firms are customer satisfaction of both internal and external customers. Further, while traditional financial control measures are still important, others have been added to measure the success of the firm in pleasing customers, employees and other stakeholders. Other criteria may include the contribution the firm is making to society or improvements in the quality of the environment.
2. A corporate scorecard is a broad measurement tool that measures customer satisfaction, financial progress, return on investment and everything else that needs to be managed for a firm to be profitable.
3. a. Comparing to standards
    b. Monitoring results
    c. Setting clear standards
    d. Communicating results and deviations
    e. Taking corrective action
4. *Possible Answers*
    a. Increase sales of product X by 20% for the next quarter.
    b. Decrease the number of rejects by 10% per week in 30 days.
    c. Get a bachelor's degree in business in four years.
    d. Study four hours every day for the spring term.
    e. Spend three hours a week reading articles on management. Praise employees once a week.

Tasks and Skills at Different Levels of Management

1. Technical skills involve the ability to perform tasks of a specific discipline or department.
2. Human relations skills include skills such as communication and motivation, leadership, coaching, morale building, training and development, and being supportive.
3. Conceptual skills refer to a manager's ability to picture the organization as a whole and the relationship of various parts, to perform tasks such as planning, organizing, controlling, decision-making, problem analysis, coordinating and delegating.
4. Managers need to be skilled in all three skill areas. First-line managers spend most of their time on technical and human relations tasks, but they spend little time on conceptual tasks. Middle managers need to use few conceptual skills. Instead, almost all their time is devoted to human relations and conceptual tasks. Top managers use considerable time on conceptual skills and human relations tasks.

5.

Management Level	Skills
a. Supervisory level	Technical
	Human relations

		Communications (verbal)
b.	Top management	Communications (writing)
		Conceptual (delegating)
		Time management
c.	Middle management	Human relations
		Communications
		Conceptual
d.	Middle management	Interpersonal
		Technical (computer)
e.	Supervisory level	Time management
		Computer skills

6. Delegating is one of the most difficult tasks for a manager to learn. The inclination for many managers is to pitch in and help others do their job. The progressive manager of today is a team leader. The manager will set specific goals in cooperation with team members, set up control procedures, and then basically allow the team a great deal of freedom to decide the "hows and whens" of completing certain tasks, as long as the goals are accomplished on time.

7. a. Develop alternatives
   b. Evaluate
   c. Define the situation
   d. Implement the best alternative
   e. Decide which alternative is best
   f. Describe and collect needed information

CHAPTER CHECK ANSWERS

1. a. Planning, Organizing, Leading, Controlling
   b. i. Planning
         a. Setting goals
         b. Developing strategies
         c. Determining resources needed
         d. Setting standards
      ii. Organizing
         a. Allocate resources, assign tasks, establish procedures
         b. Develop structure
         c. Recruit, select, train, develop employees
         d. Place employees
      iii. Leading
         a. Guide and motivate employees
         b. Give assignments
         c. Explain routines
         d. Clarify policies
         e. Provide feedback
      iv. Controlling
         a. Measure results against objectives
         b. Monitor performance
         c. Reward outstanding performance
         d. Take corrective action

2. Answers may vary, but should include being a skilled communicator, planner, organizer, coordinator, and supervisor.

3. What is the situation now?
   Where do we want to go?
   How can we get there from here?

4. Strategic planning, tactical planning, contingency planning

5. Top level management, develops strategic plans; tasks include structuring, controlling, and rewarding.
   Middle managers, responsible for tactical plans.
   Supervisory (first-line) management, is directly responsible for assigning specific jobs to workers and evaluating their daily performance.

6. Giving assignments, explaining routines, clarifying policies, and providing feedback on performance.

7. a. Setting clear performance standards, monitoring and recording actual performance results, comparing results against plans and standards, communicating results and deviations to the employees involved, taking corrective action when needed.
   b. They must be specific, attainable, and measurable.

8. a. Leaders: do the right thing; inspire and empower; seek flexibility, change, and stability; are externally oriented.
      Managers: do things right; command and control; seek predictability; are internally focused.
   b. Autocratic, democratic, laissez-faire.

9. a. Verbal
   b. writing
   c. computer
   d. human relations
   e. time management
   f. technical skills

10. They need to be multilingual and have a knowledge of other cultures.

PRACTICE TEST

Multiple Choice		True/False	
1.	c	1.	T
2.	a	2.	F
3.	b	3.	F
4.	d	4.	T
5.	c	5.	T
6.	b	6.	T
7.	b	7.	T
8.	a	8.	F
9.	b	9.	T
10.	a	10.	T
11.	d	11.	F
12.	d	12.	T
13.	d	13.	T
14.	b	14.	T
15.	b	15.	T
16.	d	16.	F
17.	b		

CHAPTER 9

Managing the Move Toward Customer-Driven Business Organizations

Learning Goals

After you have read and studied this chapter, you should be able to

1. Explain the organizational theories of Fayol and Weber.
2. Discuss the various issues involved in structuring and restructuring organizations.
3. Describe traditional organizations and their limitations.
4. Show how matrix-style organizations and cross-functional teams help companies become more customer oriented.
5. Defend the use of various organizational tools and techniques such as networking, reengineering, and outsourcing.
6. Give examples to show how organizational culture and the informal organization can hinder or assist organizational change.

Key Terms and Definitions

Listed here are important terms found in this chapter. Choose the correct term for each definition and write it in the space provided.

Bureaucracy
centralized authority
– competitive
⌐ benchmarking
continuous improvement
core competencies
cross-functional teams
decentralized authority
Departmentalization
Downsizing ✓
economy of scale
Extranet

formal organization
functional structure
grapevine

hierarcy
informal organization
intranet
inverted organization
line organization
line personnel
matrix organization
networking

organizational culture
organizational design
outsourcing

real time
reengineering ✓
restructuring ✓
span of control ✓
staff personnel ✓
total quality management (TQM)
transparency
virtual corporation

✗ 1. ___Span of control___   The optimum number of subordinates a manager supervises or should supervise.

2. ___Staff personnel___   Employees who perform functions that advise and assist line personnel in achieving their goals.

✗ 3. ___Functional structure___   Grouping of workers into departments based on similar skills, expertise, or resource use.

4. ___decentralized authority___   Delegating decision-making authority to lower-level managers who are more familiar with local conditions.

5. ___Cross-functional teams___   Groups of employees from different departments who work

together on a semipermanent basis.

6. ___networking___ Using communications technology and other means to link organizations and allow them to work together on common objectives.

7. ___TQM___ Striving for maximum customer satisfaction by ensuring quality from all departments.

8. ___informal organization___ The system of relationships and lines of authority that develops spontaneously as employees meet and form power centres; it is the human side of the organization that does not appear on any organization chart.

9. ___departmentalization___ Dividing an organization's structure into homogeneous units.

10. ___centralized authority___ Maintaining decision-making authority at the top level of management.

11. ___organizational culture___ Widely shared values within an organization that provide coherence and co-operation to achieve common goals.

12. ___matrix organization___ Organization in which specialists from different parts of the organization are brought together to work on specific projects but still remain part of a line and staff structure.

13. ___line personnel___ Employees who perform functions that contribute directly to the primary goals of the organization.

14. ___formal organization___ The structure that details lines of responsibility, authority, and position. It is the structure shown on organization charts.

15. ___organizational design___ The structuring of workers so that they can best accomplish the firm's goals.

16. ___continuous improvement___ Constantly improving the way the organization does things so that customer needs can be better satisfied.

17. ___reengineering___ The fundamental rethinking and radical redesign of organizational processes to achieve dramatic improvements in critical measures of performance.

18. ___inverted organization___ An organization that has contact people at the top and the chief executive officer at the bottom of the organization chart.

19. ___competitive benchmarking___ Rating an organization's practices, processes, and products against the world's best.

20. ___outsourcing___ Assigning various functions, such as accounting and legal work, to outside organizations.

21. ___core competencies___ Functions that the organization can do as well as or better than any other company in the world.

22. ___bureaucracy___ An organization with many layers of managers who set rules and regulations and oversee all decisions.

23. ___restructuring___ The process of reorganizing the structure of companies to make them more efficient.

24. ___hierarchy___ A system in which one person is at the top of the organization

and there is a ranked or sequential ordering from the top down of managers who are responsible to that person.

25. ___downsizing___ The process of eliminating managerial and non-managerial positions.

26. ___virtual corp.___ A temporary, networked organization made up of replaceable firms that join the network and leave it as needed.

27. ___transparency___ A concept that describes a company being so open to other companies working wit it that the once solid barriers between them become "see-through" and electronic information is shared as if the companies were one.

28. ___grapevine___ The system through which unofficial information flows between and among managers and employees.

29. ___line organization___ An organization that has direct two-way lines of responsibility, authority, and communication running from the top to the bottom of the organization, with all people reporting to only one supervisor.

30. _____ The present moment or the actual time in which something takes place

31. ___economies of scale___ The situation in which companies can produce goods more inexpensively if they can purchase raw materials in bulk.

32. ___extranet___ An extension of the Internet that connects suppliers, customers, and other organizations via secure websites.

33. ___intranet___ A set of communication links within a company that travel over the Internet but are closed to public access.

The Changing Organization

1. How were organizations designed in the past?
   managers could control workers. hierarchy

2. What is a hierarchy?
   one person is in charge

3. What impact did a traditional hierarchy have on decision making?
   if an employee wanted change, he would ask manager and so on. Solution could take days, weeks.

4. What are organizations doing about the layers of management? What is the term used to describe that trend?

organizations are eliminating managers and giving more power to lower-level employees. DOWNSIZING

5. What are the characteristics of a bureaucratic organization?
   a. _many rules/regulations for employees to follow_
   b. _organization set up by function_
   c. _people specialize in a specific function_
   d. _communication between dep. is minimal_

6. What is a problem with a typical bureaucratic structure?

not very responsive to customers. Employees tend to follow rules and aren't flexable when responding to customer complaints etc.

7. What have firms done to resolve the problems created by a bureaucratic structure?

restructuring, give more authority to lower-level people

8. You learned in earlier chapters of the success of such ideas as "skunkworks" and intrapreneuring in today's large corporate structures. This chapter discusses the trend in large corporations towards smaller, more responsive units.

   Discuss how these two trends complement one another in today's work environment, and why you think they can lead to a more successful organization in today's marketplace.

9. Many organizations today are organized around principles developed in the late 1940s by Henri Fayol and Max Weber. In the 1950s, Joan Woodward emerged as an organizational design specialist.

   Read the following statements and determine whose ideas they represent.
   a. _Fayol_ — Developed several "principles" of organizing.
   b. _~~woodward~~ weber_ — Designed what is known as the bureaucratic organization.
   c. _woodward_ — Found that there is no one best way to organize.
   d. _weber_ — Detailed, written job descriptions are essential.
   e. _____ — The creation of a spirit of pride and loyalty among

people in the firm is important.

f. ______________ Each worker should report to only one boss.

g. ______________ Staffing and promotions should be based upon qualifications.

h. ______________ Functions of the organization should be divided into specialized areas such as production, marketing, finance, and management.

i. ______________ Believed in good relations between managers and workers.

j. ______________ Studied the relationship among organizational structure, technology, and success.

k. ______________ Each person should know to whom they report. Managers have a right to give orders and expect others to follow.

l. ______________ There should be three layers of management.

m. ______________ Clear, written, consistent procedures, regulations, and policies.

n. ______________ A firm using a complex technology was more successful with a bureaucratic structure.

o. ______________ Clear definitions of channels of communication.

Issues Involved in Structuring and Restructuring Organizations

1. What is the trend in organizations today regarding management layers?

eliminate several layers of management managers and create teams

2. How does span of control vary at different levels in an organization?

as you go ↑ in an organization, span of control narrows gradually

3. What is the trend in breadth of span of control?

expand span of control to get rid of middle managers ~~IT makes it possible to handle more info~~ w/o managers

4. What determines the decision about which way to departmentalize?

nature of product & customers served.

5. Think of an organization to which you belong — a club, a church, an athletic team, fraternity or sorority, the company you work for.
   a. Who has the responsibility, and authority, to make important decisions in that organization?

   _____

   _____

   _____

   _____

   b. Draw an organizational chart showing who reports to whom.

   _____

   _____

   _____

   _____

   c. How are jobs and authority delegated by the top manager to lower levels in the organization?

   _____

   _____

   _____

   _____

6. There are five methods that a firm uses to group the work units of an organization:
   ☐ Product
   ☐ Function
   ☐ Customer group
   ☐ Geographic location
   ☐ Process

   Match each of the following examples to the correct type of departmentalization.

   a. _____product_____   General Motors has the Saturn, Chevrolet, and Pontiac division, and the Oldsmobile and Buick divisions. Small cars are designed and manufactured by the first division, intermediate and large cars by the latter.

   b. _____function_____   At the highest corporate levels, G.E. has a corporate strategic planning staff, production resources staff, technical resources staff, and financial resources staff.

   c. _____process_____   Apple Computer, in manufacturing the Macintosh Computer System, begins with an assembly line that makes the logic board; another line makes the analog board. Once assembled, the boards go through diagnostic tests before being assembled into a computer unit.

   d. _Geographic location_   When Wendy's made the decision to expand into the European market, the company created a separate European division.

   e. _customer group_   Most banks have commercial loan officers who deal only with business customers, and consumer loan specialists for personal loans.

7. Generally, the more decision-making authority that is delegated to lower-level managers, the more

decentralized an organization is.

Read the following situations, and decide whether the organization appears to be centralized or decentralized in its decision making.

a. _decentralized_ In the U.S., the headquarters for IBM is located in New York State. When a new salesperson is hired, he or she is hired by the branch manager in whatever location the person will be working.

b. _decentralized_ Laura Ashley, founder of a company that makes home furnishings and women's clothing, turned over the management of the firm to professional managers, licensed the production of sheets and upholstered furniture to other firms, and relinquished control over the design of clothes and fabrics.

c. _centralized_ Companies such as Kentucky Fried Chicken make decisions about menu offerings, store decor, pricing, and advertising at the corporate headquarters.

8. How is the trend toward making firms more responsive to the market enhanced by decentralization?

_____

_____

_____

Organization Models

1. a. What areas of a business are considered "staff"?
   safety, quality control, comp tech, HR mangement

   _____

   _____

   _____

   b. What disadvantage is common to both line, and line and staff organizational structures?
   inflexability

   _____

   _____

   c. What benefits do both types of organizations have in common?
   created lines of authority & communication

   _____

   _____

   _____

2. Describe cross-functional teams.
   employees from different departments who together as a team on a semipermanent basis

_____

_____

3. What are the advantages and disadvantages of cross-functional, self-managed teams?

   Advantages
   a. increase in indepartmental relations
   b. quicker response to customers
   c. + increased employee motivation.

   Disadvantages
   a. confusion over authority
   b. loss of control by management
   c. difficult to evaluate employees individually
   d. _____

4. What are five kinds of teams?
   a. management
   b. virtual
   c. quality circles
   d. work teams
   e. problem-solving teams

5. What is an extranet?

   _____

   _____

   _____

6. What is an intranet?

   _____

   _____

   _____

   _____

7. There are four types of organizational structures:

   ☐ Line   ☐ Matrix
   ☐ Line and Staff   ☐ Cross-functional

   Read the following brief descriptions of several companies and decide which form of organizational structure would be most suitable for each.

   a. matrix   A small company, Dynalink is in the biotechnology industry. Competition is fierce, and new product development is of highest importance. The field is changing and growing so rapidly that new product ideas must come fast and furiously. The firm employs highly skilled, very creative people.

   b. _____   Another small firm is Cleanem Up, a dry cleaning establishment, with one owner and one store. They are located in a suburban area and have a loyal clientele. The store is known for its quality and courteous service.

c. _____   Wells Industries is a medium-sized firm employing about
                                1,500 people. Wells makes a variety of business-related
                                products such as stationery, forms, and so forth. They have
                                a good sales force which knows the product very well. While
                                this is a fairly competitive industry, new product develop-
                                ment happens as the need arises, such as when firms go
                                from sophisticated word processing machines to even more
                                sophisticated computerized office management.

d. _____   Chrysler wants to develop a new luxury car to compete with
                                Lexus, Infiniti, and others. Time is important, as they want to
                                enter the market within 18 months.

8. What impact will cross-functional teams have on organizational designs of the future?
   more competitive edge with better linkages with
   customers, suppliers & distributors

9. What problems are sometimes associated with cross-functional teams?
   members might be unsure with what their duties are

The Restructuring Process and Total Quality

1. "When an organization needs dramatic changes, only reengineering will do."
   What is the difference between "restructuring" and "reengineering"?

2. How does the upside-down (inverted) organizational structure relate to the other kinds of changes we
   have read about in this chapter, such as wider spans of control, decentralization, cross-functional self-
   managed teams, and so on? What does it accomplish?

3. How does the "internal" customer concept help a business become more competitive?

Establishing a Service-Oriented Culture

1. What kind of organizational cultures do the best organizations have?

   _____

   _____

   _____

   _____

2. What are two organizational systems that all companies have?

   a. _____   b. _____

3. Describe the difference between the formal and the informal organization.

   _____

   _____

   _____

   _____

4. What is the relationship among leadership style, the organizational structure (such principles as flat vs. tall organizations, span of control, and delegation of authority), and the creation of an organizational culture?

   _____

   _____

   _____

   _____

5. How does the informal organization help to create the corporate culture?

   _____

   _____

   _____

   _____

6. As a "customer" of the products your school offers, describe the organizational climate. How does the school and its employees (faculty, staff, and administrators) emphasize service to its customers?

   _____

   _____

   _____

   _____

7. Read the following situations, and determine whether the formal or informal structure is being described.

   a. _____ A disgruntled employee files a grievance with his supervisor.

   b. _____ Ford reduces the number of management levels in a plant from 15 to 10.

   c. _____ The plant manager at the White Motor plant in Kelowna, B.C., takes time to walk around the production facility to talk to the people on the line about their concerns.

   d. _____ Rather than making a formal written request, a college professor talks to the data processing lab supervisor about getting a computer in her office when old equipment is being replaced.

   e. _____ Monsanto completely reorganizes, eliminating 1,500 management

f. _____ A manager of a small plant recognizes that if he wants to make any changes, he has to get the support of the first-line supervisor on the second shift. That supervisor is the most influential in determining attitudes among workers on both shifts.

8. Music-stor is in a growth state, and Eric, the founder, wants to be sure to build on a good foundation. You are already familiar with the product, and have reengineered the production area. Eric is now interested in the organizational design of the entire company. What suggestions can you give him, knowing what you already know about the company and its employees?

_____
_____
_____
_____
_____
_____
_____
_____
_____
_____

CHAPTER CHECK

1. a. Describe the current trends in organizational design.

   trend is toward restructuring/reengineering business processes
   - smaller, more responsive units → downsizing

   b. Discuss two examples of Canadian companies that have adopted new organizational designs reflecting these trends.

   _____
   _____
   _____
   _____

2. List 10 principles of organizing outlined by Fayol.
   a. utility of command
   b. hierarchy of authority
   c. division of labour
   d. order
   e. equity
   f. authority degree of centralization
   g. esprit de corps
   h. _____
   i. _____
   j. _____

3. List four characteristics of Max Weber's bureaucracy.
   a. job descriptions
   b. written rules
   c. consistent policies, procedures and regulations
   d. staffing & promotions based on qualifications

4. What did Joan Woodward find in her studies of organizational design?

   no best way to organize a corporation

5. What are four organizational issues that have resulted from the process of firms reorganizing?
   a. tall vs flat
   b. span of control
   c. ~~departmentalization~~ departmentalization
   d. centralization vs. decentralization

6. Describe what is meant by "tall" and "flat" organizations.

   -tall = many layers of management, $$$ of management

   -flat = todays trend, creation of teams

7. List seven factors in determining the appropriate span of control.
   a. capabilities of manager
   b.   "   of subordinates
   c. functional complexity
   d.   "   similarity
   e. need for coordination
   f. planning demands
   g. geographical closeness

8. What are the advantages and disadvantages of a functional structure?

Advantages	Disadvantages
a. economies of scale	a. lack of coord. between depts
b. development of skills/	b. emp. identify w/ dept goals, not org.
c. good coordination w/function	c. external change response is slow
d.	d.

9. List five methods of departmentalization.
   a. product
   b. function
   c. process
   d. geographical
   e. customer group

10. Describe the difference between centralized and decentralized authority.

Centralized _____ decision making at top level _____

Decentralized _____ ″ ″ lower level management managers _____

11. Name three types of organizational structures.

a. line _____
b. line & staff _____
c. matrix _____

12. Describe the difference between line and staff personnel.

a. Line _____ functions that contribute directly to goals _____

b. Staff _____ perform functions that contribute line personnel in achieving the goals _____

13. List three advantages and three disadvantages of each form of organizing.

Line

Advantages

a. _____
b. _____
c. _____

Disadvantages

a. _____
b. _____
c. _____

Line and Staff

Advantages

a. _____
b. _____
c. _____

Disadvantages

a. _____
b. _____
c. _____

Matrix

Advantages

a. _____
b. _____
c. _____

Disadvantages

a. _____
b. _____
c. _____

Cross-functional, self-managed teams
  Advantages
  a. _____
  b. _____
  c. _____
  Disadvantages
  a. _____
  b. _____
  c. _____

14. In what circumstances does a matrix system of organizing function most effectively?
  a. _____
  b. _____
  c. _____
  d. _____

15. Describe the difference between formal and informal organizations.
  Formal organization _____
  _____
  Informal organization _____
  _____

16. What are two important aspects of the informal organization?
  a. _____
  b. _____

PRACTICE TEST

Multiple Choice: Circle the best answer.

1. In general, organizations today are
   a. eliminating managers and giving power to lower-level employees
   b. getting bigger, more international, and so are adding management layers
   c. becoming more bureaucratic
   d. managing employees more closely as they reduce the layers of management
2. Which of the following does NOT fit in when describing a bureaucratic organization?
   a. many rules and regulations that everyone is expected to follow
   b. people tend to specialize in many functions
   c. communication is minimal
   d. the organization is set up by function, with separate departments for marketing, engineering, and so on
3. When IBM changed its organizational design, the company gave more authority to lower-level employees, to become more flexible in responding to customer needs. The company broke down barriers between functions, and ended top-down management. This process is known as
   a. downsizing
   b. changing span of control
   c. restructuring
   d. becoming more bureaucratic
4. According to Henry Fayol, the principle of _____ means that each person should know to

whom they report, and that managers should have the right to give orders and expect others to follow.
   a. unity of command
   b. division of labour
   c. order
   d. hierarchy of authority
5. Max Weber believed that
   a. large organizations demanded clearly established rules and guidelines
   b. workers and supervisors should make decisions together
   c. rules were to be considered only as guidelines, and employees should be flexible
   d. there was no need for job descriptions
6. Robin Banks is a supervisor for a large, bureaucratic organization on the West Coast. According to the views of a bureaucratic organization held by Max Weber, this means that Robin should
   a. be included on decision making when decisions affect her workers
   b. have a wide span of control
   c. try to get her workers organized into cross-functional teams
   d. do her work and let middle and upper-level managers do the decision making
7. The process of reorganizing firms into smaller, less complex units is the result of
   a. new technologies and international competition
   b. employees rebelling against too many rules
   c. upper-level managers who were not good decision makers
   d. bureaucrats changing their way of thinking
8. Who Dunnit is a new firm which makes murder mystery games for sale in retail stores and through catalogs. The company is run by a very few people, and most everybody pitches in when they need to, to get the job done. It is really a "team" effort, with very few layers of management. Who Dunnit is an example of a
   a. tall organization
   b. bureaucratic organization
   c. centralized organization
   d. flat organization
9. A manager's span of control
   a. can narrow as subordinates need less supervision
   b. will narrow as the manager gets to higher levels in the organization and work becomes less standardized
   c. will broaden as work is less geographically concentrated
   d. will broaden as functions become more complex
10. Dewey, Cheatum and Howe is a car company that makes four models, a sport utiity, a sports car, a four-door sedan, and a compact car. Workers at Dewey basically work on only one type of vehicle, and separate marketing and product development processes are designed for each type of vehicle, to better serve the customers for each type of vehicle. Dewey, Cheatum and Howe is departmentalized by
   a. customer
   b. function
   c. process
   d. product
11. The form of organizational structure that is most flexible, and allows the organization to take on new projects without adding to the organizational structure is the
   a. line
   b. line and staff
   c. martix

    d. cross-functional self-managed team

12. The line structure has the disadvantage of

    a. being too inflexible

    b. being costly and complex

    c. perceived loss of control for a manager

    d. requiring self-motivated, highly trained employees

13. Banana Computers is restructuring, and intends to implement cross-functional teams. All of the following are likely to serve on a cross-functional team EXCEPT

    a. a Banana engineer

    b. an employee of Peelit, Inc. one of Banana's competitors

    c. an employee of Monkeyshine, one of Banana's suppliers

    d. a Banana salesperson

14. Ima Doogooder works for Banana Computers and is very good at her job. However, Ima believes that there is always something she can do better, and she is constantly looking for better ways to satisfy customer needs. Ima is apparently a practitioner of

    a. reengineering

    b. restructuring

    c. continuous improvement

    d. benchmarking

15. In an inverted, or "upside-down" organization, the manager's job is to

    a. maintain direct contact with customers

    b. direct and closely monitor employee performance

    c. look for the best ways to outsource functions

    d. assist and support sales personnel and other employees who work directly with customers

16. When a firm is rating its processes and products against the best in the world, the firm is practising

    a. total quality management

    b. outsourcing

    c. their core competencies

    d. competitive benchmarking

17. Companies based on an inverted pyramid

    a. support front-line personnel with data, communication, and professional assistance

    b. need employees who are unskilled, so they can be trained in new ways

    c. insist that managers keep close watch on those employees who have direct contact with customers

    d. have difficulty with slow decision making and with meeting customer needs

True/False

1. ____ A typical hierarchy will consist of top management, middle managers, and supervisory or first-line managers.

2. ____ A bureaucratic organizational system is good when workers are relatively well educated and trained to make decisions.

3. ____ Henri Fayol and Max Weber are best known for such organizational concepts as division of labour, unity of command and strict rules, guidelines, and policies.

4. ____ An organization with many layers of management, such as the Canadian army or a large corporation, is a good example of a flat organization.

5. ____ Companies that cut management layers are tending to create cross-functional and self-managed teams.

6. ____ The more experienced a manager is, the broader the span of control can be.

7. _____ One of the advantages of a functional structure is an ability to respond quickly to external changes.
8. _____ Today's rapidly changing markets tend to favour centralization of authority, so decisions can be made quickly.
9. _____ Safety, quality control and human resource management are examples of staff positions in a manufacturing firm.
10. _____ An extranet is a communication link within a specific company that travels over the Internet.
11. _____ Total quality management calls for continuous improvement of processes to deal with both internal and external customers.
12. _____ When a company can't perform a certain function as well as the best, the company may outsource that function, in order to concentrate on the functions at which they are the best.
13. _____ To improve internal services, some companies will set up a buy-sell relationship between teams and business units in the company, thus creating internal customers.
14 _____ In general, an organizational culture cannot be negative.
15. _____ The informal organization in most organizations is not particularly powerful.

ANSWERS

Key Terms and Definitions

1. span of control
2. staff personnel
3. functional structure
4. decentralized authority
5. cross-functional teams
6. Networking
7. total quality management
8. informal organization
9. Departmentalization
10. centralized authority
11. organizational culture
12. matrix organization
13. line personnel
14. formal organization
15. organizational design
16. continuous improvement
17. reengineering
18. Inverted organization
19. competitive benchmarking
20. outsourcing
21. core competencies
22. bureaucracy
23. restructuring
24. hierarchy
25. downsizing
26. virtual corporation
27. transparency
28. grapevine
29. line organization
30. real time
31. economy of scale
32. extranet
33. intranet

The Changing Organization

1. In the past, many organizations were designed so that managers could control workers. Everything was set up in a hierarchy.
2. A hierarchy means that there is one person at the top of the organization. There are many levels of managers who are responsible to that one person. Since one person can't keep track of thousands of workers, the top manager needs many lower-level managers to help.
3. In a traditional hierarchy, when an employee wanted to introduce a change, the employee would ask their manager. That manager would, in turn, ask his or her manager, and so on. Eventually a decision would be passed down. This type of decision making could take days, weeks, or months.

4. Organizations are eliminating managers and giving more power to lower-level employees. This process is called downsizing, because the organization is able to operate with fewer employees.
5. The characteristics of a bureaucratic organization are
   a. many rules and regulations which everyone is expected to follow
   b. the organization is set up by function
   c. people tend to specialize in one function
   d. communication among departments is minimal
6. The problem today with bureaucratic organizations is that such organizations are not very responsive to customers. Employees tend to follow the rules and aren't very flexible in responding to customer needs and wants.
7. Slow response to consumer demands cuts into sales. Companies have responded by restructuring, or redesigning the organization so it can more effectively and efficiently service customers. Often that will mean breaking down barriers between functions, and giving more authority to lower-level employees.
8. *Suggested Answer*
   Part of the success of skunkworks and intrapreneuring is due to the small group structure, which allows for effective communication and quick decision making. These seem to be the benefits that larger organizations are looking for in smaller, self-contained business units. In smaller groups, employees feel a sense of "camaraderie, involvement, flexibility, and a feeling of oneness." Members of these small groups, as in skunkworks and intrapreneuring, tend to feel more motivated and committed to realizing the goals of the organization.
9. a. Fayol   i. Fayol
   b. Weber   j. Woodward
   c. Woodward   k. Fayol
   d. Weber   l. Weber
   e. Fayol   m. Weber
   f. Fayol   n. Woodward
   g. Weber   o. Fayol
   h. Fayol

Issues Involved in Structuring and Restructuring Organizations

1. The trend is to eliminate several layers of management. Throughout the 1990s, companies fired managers in an attempt to become more efficient. Companies that cut management are tending to create teams.
2. Span of control narrows gradually at higher levels of the organization. Because work is standardized at lower levels, it is possible to implement a wider span of control.
3. The trend is to expand span of control as organizations get rid of middle managers. This will be possible as employees become more professional, information technology makes it possible for managers to handle more information, and employees take on more responsibility for self-management.
4. The decision about which way to departmentalize depends upon the nature of the product and the customers served.
5. Answers will vary.
6. a. Product
   b. Function
   c. Process
   d. Geography
   e. Customer
7. a. Decentralized
   b. Decentralized

c. Centralized
8. Today's rapidly changing markets tend to favour decentralized decision making, because decision making is faster, and changes can be implemented more rapidly.

Organization Models

1. a. Areas such as safety, quality control, computer technology, human resource management, and investing would be considered staff.
   b. Both line, and line and staff structures have a certain amount of inflexibility.
   c. Both types of organizations have established lines of authority and communication and both work well in companies with a relatively unchanging environment and slow product development.
2. Cross-functional teams are groups of employees from different departments who work together on a semipermanent basis. Often the teams are empowered to make decisions on their own without seeking approval of management.
3. Cross-functional, self-managed teams
   Advantages
   a. Greatly increases interdepartmental coordination and cooperation
   b. Quicker response to customers and market conditions
   c. Increased employee morale and motivation
   Disadvantages
   a. Some confusion over responsibility and authority
   b. Perceived loss of control by management
   c. Difficult to evaluate employees and set up reward systems
   d. Requires self-motivated and highly trained workers
4. Five kinds of teams are
   a. management teams
   b. virtual teams
   c. quality circles
   d. work teams
   e. problem-solving teams
5. An extranet is an extended Internet that connects suppliers, customers, and other organizations via secure Web sites.
6. Intranets are secure communication links within companies that travel over the Internet.
7. a. The *best answer* is most likely a matrix system.
   b. Line
   c. Line and staff
   d. Cross-functional
8. Cross-functional teams will have a major impact on organizational designs of the future. Companies will be linked with customers, suppliers, and distributors through these teams, creating an integrated system of firms working together to create products and services designed to exactly meet customers' needs. Firms designed in such a manner will have a real competitive edge over more traditional corporations.
   9. Managers may resist the move toward teams, and team members themselves may be unsure of what their duties are, how they will be compensated, and who is responsible for mistakes. Workers need different skills from those required for working alone, and companies can falter while a change-over is in process. Firms run the risk of overusing teams, which may hinder creativity and problem solving.

The Restructuring Process and Total Quality

1. Restructuring most often refers to grouping employees differently than in the traditional ways, using a team approach and implementing a customer focus through continuous improvement in the way the organization does things. Reengineering is rethinking and redesigning the whole process of doing business in order to improve performance.

2. These organizational changes are all focused on designing the organization with meeting the needs of the customer as the most important objective. Inverted organizations empower front-line workers, who deal directly with customers, and provide them with the information and support needed to satisfy customers. Turning the organization inside out again focuses on customer service because the firm concentrates on its "core competencies," and outsources the functions at which the company is less proficient. The idea of turning the organization inside out is to rate your practices, processes, and products against the world's best. If you don't measure up, it's important to either outsource the function or reengineer the function.

3. The internal customer "buys" his "product" from another business unit in the organization. If the team (customer) is not happy with products or services provided by the internal unit, the team (customer) can purchase the services from an outside vendor.

Establishing a Service-Oriented Culture

1. The best organizations have cultures that emphasize service to others; the atmosphere is one of friendly, concerned, caring people who enjoy working together to provide a good product at a reasonable price. Those companies have less need for close supervision of employees, policy manuals, organization charts and formal rules, procedures and controls.

2. All companies have a(n)
   a. formal organization
   b. informal organization

3. The formal organization details each person's responsibility, authority, and position. The informal organization consists of relationships and line of authority that develop outside the formal organization.

4. The text states that companies that have good organizational cultures have less need for close supervision of employees, policy manuals, organization charts, and formal rules, procedures, and controls. That would indicate broad spans of control, with decision-making authority delegated to lower levels of management. This creates a flatter organization and calls for a participative management style, which we learned in earlier chapters creates a climate of cooperation and self-motivation.

5. The informal organization can help to create a spirit of cooperation between managers and employees. Studies suggest that worker productivity is increased by a feeling of belonging to a group. If there is a sense of loyalty to the group, members will follow group norms (the group in this case being the organization and/or specific work groups) and will develop a cohesiveness that creates and enhances a positive and corporate culture.

6. Answers will vary.

7. a. Formal
   b. Formal
   c. Informal
   d. Informal
   e. Formal

f. Informal

8. How you would design the organization is up to you. Many of the ideas presented in the chapter could be helpful. This is a small company, so a line organization might be appropriate. We noted earlier that the workers are a "new breed" who don't need a lot of supervision, however, so close monitoring probably could prove to be counter-productive. There doesn't seem to be an immediate need for new product development, so a matrix structure probably wouldn't be necessary. The emphasis on customer service has been apparent throughout the chapter, so however you design the company, the focus should be on whatever design will most effectively help the company to meet customer needs.

CHAPTER CHECK ANSWERS

1. a. The trend in organizational design is toward smaller, more responsive units. This is being accomplished through downsizing in large firms, eliminating layers of management, and reducing the number of workers. This tends to create faster decision making. Particular attention is being given to communication, employee morale, and manageability.
    b. Answers will vary.
2. a. Unity of command
    b. Hierarchy of authority
    c. Division of labour
    d. Subordination of individual interest to the general interest
    e. Authority
    f. Degree of centralization
    g. Clear communication channels
    h. Order
    i. Equity
    j. Esprit de corps
3. a. Job descriptions
    b. Written rules, guidelines, and detailed records
    c. Consistent procedures, regulations, and policies
    d. Staffing and promotions based on qualifications
4. Woodward found that there is no one best way to organize a corporation. The structure of the organization depends upon the technical complexity of the company's production process.
5. a. Tall vs. flat structures
    b. Span of control
    c. Departmentalization
    d. Centralization vs. decentralization
6. Companies that have many layers of management have a tall organization structure. Companies with fewer layers of management have a flat structure.
7. a. Capabilities of the manager
    b. Capabilities of the subordinates
    c. Functional complexity
    d. Functional similarity
    e. Need for coordination
    f. Planning demands
    g. Geographical closeness
8. *Advantages*
    a. Skills can be developed and employees can progress as skills develop
    b. Allows for economies of scale

c. Good coordination within the function

　　Disadvantages

　　a. Lack of communication between departments

　　b. Employees identify with the department goals, not the organizational goals

　　c. Response to external change is slow

　　d. People not trained to take different managerial responsibilities

9. a. Product

　　b. Function

　　c. Customer group

　　d. Geographic

　　e. Process

10. "Centralized authority means that decision-making authority is maintained at the top level of management."
　　"Decentralized authority means that decision-making authority is delegated to lower-level managers."

11. a. Line

　　b. Line and staff

　　c. Matrix

12. a. Line personnel perform functions that contribute directly to the goals of the organization.

　　b. Staff personnel perform functions that assist line personnel in performing their functions.

13. Line

　　Advantages

　　a. Clearly defined responsibility and authority

　　b. Easy to understand

　　c. One supervisor for each person

　　Disadvantages

　　a. Too inflexible

　　b. Few specialists to advise

　　c. Long lines of communication

　　d. Unable to handle complex questions quickly

Line and staff

　　Advantages

　　a. Expert advice from staff to line personnel

　　b. Established lines of authority

　　c. Encourages cooperation and better communication at all levels

　　Disadvantages

　　a. Potential overstaffing

　　b. Potential overanalyzing

　　c. Lines of communication can get blurred

　　d. Staff frustrations because of lack of authority

Matrix

　　Advantages

　　a. Flexible

　　b. Encourages cooperation among departments

　　c. Can produce creative solutions to problems

　　d. Allows organization to take on new projects without adding to the organizational structure

　　Disadvantages

　　a. Costly and complex

　　b. Can confuse employees

　　c. Requires good interpersonal skills and cooperative managers and employees

d. Difficult to evaluate employees and to set up reward systems

Cross-functional, self-managed teams

Advantages

   a. Greatly increases interdepartmental coordination and cooperation
   b. Quicker response to customers and market conditions
   c. Increased employee motivation and morale

Disadvantages

   a. Confusion over responsibility and authority
   b. Perceived loss of control by management
   c. Difficult to evaluate employees and set up reward systems
   d. Requires self-motivated and highly trained workers

14. a. Underlying the matrix system is a traditional line and staff organization with recognized lines of authority.
    b. A project manager may be given temporary authority to borrow line personnel from functional departments, but the line personnel will report to their regular position upon completion of the project. Therefore, personnel do not in fact report to more than one manager.
    c. A matrix system evolves easily in an organization where there is a strong informal communication system within the formal structure.
    d. The unit of operation must be small enough to be flexible and enable everyone to stay informed.

15. The formal organization is "the structure that details lines of responsibility, authority, and position. It is the structure shown on organization charts."

    The informal organization is the "system of relationships and lines of authority" that develops outside the formal organization and is not shown on the organization chart.

16. a. Group norms
    b. Group cohesiveness

PRACTICE TEST

Multiple Choice	**True/False**
1. a	1. T
2. b	2. F
3. c	3. T
4. d	4. F
5. a	5. T
6. d	6. T
7. a	7. F
8. d	8. F
9. b	9. T
10. b	10. F
11. c	11. T
12. a	12. T
13. b	13. T
14. c	14. F
15. d	15. F
16. d	
17. a	

CHAPTER 10

Managing Production and Operations

Learning Goals

After you have read and studied this chapter, you should be able to

1. Define *operations management*.
2. Describe the operations management functions that are involved in both the manufacturing and service sectors.
3. Discuss the problem of measuring productivity in the service sector, and tell how new technology is leading to productivity gains in service companies.
4. Explain process planning and the various manufacturing processes being used today.
5. Describe the seven new manufacturing techniques that have made companies more productive: just-in-time inventory control, Internet purchasing, flexible manufacturing, lean manufacturing, mass customization, competing in time, and computer-aided design and manufacturing.
6. Explain the use of PERT and Gantt charts.

Key Terms and Definitions

Listed here are important terms found in this chapter. Choose the correct term for each definition and write it in the space provided.

Assembly process ✓
Competing in time
computer-aided design (CAD) ✓
Computer-aided manufacturing (CAM) ✓
Computer-integrated manufacturing (CIM)
Continuous process
Critical path ✓
enterprise resource planning (ERP)
facility layout
facility location

Flexible manufacturing ✓
form utility
Gantt chart ✓
Intermittent process
ISO 9000
ISO 14000
just-in-time (JIT) inventory control ✓
lean manufacturing
manufacturing
mass customization
mass production ✓
materials requirement planning (MRP)

Operations management ✓
process planning
process manufacturing
production ✓
program evaluation and review technique (PERT)
purchasing ✓
quality control
robot ✓

1. ___Robot___ — A computer-controlled machine capable of performing many tasks.

2. ___Gantt chart___ — Bar graph that shows managers what projects are being worked on and what stage they are at on a daily basis.

3. ___Flexible manufacturing___ — Designing and using individual machines that can do multiple tasks so that each can produce a variety of products.

4. ___purchasing___ — The function in a firm that searches for quality material

resources, finds the best suppliers, and negotiates the best price for goods and services.

5. Computer Aided Manufact. The use of computers in the manufacturing of products.

6. operations management A specialized area in management that converts or transforms resources into goods and services.

7. mass production The process of making a large number of a limited variety of products at very low cost.

8. CA Design (CAD) The use of computers in the design of products.

9. PERT A method for analyzing the tasks involved in completing a given project, estimating the time needed to complete each task, and identifying the minimum time needed to complete the total project.

10. process manufacturing Production process that physically or chemically changes materials.

11. JIT inventory control Delivery of the smallest possible quantities at the latest possible time, to keep inventory as low as possible.

12. ERP enterprise resource planning Computer-based production and operations system that links multiple firms into one integrated production unit.

13. critical path The sequence of tasks that takes the longest time to complete.

14. production The creation of goods and services using the factors of production: land, labour, capital, entrepreneurship, and information.

15. form utility The value added to inputs by the creation of outputs.

16. assembly process Production process that puts together components.

17. competing in time Being as fast or faster than competition in responding to consumer wants and needs and getting goods and services to them.

18. MRP A computer-based operations management system that uses sales forecasts to make sure that needed parts and materials are available at the right time and place.

19. intermittent process A production process in which the production run is short and the machines are changed frequently to make different products.

20. mass customization Tailoring products to meet the needs of individual customers.

21. manufacturing An important part of production: people producing goods using materials, machinery, robots, and computers.

22. continuous process A production process in which long production runs turn out finished goods over time.

23. lean manufacturing The production of goods using less of everything compared to mass production.

24. quality control The measurement of products and services against set standards.

25. C Intergrated Manufact. The uniting of computer-aided design with computer-aided manufacturing.

26. _facility location_ — The process of selecting a geographic location for a company's operations.

27. _facility layout_ — The physical arrangement of resources in the production process.

28. _ISO 9000_ — The common name given to quality management and assurance standards.

29. _ISO 14000_ — A collection of the best practices for managing an organization's impact on the environment.

30. _process planning_ — Choosing the best means for turning resources into useful goods and services.

Canada's Evolving Manufacturing and Services Base

1. What are five things manufacturers have done in search of a competitive lead in the world marketplace?

   a. Customer focus

   b. cost saving through site selection

   c. TQM using ISO 9000 & 14000 standards

   d. new manufacturing techniques

   e. reliance on internet to unite companies

2. What is _production management_?

   all the activities managers do to help their firms create products

3. What is the difference between _goods_ and _services_?

   - goods are tangible products such as car, computer
   - service is provided, such as engineering service (intangible products)

4. What is a _service economy_?

   economy dominated by service sector, such as financial & consulting businesses

5. How have companies such as IBM, General Electric and Dell changed what they do to grow and prosper?

   expanded operations management out closer to customers
   - fast delivery
   - customization eg

6. What are _Application Service Providers (ASP's)_?

Companies who provide software services online, so they don't have to buy software, but instead can have instant access to programs

7. In earlier chapters you learned about trends in Canadian businesses and how they have changed. How has the trend toward smaller units in businesses contributed to the change and rebuilding of Canada's manufacturing base?

8. The three elements of the production process are inputs, production control, and outputs. The key to increasing productivity is to keep costs low and produce more. What are the ways Canadian manufacturers are meeting the challenge of increasing productivity?

   - lower labour costs, inexpensive resources, etc.
   - extensively automate production processes
   - concentrate on quality control

Operations Management Functions

1. What are three major reasons why firms shift facilities from one area to another?
   a. _lower wages_
   b. _access to energy_
   c. _market proximity_

2. What are some issues surrounding moving to foreign countries in search of cheap labour?
   - child labour & unsafe conditions

3. What elements are giving firms flexibility in choosing locations, while remaining competitive?
   IT - email, voicemail, internet
   → TELECOMMUNICATIONS

4. Businesses may choose to locate close to where the buying power for their product is located, where labour is cheap, or where land and resources are inexpensive and readily available.
   Evaluate the area in which you live based on the site-selection criteria listed in the text. Does your area have an advantage in the variables considered for site selection? If so, which ones? Are you located close to the buying power? How would you convince a producer to locate a plant in your area?

5. What are three functions of operations management?

a. facility location

b. facility layout

c. quality control — ISO 9000 / ISO 14 000

6. What do brick and mortar stores have to do to compete with services offered over the Internet?

—choose good service & offer outstanding service for those who come to the store

7. What might provincial and local governments do to provide incentives for companies that are considering locating in their area?

tax reductions, financial aid, zoning changes

8. What is important in terms of facilities layout for service businesses?

layout is designed for customers to find and buy what they need

9. In manufacturing, what kind of layout is replacing the assembly line?

modular layout — teams work together to produce more complex units of the final product

10. What is a *fixed position layout*? When is it used?

when workers congregate around the product to be completed —major product

11. How has the Internet affected operations management, and what kinds of companies are facilitating the process?

12. How has quality control changed from the earlier days of manufacturing? What is the major purpose of quality control?

go from QC at final product to beginning
- quality, on production, purchasing, sales, and service

Emphasis on customer satisfaction

13. What do the ISO 9000 standards require?

- determine customer needs
- Communication arrangements to handle customer complaints
- Storage, delivery

14. Why is ISO certification so important for Canadian companies?

European companies will only do business w/ ISO certified companies

15. What is the difference between ISO 9000 and ISO 14000?

9000 - name for quality & assurance standards
14000 - collection of best practices for managing impact on society

16. What are the requirements for ISO 14000 certification?

audits, enviro. policy, top management review

Operations Management in the Service Sector

1. According to the text, what has become the quality standard for luxury hotels, as well as for other service businesses?

Anticipating customer needs & delighting customers

2. In what sector of the economy is the greatest productivity problem?

Service

3. What is the difficulty in measuring productivity increases in the service sector?

traditional methods don't work

4. What are some examples of how technology has begun to improve productivity in the service sector?

- ATMs have made banking easier
- Computers process info for airline passengers ie tickets etc.

5. How is the Internet changing the service industry?

- buy CD's & movies over internet

6. How do the changes in technology affect workers outside work?

greater standard of living and new opportunities

7. Why is improving productivity in non-profit organizations, particularly government agencies, important today?

8. Because most services tend to be people-oriented and labour-intensive, traditional thinking has been that increased productivity through the increased use of automation (mainly computers) is not feasible. However, many services have made use of automation to serve their customers more quickly and efficiently.
   From your own experience, give an example of how three services you use have increased efficiency through the use of high-technology.
   a. _____

b. _____

c. _____

c. _____

Operations Management in the Manufacturing Sector

1. What are the three basic requirements of production, according to Andrew Grove?
   a. build & deliver products in response to customer demands
   b. provide acceptable quality level
   c. a everything at the lowest possible cost

2. What did MRP do for manufacturers?

   Material requirement planning

   right parts are available at right time & place

3. What are two production processes?
   - process manufacturing
   - assembly process

4. What is the difference between a *continuous* production process and an *intermittent* one?
   production
   - long run turns out goods over time

   - production is short and machines changed

5. Why do most manufacturers today use intermittent processes?
   computers/robots do it faster

6. How is enterprise resource planning (ERP) different from materials requirement planning (MRP) and MRPII?
   ERP is newer version of MRP - computer based - monitors processes in multiple firms at same time

7. What is DNP?
   dynamic performance monitoring - plant operators can monitor use of power, chemicals etc to make needed adjustments

8. Describe *sequential delivery* in manufacturing.

provide components in sequence to the building process

9. Music-stor is beginning to really gear up for production. It has two main product lines: a component part, for built-in tape and CD storage, designed to be installed during the automotive assembly process, and an "after-market" product, to be sold in auto parts stores, which can be installed by the consumer. Music-stor buys the raw material from a plastic supplier. They then melt the plastic down and pour it into molds, which are then allowed to cool. During the process, colour is added that's coded to the colours offered by the car company they have contracted with. Later, clips and other parts are added which are needed for installation. The process is similar for both product lines, with some alterations needed for the retail version. What type of production process is Music-stor likely to be using? How can the company ensure their product is available when the assembly plant needs it, and when the retailer wants to sell it?

Modern Production Techniques

1. What will be the benefit of programs such as ERP?

link suppliers, manufacturer, retailers

2. What is the main reason companies must make a wide variety of high-quality custom products at a very low cost?

global competition

3. What are five major developments that have radically changed the production process?
   a. _JIT inventory_
   b. _flexible manufacturing_
   c. _____
   d. _____

e. _____

4. How does a JIT program work?

_____
_____
_____
_____

5. What does ERP, in combination with JIT systems, provide?

_____
_____
_____
_____

6. What are the responsibilities of the purchasing department?

_____
_____
_____
_____

7. What are three forms of Internet marketplaces?
   a. trading exchange platform
   b. industry sponsored exchanges
   c. net market makers
   _____

8. What is the benefit flexible manufacturing systems provide to manufacturers?

_____
_____
_____
_____

9. What is the objective of *lean manufacturing?*

_____
_____
_____
_____

10. How does a company become "lean"?

_____
_____
_____
_____

11. What is the difference between lean manufacturing and flexible manufacturing?

_____
_____

_____
_____

12. What has *mass customization* allowed manufacturers to do?

_____
_____
_____
_____

13. What one development changed production techniques more than any other?

_____
_____
_____
_____

14. What is meant by *competing in time?*

_____
_____
_____
_____

15. What has CAD/CAM made possible?

_____
_____
_____

16. What is CIM?

_____
_____
_____
_____

17. In the production process, two ways of controlling costs are
    ] Materials requirement planning (MRP)
    ] Just-in-time inventory control (JIT)
    a. Read the following situations and indicate whether MRP or JIT is being described.

    i. _____ Another name for this is *kanban*, a Japanese word, used to describe a parts supply system that keeps inventory to a bare minimum.

    ii. _____ To keep an important customer, United Electric. Co., a distributor of electrical supplies, guaranteed delivery of electrical controls a day before they were needed on the production line. This enabled the customer to cut his inventory carrying costs.

    iii. _____ Black & Decker uses a master scheduling plan, integrating the needs of marketing and manufacturing.

iv. _____ From this master plan, the company determines how much inventory the company will need and when. A scheduling technique for making sure that the right inventory is at the right place at the right time.

b. What problems can you identify with JIT inventory control?

   i. Supplier side

_____

_____

   ii. Manufacturer side

_____

_____

18. Five areas that will be the focus of production and operations management for the coming decade are

   ☐ Competing in time
   ☐ Internal and external customer orientation
   ☐ Total quality
   ☐ Constant improvement
   ☐ Productivity

Several business people from the newly formed Commonwealth of Independent States (formerly the Soviet Union) and other Eastern European countries are visiting your company for some badly needed manufacturing assistance. As a production and operations management consultant, how can you explain these issues to your Eastern European visitors?

_____

_____

_____

_____

_____

_____

_____

_____

_____

_____

_____

_____

_____

_____

_____

_____

Control Procedures: PERT and Gantt Charts

1. How are PERT Charts generally developed?

_____

_____

_____

_____

2. Where does the critical path fit in a PERT Chart?

_____
_____
_____
_____

3. What is the difference between a Gantt Chart and a PERT Chart?

_____
_____
_____
_____

4. What can a manager do with a Gantt Chart?

_____
_____
_____
_____

5. a. How was quality control handled in the past?

_____
_____
_____
_____

   b. How are things different today with regard to quality control?

_____
_____
_____
_____

6. What are three steps involved in the quality control process?
   a. _____
   b. _____
   c. _____

CHAPTER CHECK

1. What are three issues surrounding the rebuilding of Canada's manufacturing base?
   a. debates on moving production overseas
   b. Q's about replacing workers with machines
   c. protection through quotas and trade restrictions

2. Name the three fundamental components of the manufacturing process.
   a. input
   b. output
   c. production process

3. What two things must be done to increase productivity?
   a. _increase outputs_
   b. _lower cost of outputs_

4. What are the five inputs to the production process?
   a. _land_
   b. _labour_
   c. _capital_
   d. _entrepreneurship_
   e. _informati_

5. Identify eight considerations in site selection.
   a. _wages_
   b. _market proximity_
   c. _energy access_
   d. _$ of living_
   e. _gov't inducements_
   f. _____
   g. _____
   h. _____

6. List four production processes.
   a. _product process mar._
   b. _assembly process_
   c. _continuous/intermittent process_
   d. _____
   e. _____

7. What five indicators do managers use to determine if they can meet production goals on a given day?
   a. _____
   b. _____
   c. _____
   d. _____
   e. _____

8. Name two ways of reducing inventory costs.
   a. _JIT_
   b. _MRP_

9. What does *quality* mean in the context of modern business activities?
   _____
   _____
   _____

10. Identify two methods used for production control.
    a. _PERT charts_
    b. _GANTT Chart_

11. Identify the four steps involved in using a PERT chart.

a. _____
b. _____
c. _____
d. _____

12. List five steps that must be taken before people and machines can be combined to revolutionize manufacturing.
    a. _____
    b. _____
    c. _____
    d. _____
    e. _____

13. What are five production and operations management issues that will be emphasized in the next decade?
    a. _____
    b. _____
    c. _____
    d. _____
    e. _____

14. List five important elements of total quality control.
    a. involves everyone in company
    b. lower costs
    c. ind. & team workers
    d. part of a total system
    e. _____

15. List four industries in the service sector that have improved productivity through automation.
    a. FF (McD)
    b. banking
    c. grocery store
    d. airline

PRACTICE TEST

Multiple Choice: Circle the best answer.

1. What statement does NOT fit in when describing the trend in manufacturing in Canada?
   a. The heart of the free enterprise system has always been manufacturing.
   b. Manufacturing produces less than one-fourth of the Canadian Gross Domestic Product.
   c. Traditional manufacturing leaders have declined through much of the last two decades.
   d. Foreign competition has not affected Canadian manufacturers.

2. New production techniques have
   a. been difficult and costly to implement, and so have been largely ignored
   b. made it possible to virtually custom-make products for individual industrial buyers
   c. have been implemented primarily by foreign manufacturers
   d. have not been shown to be effective in making Canadian manufacturers competitive

3. Music-stor is beginning to see some competition for their portable compact disc storage units. In order to remain competitive, Music-stor must be sure to
   a. replace all workers with automated equipment
   b. move all manufacturing to foreign countries
   c. train all salespeople in aggressive selling techniques
   d. keep the costs of inputs down
4. Which of the following is NOT considered a strong reason for companies to move production facilities from one area to another?
   a. availability of cheap labour
   b. cheaper natural resources
   c. the level of unemployment in a geographic area
   d. reducing the time it takes to deliver products to the market
5. What are the benefits manufacturers see in locating close to larger markets, according to the text?
   a. businesses can lower transportation costs and be more responsive to customers
   b. more availability of skilled labour
   c. guaranteed lower tax rates in the suburban areas
   d. cheaper natural resources
6. Boiling an egg is an example of
   a. assembly process
   b. process manufacturing
   c. analytic system
   d. continuous process
7. Music-stor wants to link its resource planning and manufacturing with its suppliers in order to develop a more integrated system. Music-stor could use
   a. enterprise resource planning
   b. continuous process manufacturing
   c. PERT charts
   d. total quality control
8. Tony Ruggali is in the process of opening a new restaurant. Tony wants to be sure that his new place, The Fresh Place, always has the freshest ingredients, and will always be known for being the "freshest place in town." He also wants to devote most of the space in the restaurant to tables for diners, not to storing produce. Tony could make use of
   a. analytic production
   b. Gantt charts
   c. just-in-time inventory
   d. mass production
9. _____ enable manufacturers to custom-make goods as quickly as mass-produced items once were.
   a. PERT techniques
   b. Flexible manufacturing systems
   c. Lean manufacturing
   d. Computer-aided design
10. Quon Ho believes that there must be a way to cut down on the amount of resources his company uses in the production process. Quon feels that the company uses more space, tools, and time to make their product than is necessary. Quon should examine the benefits of
    a. lean manufacturing
    b. CAD/CAM

c. mass customization
d. competing in time

11. A _____ is a bar graph that shows which projects are being worked on and how much has been completed.
   a. PERT chart
   b. flexible manufacturing system
   c. Gantt chart
   d. CAD/CAM system

12. Munchin A. Pickle is a production supervisor at the local cucumber processing plant. Munchin is looking at a chart which illustrates for him the sequence of tasks involved in processing the cukes. He is especially interested in the sequence of tasks that take the longest time to complete. Munchin is interested in the
   a. Gantt chart
   b. total quality management process
   c. critical path
   d. lean manufacturing process

13. Which of the following is NOT a part of the TQM process?
   a. continual employee evaluations
   b. analyzing the consumer to determine quality demands
   c. incorporating quality features into the product design
   d. ensuring quality standards are met during the entire production process

14. What is the difficulty in measuring productivity growth in the service sector?
   a. incorporating automation
   b. unemployment caused by using computers in services
   c. measuring improvements in quality of service provided
   d. finding trained workers

15. The success of service organizations in the future depends upon
   a. keeping out foreign competition
   b. automating even more elements of providing the service
   c. listening to consumers in order to adapt to consumer demands more quickly
   d. training workers in how to sell services to customers

True/False

1. It could be said that we are actually in a new era in the industrial revolution.
2. The key to success in the future is for Canadian producers to combine effective marketing with effective production and management.
3. Form utility is the value added by the creation of finished goods and services using raw materials, components, and other inputs.
4. Many firms in Canada are moving to the U.S. and Mexico in the search for inexpensive labour.
5. Telecommuting has not had much impact on site selection.
6. Eventually, suppliers will be linked with manufacturers and retailers in a completely integrated system to facilitate the smooth flow of goods to the consumer.
7. Global competition has had little impact on Canadian manufacturers.
8. Flexible manufacturing systems are so flexible that a special order, even a single item, can be produced without slowing down the manufacturing process.
9. It is likely that robots will totally replace manufacturing workers in the future.
10. Computer-integrated manufacturing allows computer-aided design machines to "talk" to

computer-aided manufacturing machines.

11.   A Gantt computer program will allow a manager to trace the production process minute by minute to determine which tasks are on time and which are behind.

12.   In manufacturing, it is still the company itself which determines what the standard for quality should be.

13.   Productivity in the service sector is going down.

14.   The government doesn't yet know how to measure productivity gains in the service sector.

15.   One of the results of technology in the workplace will be that people will need more contact with people outside the work environment.

ANSWERS

Key Terms and Definitions

1.   Robot
2.   Gantt chart
3.   flexible manufacturing
4.   Purchasing
5.   computer-aided manufacturing (CAM)
6.   operations management
7.   mass production
8.   computer-aided design (CAD)
9.   PERT
10. process manufacturing

11. just-in-time inventory control (JIT)
12. enterprise resource planning (ERP)
13. critical path
14. Production
15. form utility

16. assembly process
17. competing in time
18. materials requirement planning (MRP)
19. intermittent process
20. mass customization
21. manufacturing
22. continuous process
23. lean manufacturing
24. quality control
25. computer-integrated manufacturing (CIM)
26. facility location
27. facility layout
28. ISO 9000
29. ISO 14000
30. process planning

Canada's Evolving Manufacturing and Services Base

1.   Manufacturers today have:
     a. taken a customer focus
     b. created cost savings through site selection
     c. total quality management using ISO 9000 and ISO 14000 standards
     d. used new manufacturing techniques
     e. relied on the Internet to unite companies.

2.   Production management is the term used to describe all the activities managers do to help their firms create goods.

3.   Goods are tangible products such as cars and furniture. Services are intangible products such as engineering services and the service you receive in retail stores.

4. A service economy is one that is dominated by the service sector, such as financial and consulting businesses.

5. These companies have expanded operations management out of the factory and moved it closer to the customer. They are providing services such as custom manufacturing, fast delivery, credit, installation, and service repair.

6. Application Service Providers are companies that provide software services online so that companies do not have to buy their own software but can have instant access to the latest programs.

7. *Suggested Answer*
The trend toward smaller units has created a tremendous amount of restructuring in major Canadian manufacturing businesses.
Large companies are focusing on more productive, smaller units which allow them to respond more quickly to customer demands. The text states that "The job ... becomes one of getting closer to ... customers to find out what the product needs are." The restructuring is enabling Canadian manufacturers to perform that job.

8. This chapter focuses on the many techniques Canadian firms have implemented to increase productivity and become more competitive. The first is concentrating on elements important in site selection, such as lower labour costs, inexpensive resources, lower taxes, and low cost of land. Second, Canadian firms have begun to extensively automate their production processes. Using sophisticated materials, requirement planning management systems, and just-in-time inventory control, as well as other computer-based manufacturing processes, Canadian firms have begun to increase their levels of productivity and to reduce production time and labour costs.
Last, Canadian firms are concentrating on production control techniques to ensure that products are produced in a timely fashion. Total quality control and quality circles help Canadian firms to maintain as high a quality level as many of their foreign competitors.

Operations Management Functions

1. Any three of
   ] lower wages
   ] market proximity
   ] proximity to materials and parts
   ] access to energy
   ] government inducements
   ] availability of workforce
   ] quality of life

2. Cheap labour is a key reason why less technologically advanced producers move their plants to foreign locations. This has caused problems for some firms, as they have been charged with using child labour and unsafe labour practices in other countries. It is important for firms to maintain the same quality standards and fair labour practices wherever they produce.

3. New developments in information technology, such as computers, modems, e-mail, voice mail, and so forth are enabling firms and employees to be more flexible in choosing locations while remaining

competitive. These innovations have made telecommuting a major trend in business.

4. The area in which you live may meet a number of the important criteria. Look for a large available workforce population. New immigrants seem more willing to work hard for less pay. Are other resources plentiful and inexpensive?
   If you live in a large urban area, such as Montreal, Toronto, or Vancouver, businesses may be attracted because that's where their customers are. However, land is more expensive in those areas, so a large production facility is unlikely to be built. Government support will vary from one area to another in the form of tax incentives and zoning laws.
   All of these factors will affect a company's decision in selecting a site.

5. a. facility location
   b. facility layout
   c. quality control

6. In order for bricks and mortar stores to compete with Internet shopping they have to choose good locations and offer outstanding service to those who come to the store.

7. Provincial and local governments may compete with one another by giving tax reductions and other support such as zoning changes and financial aid so that businesses will locate there.

8. Facilities layout depends on the processes that are to be performed. For services, the layout is designed to help the consumer find and buy what they need. Often this means helping consumers to find and buy things on the Internet.

9. In manufacturing, many companies are moving from an assembly line layout to a modular layout, where teams of workers combine to produce more complex units of the final product.

10. A fixed-position layout is where workers congregate around the product to be completed. This type of layout is used when working on a major project.

11. With the Internet, companies have been able to create new relationships with suppliers, so that operations management is becoming an interfirm process, where companies work together to design, produce and ship products to customers. To facilitate such transactions companies called "e-hubs" have emerged to make the flow of goods among firms faster and smoother.

12. In the past quality control was often done at the end of the production line in a quality control department. Today, quality means satisfying customers by building in and ensuring quality from product planning to production, purchasing, sales, and service. Emphasis is placed on customer satisfaction so quality is everyone's concern, not just the people at the end of the assembly line.

13. ISO 9000 standards require that a company must determine what customer needs are, including regulatory and legal requirements. There must also be communication arrangements to handle issues like complaints. Other standards involve process control, product testing, storage, and delivery.

14. ISO certification is important because the European Union is demanding that companies that want to do business with the EU be certified by ISO standards.

15. ISO 9000 is the name given to quality management and assurance standards. ISO 14000 is a collection of the best practices for managing an organization's impact on the environment. It does not prescribe a performance level like ISO 9000 does.

16. The requirements for ISO 14000 include having an environmental policy, having specific improvement targets, conducting audits of environmental programs, and maintaining top management review of the processes.

Operations Management in the Service Sector

1. The quality standard for luxury hotels and for other service businesses has become anticipating customer needs and delighting customers.

2. The greatest productivity problem is reported to be in the service sector of the economy.

3. While there is some evidence that productivity in the service sector is rising, the difficulty lies in measuring the quality of the service. Traditional productivity measures don't work.

4. Technology has changed productivity in the service sector in a number of ways. ATMs have made banking easier, and the new system of universal product codes has allowed computerized retail checkout so the process goes much faster. In the airline industry, computers are used to process reservations with the use of prepackaged meals on board, handling luggage, servicing passengers and so on.

5. The Internet has changed retailing in particular. A greater variety of books and CDs is available on the Internet than in retail stores, for example. Jet travel has enabled FedEx to deliver goods overnight. Computer databases enabled AT&T to have individualized customer service.

6. Technology will allow for a greater standard of living and new opportunities. In the future, people will need more contact with people outside work. There will be new demands for recreation, social clubs, travel, and other diversions.

7. Increased efficiency in government agencies is crucial in a time of increased deficits, balanced-budget requirements, slowdowns in government revenues, and increased demand for government services. If Canada is going to remain competitive with the rest of the world, inefficient government agencies cannot keep draining funds away from business.

8. Multiple answers. Suggestions include banking, grocery stores, gas stations, retail stores, tax preparation, school registration.

Operations Management in the Manufacturing Sector

1. According to Andrew Grove, the three basic requirements of production are
   a. Build and deliver products in response to demands of a customer at a scheduled delivery time.
   b. Provide an acceptable quality level.
   c. Provide everything at the lowest possible cost.

2. MRP allowed manufacturers to make sure that needed parts and materials are available at the right place and the right time.

3. Two types of production processes are:
   a. process manufacturing
   b. assembly process

4. A continuous process is one in which long production runs turn out finished goods over time. An intermittent process is an operation where the production run is short and the machines are changed frequently to produce different products.

5. Most new manufacturers use intermittent processes because the use of computers, robots, and flexible manufacturing processes makes it possible to make custom-made goods almost as fast as mass-produced goods were once made.

6. ERP is the newest version of MRP. Enterprise resource planning is a computer-based production and operations system that links multiple firms into one integrated production unit. MRPII is a system that monitors systems within a single firm. ERP is much more sophisticated than MRPII because it monitors processes in multiple firms at the same time.

7. Dynamic performance monitoring, or DNP, enables plant operators to monitor the use of power, chemicals and other resources and to make needed adjustments.

8. Sequential delivery is a system where suppliers provide components in an order sequenced to the customer's production process.

9. It sounds like Music-stor uses an intermittent process, as the machines or molds may need to be changed when they go from producing the retail version to the built-in version, or when they change colors according to manufacturer.
   Music-stor needs to keep track of its own inventory, as well as that of the auto assembly plants and their retail customers. Enterprise resource planning is a sophisticated computer-based operations system that would link Music-stor with their suppliers, as well as with their customers.
   With this system, Music-stor could track the availability of the plastic they need from their supplier. They could monitor their own inventory to ensure adequate stock at crucial times, and be sure that their customers have what they need when they need it to keep production flowing smoothly, and to keep sales at the retail level from slacking off.

Modern Production Techniques

1. Programs such as ERP will link suppliers, manufacturers, and retailers in a completely integrated manufacturing and distribution system that will be constantly monitored for the smooth flow of goods from the time they're ordered to the time they reach the ultimate consumer.

2. Companies must make a wide variety of high-quality custom-designed products at a very low cost because of global competition.

3. These developments have changed the production process:
   a.   just-in-time inventory control   d.   mass customization

b. flexible manufacturing   e. competing in time
c. lean manufacturing

4. In a JIT program, a manufacturer sets a production schedule using enterprise resource planning or a similar system, and determines what parts and supplies will be needed. It then informs its suppliers of what will be needed. The supplier delivers the goods just in time to go on the assembly line. The supplier becomes more like another department in the firm because it is linked to the manufacturer by computer.

5. ERP in combination with JIT makes sure the right materials are at the right place at the right time at the cheapest cost to meet customer needs and production needs. This is the first step in modern production innovation.

6. The purchasing department is responsible for finding suppliers, negotiating long-term contracts with them, and getting the best price possible.

7. Three forms of Internet marketplaces are:
   a. trading exchange platforms
   b. industry sponsored exchanges
   c. net market makers

8. Flexible manufacturing systems enable manufacturers to custom-make goods as quickly as mass-produced items were once made. This enables producers to more closely meet the wants and needs of customers.

9. The objective of lean manufacturing is to use less human effort, less manufacturing space, less investment in tools, and less engineering time to develop a new product. A company becomes lean by continuously increasing its capacity to produce more, higher quality products with fewer resources.

10. A company becomes lean by continuously increasing the capacity to produce more, higher quality products with fewer resources.

11. Lean manufacturing allows for producing goods using less of everything, when compared to mass production — half the labour, half the space, half the time. Flexible manufacturing is using fewer machines to do more work, and so could be considered a part of lean manufacturing.

12. Mass customization has allowed manufacturers to meet the needs of individual customers with virtually customized products.

13. The one development that has changed production techniques more than any other has been the integration of computers into the design and manufacture of products.

14. Competing in time means being as fast or faster than the competition in responding to consumer wants and needs and getting goods and services to them.

15. CAD/CAM has made it possible to custom-design products to meet the needs of small markets with very little increase in cost. A producer can program the computer to make a simple design change, and that change can be incorporated indirectly into the production line.

16. Computer-integrated manufacturing is software that enables machines involved with computer-aided design to "talk" with machines involved with computer-aided manufacturing.

17. a. i.   JIT
       ii. JIT
       iii. MRP
       iv. MRP
    b. i.   Suppliers (rather than manufacturers) have to hold inventory
             Added costs of smaller, more frequent deliveries
        ii. Need for increased planning
             No back-up inventory in case of supplier problems

18. Our visitors from the former communist countries will learn that in a global marketplace it is essential to get products out to your customers before your competitors.

    An external customer orientation helps us to find out customer needs and to meet those needs better than our competitors. When we act as if other departments within our company are valued customers, we are acting with an internal customer orientation. The needs of all departments are then filled. This creates an atmosphere of teamwork and cooperation which will enhance our relationships with our outside customers.

    Total quality control means building in and ensuring quality in all aspects of product planning and production. Within this context, quality is everyone's responsibility and everyone is permitted and expected to contribute. Again the customer is at the forefront, by beginning with determining consumer needs. Quality is then designed into our products.

    To stay competitive, employees must always be looking for ways to improve the way jobs are done, focusing on time- and money-saving programs. This kind of continuous improvement takes a great deal of long-term training.

    Productivity growth encompasses all the previously mentioned ideas — producing high-quality output at the least possible cost. If our visitors can implement those and other concepts we have dis-cussed, they will be on their way to increasing productivity and the ability to enter into global competition.

Control Procedures: Pert and Gantt Charts

1. PERT charts are generally developed by computer.

2. The critical path in a PERT Chart identifies the sequence of tasks that takes the longest time to complete. It is the last step in the development and is critical because a delay in the time needed to complete this path would cause the project or production run to be late.

3. A PERT Chart analyzes the tasks involved in completing a given project, estimating the time needed to complete each task, and identifying the minimum time needed to complete the total project. A Gantt Chart is more basic, and is used to measure production progress using a bar chart that shows what projects are being worked on and how much has been completed.

4. A manager can trace the production process minute by minute to determine which tasks are on time and which are behind, so that adjustments can be made to stay on schedule.

5. a. In the past, quality control was often done at the end of the production line in the quality control department.

b. Today, quality means satisfying customers by building in and ensuring quality from product planning to production, purchasing, sales, and service.

6. A total quality program involves
   a. analyzing the consumer to see what quality standards need to be established.
   b. ensuring quality is designed into products.
   c. specifying products must meet the quality standards every step of the way in the production process.

CHAPTER CHECK ANSWERS

1. a. Debates about moving production facilities overseas, or to Mexico or the U.S.
   b. Questions about replacing workers with robots and other machinery
   c. Protection of Canadian manufacturers through quotas and trade restrictions
2. a. Inputs
   b. Outputs
   c. Production process
3. a. Increase outputs
   b. Lower the cost of inputs
4. a. Land
   b. Labour
   c. Capital
   d. Entrepreneurship
   e. Information
5. a. Wage rates
   b. Proximity to markets
   c. Access to raw materials and parts
   d. Access to energy
   e. Government inducements
   f. Availability of workforce
   g. Cost of living
   h. Quality of life
6. a. Process manufacturing
   b. Assembly process
   c. Analytic system
   d. Continuous process
   e. Intermittent process
7. a. Sales forecast
   b. Raw material inventory
   c. Equipment
   d. Manpower
   e. Quality
8. a. Materials requirement planning
   c. Just-in-time inventory control
9. *Quality* means satisfying customers by building in and ensuring quality from product planning to production, purchasing, sales and service. Emphasis is placed on customer satisfaction, so quality is everyone's concern, not just the concern of the quality control people at the end of the assembly line.
10. a. PERT Charts
    b. Gantt Chart

11. a. Analyzing tasks that need to be done and sequencing the tasks.
    b. Estimating the time needed to complete each task.
    c. Drawing a PERT network illustrating steps one and two.
    d. Identifying the critical path.
12. a. Train future production workers in the use and repair of computers, robots, and automated machinery.
    b. Retrain or relocate today's production workers to adapt to the new high-tech systems.
    c. Make adjustments in the relationships between suppliers and producers to implement concepts such as just-in-time inventory programs and enterprise networking.
    d. Retrain production managers to deal with more highly skilled workers who demand a much more participative managerial style.
    e. Train employees to work in teams and to understand the concepts of competing in time, constant improvement, total quality, and continuous improvement.
13. a. "Competing in time." Tardy companies will be put out of business.
    b. Organizations are adopting a customer orientation internally and externally.
    c. Emphasis is on total quality.
    d. Focus on constant improvement. Everything is subject to change and improvement.
    e. Productivity will become a major issue, along with quality improvement.
14. a. Quality is a company-wide process involving everyone in the company.
    b. Quality means lower costs.
    c. Quality involves both individual workers and teams of workers. It is part of the corporate culture.
    d. Philosophy of continuous improvement, empowering employees to implement quality changes on a constant or regular basis.
    e. Quality is part of a total system, involving suppliers, distributors, and all organizations that affect consumer satisfaction.
15. a. Fast food
    b. Banking
    c. Airlines
    d. Grocery stores

PRACTICE TEST

Multiple Choice		True/False	
1.	d	1.	T
2.	b	2.	T
3.	d	3.	T
4.	c	4.	T
5.	a	5.	F
6.	b	6.	T
7.	a	7.	F
8.	c	8.	T
9.	b	9.	F
10.	a	10.	T
11.	c	11.	T
12.	c	12.	F
13.	a	13.	F
14.	c	14.	T
15.	c	15.	T

CHAPTER 11

Using Technology to Manage Information

Learning Goals

After you have read and studied this chapter, you should be able to

1. Outline the changing role of business technology.
2. Compare the scope of the Internet, intranets, and extranets as tools in managing information.
3. List the steps in managing information and identify the characteristics of useful information.
4. Review the hardware most frequently used in business and outline the benefits of the move toward computer networks.
5. Classify the computer software most frequently used in business.
6. Evaluate the human resource, security, and privacy issues in management that are affected by information technology.
7. Identify the careers that are gaining or losing workers due to the growth of information technology.

Key Terms and Definitions

Listed here are important terms found in this chapter. Choose the correct term for each definition and write it in the space provided.

broadband technology ✓

business-to-business (B2B) ✓
business-to-consumer (B2C) ✓
cookies ✓
data processing (DP) ✓
e-business ✓
e-commerce ✓

extranet ✓

information systems (IS) ✓
information technology (IT) ✓
Internet 2 ✓
Intranet ✓
Knowledge management ✓
Knowledge technology (KT) ✓

network computing system (client/server computing) ✓
public domain software ✓
push technology ✓
shareware ✓
spam ✓
virtualization ✓
virtual private network (VPN) ✓
virus ✓

1. _data processing_ — 1970's term for business technology; technology that supports an existing business, primarily used to improve the flow of financial information.

2. _Knowledge management_ — Sharing, organizing and disseminating information in the simplest and most relevant way possible for the users of information.

3. _broadband tech._ — Technology that delivers voice, video and data through the Internet.

4. _Knowledge Technology_ — Technology that adds a layer of intelligence to information technology, to filter appropriate information and deliver it when it is needed.

5. _E-Commerce_ — The process of managing online financial transactions by individuals and companies.

6. _virtualization_   Accessibility through technology that allows business to be conducted independent of location.

7. _extranet_   A semiprivate network that uses Internet technology and allows more than one company to access the same information or allows people on different servers to collaborate.

8. _shareware_   Software that is copyrighted but distributed to potential customers free of charge.

9. _virus_   A piece of programming code inserted into other programming to cause some unexpected and, for the victim, usually undesirable event.

10. _information systems_   Technology that helps companies do business; includes such tools as automated bank machines and voice mail.

11. _B2B_   E-business in which the focus is on transactions between businesses.

12. _B2C_   E-business in which the focus is on purchases made by consumers for personal use.

13. _Network Computing Sys._   Computer systems that allow personal computers (clients) to obtain needed information from huge databases in a central computer (the server).

14. _information technology_   Technology that helps companies change business by allowing them to use new methods.

15. _push technology_   Web software that delivers information tailored to a previously defined user profile; it pushes the information to users so that they don't have to pull it out.

16. _Internet 2_   The new internet system that links government supercomputer centres and a select group of universities; it will run more than 22,000 times faster than today's public infrastructure and will support heavy-duty applications.

17. _E-business_   The production, advertising, sale, and distribution of products via telecommunication networks.

18. _intranet_   A companywide network, closed to public access, that uses internet-type technology.

19. _Cookies_   Pieces of information, such as registration data or user preferences, sent by a Web site over the Internet to a Web browser that the browser software is expected to save and send back to the server whenever the user returns to that Web site.

20. _Public domain software_   Software that is free for the taking.

21. _Virtual Private Network_   A private data network that creates secure connections, or "tunnels," over regular Internet lines.

22. _Spam_   Unsolicited commercial e-mail; a message sent over the Internet to someone that wold not otherwise choose to receive it.

The Role of Information Technology

1. What is the primary role and use of data processing?

   improving flow of financial information

2. How do information systems differ from data processing?

   IS went from supporting business processes to actually doing business

3. What does information technology allow businesses to do?

   deliver products & services when & where its convienient for customer

4. a. What two barriers to doing business are being broken by information technology?

   Communication, time & location

   b. How does breaking these barriers change the way business is done?

   - location brings work to people instead of visa versa

   -faster

5. What is a *virtual office?*

   includes cell phones, pagers, laptops & PDA

6. How does knowledge technology change the flow of information?

   from individual going to database to data going to ind.

7. How does KT change a businessperson's job?

Thinks about ind. needs & reduce the time of getting info

The Road to Knowledge: The Internet, Intranets, Extranets and Virtual Private Networks

1. What is a key issue for business today regarding information?

   how to get right into the the right people at the right time

   Knowledge Key to successful competition.

2. What are some applications of an intranet?

3. How have companies solved the problem of competitors getting into their intranets?

   firewall — hardware and/or software

4. How does the Internet change the way we do business?

5. How can an extranet be used?

6. What is the potential problem with an extranet?

   Can be accessed by outsiders with knowledge to break in

7. How does a virtual private network solve the problems involved with the use of an extranet?

    creates secure connections/or tunnels over regular internet lines

8. Compare the Internet, intranets, and extranets. Do you know a company that has an intranet? How is it used? What are the applications in this company?

9. How does broadband technology solve the problem of a "traffic jam" on the Internet?

    offers users continuous connection to Internet and allowing them to send files faster

10. What is a vBNS?

    Very high speed backbone network service links gov't supercomp centres and a select group of universities

11. What is one of the biggest problems with the age of information technology in terms of managing the information?

Managing Information

1. What is "high quality information?"

    accurate/reliable

2. When is information complete?

    when theres enough for you to make a decision but not so much that you get lost or confused

3. What is meant by *timeliness and relevance*, regarding information?

_____
_____
_____
_____

4. What is knowledge mail, and how does it work?

_____
_____
_____
_____

5. What does push technology do?

_____
_____
_____
_____

6. What is important to remember about information overload?

_____relax. Set goals and do best as you can_____
_____
_____
_____

7. Help! You are swamped by the data, reports, facts, figures, and tons of paper and e-mail being sent to you! It's your job as a low-level sales employee to manage the dissemination of all this "stuff" and make sure it makes sense to everyone who gets it. In other words, your job is to manage all that information! What can you do to make this information useful? How does push technology help to solve information overload?

_____
_____
_____
_____
_____
_____
_____
_____
_____

The Enabling Technology: Hardware

1. What does *Moore's Law* predict? How did Moore revise his statement?

_____capacity of computer chips will double every year_____
_____
_____
_____

2. What are some hardware components?

_____

_____

_____

_____

3. What will a *human computer interface* do?

Combines video camera and computer, it recognises you
and determines what tasks you want to complete that day

_____

_____

4. Identify the major benefits of computer network systems.
   a. Save time & $
   b. provides easier links to other areas of company
   c. companies see products more clearly

5. What are Internet appliances designed to do?

_____

_____

_____

_____

6. How is the way we access the Internet changing, and what effect does this have on information we get from the Internet?

_____

_____

_____

_____

7. Describe the drawbacks of networks. What have some companies looked into to avoid these drawbacks?

_____

_____

_____

_____

8. What is a *thin client network?* What are its benefits?

_____

_____

_____

_____

9. What is another option for companies looking to avoid problems with networks, besides thin client networks? What is the benefit?

_____

_____

Software

Identify the major elements of:

1.   Word processing programs

_____

2.   Desktop Publishing Software (DTP)

_____

3.   Spreadsheet programs

_____

4.   Database programs

_____

5.   Personal information managers (PIMs)

_____

6.   Graphics and presentation programs

_____

7.   Communications programs

_____

8.   Message centre software

_____

9.   Accounting and finance programs

_____

10.   Integrated programs

_____

11.   Groupware

ppl collaborate and share ideas by working on same project at same time.

Effects of Information Technology on Management

1. What impact has technology had on the human resource area?

eliminates middle management

_____

2. What is the challenge technology poses for human resource managers? How is the problem being addressed?

_____

_____

_____

_____

3. What are three areas that are being affected by the growing reliance on information technology?
   a. HR changes
   b. Security threats
   c. privacy concerns

4. What are some benefits of telecommuting?

_____

_____

_____

_____

5. What are some drawbacks of telecommuting?

_____

_____

_____

_____

6. How are companies attempting to alleviate the problems of telecommuting?

_____

_____

_____

_____

7. Why are antivirus programs not always effective? How do you avoid the problem?
   new viruses are always being developed.

_____

_____

_____

8. What kind of personal information can be obtained from certain Web sites?

_____

_____

_____

9. What is a key issue being debated over Internet privacy?

_____

_____

10. What has happened to organizational structures as a result of the increased use of technology?

_____

_____

_____

_____

11. What are some of the security and privacy issues that are important to recognize with the increasing use of information technology?

_____

_____

_____

_____

_____

_____

12. What is causing computer glitches?

comb. of human error, computer terror, bugs etc.

_____

_____

_____

13. How expensive are computer glitches?

$100 billion in lost production/year

_____

_____

_____

Technology and You

1. What are some of the reasons why being computer illiterate could be "occupational suicide?"

_____

_____

_____

_____

2. What has been the impact of a shortage of information technology workers?

_____

_____

_____

_____

CHAPTER CHECK

1. What is the difference between data and information?

   data - raw, unprocessed facts

   info - processed & summarized data

2. What is the difference between information technology and knowledge technology?

3. How is an intranet different from an extranet?

4. What is the Internet 2 used for?

5. What is "infoglut"?

   information overload resulting from deluge of info from wide variety of sources

6. List four qualities of useful information.
   a. *quality*   c. *timeliness*
   b. *Completeness*   d. *relevance*

7. How is a network computing system different from mainframe computing?

8. How could a network computing system help with information overload?

9. What are six major business uses of software?
   a. writing in WORD
   b. spreadsheets
   c. filing/retrieving data for databases
   d. presenting info with graphics
   e. communicating
   f. accounting/financial info

10. What is a spreadsheet?

11. What does a database program allow you to do?

12. What is a personal information manager (PIM)?

13. What can a graphics program add to a presentation?

14. What does communications software enable a computer to do?

15. What is the next generation of communications software?
    message centre software

16. What is accounting software used for?

_____

17. What can you do with integrated software packages?

_____
_____
_____
_____

18. What does groupware make possible?

_____
_____
_____
_____

19. Name two ways that computers will change the structure of organizations and jobs.
    a. _eliminate middle management, reduce managerial layers_
    b. _telecommuting_

20. What is a hacker?

_____
_____
_____
_____

21. How are computer viruses spread?

_____
_____
_____
_____
_____

22. What does a cookie do?

_____
_____
_____
_____

PRACTICE TEST

Multiple Choice: Circle the best answer.

1. In the 1980s, business technology changed from supporting business to doing business by using

   _____.
   a. data processing   c. information systems
   b. information technology   d. knowledge technology

2. Using _____, a new employee can sit at a workstation and let the system take over doing everything from laying out a checklist of each thing required on a shift to answering questions and

offering insights that once would have taken up a supervisor's time.

a. data processing   c. knowledge technology

b. information technology   d. virtualization

3. At MEMC Electronics, employees can update their addresses, and submit requisitions, timesheets, and payroll forms online. The company's system is closed to public access, but all employees have access. MEMC is using an _____ .

a. intranet   c. internet

b. extranet   d. electronic data interchange system

4. A problem managers have with the rapid advance of information technology has been

a. the skyrocketing cost of information

b. the hardware and software products available can't keep up with the expansion

c. the increased layers of management

d. information overload, with the deluge of information available

5. Which of the following is NOT included in a list of characteristics of useful information?

a. timeliness   c. completeness

b. quality   d. accessibility

6. When facing information overload a manager should

a. set goals and do the best he or she can

b. hire an intern to take care of information which is not needed

c. look for a system which will handle the information more readily

d. make use of a file management system

7. _____ includes pagers, cellular phones, printers and scanners, and personal digital assistants.

a. software   c. extranets

b. multimedia   d. hardware

8. In recent years, businesses have moved from

a. network computing systems to mainframe systems

b. client/server computing to network computing systems

c. database systems to information processing

d. mainframe systems to network computing systems

9. Which of the following is NOT a benefit of networks?

a. more information is available

b. saving time and money

c. networks provide easy links across boundaries

d. companies can see their products more clearly

10. Which of the following projects would be best suited to a spreadsheet program?

a. personalizing a standardized letter to clients

b. recording the sales figures from several different stores, and calculating profits

c. updating lists and schedules, keeping track of inventory

d. making a presentation more appealing with sound clips, video clips, and clip art

11. A major difference between groupware and other types of software is that groupware

a. is less expensive than other forms of software because it is distributed free

b. can replace more management functions than others

c. allows computers to talk to one another

d. runs on a network and allows several users to work on the same project at the same time

12. Perhaps the most revolutionary effect of computers and increased use of the Internet is

a. the amount of information which has been made available to managers

b. the ability to allow employees to work from home

c. the spread of viruses

d. the amount of personal information available and people who can access it

13. Which of the following is NOT considered a benefit of telecommuting?

   a. saves money by retaining valuable employees during long leaves

   b. involves less travel time and cost

   c. can increase productivity

   d. avoids isolation of workers

14. In the movie *Sneakers*, two young guys broke into a government computer and accessed some sensitive government documents. The term to describe these young guys would be

   a. hackers   c. cookies

   b. viruses   d. computer illiterates

15. One of the problems with today's direct, real-time communication is

   a. existing laws do not address the legal issues

   b. public information is more difficult to obtain

   c. communication is not face to face

   d. having to be careful to constantly update antivirus programs

True/False

1.   A virtual office would include cellular phones, pagers, laptop computers, and personal digital assistants.

2.   Information technology creates organizations and services that are independent of location.

3.   An extranet is a companywide network which is closed to everyone outside the specific company using the intranet.

4.   Only the largest companies can use the Internet to do business.

5.   The Internet 2 will support heavy-duty applications, such as videoconferencing, research, distance education, and other sophisticated applications.

6.   With the increased use of the Internet, information has become easier to manage.

7.   Push technology will allow for customized news delivery to your computer after sorting through thousands of new sources.

8.   Companies are moving toward mainframe computer systems for the next century.

9.   A computer network will help a company file, store, and access data more easily.

10. Desktop publishing combines word processing with graphic capabilities.

11. Personal information managers are actually word processing programs.

12. Message centre software teams up with modems to provide a way of making certain that phone calls, e-mail, and faxes are received, sorted, and delivered on time.

13. Computers have created more middle management layers.

14. Antivirus programs need to be updated on a regular basis.

15. In the future, being computer illiterate will be "occupational suicide."

ANSWERS

Key Terms and Definitions

1. data processing (DP)
2. knowledge management
3. broadband technology
4. knowledge technology
5. e-commerce

12. business-to-consumer (B2C)
13. network computing system
14. information technology
15. push technology
16. Internet 2

6.	virtualization	17.	e-business
7.	extranet	18.	intranet
8.	shareware	19.	cookies
9.	virus	20.	public domain software
10.	information systems	21.	virtual private network (VPN)
11.	Business-to-business (B2B)	22.	Spam

The Role of Information Technology

1. The primary role of data processing was to support existing business by improving the flow of financial information.
2. Information systems went from supporting business to actually doing business, through such means as ATMs and voice mail.
3. Information technology allows businesses to deliver products and services where and when it is convenient for the customer.
4. a. Information technology breaks time and location barriers.
   b. Breaking these barriers creates organizations and services that are independent of location. Being independent of location brings work to people instead of people to work. With information technology, businesses can conduct work around the world continuously.
5. A virtual office includes cellular phnes, pagers, laptop computers, and personal digital assistants. This technology allows you to access people and information as if you were in an actual office.
6. Knowledge technology changes the traditional flow of information from an individual going to the database to the data coming to the individual. Using KT business training software a company can put a new employee at a workstation and then let the system take over.
7. It will "think" about individual needs and reduce the amount of time finding and getting information. Businesspeople an then focus on decision-making, rather than spending time on just finding the information they need to make decisions.

The Road to Knowledge: The Internet, Intranets, Extranets and Virtual Private Networks

1. The key issue for business today is how to get the right information to the right people at the right time. Knowledge is now the key to successful competition.
2. Intranet applications can include allowing employees to update their addresses or submit company forms such as requisitions, timesheets, or payroll forms online.
3. To solve the problem of other companies getting into an intranet, companies can construct a "firewall" between themselves and the outside world to protect corporate information from unauthorized users. A firewall can be hardware, software, or both.
4. Almost all companies can use the Internet to share and process data such as orders, specifications, invoices, and payments. The Internet creates a critical mass of people who can exchange data over the network. The Internet also makes it easier for small businesses to sell their goods and services globally.
5. One of the most common uses of extranets is to extend an intranet to outside customers. It can be used to share data and process orders, specifications, invoices and payments.
6. An extranet can be accessed by outsiders with enough knowledge to break into the system.
7. Most companies want a network that is as secure as possible. A dedicated line is a way to achieve that, but a dedicated line is costly and limits use to computers directly linked to that line. A virtual private network solves the problem by creating secure connections, or "tunnels" over regular Internet lines. The idea is to give the company the same capabilities as dedicated lines at a much

lower cost.

8. The Internet is a network of computer networks, available to anyone with the right equipment and software. An intranet is a companywide network closed to public access, which uses internet-type technology. An extranet is a semiprivate network that uses internet technology so more than one company can access the same information, or so people on different servers can collaborate. One of the most common uses of extranets is to extend an intranet to outside customers.

9. Broadband technology solves the Internet traffic jam problem by offering users a continuous connection to the Internet, and allowing them to send and receive large files faster than before. The more bandwidth, the bigger the pipe for the data to flow through. The bigger the pipe, the faster the flow.

10. vBNS, or very high speed Backbone Network Service links government supercomputer centres and a select group of universities.

11. One of the biggest problems of information technology and the information highway is the overwhelming amount of information available. Today business people are deluged with information from voice mail, the Internet, fax machines, and e-mail. Business people refer to this information overload as "infoglut."

Managing Information

1. High quality information is accurate and reliable.

2. Information is complete when there is enough information for you to make a decision but not so much information that the issue is lost or confused.

3. Timeliness means that information must reach managers quickly. Relevance refers to the fact that different managers have different information needs. Because there is so much information available, managers must learn which questions to ask to get the answers they need.

4. Knowledge-mail sorts through the millions of e-mail messages going through a company's system and tracks users' work. It can then alert an individual when others in the company are doing similar work, so that people can share information to solve problems.

5. Push technology consists of software and services that filter information so that users can get the customized information they need. Push technology pushes the information to you so you don't have to pull it out. These services deliver customized news to your computer after sorting through thousands of news sources to find information that suits your identified needs.

6. The important thing to remember when facing information overload is to relax. Set goals for yourself and do the best you can.

7. The first thing you need to do is to improve the quality of the information by combining the facts and figures and so on into something that is meaningful. Put sales reports together and summarize weekly or monthly figures. Note any trends in sales over a given period, and double-check for accuracy in all the information you use. (Quality)

Second, you need to make sure that you are using the latest sales reports, and double-check your figures. Since you will be sending this information to various sales managers, check to be sure that you have included all the data needed to give the managers an accurate picture of how sales are going and why. You don't need to include anything that may not be relevant, such as reports from committees or other areas that don't pertain to sales. (Completeness)

In addition, you need to work fast! If a salesperson is not meeting quotas, a few weeks is too long to wait to find out why. With e-mail, your reports can be sent out almost as soon as they're finished. (Timeliness)

Lastly, be sure that the sales reports you are sending are appropriate to the management level at which they'll be received. Lower level managers will need inventory information, perhaps, but not industry trends. Middle level managers may want your sales forecasts based upon past trends, but not vacation schedules for various salespeople. (Relevance)

The Enabling Technology: Hardware

1. Moore's Law predicts that the capacity of computer chips will double approximately every year. That has been true, but recently the speed of evolution has slowed. Moore said in 1997 that his prediction cannot hold good for much longer because chipmakers will run into a fundamental law of nature: the finite size of atomic particles will prevent infinite miniaturization.
2. Hardware components include computers, pagers, cellular phones, printers, scanners, fax machines, and personal digital assistants.
3. A human computer interface combines a video camera and computer. When you approach the PC it recognizes you, and determines what tasks you want to complete that day.
4. Computer network systems
   a. save time and money
   b. provide easy links to other areas of the company
   c. permit companies to see their products more clearly.
5. Internet appliances are designed to connect people to the Internet and to e-mail.
6. Wireless handheld devices like the Palm Pilot, smart phones and two-way paging devices allow people to take the Internet with them wherever they go. Because these devices are meant for mobile Internet access, they must be small. This changes the format in which Internet information can be delivered. The traditional format designed for big, high resolution monitors must be changed to deliver small bits of information using brief lines of text and tiny images.
7. Maintaining a large number of desktop computers can be expensive. Studies show that maintaining one corporate Windows-based desktop computer costs between $5,000 and $10,000 a year. This incurs a cost in lost productivity, when computers are down, or being updated with new software. Adding new software often causes problems with PC's, as it often conflicts with, or even disables, existing software.
   Some companies have looked at using a thin-client network, which is a hybrid of mainframe and network computing systems. In this system, the individual PCs lack the processing power to handle applications on their own.
8. It's a hybrid of mainframe and network computing. Applications and data reside on a server, which handles all of the processing needs for all the client machines on the network.
   With a thin client network, software changes and upgrades only need to be made on the server, so the cost is lower.
9. Another option is to not maintain a server on site. Contract with a remote service provider, or lease specific software applications. When you lease software from an applications service provider, or ASP, the provider maintains and upgrades the software on its servers. You connect to their servers via the Internet. You are then using the most current software without the hassles of upgrading software yourself.

Software

1. Standardized letters can be personalized, documents can be updated by changing only the outdated text and leaving the rest intact, and contract forms can be revised to meet the stipulations of specific customers.
2. Desktop publishing software combines word processing with graphics capabilities to produce designs.
3. Spreadsheets allow for quick calculations; they are the electronic equivalent of an accountant's worksheet, combined with other features.
4. A database allows users to work with information normally kept in lists. Can be used to create

customized reports.

5. PIMs are specialized databases, allowing users to track business contacts.
6. Graphics/Presentation programs allow for visual summary of spreadsheet data.
7. Communications programs allow computers to exchange files with other computers, retrieve database information, and send and receive mail.
8. Message centre software is more powerful than traditional communications packages. It provides a more efficient way of delivering messages from phone, fax, or e-mail.
9. Accounting/finance software helps users record financial transactions and generate financial reports.
10. Integrated programs offer two or more applications in one package.
11. Groupware allows people to collaborate and share ideas by working on the same project at the same time.

Effects of Information Technology on Management

1. Technology has made the work process more efficient as it replaces many bureaucratic functions. Computers often eliminate middle management functions and flatten organizational structures.
2. One of the major challenges technology poses for human resources management is the need to recruit and/or train employees proficient in technology applications. Often managers hire consultants to address these concerns, and outsource the technology training.
3. a. human resource changes
   b. security threats
   c. privacy concerns
4. Companies can retain valuable employees while they are on leave and take advantage of the experience offered by retired employees. Workers with disabilities can be gainfully employed, men and women with small children can stay home, and employees can work extra hours at home rather than at work. This may help to improve morale and reduce stress.
5. Some telecommuters report that a consistent diet of long-distance work gives them a dislocated feeling of being left out of the office loop. Some feel a loss of the increased energy people can get through social interaction. In addition to isolation, the intrusion that work makes into personal lives is an issue. Often people who work from home don't know when to turn off the work.
6. Companies are using telecommuting as a part-time alternative to alleviate some of the problems and complaints of this kind of work schedule.
7. New viruses are being developed constantly, and the antivirus programs may have difficulty detecting them. It is important to keep your antivirus protection program up-to-date and not download files from an unknown source.
8. The Internet allows Web surfers to access all sorts of personal information. For example, Web sites allow a person to search for vehicle ownership from a license number, find real estate property records on individuals, or find the vehicles owned by a person.
9. One of the key issues in the debate over protecting our privacy is this: Isn't this personal information already public anyway? The difference is that the Net makes getting public information too easy.
10. Computers have often enabled businesses to eliminate middle management functions, and thus flatten organization structures. Perhaps the most revolutionary effect of computers and the increased use of the Internet and intranets may be the ability to allow employees to stay home and do their work from there, or telecommute. Using computers linked to the company's network, workers can transmit their work to the office and back easily.
11. One problem today is hackers, who break into computer systems for illegal purposes. Today, computers not only make all areas of the company accessible, but also other companies with which the firm does business. Another security issue involves the spread of computer viruses over the

Internet. Viruses are spread by downloading infected programming over the Internet or by sharing an infected disk. A major concern is a problem with privacy as more and more personal information is stored in computers and people are able to access all sorts of information about you. One of the key issues in the privacy debate is this: Isn't this personal information already public anyway?

12. Experts say that computer glitches are combinations of human error, computer error, malfunctioning software, overly complex equipment, bugs in systems, and naiive executives who won't challenge consultants or in-house specialists.

13. It has been estimated that computer glitches account for as much as $100 billion in lost productivity each year.

Technology and You

1. Being computer illiterate could be occupational suicide because workers in every industry are exposed to computers somewhat. It is estimated that by 2006 half of all North American workers will be employed in information technology positions or within industries that intensively use information technology products and services.

2. A shortage of information technology workers could have severe consequences for Canadian competitiveness, economic growth and job creation. As the demand has increased and worsened the shortage, pay scales have gone up dramatically.

CHAPTER CHECK ANSWERS

1. Data are raw, unanalyzed, and unsummarized facts and figures. Information is the processed and summarized data that can be used for managerial decision making.

2. Knowledge technology is information with enough intelligence to make it relevant and useful. It adds a layer of intelligence to filter appropriate information and deliver it when it is needed. Information technology makes information available, as long as you know how to use it and where to find it. Knowledge technology brings the information to the individual. It will "think" about individual needs and reduce the amount of time finding and getting information.

3. An intranet is only within the company. An extranet is a semiprivate network that uses Internet technology so that more than one company can access the same information or so people on different servers can collaborate.

4. The Internet 2 supports heavy-duty applications, such as videoconferencing, collaborative research, distance education, digital libraries, and full-body simulation environments known as tele-immersion.

5. Infoglut refers to information overload resulting from a deluge of information from a variety of sources.

6. a. Quality
   b. Completeness
   c. Timeliness
   d. Relevance

7. In a mainframe system, the central computer performed all the tasks and sent the results to a terminal that could not perform the task itself. In the network computing system, the tasks, such as searching sales records, are handled by personal computers. The information needed to complete the tasks is stored in huge databases controlled by the server. Networks connect people to people and people to data.

8. The network would allow you to communicate quickly with other areas of the company through e-mail, which we already mentioned. You may more easily find someone in the company who could either answer questions you may have, or could tell you exactly what kind of information they need, and in

what format. Using a network means that you could put all the information you have into a database and anyone who needs it could access it. The network could, in fact, eliminate the need for your job altogether!

9. a. Writing by using word processing
    b. Manipulating numbers using spreadsheets
    c. Filing and retrieving data using databases
    d. Presenting information visually using graphics
    e. Communicating
    f. Accounting and financial information

10. A spreadsheet is a table made up of rows and columns that enable a manager to organize information. Using the computer's speedy calculations, managers have their questions answered almost as fast as they can ask them.

11. Database programs allow you to work with information you normally keep in lists: names and addresses, schedules, and inventories, for example. Simple commands allow you to add new information, change incorrect information, and delete out-of-date or unnecessary information. Using database programs, you can create reports with exactly the information you want and the way you want the information to appear.

12. Personal information managers, or contact managers, are specialized database programs that allow users to track communication with their business contacts. These programs keep track of people, phone calls, e-mail messages, and appointments.

13. Graphics can add sound clips, video clips, clip art, and animation.

14. Communications software makes it possible for different brands of computers to transfer data to each other.

15. Message centre software is more powerful than traditional communications packages. This generation of programs has teamed up with fax/voice modems to provide an efficient way of making certain phone calls, e-mail, and faxes are received, sorted, and delivered on time, no matter where you are.

16. Accounting software helps users record financial transactions and generate financial reports. Some programs include online banking features that allow users to pay bills through the computer.

17. Integrated software packages offer two or more applications in one package. With these programs, you can share information across applications easily. Most such packages include word processing, database management, spreadsheet, graphics, and communications.

18. Groupware runs on a network and allows people to work on the same project at the same time. Groupware also makes it possible for work teams to communicate together over time. Team members can swap leads, share client information, monitor news events, and make suggestions to one another. The computer becomes a kind of team memory.

19. a. Computers will decrease the number of management layers, eliminating middle management functions, and flattening organizational structures.
    b. Computers will allow employees to work at home (telecommuting).

20. A hacker is a person who breaks into computer systems for illegal purposes.

21. Computer viruses are spread by downloading infected programming over the Internet or by sharing an infected disk.

22. A cookie contains your name and password that the Web site recognizes the next time you visit the site so that you don't have to re-enter the same information every time you visit. Other cookies track your movements around the Web and then blend that information with their databases and tailor the ads you receive accordingly.

PRACTICE TEST

Multiple Choice		True/False	
1.	C	1.	T
2.	C	2.	T
3.	A	3.	F
4.	D	4.	F
5.	D	5.	T
6.	A	6.	F
7.	D	7.	T
8.	D	8.	F
9.	A	9.	T
10.	B	10.	T
11.	D	11.	F
12.	B	12.	T
13.	D	13.	F
14.	A	14.	T
15.	A	15.	T

CHAPTER 12

Motivating Employees and Building Self-Managed Teams

Learning Goals

After you have read and studied this chapter, you should be able to

1. Explain Taylor's scientific management.
2. Describe the Hawthorne studies and relate their significance to human-based management.
3. Identify the levels of Maslow's hierarchy of needs and relate their importance to employee motivation.
4. Differentiate among Theory X, Theory Y, and Theory Z.
5. Distinguish between motivators and hygiene factors identified by Herzberg.
6. Explain how job enrichment affects employee motivation and performance.
7. Identify the steps involved in implementing a management-by-objectives (MBO) program.
8. Explain the key factors involved in expectancy theory.
9. Examine the key principles of equity theory.
10. Explain how open communication builds teamwork, and describe how managers are likely to motivate teams in the future.

Key Terms and Definitions

Listed here are important terms found in this chapter. Choose the correct term for each definition and write it in the space provided.

equity theory	Job enlargement	principle of motion economy
expectancy theory	Job enrichment	reinforcement theory
extrinsic reward	Job rotation	scientific management
goal-setting theory	Job simplification	time-motion studies
Hawthorne effect	Management by objectives (MBO)	
hygiene factors	Maslow's hierarchy of needs	
intrinsic reward	Motivators	

1. _____ Theory that every job can be broken down into a series of elementary motions.

2. _____ Factors that provide satisfaction and motivate people to work.

3. _____ Something given to you by someone else as recognition for good work, including pay increases, praise, and promotions.

4. _____ A system of goal setting and implementation that involves a cycle of discussion, review, and evaluation of objectives among top and middle-level managers, supervisors, and employees.

5. _____ Factors that cause dissatisfaction but do not motivate if they are removed.

6. _____ Studies of the tasks performed to complete a job and the time needed to do each task.

7. _____ Theory that the amount of effort employees exert on specific tasks depends on their expectations of the outcome.

8. _____ Theory that employees try to maintain equity between inputs and outputs compared to others in similar positions.

9. _____ Job enrichment strategy involving combining a series of tasks into one assignment that is more challenging and interesting.

10. _____ The study of workers to find the most efficient way of doing things and then teaching people those techniques.

11. _____ States that positive and negative reinforcers will motivate a desired behaviour.

12. _____ Theory that setting specific ambitious but attainable goals can motivate workers and improve performance if the goals are accepted, are accompanied by feedback, and are facilitated by organizational conditions.

13. _____ Theory of motivation that places different types of human needs in order of importance, from basic physiological needs to safety, social, and esteem needs, to self-actualization needs.

14. _____ A motivational strategy that emphasizes motivating the worker through the job itself

15. _____ The good feeling you have when you have done a job well.

16. _____ The tendency for people to behave differently when they know they are being studied.

17. _____ Job enrichment strategy involving moving employees from one job to another.

18. _____ Process of producing task efficiency by breaking down the job into simple steps and assigning people to each of those steps.

The Importance of Motivation

1. Early management studies were done by individuals such as Frederick Taylor (scientific management), Elton Mayo (Hawthorne experiments), H.L. Gantt (Gantt charts), Frank & Lillian Gilbreth (motion economy).

   Read the following and indicate which person's ideas are being described.

   a. _____ Developed a test to measure the effect of environmental factors on worker productivity.

   b. _____ His studies became the basis for later human-based management studies.

   c. _____ Created "therbligs."

   d. _____ Developed the idea of time-motion studies.

   e. _____ Discovered that worker productivity increased despite adverse conditions.

f.	_____	Studied the most efficient method of completing a task.
g.	_____	Developed a chart plotting employees' work.
h.	_____	The principle of motion economy, developed by the Gilbreths, was based upon his theory.
i.	_____	Developed the principle of scientific management.
j.	_____	Discovered that when workers are involved in planning and decision making, productivity tends to increase.
k.	_____	Believed that the way to increase productivity was to train workers in the most efficient way of doing things.
l.	_____	Ignored the human and psychological aspects of work.
m.	_____	Discovered the impact of work groups and social interaction on productivity.
n.	_____	Broke down each job into a series of motions, then studied each motion to make it more efficient.
o.	_____	Developed the term that refers to the tendency of people to behave differently when they know they are being studied.

Early Management Studies — Taylor

1. Who is known as the "father of scientific management"?

_____
_____
_____
_____

2. What did Taylor believe was the key to improving productivity?

_____
_____
_____
_____

3. What is Gantt known for?

_____
_____
_____
_____

4. What contribution to scientific management was made by Frank and Lillian Gilbreth?

_____
_____
_____
_____

5. What view of workers was held by proponents of scientific management?

_____
_____
_____
_____

The Hawthorne Studies — Mayo

1. How did scientific management view people? How does that compare to Mayo's Hawthorne studies?

_____
_____
_____
_____

2. What did the Hawthorne experiments originally set out to test?

_____
_____
_____
_____

3. What was the problem with the initial experiments?

_____
_____
_____
_____

4. Why did the researchers believe the Hawthorne studies were a failure after the second series of experiments?

_____
_____
_____
_____

5. What is the Hawthorne effect?

_____
_____
_____
_____

6. How did research change after the Hawthorne experiments?

_____
_____
_____
_____

Motivation and Maslow's Hierarchy of Needs

1. What did Maslow believe about motivation?

_____
_____
_____
_____

2. According to Maslow, what kinds of needs are people motivated to satisfy? What happens when a need *is* satisfied?

_____

_____

_____

_____

_____

_____

_____

3. What must Canadian firms do with regard to motivation, in order to compete successfully?

_____

_____

_____

_____

_____

4. According to Andrew Grove, where does motivation come from? What kind of people are achievers, according to Grove?

_____

_____

_____

_____

_____

McGregor's Theory X and Theory Y

1. Douglas McGregor observed that managers had two different attitudes that lead to entirely different managerial styles. Those attitudes are based upon a manager's assumptions about his workers, and are labelled Theory X and Theory Y.

   Match the following statements to the type of management attitude.

   a. _____ "Joe is pretty good at solving these kinds of problems. Let's get his input."

   b. _____ "Ann, I know you'd like that promotion. Keep up the good work and I think you'll be the next new product manager."

   c. _____ "Tell that secretary that if she values her job, she'll keep those coffee breaks down to 15 minutes."

   d. _____ "Joe, you've got one week to get this problem solved. I want your input Friday at 8 a.m."

   e. _____ "I think that secretary takes long coffee breaks because she gets her work done so quickly and then doesn't have much to do. She's been asking about working on the new product project. I'll talk to her about it and see what she thinks."

   f. _____ "Ann, new product managers have to work a lot of weekends and evenings. If you think you want that job, you'll have to prove to me you're willing to work extra hours."

2. What kind of management assumptions do you think Frederick Taylor had?

_____
_____
_____
_____

3. How do the attitudes of a Theory X manager affect his/her behaviour toward employees?

_____
_____
_____
_____

4. How do the attitudes of a Theory Y manager affect his/her behaviour toward employees?

_____
_____
_____
_____

5. What steps should management follow in order to use "empowerment" as a motivator?
   a. _____
   b. _____
   c. _____

Ouchi's Theory Z

1. William Ouchi believes that North American firms would be able to compete more effectively with Japanese firms if they implemented the Japanese management style, known in North American as Theory Z.

   Determine whether each statement below applies to Theory Z organizations or to "typical" North American firms.
   a. _____ Virtually guaranteed lifetime employment.
   b. _____ Strong sense of corporate loyalty within a "family atmosphere"
   c. _____ Individual decision making
   d. _____ Very few layers of management
   e. _____ Rapid evaluation and promotion
   f. _____ Collective decision making
   g. _____ Workers changing firms to advance careers
   h. _____ Relatively short-term employment
   i. _____ Trust between management and workers
   j. _____ Clear distinctions and barriers between management and employees

2. Theory Z is based on a Japanese cultural heritage of humility, loyalty, and a strong sense of identification with group, rather than individual, needs.
   Identify four potential problems associated with implementing Theory Z management style in Canadian firms.
   a. _____
   b. _____
   c. _____
   d. _____

3. There have been questions as to the effectiveness of a Theory Z approach in "typical" Canadian firms. You have been learning about all the changes taking place in "typical" Canadian firms, and of the many changes made necessary by increasing global competition. Compare the philosophy of Theory Z to those changes and to the ideas in this chapter. Do you see any similarities?

_____
_____
_____
_____

4. List the major elements of Ouchi's "Type J" management approach.

a. _____
b. _____
c. _____
d. _____
e. _____
f. _____
g. _____

5. How do the ideas of Type J contrast with Ouchi's "Type A?"

_____
_____
_____
_____
_____

6. What is the difference between a Type J firm and a Type A firm?

_____
_____
_____
_____
_____

7. How is the Japanese management system changing? Why?

_____
_____
_____
_____
_____

Herzberg's Motivating Factors

1. From his study, Herzberg categorized factors influencing job performance into two areas: motivators, relating primarily to job content; and hygiene factors, relating primarily to job environment.

Motivators include
☐ Work itself
☐ Achievement
☐ Recognition

Hygiene factors include
☐ Company policy and administration
☐ Supervision
☐ Working conditions

□ Responsibility   □ Interpersonal relations
□ Growth and advancement   □ Salary, status, and job security

Match the correct factor to each of the following situations.

a. _____   In recent contract negotiations with its administration, faculty representatives for a large community college focused on pay raises as the primary issue.

b. _____   The Wal-Mart Corporation presents the "employee of the month" with a plaque, and has a weekly "honour roll" for its stores.

c. _____   During a period of slow sales, management and employees at Hewlett-Packard took a 10% pay cut to avoid layoffs.

d. _____   Upper management at Canadian Hunter has an "open door policy" encouraging face-to-face communication with employees at all levels.

e. _____   At Mars, Inc., every employee gets a weekly 10% bonus if he comes to work on time each day.

f. _____   At GM's Saturn plant, the typical assembly-line structure is being changed to modular construction. Workers perform a "cluster" of tasks that require a greater variety of skills.

g. _____   At the 3M Company, an individual associated with a new product venture gets promoted each time his product reaches a specified sales volume.

h. _____   At Dana Corporation, factory managers have control over tasks that are normally done by corporate headquarters, such as purchasing and financial control systems.

2. Make your own personal ranking of the 14 job-related factors listed in your text.

a. _____   h. _____
b. _____   i. _____
c. _____   j. _____
d. _____   k. _____
e. _____   l. _____
f. _____   m. _____
g. _____   n. _____

Evaluate your list. Are the factors most important to you primarily motivators or hygiene factors?

_____

Relate these factors to a job you have had, to explain why you were or were not motivated, or satisfied with that job.

_____
_____
_____
_____

3. What impact do hygiene factors have on workers? What about motivating factors?

_____
_____
_____

_____

_____

_____

_____

_____

4. What conclusions come from combining Theory Y with Herzberg's motivating factors?

_____

_____

_____

_____

5. Is money the number one motivator for most people? Why or why not?

_____

_____

_____

_____

_____

Job Enrichment

1. How is job enrichment implemented?

_____

_____

_____

_____

2. What is the difference between job enlargement and job rotation?

_____

_____

_____

_____

3. How does job design (including job enlargement and job rotation) fit into Herzberg's motivating factors and Maslow's needs hierarchy?

_____

_____

_____

_____

4. The design of job enrichment programs revolves around five characteristics of work:
   - ☐ Skill variety
   - ☐ Task identity
   - ☐ Task significance
   - ☐ Autonomy
   - ☐ Feedback

   Match each of the following examples to the correct job enrichment characteristic.

a. _____ Scott Paper has implemented a program allowing workers to complete their jobs within a 40-hour workweek arranged by the worker.

b. _____ At Travelers Insurance Company, computer operators (not their supervisors) receive a weekly computer printout summarizing errors and productivity.

c. _____ At 3M, a new venture team stays together from the initiation phase to the eventual national introduction.

d. _____ At Sherwin-Williams, all the members of a work group are trained to do all the jobs assigned to the team.

e. _____ At the Dana Corporation, all employees share in any savings realized by productivity increases that reduce costs.

5. Things have really been happening at Music-stor. Lots of changes have been made and it would seem that things ought to be going smoothly. However, there are problems with the workers, and you just can't figure out what's wrong. People don't seem to be motivated, although they are being paid well. You have been in charge, made the decisions you thought were best for the company and the workers, and have even pitched in and shown people how you want things done from time to time. Everybody has their own job, and they know exactly how it's supposed to be done. You have heard some people complain that their job is boring, but you know that the way you have shown them is the best way to get things done. People come in late, and sometimes seem to actually resent your help! You would really like the employees of this company to feel like they are a team. How will you solve this problem?

_____
_____
_____
_____

Re-read your answer — Are you a Theory X or a Theory Y manager?

_____
_____
_____
_____

Goal-Setting Theory and Management by Objectives

1. What is the basic principle of goal-setting theory?

_____
_____
_____
_____

2. What is the difference between helping and coaching?

_____
_____
_____
_____

3. What four things does a manager do in an MBO program?

a. _____

b. _____

c. _____

d. _____

_____

4. Review the six steps of implementing an MBO program described in your text. How does an MBO program fit into the ideas of Maslow and Herzberg? Why is the third step a key step in the program?

_____

_____

_____

_____

5. Based upon what you've learned about motivation in this chapter, list four benefits of a well-run MBO program.

a. _____

b. _____

c. _____

d. _____

6. List four problems you can see with MBO programs.

a. _____

b. _____

c. _____

d. _____

Meeting Employee Expectations: Expectancy Theory

1. According to expectancy theory, what are three questions employees ask before exerting maximum effort to a task?

a. _____

b. _____

c. _____

2. What are the steps to improving employee performance, according to expectancy theory?

a. _____

b. _____

c. _____

d. _____

e. _____

3. Think about expectancy theory and how it works for you. What is something you really want? How likely is it that you can reach the goal? Will the hard work be worth the effort? For example:

_____

_____

_____

_____

What kind of job do you want as a career?

_____
_____
_____
_____

What do you need to do to get that kind of job? Is it possible to get that job if you exert the effort?

_____
_____
_____
_____

What intrinsic and extrinsic benefits will you get from this kind of job?

_____
_____
_____
_____

Treating Employees Fairly: Equity Theory

1. What is the basic principle of equity theory? What role do perceptions play in equity theory?

_____
_____
_____
_____
_____
_____

2. What do people do when they perceive an inequity?

_____
_____
_____
_____

3. What is a key point to remember about equity theory? How might organizations address the challenge?

_____
_____
_____
_____
_____

4. Hal Yard is in marketing with a major manufacturer of sailboats. He has been happy with his job since he started there three years ago. He has received several raises, and has always gotten very good reviews. He is in line for a good promotion, which he should know about soon. Hal recently went to lunch with a new co-worker, Donna Telli. Donna just got her degree at night school, and this is her

first "real" job. During the course of their conversation, Donna mentioned her starting salary is only $40 per month lower than Hal's!

How would you feel if you were Hal? Why? What would you do? What theories of motivation may come into play here?

_____

_____

_____

_____

5. In the end, who is most likely to motivate any individual? Where does a manager fit in?

_____

_____

_____

_____

Reinforcement Theory

1. According to reinforcement theory, what two kinds of things can be used to motivate a desired behaviour?

   a. _____

   _____

   b. _____

   _____

   _____

2. According to reinforcement theory, what two types of actions can be taken by managers to motivate an employee to change an undesireable bahaviour pattern?

   a. _____

   _____

   b. _____

   _____

Building Teamwork Through Open Communication

1. Two-way communication provides an opportunity for managers and employees to work together to solve problems and increase productivity through improved employee relations. It encourages a feeling of teamwork among employees and can help to break down the barriers of an "us versus them" attitude.

   Based on what you have read in this and previous chapters, identify five techniques that managers can use to encourage a two-way flow of communication.

   a. _____

   b. _____

   c. _____

   d. _____

   e. _____

2. There are several executives cited in the text that have attempted to create an effective communications system. Can you identify what they have in common?

3. What are ways that communication could be improved where you work, or in one of your classes?

Reinventing Work

1. What is meant by "reinventing work"?
   a. _____
   b. _____
   c. _____
   d. _____
   e. _____

2. In their book (discussed in your text), Naisbitt and Aburdene state that "the goal of management ... is to adopt new humanistic values."
   a. Review the points made in your text about rethinking the corporation and reinventing work. How do these specific points relate to the motivation theories you have learned in this chapter? (i.e., What needs in Maslow's hierarchy? What elements of Herzberg, McGregor, Ouchi, etc.)

   b. Why is it difficult for some managers to change over to the new style of management?

   c. What are six additional points made by Naisbitt and Aburdene?
      i. _____
      ii. _____
      iii. _____
      iv. _____
      v. _____
      vi. _____

CHAPTER CHECK

1. What is the difference between an intrinsic reward and an extrinsic reward?

   _____
   _____
   _____
   _____

2. Identify four early management writers and what they are known for.
   a. _____   _____
   b. _____   _____
   c. _____   _____
   d. _____   _____

3. List the three basic elements of Frederick Taylor's approach to management.
   a. _____
   b. _____
   c. _____

4. Identify three conclusions drawn from Mayo's Hawthorne experiments.
   a. _____
      _____
   b. _____
      _____
   c. _____
      _____

5. What are the five need levels in Maslow's hierarchy of needs?
   a. _____
   b. _____
   c. _____
   d. _____
   e. _____

6. Douglas McGregor described two kinds of managerial attitudes, Theory X and Theory Y.
   a. List the assumptions made by a Theory X manager.
      i. _____
      ii. _____
      iii. _____

   b. List the assumptions of a Theory Y manager.
      i. _____
      ii. _____
      iii. _____
      iv. _____
      v. _____
      vi. _____

c.   What is the trend today in management style in Canadian business? Why?

_____
_____
_____
_____

7.   What are the major elements of Theory Z?
     a. _____
     b. _____
     c. _____
     d. _____
     e. _____
     f. _____
     g. _____

8.   Compare five essential elements of Theory X, Y, and Z.
     Theory X
     a. _____
     b. _____
     c. _____
     d. _____
     e. _____
     Theory Y
     a. _____
     b. _____
     c. _____
     d. _____
     e. _____
     Theory Z
     a. _____
     b. _____
     c. _____
     d. _____
     e. _____

9.   List Herzberg's five motivators.
     a. _____
     b. _____
     c. _____
     d. _____
     e. _____

10. List Herzberg's five hygiene factors.
     a. _____
     b. _____
     c. _____
     d. _____
     e. _____

11. List five characteristics of work, important in individual motivation and performance, that are used as a basis for job-enrichment programs.

a. _____

b. _____

c. _____

d. _____

e. _____

12. What are the six steps in implementing an MBO program?

a. _____

b. _____

c. _____

d. _____

e. _____

f. _____

13. Identify three ways to encourage two-way communication in the workplace.

a. _____
   _____

b. _____
   _____

c. _____
   _____

14. a. What are six ways to "reinvent" the corporation?

   i. _____

   ii. _____

   iii. _____

   iv. _____

   v. _____

   vi. _____

   b. What are six ways to "reinvent" work?

   i. _____

   ii. _____

   iii. _____

   iv. _____

   v. _____

   vi. _____

15. What are three lessons to be learned from the Wal-Mart example in the text?

a. _____

b. _____

c. _____

PRACTICE TEST

Multiple Choice: Circle the best answer.

1. Time and motion studies, methods of work, and rules of work were all part of the ideas of
    .
    - a. Maslow's hierarchy of needs
    - b. Herzberg's two-factor theory
    - c. Taylor's scientific management
    - d. the Hawthorne experiments

2. Which of the following was NOT determined as part of the Hawthorne experiments:
    - a. Workers enjoyed the atmosphere of their special room.
    - b. The workers thought of themselves as a social group.
    - c. The workers were not involved in the planning of the experiment.
    - d. Workers felt their ideas were respected.

3. Frederick Taylor believed the best way to improve worker productivity was to
    - a. scientifically determine the most efficient way to do things and then teach people
    - b. design jobs to be interesting and challenging
    - c. determine people's needs at work and find ways to meet those needs
    - d. give people the authority to make decisions

4. Which of the following is NOT included as one of Maslow's needs?
    - a. self-actualization
    - b. social
    - c. monetary
    - d. esteem

5. Harry Leggins has worked for Shavem'Up for a number of years. He has just been passed over for promotion, again, and is considering leaving because it seems that his managers don't appreciate his abilities. The only problem is that he really likes his co-workers, and they have an undefeated softball team. Harry is concerned with filling
    - a. esteem needs
    - b. social needs
    - c. self-actualization needs
    - d. safety needs

6. Douglas McGregor believed that managers with a Theory X attitude believed
    - a. workers prefer to be directed
    - b. people seek responsibility
    - c. people will use imagination in problem solving
    - d. workers like work

7. At Flo Valley Manufacturing, workers are encouraged to find their own solutions to problems, and to implement their solutions when practical. They work with little supervision because management feels they are committed workers, and pretty creative workers. Flo Valley reflects a
    attitude about workers.
    - a. Theory Z
    - b. autocratic
    - c. scientific
    - d. Theory Y

8. _____ emphasizes lifetime employment, collective decision making, and few levels of management.
    - a. Theory Z
    - b. Theory X
    - c. Theory Y
    - d. Theory M

9. Herzberg motivators include
    - a. job security
    - b. salary
    - c. working conditions
    - d. recognition

10. According to Herzberg, workers felt that good pay and job security
    - a. are the most important motivators for most workers
    - b. were important for participative management
    - c. provided a sense of satisfaction, but did not motivate them

d. were the best way to keep jobs interesting and to help them achieve their objectives

11. Which statement does NOT fit with the ideas of Herzberg and McGregor regarding the most effective way to motivate workers?
    a. Employees work best when managers assume employees are self-motivated.
    b. The best way to motivate employees is to make sure they know what to do and how to do it.
    c. Interesting jobs is one of the best ways to motivate workers.
    d. It is important to recognize achievement through advancement and added responsibility.

12. The strategy of making work interesting and motivating employees by moving them from one job to another is called
    a. job enlargement
    b. job simplification
    c. job rotation
    d. job enrichment

13. The degree to which a job has a substantial impact on the work of others in the company is called
    a. skill variety
    b. task identity
    c. autonomy
    d. task significance

14. At the NOVA car manufacturing company, workers are grouped into self-managed teams, which are responsible for completing a significant portion of the automobile. Unlike the typical assembly plant, the car stops along the way, and the team completes their portion of the car before the vehicle moves on. The team is given the freedom to decide who does which job, and they receive constant feedback from the company. NOVA is using a job strategy of
    a. job rotation
    b. job enlargement
    c. job enrichment
    d. job simplification

15. Management by objectives calls for managers to do all of the following EXCEPT
    a. set goals for employees
    b. commit employees to goals
    c. monitor results
    d. reward accomplishment

16. Which of the following is NOT one of the questions employees will ask themselves before committing a maximum effort toward a task?
    a. Can I accomplish this task?
    b. Is the reward worth the effort?
    c. What do I need to do to accomplish this task?
    d. If I do accomplish the task, what is the reward?

17. Expectancy theory indicates that
    a. people's needs affect their level of motivation
    b. the amount of effort an employee puts forth depends on their expectations of the outcome
    c. the perception of fairness will affect an employee's willingness to perform
    d. employees expect to be involved in setting objectives

18. According to equity theory, when workers perceive an inequity, they will
    a. try to reestablish an equitable feeling in a number of ways
    b. always reduce their efforts in the future
    c. always increase their effort in the future
    d. generally be mistaken in their perceptions

True/False

1.   The problem with the initial experiments of the Hawthorne study was that the productivity of the experimental group actually decreased when lighting was changed.

2.   The satisfaction you feel when you have finished a term paper and done a good job is an example of an extrinsic reward.

3. Frank and Lillian Gilbreth developed the principle of motion economy and therbligs.
4. The Hawthorne experiments led to new assumptions about workers, including that pay was not the only motivator.
5. According to Maslow, people will always try to satisfy higher-level needs before they focus on lower-level needs.
6. In developed countries, basic needs such as those for food and shelter dominate workers' motivation.
7. A Theory X manager believes that employees should be involved in both defining problems and in designing the solutions.
8. Theory Z principles have been widely adopted by companies in Canada and the U.S.
9. Herzberg's research results showed that the most important factors that motivate workers were a sense of achievement and earned recognition.
10. Goal-setting theory is based on the notion that managers should set specific goals to be reached.
11. The basic principle of expectancy theory is that workers try to maintain equity when they compare what they expect to gain to that gained by people in similar situations.
12. The concept of reinventing work involves respecting workers, rewarding good work, developing worker skills, and decentralizing authority.

ANSWERS

Key Terms and Definitions

1. principle of motion economy
2. Motivators
3. extrinsic rewards
4. management by objectives (MBO)
5. hygiene factors
6. time-motion studies
7. expectancy theory
8. equity theory
9. job enlargement
10. scientific management
11. reinforcement theory
12. goal-setting theory
13. Maslow's hierarchy of needs
14. job enrichment
15. intrinsic rewards
16. Hawthorne effect
17. job rotation
18. job simplification

The Importance of Motivation

1. a. Mayo
   b. Mayo
   c. Gilbreth
   d. Taylor
   e. Mayo
   f. Taylor
   g. Gantt
   h. Taylor
   i. Taylor
   j. Mayo
   k. Taylor
   l. Taylor
   m. Mayo
   n. Gilbreth
   o. Mayo

Early Management Studies — Taylor

1. Frederick Taylor is known as the Father of Scientific Management.
2. The way to improve productivity according to Taylor was to scientifically study the most efficient way to do things and then teach people those methods.
3. Gantt is known for charts which managers use to plot the work of employees a day in advance down

to the smallest detail.

4. Frank and Lillian Gilbreth used Taylor's ideas to develop the principle of motion economy, which showed that every job could be broken down into a series of elementary motions called therbligs.

5. Scientific management viewed people largely as machines that needed to be programmed. There was little concern for psychological or human aspects of work.

The Hawthorne Studies — Mayo

1. Scientific management viewed people largely as machines that needed to be properly programmed. The Hawthorne studies showed that productivity is largely determined by motivation.

2. Elton Mayo and his colleagues wanted to test the degree of lighting associated with optimum productivity.

3. The problem with the initial experiments was that productivity of the experimental group compared to other workers doing the same job went up regardless of whether the lighting was bright or dim.

4. The second series of experiments added a number of other environmental factors to the experiment, such as temperature and humidity. Productivity went up with each experiment. No matter what the experimenters did, productivity went up, thus proving the initial ideas were invalid.

5. The Hawthorne effect refers to the tendency for people to behave differently when they know they're being studied.

6. After the Hawthorne experiments, the emphasis of research shifted away from Taylor's scientific management to a new human-based management.

Motivation and Maslow's Hierarchy of Needs

1. Maslow believed that motivation arises from need.

2. Maslow believed that people are motivated to satisfy unmet needs. When one need is satisfied another, higher level need emerges, and a person will attempt to satisfy that need. Needs that have been satisfied do not provide motivation.

3. To compete successfully, Canadian firms must create a work environment that motivates the best and brightest workers. This means establishing a work environment that includes goals such as social contribution, honesty, reliability, service, quality, dependability, and unity.

4. According to Andrew Grove, all motivation comes from within. People who are "self-actualized" are achievers.

McGregor's Theory X and Theory Y

1. a. Y   d. X
   b. Y   e. Y
   c. X   f. X

2. *Possible Answer*
   Frederick Taylor appears to be a Theory X type of manager. His leadership style would probably be autocratic.

3. A Theory X manager will hang over people, telling them what to do and how to do it. Motivation will take the form of punishment for bad work, rather than reward for good work. Workers are given little responsibility, authority, or flexibility.

4. A Theory Y manager will emphasize a more relaxed atmosphere, in which workers are free to set objectives, be creative, be flexible, and go beyond the goals set by management. A key factor in this environment is empowerment, which gives employees the ability to make decisions and the tools to implement the decisions they make.

5. In order to use empowerment as a motivator, a manager must
   a. find out what people think the problems in the organization are
   b. let them design the solutions
   c. get out of the way and let them put the solutions into action

Ouchi's Theory Z

1. a. Z   f. Z
   b. Z   g. N.A. firms
   c. N.A. firms h. N.A. firms
   d. Z   i. Z
   e. N.A. firms j. N.A. firms
2. a. Fewer management positions
   b. No chance to change jobs
   c. Individual needs not recognized
   d. Slow decision making
3. The changes we have learned about in this and previous chapters would appear to be fundamentally similar to the philosophy found in a Theory Z type corporation. We are seeing more worker participation in decision making, for example, which could be similar to collective decision making. As companies downsize and reorganize, they are reducing layers of management, and attempting to create a "team" atmosphere. With programs such as job enrichment and self-managed work teams, managers have had to place more trust and responsibility in workers. The figure comparing theories X, Y, and Z will show that many of the characteristics of Theory Z are found in the "new" management philosophies we have been learning about.
4. The elements of Type J management include:
   a. lifetime employment
   b. consensual decision-making
   c. collective responsibility
   d. slow promotion and evaluation
   e. implicit informal control
   f. nonspecific career paths
   g. holistic concern for employees
5. Type A, American management, approach differs significantly from Type J. Type A involves short-term employment, individual decision-making, individual responsibility for the outcomes of decisions, rapid evaluation and promotion, explicit control mechanisms, specialized career paths and segmented concern for employees.
6. Type J firms are based on the culture of Japan, a focus on trust and intimacy within the group and family. Similarly, Type A firms are based on the culture of America. American culture focuses on individual rights and achievements.
7. Negative economic growth, demographic and social changes, and fierce global competition are forcing Japanese managers to reevaluate the way they conduct business. Japanese managers and firms need more dynamic ways to become more efficient in order to compete more effectively in today's changing global economy. Companies such as Hitachi, for example, have eliminated the ritual morning exercises. Managers felt that these morning exercises symbolized doing the same things the same way, reinforcing that employees avoid risks and don't exercise initiative.

Herzberg's Motivating Factors

1. a. Hygiene
   b. Motivator
   c. Hygiene
   d. Hygiene
   e. Hygiene
   f. Motivator
   g. Motivator
   h. Motivator
2. Answers will vary.
3. Workers feel that the absence hygiene factors like good pay, job security, friendly supervisors, and the like could cause dissatisfaction. The presence of these factors does not motivate workers, it just provides satisfaction and contentment in the work situation.
   Motivators cause employees to be productive and give them a great deal of satisfaction.
4. Employees work best when management assumes that employees are competent and self motivated. Theory Y calls for a participative style of management. The best way to motivate employees is to make the job interesting, help them to achieve their objectives, and recognize that achievement through advancement and added responsibility.
5. Surveys conducted to test Herzberg's theories have supported the finding that money is not the number one motivator. Number one is a sense of achievement and recognition for a job well done. The reason for this is that most organizations review an employee's performance once a year, and allocate raises only once a year. To inspire and motivate employees to perform their best, achievements and progress toward goals must be recognized more frequently.

Job Enrichment

1. In a program of job enrichment, work is assigned to individuals so that they have the opportunity to complete an identifiable task from beginning to end. They are held responsible for successful completion of the task.
2. Job enlargement combines a series of tasks into one assignment that is more challenging, interesting, and motivating. Job rotation also makes work more interesting, but does so by moving employees from one job to another.
3. These job design theories included Herzberg's motivators such as growth, challenge, and increased responsibility. These fill upper-level needs on Maslow's hierarchy such as self-esteem and self-actualization.
4. a. Autonomy
   b. Feedback
   c. Identity
   d. Variety
   e. Significance
5. How you would solve these problems is a matter of personal style. However, there are some suggestions. You may want to sit down with these people and find out exactly what *they* think the problem is, or even if they recognize that there is a problem. It will help to listen to them, ask for their suggestions about how to solve the problems, and implement those suggestions.
   It sounds like you have been making most of the decisions yourself, and not generally trusting these workers to be responsible. In other words, sounds like you have used a Theory X approach focusing on Herzberg's hygiene factors as a way to increase productivity. This may be appropriate in some instances, but you recall from previous chapters that these are the "new breed" of workers, who may prefer less direction and "bossing" and more "coaching." You can act as a resource, teaching, guiding, and recommending, but not actively participating in doing work. Allow them to decide the most appropriate way of designing their jobs. Programs such as job enlargement may be appropriate, or job rotation. You may also consider self-managed teams. Many of the programs and theories

described in this chapter may provide the solution to your problems.

Goal-Setting Theory and Management By Objectives

1. Goal-setting theory is based on the notion that setting specific but attainable goals will lead to high levels of motivation and performance if goals are accepted, accompanied by feedback and facilitated by organizational conditions.
2. Helping means working with the subordinates and doing part of the work if necessary. Coaching means acting as a resource, teaching, guiding, and recommending, but not participating or actively doing the task.
3. Management by Objectives calls on managers to formulate goals in cooperation with everyone in the organization, to commit employees to those goals, to monitor results and to reward accomplishment.
4. MBO programs would fill upper-level needs on Maslow's hierarchy and serve as a motivator in Herzberg's two factor theory. The third step is a key one because it focuses on the participative aspects of MBO, with the type of leadership or management style these theories support.
   The idea in goal setting is to involve everyone in setting goals. This motivates them by making them feel part of a team.
5. a. Motivation through participation
   b. Members feel part of a team
   c. Spirit of mutual cooperation
   d. Evaluation and promotion on objective criteria
6. a. Paperwork
   b. Time commitment
   c. Goals could be set by management
   d. Reward system could contradict objectives

Meeting Employee Expectations: Expectancy Theory

1. Before exerting maximum effort, employees will ask the following:
   a. Can I accomplish the task?
   b. If I do accomplish it, what's my reward?
   c. Is the reward worth the effort?
2. To improve employee performance according to expectancy theory, managers should
   a. determine what rewards are valued by employees
   b. determine the employee's desired performance standard
   c. ensure performance standards are attainable
   d. guarantee rewards are tied to performance
   e. be certain rewards are considered adequate
3. The answer to this question will depend on what your goals are, and how hard you are willing to work to reach them. The level of motivation you feel will be determined, according to expectancy theory, by how strongly you value what you say your goals are, and whether or not you feel like you can "make the grade," or get the kind of job you want. And last, in the end, your motivation will be determined by whether or not you feel that the effort would actually be worth it.

Treating Employees Fairly: Equity Theory

1. The basic principle of equity theory is that workers try to maintain equity between inputs and outputs compared to people in similar positions. It is based on perceptions of fairness and how those

perceptions affect employees' willingness to perform.

2. When workers perceive an inequity, they will try to make the situation more equitable. They may change their behaviour or rationalize the situation in some way.

3. A key element to equity theory is that equity, or inequity, is based upon perception of reality. Workers often overestimate their own contributions, and so they are often going to feel that there is a lot of inequity. Sometimes organizations try to deal with this by keeping salaries secret, but that can make things worse. The best remedy is clear and frequent communication.

4. If you were Hal, you might feel like there is an inequity in your level of compensation compared to Donna's. This is equity theory at work! After all, she is new, and you have been a good employee for three years. What you would do will depend upon your own view of how big the inequity is. You may choose to talk to your boss, work harder to get promoted and recognized, work a little less for a while, rationalize the inequity in some way, or take the afternoon off!

5. In the end, it is really the individual who motivates himself or herself. The manager's job is to understand that all workers are different and respond to different motivational styles. Managers will have to get to know each worker as an individual and fit the "reward" to each individual. Rewards will come from the job itself, rather than externally. Managers need to give workers what they need to do a good job: the right tools, the right information, and the right amount of cooperation.

Reinforcement Theory

1. positive reinforcement and negative reinforcement
2. a. withhold praise or recognition (extinction)
   b. publicly reprimand (punishment)

Building Teamwork Through Open Communication

1. a. Training programs in listening skills
   b. Set up facilities in such a manner as to encourage communication
   c. Eliminate "barriers" such as separate offices, designated parking spaces, etc.
   d. Sponsor company picnics and family activities
   e. MBWA
2. These executives communicate with all levels within the organization. The top-level managers make a point of interacting with employees at all levels.
3. Answers will vary.

Reinventing Work

1. Reinventing work means
   a. respecting workers
   b. providing interesting work
   c. rewarding good work
   d. developing workers' skills
   e. allowing autonomy
   f. decentralizing authority

2. a. In their book, Naisbitt and Aburdene stress eliminating, through communication, the barriers identified in this chapter as detrimental to motivation. They also stress using managers as coaches and employee ownership as new ways to run a corporation. In all, the book seems to stress recognition of higher-level needs on Maslow's hierarchy and the motivators of Herzberg's theory as well as a trend toward Ouchi's Theory Z management style.
   b. Many old-style managers are used to the traditional manner of doing business which stresses structure, barriers to communication, and decision making by management rather than

participation by employees.
- c. i. The manager's role is that of teacher, mentor, coach.
  - ii. The best people want ownership in the firm.
  - iii. The best managerial style is not top-down, but a networking, people style of management.
  - iv. Quality is the new key to success.
  - v. Successful large corporations copy the entrepreneurial flavour of small businesses.
  - vi. The information age enables firms to locate where there is a high quality of life.

CHAPTER CHECK ANSWERS

1. An intrinsic reward is a good feeling after having done a job well. It comes from within. An extrinsic reward is something given to you by someone else as recognition for good work.

2.
   - a. Taylor — Scientific management
   - b. Gantt — Gantt charts, plotting work of employees
   - c. Gilbreth — Motion economy
   - d. Mayo — Hawthorne studies

3.
   - a. Time
   - b. Methods
   - c. Rules of work

4.
   - a. People in work groups think of themselves as a social group.
   - b. Involving employees in decision making improves productivity.
   - c. Job satisfaction increases with a friendly atmosphere and additional compensation.

5.
   - a. Physiological needs
   - b. Safety needs
   - c. Social needs
   - d. Self-esteem needs
   - e. Self-actualization

6.
   - a. i. The average person dislikes work.
     - ii. People must be forced, controlled, directed, or threatened to work.
     - iii. The average person avoids responsibility, has little ambition, and wants security.
   - b. i. The average person likes work.
     - ii. The average person works toward goals.
     - iii. The depth of commitment to goals depends on the perceived rewards for achieving them.
     - iv. The average person seeks responsibility.
     - v. People are capable of creativity, imagination, and cleverness in solving problems.
     - vi. In industry the average person's intellectual potential is only partially realized.
   - c. The trend today is toward Theory Y management style. There are two basic reasons for this: one reason is that many service industries are finding Theory Y is more conducive to dealing with on-the-spot problems. Another reason for a more flexible managerial style is to meet competition from foreign firms.

7.
   - a. Long-term employment
   - b. Collective decision making
   - c. Relatively slow evaluation and promotion
   - d. Creation of a sense of involvement, closeness, and cooperation (family atmosphere)
   - e. Expectation of individual responsibility
   - f. Trust among workers
   - g. Few levels of management

8. *Theory X*
   - a. Employees dislike work and will try to avoid it.
   - b. Employees prefer to be controlled and directed.

c. Employees seek security, not responsibility.

d. Employees must be intimidated by managers to perform.

e. Employees are motivated by financial rewards.

Theory Y

a. Employees view work as a natural part of life.

b. Employees prefer limited control and direction.

c. Employees will seek responsibility under proper work conditions.

d. Employees perform better in work environments that are non-intimidating.

e. Employees are motivated by many different needs.

Theory Z

a. Employee involvement is the key to increased productivity.

b. Employee control is implied and informal.

c. Employees prefer to share responsibility and decision making.

d. Employees perform better in environments that foster trust and cooperation.

e. Employees need guaranteed employment and will accept slow evaluations and promotion.

9. a. Work itself
   b. Achievement
   c. Recognition
   d. Responsibility
   e. Growth and advancement

10. a. Company policy and administration
    b. Supervision
    c. Working conditions
    d. Interpersonal conditions
    e. Salary

11. a. Skill variety
    b. Task identity
    c. Task significance
    d. Autonomy
    e. Feedback

12. a. Top management consults with other managers to set long-range goals.
    b. Overall goals are formulated, and subgoals are determined for each department.
    c. Managers and workers develop ways to reach the objectives.
    d. Periodic review of progress.
    e. Compare progress with objectives; take corrective action if needed.
    f. Reward employees for reaching their goals.

13. a. Top management must create a good organizational culture by creating a two-way communication system.
    b. Supervisors and managers must be trained in listening skills.
    c. Remove barriers to open communication and install facilitating mechanisms.

14. a. i. Call everyone by his or her first name.
       ii. Eliminate executive parking spots and bathrooms.
       iii. Have everyone answer their own phone.
       iv. Eliminate files.
       v. Do business only with pleasant people.
       vi. Throw out the organization chart.
    b. i. Respect workers.
       ii. Provide interesting work.
       iii. Reward good work.
       iv. Develop workers' skills.

v. Allow some autonomy.

vi. Decentralize authority.

15. a. The future growth of industry and business in general depends on a motivated, productive workforce.

b. Motivation is largely internally generated by workers themselves.

c. The first step in any motivational program is to establish open communication among workers and managers to generate a feeling of cooperation and teamwork.

PRACTICE TEST

Multiple Choice		**True/False**	
1.	c	1.	F
2.	c	2.	F
3.	a	3.	T
4.	c	4.	T
5.	a	5.	F
6.	a	6.	F
7.	d	7.	F
8.	a	8.	F
9.	d	9.	T
10.	c	10.	F
11.	b	11.	F
12.	c	12.	T
13.	d		
14.	c		
15.	a		
16.	c		
17.	b		
18.	a		

CHAPTER 13

Human Resource Management: Managing the Most Important Asset — People

Learning Goals

After you have read and studied this chapter, you should be able to

1. Explain the importance of human resource management and describe current issues in managing human resources.
2. Describe methods companies use to recruit new employees and explain some of the problems that make recruitment challenging.
3. Illustrate the various types of employee training and development methods.
4. Summarize the objectives of employee compensation programs, and describe various pay systems and benefits.
5. Explain scheduling plans managers use to adjust to workers' needs.
6. Describe training methods used in management development programs.
7. Illustrate the effects of legislation on human resource management.

Key Terms and Definitions

Listed here are important terms found in this chapter. Choose the correct term for each definition and write it in the space provided.

affirmative action	job analysis	online training
apprentice programs	job description	on-the-job training
cafeteria-style benefits	job sharing	performance appraisal
compressed workweek	job simulation	recruitment
contingent workers	job specifications	reverse discrimination
core time	management development	selection
employee orientation	mentor	training and development
flextime plans	networking	vestibule training
human resource	off-the-job training	
management (HRM)		

1. _____ Training done in schools where employees are taught on equipment similar to that used on the job.

2. _____ An experienced employee who supervises, coaches, and guides lower-level employees by introducing them to the right people and generally being their organizational sponsor.

3. _____ Training program in which the employee immediately begins his or her tasks and learns by doing, or watches others for a while and then imitates them, all right at the workplace.

4. _____ The period when all employees are present in a flextime system.

5. _____ Work schedule that gives employees some freedom to adjust when they work, within limits, as long as they work the

required number of hours.

6. _____ The use of equipment that duplicates job conditions and tasks so that trainees can learn skills before attempting them on the job.

7. _____ An evaluation in which the performance level of employees is measured against established standards to make decisions about promotions, compensation, additional training, or firing.

8. _____ Training that occurs away from the workplace and consists of internal and external programs to develop any of a variety of skills to foster personal development.

9. _____ Benefit plans that allow employees to choose which benefits they want up to a certain dollar amount.

10. _____ Training programs involving a period during which a learner works alongside an experienced employee to master the skills and procedures of a craft.

11. _____ Work schedule made up of four 10-hour days.

12. _____ Employment activities designed to right past wrongs endured by females and minorities by giving them preference in employment.

13. _____ The unfairness unprotected groups may perceive when protected groups receive preference in hiring and promotion.

14. _____ The process of gathering information to decide who should be hired, under legal guidelines, for the best interests of the organization and the individual.

15. _____ Training programs in which employees "attend" classes via the Internet.

16. _____ A summary of the objectives of a job, the type of work to be done, the responsibilities, the working conditions, and the relationship of the job to other functions.

17. _____ The process of training and educating employees to become good managers and then developing managerial skills over time.

18. _____ The set of activities used to obtain a sufficient number of the right people at the right time and to select those who best meet the needs of the organization.

19. _____ A study of what is done by employees who hold various job titles.

20. _____ The process of evaluating human resource needs, finding people to fill those needs, and motivating employees to get the best work from each one by providing the right incentives and job environment, all with the goal of meeting the organization's objectives.

21. _____ The process of establishing and maintaining contacts with key

managers in one's own organization and in other organizations and using those contacts to weave strong relationships that serve as an informal development system.

22. _____ An arrangement whereby two part-time employees share one full-time job.

23. _____ All attempts to improve productivity by increasing an employee's ability to perform.

24. _____ The activity that introduces new employees to the organization, to fellow employees, to their immediate supervisors, and to the policies, practices, and objectives of the firm.

25. _____ Written summary of the minimum qualifications required of a worker to do a particular job.

26. _____ Workers who are not regular, full-time employees.

The Human Resource Function

1. How has the role of human resource management changed in recent years?

   _____
   _____
   _____
   _____

2. What are the challenges facing human resource management?

   a. _____
   b. _____
   c. _____
   d. _____
   e. _____
   f. _____
   g. _____
   h. _____
   i. _____
   j. _____
   k. _____

3. Why has human resource management received increased attention in recent years?

   _____
   _____
   _____
   _____

Determining Human Resource Needs

1. What information is included in a human resource inventory?

   _____
   _____
   _____

2. What's the difference between a job description and job specifications?

_____

_____

_____

_____

3. What affects future demand for employees?

_____

_____

_____

_____

4. What is likely to happen regarding supply of future employees?

_____

_____

_____

_____

Recruiting Employees

1. Recruiting has become more difficult in the last few years.
   Name four issues important in the area of recruiting.
   a. _____
   b. _____
   c. _____
   d. _____

2. What are three activities used in recruiting?
   a. _____
   b. _____
   c. _____
   d. _____

3. What are two general sources for recruiting?
   a. _____
   b. _____

4. What are some internal methods of recruiting?
   a. _____
   b. _____
   c. _____

5. What are some external methods of recruiting?
   a. _____
   b. _____
   c. _____
   d. _____
   e. _____

f. _____

g. _____

6. What are some of the newest tools used to recruit employees?

_____

_____

_____

_____

7. Most organizations use a variety of methods to recruit potential employees.

    If you have a job now, talk to the director of human resources (your company may call it the personnel department) and find out what kinds of sources your firm uses.

    If you don't have a job, ask people you know how they found their jobs. That can give you an idea of the recruitment methods companies use.

_____

_____

_____

_____

Selecting Employees

1. Why is the selection process such an important element in the human resource program?

_____

_____

_____

_____

2. How do legal issues make the steps in the selection process more challenging?

_____

_____

_____

_____

3. What are employment tests used to measure? What is the important element of employment tests?

_____

_____

_____

_____

_____

4. What is the benefit, for the firm, of a trial period?

_____

_____

_____

_____

5. a. What are "contingent workers"?

_____

_____

b. When do firms hire contingent workers?

_____

_____

_____

c. What are the ups and downs of being a contingent worker?

_____

_____

_____

_____

6. "Selection is the process of gathering information to decide who should be hired … for the best interests of the individual and the organization."

    A typical process involves six steps:

    ☐ Application
    ☐ Initial and follow-up interviews
    ☐ Employment tests
    ☐ Background investigations
    ☐ Physical exams
    ☐ Trial periods

    Match each of the following statements to the correct step in the selection process.

    a. _____ Contributes to the high cost of turnover, but enables a firm to fire incompetent employees after a certain period of time.

    b. _____ Helps a firm to determine the information about an employee that is pertinent to the requirements of the job, but companies are limited by legal guidelines.

    c. _____ An investigation of previous work records and school records, and follow-up on recommendations.

    d. _____ These have been severely criticized because of cultural discrimination. They are used to test specific job skills.

    e. _____ Help to assess an applicant's ability to communicate clearly, to adapt to stress situations, and to clarify information.

    f. _____ A major controversy in this step was a proposal to use drug tests to screen employees in industry and government.

7. Music-stor needs the human resource manager to begin developing some job descriptions, identify the various skills needed to perform the different jobs in the company, and to start to develop a recruitment and selection process. Select at least one job that will be a part of Music-stor's organization, write a job description, job specifications, and develop a plan for recruiting and selecting job candidates.

_____

_____

_____

_____

Training and Developing Employees for Optimum Performance

1. What are three steps in the process of creating training and development programs?

   a. _____

   b. _____

   c. _____

2. What is the difference between training and development?

   _____

   _____

   _____

   _____

3. Identify the activities in an employee orientation program.

   _____

   _____

   _____

   _____

4. In what type of situation is on-the-job training effective? How have intranets affected on-the-job training programs?

   _____

   _____

   _____

   _____

   _____

5. a. What types of jobs would you train for in an apprenticeship?

   _____

   _____

   _____

   b. What job classification comes after apprenticeship?

   _____

   c. How will apprenticeship programs change?

   _____

   _____

   _____

   _____

6. What is another name for Internet training?

   _____

7. When is vestibule training used?

   _____

   _____

_____

_____

8. What kinds of jobs use job simulation training?

_____

_____

_____

_____

9. What are the two basic elements of management development?
   a. _____
   b. _____

10. List four types of training included in management training programs.
    a. _____
    b. _____
    c. _____
    d. _____

11. What are three reasons for companies to develop mentoring and networking programs for women and minorities in the workplace?
    a. _____
    b. _____
    c. _____

12. A good manager needs to develop many skills. Management development programs include the following types of training:
    ☐ On-the-job coaching
    ☐ Understudy positions
    ☐ Job rotation
    ☐ Off-the-job courses and training

Match the correct type of training program to each of the following statements:
    a. _____ Bernie Breen, an executive with Air Canada, spent three weeks in a course on communication techniques for middle managers.
    b. _____ Managers at Hewlett-Packard move from one department to another every three years without exception.
    c. _____ The Assistant Dean of Instruction often fills in for the Dean when he isn't available.
    d. _____ Many young business people try to find a mentor in their organizations as they "learn the ropes."

13. Networking has been an important aspect in the career of many young aspiring business people. Once you're on the job, another way to enhance your career is to find a mentor, or "coach."
    If you are working now, what are the ways you could begin to develop a network which could be beneficial in the future? If you're in school, where do you think is the best place to look to develop a network?

_____

_____
_____
_____

Appraising Employee Performance to Get Optimum Results

1. What three characteristics must performance standards have?

   a. _____ b. _____ c. _____

2. What decisions are based upon a performance appraisal?

   _____
   _____
   _____
   _____

3. What is the latest form of performance appraisal?

   _____
   _____
   _____
   _____

Compensating Employees to Attract and Keep the Best

1. Why have compensation and benefit packages become a major challenge at the beginning of the 21st century?

   _____
   _____
   _____
   _____

2. In looking at team compensation, what is the problem when pay is based strictly on individual performance?

   _____
   _____
   _____
   _____

3. What are the two most common compensation methods for teams?

   _____
   _____
   _____
   _____

4. Describe a skill-based pay system for teams.

   _____
   _____
   _____
   _____

5. What are two problems with skill-based pay systems?

_____

_____

_____

_____

6. Describe a profit sharing, or gain sharing, system of compensation for teams.

_____

_____

_____

_____

7. Where does individual compensation fit into these team-based plans?

_____

_____

_____

_____

8. What are some of the things included in a fringe benefits package? How big a part of companies' compensation plans are fringe benefits?

_____

_____

_____

_____

9. What are "soft benefits?"

_____

_____

_____

_____

10. Why have companies implemented cafeteria-style benefits packages? What is the key to offering these types of plans?

_____

_____

_____

_____

11. In the competitive environment today, compensation and fringe benefit packages are being given special attention. A good program can accomplish several benefits for an organization, including attracting and keeping skilled employees.

Basic pay systems include

] Salary systems	] Profit sharing plans
] Hourly wage	] COLAs
] Piecework	] Bonus plans
] Commission plans	

   a. Give a suggested pay system for each situation described below. Your suggestion can be a combination of systems.

i. _____ A sales job that includes a variety of non-selling functions such as advising, keeping records, and setting up displays.

ii. _____ An assembly-line operation in which each worker completes several tasks before the product moves to the next station.

iii. _____ An office manager just starting out with a new word-processing program designed to increase productivity.

iv. _____ The president of a small firm that makes computer chips.

v. _____ A worker in a garment-making plant, making shirts.

b. Name eight employee benefits that companies can provide for their employees.

i.   _____   v.   _____

ii.   _____   vi.   _____

iii. _____   vii. _____

iv.   _____   viii. _____

12. How can a company ensure that their benefit program meets the needs of a changing workforce?

_____

_____

_____

_____

Adopting Flexible Work Schedules

1. What are four alternatives for job scheduling?

a. _____

b. _____

c. _____

d. _____

2. The changing nature of the workforce has created the need for more flexible work scheduling. Four ways to meet those needs are

☐ Job sharing
☐ Flextime plans
☐ Compressed workweeks
☐ Working at home

a. List the advantages of job sharing.

For employees:

i.   _____

ii. _____

iii. _____

For organizations:

i.   _____

ii. _____

iii. _____

b. List the advantages of flextime plans.

For employees:

i. _____

ii. _____

iii. _____

For organizations:

i. _____

ii. _____

iii. _____

c. List the disadvantages of job sharing and flextime.

Job sharing:

i. _____

ii. _____

Flextime:

i. _____

ii. _____

iii. _____

d. There are obvious advantages to working four days and having three days off. They are much the same as with job sharing and flextime.

List two disadvantages of a compressed workweek.

i. _____

ii. _____

3. Why do people work at home? Can you think of any disadvantages to this type of work?

_____

_____

_____

_____

Moving Employees Up, Over, and Out

1. What are four ways of moving employees through the organization?

a. _____   c. _____

b. _____   d. _____

2. What are the benefits of promotion from within a company?

_____

_____

_____

_____

3. What events have created a need for managers to manage layoffs and firings?

_____

_____

_____

_____

4. Why are companies hesitant to rehire permanent employees?

_____

_____
_____
_____
_____

5. What is the doctrine of "employment at will"?

_____
_____
_____
_____

6. How has the "employment at will" doctrine changed?

_____
_____
_____
_____

7. What are two tools used to downsize companies?

_____
_____
_____
_____

8. What are two advantages of early retirement programs?

_____
_____
_____
_____

Laws Affecting Human Resource Management

1. List six types of businesses that are subject to federal law regarding matters associated with employment.
   a. _____
   b. _____
   c. _____
   d. _____
   e. _____
   f.

2. List six grounds of discrimination that are illegal in Canada.
   a. _____
   b. _____
   c. _____
   d. _____
   e. _____
   f. _____

3. What is the purpose of affirmative action programs?

_____

_____

_____

_____

4. How do affirmative action programs result in charges of reverse discrimination?

_____

_____

_____

_____

5. Identify four important aspects of the impact of legislation on human resource management.
   a. _____
   b. _____
   c. _____
   d. _____

CHAPTER CHECK

1. Name six functions of human resource management.
   a. _____ d. _____
   b. _____ e. _____
   c. _____ f. _____

2. Identify 10 problems that human resource managers will face in the future.
   a. _____

   b. _____

   c. _____

   d. _____

   e. _____

   f. _____

   g. _____

   h. _____

   i. _____

   j. _____

3. List six steps in human resource planning.

a. _____

b. _____

c. _____

d. _____

e. _____

f. _____

4. List six steps in the selection process.

   a. _____

   b. _____

   c. _____

   d. _____

   e. _____

   f. _____

5. Name six types of training programs.

   a. _____

   b. _____

   c. _____

   d. _____

   e. _____

   f. _____

6. Identify nine areas which may be covered in employee orientation programs.

   a. _____

   b. _____

   c. _____

   d. _____

   e. _____

   f. _____

   g. _____

   h. _____

   i. _____

7. What are six steps in the performance appraisal process?

   a. _____

   b. _____

   c. _____

   d. _____

   e. _____

   f. _____

8. What are six do's and don'ts for managers conducting performance appraisals?

   a. _____

   b. _____

   c. _____

   d. _____

   e. _____

f. _____

9. List six objectives that can be achieved through a carefully managed compensation program.
   a. _____
   b. _____
   c. _____
   d. _____
   e. _____
   f. _____

10. Identify six pay systems.
    a. _____
    b. _____
    c. _____
    d. _____
    e. _____
    f. _____

11. List four job designs companies have created to accommodate workers' needs for flexibility of scheduling.
    a. _____
    b. _____
    c. _____
    d. _____

12. What are four kinds of management development programs?
    a. _____
    b. _____
    c. _____
    d. _____

13. What are the four skills managers need that require different training from that of most employees?
    a. _____
    b. _____
    c. _____
    d. _____

14. a. What is affirmative action?

    _____
    _____
    _____
    _____

   b. Why does the Canadian Charter of Rights and Freedoms permit affirmative action?

    _____
    _____
    _____
    _____

PRACTICE TEST

Multiple Choice: Circle the best answer.

1. Human resource management does not include
   a. leading
   b. evaluation
   c. recruitment
   d. selection

2. Which of the following would NOT be included in a discussion of the challenges faced by human resource managers?
   a. shortages of people trained to work in growth areas
   b. a growing population of workers who need retraining
   c. challenges from an overseas labour pool available for lower wages
   d. fewer older workers, and too many of them that want to retire, making it difficult to fill their jobs

3. A human resource inventory will provide information about
   a. what is done by various employees who fill different job titles
   b. whether or not the labour force is paid adequately
   c. the strategic plan for recruiting, selecting, training, and development
   d. education, capabilities, training, and specialized skills to determine if the company labour force is technically up-to-date

4. "Clerical worker, with responsibilities of answering phones, greeting clients, and filing for human resource department. Some weekends required." This is an example of a
   a. job analysis
   b. job specification
   c. job description
   d. job evaluation

5. According to the text, the greatest advantage of hiring from within is
   a. it is quick
   b. it requires less training
   c. it helps maintain employee morale
   d. it keeps the firm from having an oversupply of workers trained in certain areas

6. Which of the following is NOT included in a list of reasons why recruiting has become difficult?
   a. Sometimes people with necessary skills aren't available.
   b. The number of available recruiting tools has begun to shrink.
   c. The emphasis on participative management makes it important to hire people who fit in with corporate culture.
   d. Some companies have unattractive workplaces and policies which make it difficult to recruit.

7. What is the first step in the selection process?
   a. completing an application form
   b. contacting an employment agency
   c. background investigation
   d. interviews

8. Background investigations
   a. are no longer legal
   b. help weed out candidates that are not likely to succeed
   c. include an investigation of skill
   d. are not good predictors of who will be successful

9. The use of contingent workers
   a. is more expensive than hiring full-time workers
   b. is appropriate when jobs require minimum training
   c. is declining
   d. is not a good way to find good employees

10. Internal and external programs to develop a variety of skills and to foster personal development away from the job is called
    a. off-the-job training
    b. vestibule training
    c. an apprentice program
    d. employee orientation

11. _____ is a type of training that exposes managers to different functions of the organization by giving them assignments in a variety of departments.
    a. Understudy positions
    b. On-the-job coaching
    c. Job enlargement
    d. Job rotation

12. In developing a performance appraisal, standards should have all of the following characteristics EXCEPT:
    a. They should be specific.
    b. They should be subject to measurement.
    c. They should be easily attainable.
    d. They should be reasonable.

13. The latest form of performance appraisal requires feedback from up, down, and around the employee and is called a
    a. 360-degree review
    b. turnaround review
    c. complete feedback review
    d. total review

14. Ima Gogetter is interested in making a lot of money! He is a very good salesperson. People tell him he could sell ice to an Eskimo! He is a very hard worker, and is willing to work a lot of hours to make the kind of money he wants. Ima should look for the kind of job that is paid
    a. on salary with overtime
    b. hourly
    c. with profit sharing
    d. on commission

15. Studies of compensation for teams have shown that
    a. it is recommended that pay should be based on team performance
    b. team-based pay programs are pretty well developed and need not be changed
    c. team members should be compensated as individuals
    d. skill-based pay programs are relatively easy to apply

16. A program that gives employees freedom to adjust when they work, as long as they work the required numbers of hours, is called
    a. job sharing
    b. flextime
    c. a compressed workweek
    d. home-based work

17. Which of the following is NOT a benefit of job sharing?
    a. reduced absenteeism
    b. ability to schedule people into peek demand periods
    c. a high level of enthusiasm and productivity
    d. less supervision

18. The effect of downsizing on human resource management has been that
    a. fewer layers of management make it more difficult for employees to be promoted to higher levels of management
    b. companies are now scrambling to rehire those workers who were laid off
    c. a decrease in the level of complexity of managing human resources
    d. less need to adhere to employment law

True/False

1. Qualified labour is more scarce today, which makes recruiting and selecting more difficult.
2. Job descriptions are statements about the person who does the job.
3. The newest tools used to recruit employees are Internet online services.

4.   The application form and the initial interview are good ways for a company to find out about an applicant's family and religious background.

5.   It can be more cost-effective for a company to hire contingent workers rather than hire permanent employees when more workers are needed.

6.   In an apprentice program, a worker immediately begins his or her tasks and learns by doing.

7.   In a mentoring program, an older, more experienced worker will coach and guide a selected lower-level manager by introducing him or her to the right people and groups.

8.   Decisions about promotions, compensation, additional training, and firing are all based upon performance evaluations.

9.   While compensation and benefit packages are important to keep employees, these programs play little role in attracting qualified employees.

10.   Most companies have found that compensating teams is a relatively straightforward issue.

11.   Some companies have found that telecommuting has helped the company to save money.

12.   Legislation to prevent employer abuse in firing workers has restricted management's ability to terminate workers, as it increased workers' rights to their jobs.

13.   While an early retirement program is a more expensive strategy of downsizing than laying off employees, it can increase the morale of remaining employees.

14.   Legislation and legal decisions have had little effect on human resource management.

ANSWERS

Key Terms and Definitions

1. vestibule training
2. mentor
3. on-the-job training
4. core time
5. flextime plans
6. job simulation
7. performance appraisal
8. off-the-job training
9. cafeteria-style fringe benefits
10. apprentice programs
11. compressed workweek
12. affirmative action (employment equity)
13. reverse discrimination
14. selection
15. online training
16. job description
17. management development
18. recruitment
19. job analysis
20. human resource management (HRM)
21. networking
22. job sharing
23. training and development
24. employee orientation
25. job specification
26. contingent workers

The Human Resource Function

1. Historically firms assigned the functions of human resource management, such recruiting, selecting, training, and so on, to various functional departments. "Personnel" was viewed mostly as a clerical function responsible for screening applications, keeping records, processing payroll, and finding people when necessary. Today the job of human resource management has taken on a new role in the firm. It has become so important that it is a function of all managers.

2. Challenges of human resource management include the following:
   a. Shortages of people trained to work in growth areas.
   b. Large numbers of workers from declining industries who need retraining.
   c. A growing population of new workers who are poor and undereducated.
   d. A shift in the age composition of the workforce, including older workers and baby boomers.
   e. Complex law in human resource management.

f. Increasing numbers of single-parent and two-income families who need programs like day care, job sharing, and family leave.

g. Changing employee attitudes toward work with leisure having a greater priority.

h. Downsizing and its effect on morale and need for contingency workers.

i. Challenges from an overseas labour pool.

j. Increased demand for benefits tailored to the individual.

k. Growing concern for issues such as health care, elder care, and employment for people with disabilities.

3. Human resource management has received greater attention recently because in the past, labour, or "human resources" was plentiful, and there was little need to nurture and develop the labour force. If you needed qualified people, all you had to do was hire them. If they didn't work out, you could simply hire others. Qualified labour is scarcer today, and that makes the whole area of human resource management more challenging.

Determining Human Resource Needs

1. A human resource inventory includes ages, names, education, capabilities, training, specialized skills, and other information pertinent to the organization, such as languages spoken. This information reveals whether or not the labour force is technically up-to-date and thoroughly trained.

2. A job description specifies the objectives of the job, the types of work to be done, responsibilities and duties, working conditions, and the relationship of the job to other functions. Job specifications specify the qualifications of the individual needed to fill the job. In other words, the job description is about the job, and job specifications are about the person who does the job.

3. The demand for employees will be affected by changing technology. Often training programs must be started long before the need is apparent.

4. There are likely to be increased shortages of some skills in the future, and an oversupply of other types of skills.

Recruiting Employees

1. a. Legal restrictions make it necessary to recruit the proper "mix" of qualified applicants.
   b. Emphasis on more "humanistic management" makes it necessary to hire people who have not only
      the skills needed to fill a job, but who will also fit into the corporate culture.
   c. Firing unqualified employees is getting more and more difficult legally.
   d. Some companies have workplaces or policies that make recruiting and keeping employees difficult.

2. Activities used in recruiting are
   a. finding
   b. hiring
   c. training

3. Sources for recruiting are
   a. internal sources
   b. external sources

4. Internal methods of recruiting are
   a. transfers
   b. promotions
   c. employee recommendations

5. External sources of recruiting are
   a. advertisements
   b. public and private employment agencies
   c. college placement bureaus
   d. management consultants
   e. professional organizations
   f. referrals

g. applicants who appear at the workplace ✓

6. Some of the newest tools used to recruit employees are Internet online services.

7. Answers will vary.

Selecting Employees

1. The selection process is so important because the cost of selecting and training employees has become so high.

2. Legal issues affect the selection process in a number of ways. Today, legal guidelines limit the kinds of questions one can ask on an application or in an interview. Employment tests have been challenged because of discrimination, so tests must be directly related to the job. Some states will only allow physical examinations after an offer of employment has been accepted, and such tests must be given to everyone applying for the same position. Conditional employment, where a company gives an employee a trial period, has made it easier to fire inefficient or problem employees.

3. Employment tests measure basic competencies in specific job skills and help evaluate applicants' personalities and interests. Employment tests must be directly related to the job.

4. During a trial period, a person can prove his or her worth to the firm. After the trial period, a firm has the right to discharge an employee based upon performance evaluations, so it is easier to fire inefficient employees. *(probationary period)*

5. a. Contingent workers are workers who do not have the expectation of regular, full-time employment. These workers include part-time workers, seasonal workers, temporary workers, independent contractors, interns, and co-op students.
   b. Firms have contingent workers when there is a varying need for employees, full-time employees are on leave, there is a peak demand for labour, and quick service to customers is a priority.
   c. Contingent workers are often offered full-time positions, but as contingent workers they receive few health, vacation, and pension benefits. They also earn less than permanent workers.

6. a. Trial periods
   b. Application
   c. Background investigation
   d. Employment tests
   e. Initial and follow-up interviews
   f. Physical exams

7. Your answer will depend upon what kind of job you have chosen. There are many different jobs which will be part of Music-stor: sales, production, marketing, accounting, and clerical, to name a few. For a sales job, a job description may be: Sales for a small manufacturing company, calling on automotive manufacturers and/or automotive after-market dealers. Sales territory will be primarily based on geographic location. Duties will include sales calls, follow-up reports, working directly with production manager, direct input into marketing program development. Compensation will be salary plus commission.

   Skills required include familiarity with electronic communication equipment, teamwork skills, good oral and written communications skills, presentation skills, and a bachelor's degree, preferably in marketing or a related area.

   You may make use of any of the recruiting tools list in the text. Good sources may include current employees, local colleges, a local professional marketing organization, or simply advertising. The selection process should include several interviews, in particular with the people with whom the salesperson will work, production manager, other marketing people, other members of the team he/she will work with.

Training and Developing Employees for Optimum Performance

1. Steps in creating training and development programs are
   a. Assessing the needs of the organization and the skills of the employees to determine training needs.
   b. Designing the training activities to meet the needs.
   c. Evaluating the effectiveness of the training.
2. Training is short-term skills oriented, while development is long-term career oriented.
3. During an employee orientation program, new employees will be introduced to fellow employees and to their immediate supervisors, and learn about the policies, practices and objectives of the firm. Orientation programs include everything from informal talks to formal activities that last a day or more and include visits to various departments and required reading of selected handbooks.
4. On-the-job training is the most fundamental type of training. It is the easiest kind of training to implement, and can be effective where the job is easily learned, such as clerking in a store, or performing repetitive physical tasks. Technology such as intranets is leading to cost-effective forms of on-the-job training programs that are available 24 hours a day, all year long.
5. a. As an apprentice, you would train for a craft, such as bricklaying or plumbing.
   b. Workers who successfully complete an apprenticeship earn the classification of journeyman.
   c. In the future, there are likely to be more but shorter apprenticeship programs to prepare people for skilled jobs in changing industries.
6. Another name for Internet training is distance learning, or online training.
7. Vestibule training is used when proper methods and safety procedures must be learned before using equipment on the job.
8. Job simulation is the use of equipment that duplicates job conditions and tasks so trainees can learn skills before attempting them on the job. It differs from vestibule training in that simulation attempts to duplicate the exact conditions that occur on the job.
9. Basic elements of management development are
   a. training and educating employees to become good managers.
   b. developing managerial skills over time.
10. Types of training used in management training programs are
    a. on-the-job coaching
    b. understudy positions
    c. job rotation
    d. off-the-job courses and training
11. Companies taking the initiative to develop female and minority managers understand that
    a. grooming women and minorities for management positions is a key to long-term profitability.
    b. the best women and minorities will become harder to attract and retain in the future.
    c. more women and minorities at all levels means that businesses can serve female and minority customers better.
12. a. Off-the-job course
    b. Job rotation
    c. Understudy positions
    d. On-the-job coaching
13. *Suggested Answer*
    Look for work from other departments. Eat lunch with employees from other work areas. Play on softball or golf leagues that are made up of employees from other departments. At school, make an effort to get to know classmates and instructors. Join organizations that pertain to your area of interest.

Appraising Employee Performance to Get Optimum Results

1. Performance standards must be
   a. understandable
   b. subject to measurement
   c. reasonable

264

2. Decisions about promotions, compensation, additional training, or firing are all based on performance evaluations.
3. The latest form of performance appraisal is called the 360-degree review, because it calls for feedback from superiors, subordinates, and peers.

Compensating Employees to Attract and Keep the Best

1. Compensation and benefit packages have become a main marketing tool used to attract qualified employees. At the same time, employee compensation is one of the largest operating costs for many organizations, and the firm's long-term survival may depend on how well it can control employee costs, while still attracting and keeping qualified personnel.
2. The problem with paying members of a team based on individual performance is that it erodes team cohesiveness and makes it less likely that the team will meet its goals as a collaborative effort.
3. Two types of pay systems for teams are skills-based pay and profit sharing.
4. Skill-based pay is related to the growth of the individual and of the team. Base pay is raised when team members learn and apply new skills.
5. The drawbacks of the skill-based pay system are the complexity and the difficulty of correlating skill acquisition to bottom-line gains.
6. In a profit sharing, or gain sharing system, bonuses are based on improvements over a previous performance baseline.
7. Outstanding team players that go beyond what is required and make an outstanding individual contribution to the firm should be separately recognized for their additional contribution. A good way to avoid alienating recipients who feel team participation was uneven is to let the team decide which members get what type of individual award.
8. Fringe benefits include sick-leave pay, vacation pay, pension plans, and health plans. They can also include everything from paid vacations to health-care programs, recreation facilities, company cars, country club memberships, daycare services and executive dining rooms, dental care, eye care, elder care, legal counselling, mental health care and shorter workweeks.
   Fringe benefits account for approximately one-third of payrolls today.
9. "Soft benefits" are such things as on-site haircuts and shoe repair, concierge services and free breakfasts that help workers maintain the balance between work and family life.
10. Firms have begun to offer cafeteria-style benefits to counter the growing demand for different kinds of benefits. Today employees are more varied and need different kinds of benefits. The key to cafeteria-style benefits is flexibility, where individual needs can be met.
11. a. *Suggested Answers*
    i. Salary or salary plus commission
    ii. Hourly wages plus profit sharing
    iii. Salary plus bonus for meeting objectives
    iv. Salary plus bonus
    v. Piecework plus profit sharing
    b. *Possible Answers*

i. Health insurance	v.	Sick leave
ii. Life insurance	vi.	Pension plans
iii. Paid vacations	vii.	Company cars
iv. Day-care centres	viii.	Recreation facilities

11. Cafeteria-style fringe benefit programs that allow employees to choose the benefits they want. Managers can be more cost-effective and equitable to individual employees by providing a variety of benefit choices.

Adopting Flexible Work Schedules

1. a. flextime
   b. compressed work week
   c. home-based (telecommuting)
   d. job sharing
2. a. *For employees*:
   i. Employment for people who can't or prefer not to work full time
   ii. Time to perform personal errands or solve other problems
   iii. Higher level of enthusiasm and motivation
   For organizations:
   i. Employees more likely to be motivated because of shorter work hours
   ii. Lower absenteeism and fewer problems with tardiness
   iii. Better scheduling opportunities for peak business periods
   b. *For employees*:
   i. Easier scheduling for working parents
   ii. More time to perform personal errands
   iii. A psychological boost that comes with having a choice about when to work
   For organizations:
   i. Employees can work when they're most productive
   ii. Lower absenteeism for employees having to run personal errands that can only be done during
      business hours
   iii. More motivated employees
   c. *Job sharing*:
   i. Increases costs and work involved in having to train and supervise more employees
   ii. Prorating fringe benefits
   Flextime:
   i. Doesn't work on assembly lines
   ii. Managers may have longer days
   iii. Communication difficulties
   iv. Some employees could abuse the system
   v. Increased energy use
   d. i. Longer hours
   ii. Possible decline in productivity from longer hours
3. Women, in particular, have found working at home allows them to pursue the dual goals of career and family simultaneously. Other "at home" workers appreciate having more control over their lives. One obvious disadvantage is the isolation of working at home. Many people may miss the socialization of working in an office.

Moving Employees Up, Over, and Out

1. a. Promotions ✓
   b. Terminations ✓
   c. Reassignment ✓
   d. Retirement ✓
2. Many companies find that promotion from within the company improves employee morale. Promotions are also cost-effective because the promoted employees are already familiar with the corporate culture and procedures.
3. Downsizing and restructuring, increasing customer demands for value, the pressure of global competition, and shifts in technology have made human resource managers struggle.
4. Companies are hesitant to rehire permanent employees because the cost of terminating employees is

so high that managers choose to avoid the cost of firing by not hiring in the first place. Instead, companies are using temporary employees or outsourcing.

5. "Employment at will" is an old doctrine that meant managers had as much freedom to fire workers as workers had to leave voluntarily.
6. All provinces now have written employment laws that limit the "at will" doctrine to protect employees from wrongful firing.
7. Two tools used to downsize are to offer early retirement benefits and to lay off employees.
8. Two advantages of early retirement programs are the increased morale of surviving employees and greater promotion opportunities for younger employees.

Laws Affecting Human Resource Management

1. a. banks
   b. airlines
   c. railways
   d. shipping companies
   e. radio and TV
   f. insurance companies
2. a. age
   b. sex
   c. race
   d. religion
   e. nationality
   e. marital status
3. The purpose of affirmative action is to "right past wrongs" endured by females and minorities in the administration of human resources management.
4. Charges of reverse discrimination occur when companies have been perceived as unfairly giving preference to women or minority groups in hiring and promoting, when following affirmative action guidelines.
5. Impact of legislation on human resource management includes the following:
   a. Employers must be sensitive to the legal rights of all groups in the workplace.
   b. Legislation affects all areas of human resource management.
   c. It is clear that it is sometimes legal to go beyond providing equal rights for minorities and women to provide special employment and training to correct past discrimination.
   d. New court cases and legislation change human resource management almost daily.

CHAPTER CHECK ANSWERS

1. a. Human resource planning
   b. Recruiting
   c. Selecting
   d. Training
   e. Evaluating
   f. Compensating
2. a. Shortages of people trained to work in growth areas, particularly high-tech and sciences.
   b. Large numbers of unskilled workers from declining industries who need retraining.
   c. Growing populations of minority groups who are undereducated and unprepared for jobs in today's business environment.
   d. A shift in the age composition of workers.
   e. Complex set of laws in human resource management.
   f. Demand for day care and other programs designed to meet the needs of working women.
   g. Changing employee attitudes about work.
   h. Lower labour rates and more relaxed laws overseas.

i.   Increased demand for benefits packages tailored to the individual.
   j.   Growing concern for work environment and equality issues.
3. a. Forecast human resource needs.
   b. Prepare an inventory of current human resource information.
   c. Prepare job analyses, job descriptions, and job specifications.
   d. Determine future demands, including what training programs will be needed.
   e. Determine future supply of human resources with needed skills.
   f. Establish a plan for recruiting, hiring, educating, training, motivating, and scheduling the labour force.
4. a. Completion of an application form
   b. Initial and follow-up interviews
   c. Employment tests
   d. Background investigations
   e. Physical exams
   f. Trial periods
5. a. Employee orientation
   b. On-the-job
   c. Apprenticeships
   d. Off-the-job
   e. Vestibule training
   f. Job simulation
6. a. Corporate history
   b. Product descriptions
   c. Organization chart
   d. Safety measures and regulations
   e. Human resource policies
   f. Compensation programs
   g. Routines and regulations
   h. Corporate culture
   i. Organizational objectives
7. a. Establish performance standards
   b. Communicate the standards
   c. Evaluate performance
   d. Discuss results with employees
   e. Take corrective action when needed
   f. Use results to make decisions
8. a. Don't attack the employee personally
   b. Allow for sufficient time without distractions
   c. Don't make employee uneasy, or perform the appraisal with other people present
   d. Include the employee in the process
   e. Don't let problems build up until the appraisal
   f. End the appraisal on a positive note
9. a. Attract the kind of people the organization needs
   b. Provide incentives
   c. Keep people from leaving
   d. Maintain a competitive position in the marketplace
   e. Protect employee
   f. Assure employees of retirement funds
10. a. Hourly wage   d. Commissions

b. Salary
c. Piecework
11. a. Job sharing
    b. Flextime
    c. Compressed workweeks
    d. Working at home
12. a. On-the-job coaching
    b. Understudy positions
    c. Job rotation
    d. Off-the-job courses and training
13. a. Listening skills and empathy
    b. Time management
    c. Planning
    d. Human relations skills
14. a. Giving preference to members of historically disadvantaged groups in hiring and promotion
    b. To overcome the effects of long-standing discrimination

e. Bonus plan
f. Profit sharing

PRACTICE TEST

Multiple Choice

1. a
2. d
3. d
4. c
5. c
6. b
7. a
8. b
9. b
10. a
11. d
12. c
13. a
14. d
15. a
16. b
17. d
18. a

True/False

1. T
2. F
3. T
4. F
5. T
6. F
7. T
8. T
9. F
10. F
11. T
12. T
13. T
14. F

CHAPTER 14

Dealing with Employee-Management Issues and Relations

Learning Goals

After you have read and studied this chapter, you should be able to

1. Understand that the most difficult issues facing labour and management today are retraining, job security, and job flexibility.
2. Trace the history and role of labour unions in Canada.
3. Discuss the major legislation affecting labour and management.
4. Outline the collective bargaining process.
5. Describe union and management pressure tactics during negotiations.
6. Explain a strike and a lockout and who uses these procedures.
7. Explain the difference between mediation and arbitration.

Key Terms and Definitions

Listed here are important terms found in this chapter. Choose the correct term for each definition and write it in the space provided.

agency shop (Rand formula)	Collective bargaining	open shop
arbitration	Grievance	picketing
boycott	Injunction	replacement workers
	Labour Relations Board	scabs
check-off	Lockout	union shop
closed shop	Mediation	

1. _____ Workplace in which the employer is free to hire anybody, but the recruit must then join the union within a short period, perhaps a month.

2. _____ The use of a third party to attempt to bring disputing parties to a resolution by modifying their positions.

3. _____ The process whereby strikers carrying picket signs walk back and forth across entrances to their places of employment to publicize the strike and discourage or prevent people, vehicles, materials, and products from going in or out.

4. _____ The process by which a union represents employees in relations with their employer.

5. _____ Workplace in which employees are free to join or not join the union and to pay or not pay union dues.

6. _____ A quasi-judicial body consisting of representatives of government, labour, and business. It functions more informally than a court but has the full force of law. It administers labour codes in each jurisdiction, federal or provincial.

7. _____ The process of resolving all disputes, not only grievances, through an outside, impartial third party.

8. _____ Workplace in which all new hires must already be union members.

9. _____ Union's name for strikebreakers.

10. _____ Urging union members and the public at large not to buy a particular company's products or services.

11. _____ Contract clause requiring the employer to deduct union dues from employees' pay and remit them to the union.

12. _____ A formal protest by an individual employee or a union when they believe a particular management decision breaches the union contract.

13. _____ An order from a judge requiring strikers to limit or cease picketing or stop some threatening activity.

14. _____ Workplace in which a new employee is not required to join the union but must pay union dues.

15. _____ A negotiating strategy in which the employer locks the premises against the employees.

16. _____ Management's name for strikebreakers.

The Major Issues Facing Management-Labour Relations

1. Why is retraining one of "the most critical issues in management-labour relations today"?

_____
_____
_____
_____

History and Role of Trade Unions in Canada

1. What triggered the union movement of today?

_____
_____
_____
_____

2. What were working conditions like during the Industrial Revolution?

_____
_____
_____
_____

3. a. What were the issues that concerned the early crafts unions, before and during the Industrial Revolution?

_____

_____
_____
_____

b. How do those issues compare with modern day work issues?

_____
_____
_____
_____

4. What were the objectives of organized labour a quarter century ago, and how have they changed?

_____
_____
_____
_____

Legislation Affecting Labour-Management Relations

1. List eight types of employees' rights that did not exist at the time of the Industrial Revolution, but have been established by legislation in Canada.

a. _____
b. _____
c. _____
d. _____
e. _____
f. _____
g. _____
h. _____

The Collective Bargaining Process

1. a. What is collective bargaining?

_____
_____
_____
_____

b. List the steps in the collective bargaining process.

i. _____
ii. _____
iii. _____
iv. _____
v. _____
vi. _____
vii. _____
viii. _____

2. Identify four different forms of union contracts.

a. _____   c. _____
b. _____   d. _____

3. There are four types of labour agreements:
   - closed shop agreement
   - agency shop agreement
   - union shop agreement
   - open shop agreement

   Which does each example demonstrate?
   a. When Tom Oswalt worked in an automotive factory for the summer in Ontario, he chose not to join the local union. However, he was still required to pay a fee to the union under a union-security clause.
   b. Harry Buler was hired by a manufacturing company. He was required to join the union first.

   _____

   c. When Peter Tobler went to work at Tyson Foods, he was not required to join the union, and did not have to pay any fees to the union. _____
   d. Gary Reese took a job with a brewery. He had until October to join the union. _____

4. In the mid-1990s, the National and American League baseball players went on strike, and ended the baseball season for the year. While player representatives continued to negotiate with team owners (sporadically), the strike was still not resolved by the opening of the season in the spring of the following year. Even President Bill Clinton could not convince the owners and players to come to the bargaining table and talk to one another. What options are available to labour and management for resolving agreements, which could have been used before the players went on strike, or while they were on strike?

   _____
   _____
   _____
   _____

5. What are three methods used to resolve labour-management disputes?
   a. _____
   b. _____
   c. _____

6. What are, generally, the sources of grievances?
   a. _____
   b. _____
   c. _____
   d. _____
   e. _____

7. List the six steps in the grievance procedure.
   a. _____
   b. _____
   c. _____
   d. _____
   e. _____
   f. _____

8. Describe
   a. arbitration

   _____
   _____
   _____

   b. mediation

   _____
   _____
   _____

9. When does mediation become necessary?

   _____
   _____
   _____
   _____

10. What does a mediator do?

   _____
   _____
   _____
   _____

11. How does arbitration differ from mediation?

   _____
   _____
   _____
   _____

12. What will be the focus of union negotiations in the future?
    a. _____
    b. _____
    c. _____
    d. _____
    e. _____

When Unions and Management Disagree

1. Describe three union tactics and three management tactics that are used when the parties are unable to agree on the terms of a new contract.
   a. union tactics
      i. _____
      ii. _____
      iii. _____
   b. management tactics
      i. _____
      ii. _____
      iii. _____

2. List as many categories as you can of employees that are prevented from striking in Canada. Why, do

you suppose, are these people deprived of this right?

_____
_____
_____

3. What does a strike provide?

_____
_____
_____
_____

4. What is the difference between a primary boycott and a secondary boycott?

_____
_____
_____
_____

5. What will unions have to do in order to grow in the future?

_____
_____
_____
_____

6. Several years ago, the major league baseball players in the U.S. and Canada went on strike and ended the season for the year. The strike was still not resolved by the opening of the next season the following spring. Even the U.S. President could not convince the owners and players to come to the bargaining table and talk to one another. What options were available to labour and management for resolving the dispute, either before the players went on strike, or while they were on strike?

_____
_____
_____
_____

Strikes, Lockouts, and the Law

1. What is picketing? Why do strikers picket?

_____
_____
_____
_____

2. There are two terms used for *strikebreakers*. What do unions call them? What do managers call them? In what provinces are they illegal?

_____
_____
_____
_____

3.   What is an *injunction?* Who would request one when a strike is on?

_____

_____

_____

_____

Structure and Size of Trade Unions in Canada

1.   How many Canadian workers were unionized in 1998?

_____

2.   Name the four largest Congresses with which Canadian unions are affiliated.

    a.   _____

    b.   _____

    c.   _____

    d.   _____

3.   List as many benefits as you can think of that employed workers of the future will want, causing many of them to opt for bargaining collectively as union members.

_____

_____

_____

_____

4.   How is the role of unions changing to meet the business needs of today?

_____

_____

_____

_____

Future of Labour-Management Relations

1.   What is the most important concern of average workers at the down of the 21st century?

_____

_____

_____

2.   Identify three current issues that are getting union attention.

_____

_____

_____

3.   What explains the disparity between women's pay and men's pay?

_____

_____

_____

_____

4. How important is the issue of sexual harassment in the workplace? What is the problem with harassment policies?

_____
_____
_____
_____

Executives as Employees of Companies

1. Are senior executives entitled to the relatively high level of pay and generous benefits (e.g., stock options, pensions, bonuses) they receive from their employers? Explain.

_____
_____

2. What does management consultant Peter Drucker say regarding the level of executive compensation?

_____
_____
_____
_____

Caring for Children and Elders

1. Why has the issue of elder care become important in today's workplace?

_____
_____
_____
_____

2. Identify two questions surrounding the child care debate.
    a. _____
    b. _____

CHAPTER CHECK

1. How many manufacturing jobs were lost in Canada in the early 1990s?

_____

2. Describe the role of the Labour Relations Board.

_____
_____
_____
_____

3. Distinguish among the following types of hiring conditions:
    a. closed shop _____

    b. union shop _____

c. open shop _____

d. agency shop _____

4. List nine categories of matters normally covered in a union contract.

a. _____
b. _____
c. _____
d. _____
e. _____
f. _____
g. _____
h. _____

5. What step must precede a strike or lockout in most Canadian jurisdictions?

_____

6. In what provinces is it illegal for employers to use replacement workers while a strike is in progress?

_____

7. a. What is the overall rate of unionization in Canada?

_____

b. What is the rate of unionization in Canada for men? For women?

_____

c. What province has the highest rate of unionization? The lowest?

_____

8. What developments associated with trends in Canadian business have strained union-management relationships in recent years?

_____
_____
_____

9. What is a "golden parachute"?

_____
_____
_____

10. What factors have contributed to the dramatic reduction in the number of middle managers in Canadian business?

_____
_____
_____
_____

PRACTICE TEST

Multiple Choice: Circle the best answer.

1. Most historians agree that today's union movement is an outgrowth of
   a. the Great Depression
   b. the Civil War
   c. the Industrial Revolution
   d. the Revolutionary War

2. Which of the following is NOT generally covered by a union contract?
   a. Wages
   b. Seniority rights
   c. The cost of living
   d. Working conditions

3. Minimum wage legislation
   a. is illegal in Canada
   b. can be overruled by a collective agreement
   c. distinguishes between men and women
   d. exists in all provinces

4. When Dave Sutton went to work for a printing shop, he thought he was going to have to join the union representing the shop. However, on his first day of work he was told that while there was a union representing the workers, he was not required to join, and he didn't have to pay any dues to the union if he chose not to join. Dave works in a _____ shop.
   a. union
   b. agency
   c. closed
   d. open

5. When baseball players went on strike, an individual was brought in to help resolve the dispute between management and players. This third party was involved to make suggestions, but he did not make any decisions about how the players' dispute should be settled. This is an example of
   a. arbitration
   b. grievance
   c. mediation
   d. a bargaining zone

6. When organized labour encourages its members not to buy products made by a firm in a labour dispute, it is encouraging a(n)
   a. strike
   b. primary boycott
   c. secondary boycott
   d. injunction

7. Which of the following is NOT a tactic used by management in a labour dispute?
   a. lockout
   b. injunction
   c. use of strikebreakers
   d. secondary boycott

8. For unions to grow in the future, they will have to
   a. continue to grant givebacks to management
   b. begin to organize foreign workers
   c. adapt to a more culturally diverse, white collar workforce
   d. take up the fight against continuous improvement and employee involvement

9. The issue of comparable worth deals with
   a. paying equal wages to men and women who do the same job
   b. equal pay for different jobs that require similar levels of training and education or skills
   c. assuring that men and women have equal opportunity in the job market
   d. ensuring that executive pay is not more than 20 times the pay of the lowest paid worker

10. Companies have responded to requests for assistance in child care with all of the following EXCEPT
    a. discount arrangements with national child-care chains
    b. vouchers that offer payment toward the kind of child care the employee prefers

c. on-site child-care centres

d. increases in the number of allowable sick leave days for employees to use when a child is ill

True/False

1. During the Industrial Revolution, issues such as low wages and the use of child labor made the workplace ripe for the emergence of national labour unions.
2. The CIO, Congress of Industrial Organizations, grew out of the Knights of Labor.
3. Yellow dog contracts, preventing workers from joining a union as a condition of employment, were outlawed by the Fair Labour Standards Act.
4. In arbitration, an impartial third party can make a binding decision in a labour dispute.
5. Strikebreakers are often used to replace strikers during a prolonged strike until the dispute is resolved.
6. Unions have begun to take a leadership role in encouraging cooperation of employees in employee involvement programs.

7. In the past, the primary explanation for the disparity between men's and women's pay has been that women often aren't as educated as men.
8. Women file the majority of sexual harassment cases.
9. The issue of elder care is expected to decline in importance in coming years.
10. Executives are exempt from liability for corporate actions if they are also members of the company's board of directors.
11. Many Canadian unions started as locals of U.S. unions.

ANSWERS

Key Terms and Definitions

1. union shop
2. mediation
3. picketing
4. collective bargaining
5. open shop
6. Labour Relations Board
7. arbitration
8. closed shop
9. scabs
10. Boycott
11. Check-off
12. Grievance
13. Injunction
14. Agency shop (Rand formula)
15. Lockout
16. Replacement workers

The Major Issues Facing Labour-Management Relations

1. As the economy is transformed from labour-intensive manufacturing to an automated manufacturing and service economy, machinery replaces human beings in the hardest, dirtiest, most repetitive jobs. The jobs of the future require people to use their brains rather than their muscles.

History and Role of the Trade Unions in Canada

1. Most historians agree that the union movement of today is an outgrowth of the economic transition caused by the Industrial Revolution. The workers who worked in the fields suddenly became dependent upon factories for their living.
2. Workers were faced with the reality that if you failed to produce, you lost your job. Often workers went to work when they were ill or had family problems. The average workweek expanded to 60 or as many

as 90 hours per week. Wages were low and the use of child labour was common.

3. a. The development of crafts unions, beginning in 1792, came about to discuss work issues such as pay, hours, work conditions, and job security. The Industrial Revolution led to changes and problems for workers in terms of productivity, hours of work, wages, and unemployment. If you failed to produce, you lost your job. Hours worked increased to as many as 80 per week.

   b. The issues unions face today are similar to those that concerned the early labour unions. However, union negotiators today also address such issues as drug testing, benefits such as day care and elder care, violence in the workplace, and employee stock ownership programs.

5. The primary objectives of labour unions in the 1970's were increased pay and improved benefits. The focus is now on job security and on global competition and its effects.

Legislation Affecting Labour-Management Relations

1. a. minimum wage
   b. paid minimum holidays and vacation
   c. maximum hours
   d. overtime pay
   e. health and safety conditions
   f. workers' compensation for accidents
   g. unemployment insurance
   h. CPP/QPP

The Collective Bargaining Process

1. a. The process by which a union represents employees in relations with their employer.
   b. i.   union sign-up campaign
      ii.   vote and certification
      iii.   union local is established and officers are elected
      iv.   union members vote on proposed contract
      v.   contract governs labour-management relations
      vi.   grievance committee handles complaints
      vii.   negotiations on a new contract
      viii.   if no agreement, conciliation followed by strike or lockout

2. Forms of union contracts include
   a. union shop
   b. agency shop
   c. closed shop
   d. open shop

3. a. agency shop agreement   c. open shop agreement
   b. closed shop agreement   d. union shop agreement

4. There are three options available for resolving labour disputes. The players' union could have filed grievances against the owners before going on strike, in an attempt to resolve their differences without putting an end to the season. Either side could have brought in a mediator, before or during the strike. The mediator's job is to make suggestions for resolving the dispute. Lastly, arbitration could have been used. In arbitration, the parties agree to bring a third party to make a binding decision, a decision that both parties must adhere to. The arbitrator must be acceptable to both parties. In fact, an arbitrator was discussed between the players and the owners, but neither side could agree on the choice of an arbitrator.

5. Methods used to resolve labour-management disputes include

    a. grievances

    b. mediation

    c. arbitration

6. Sources of grievances are

    a. overtime rules

    b. promotions

    c. layoffs

    d. transfers

    e. job assignments

7. a. first-level supervisor: shop steward

    b. second-level supervisor: chief steward

    c. plant manager: chief grievance officer

    d. director of industrial relations: national or international union representative

    e. CEO or president: president of union or central labour body

    f. arbitration

8. a. the process of resolving disputes through an outside, impartial third party

    b. the use of a third party to attempt to bring the parties to a resolution of their dispute

9. Mediation becomes necessary if labour-management negotiators aren't able to agree on alternatives within the bargaining zone.

10. A mediator will encourage both sides to continue negotiating and make suggestions for resolving a work dispute. Mediators make suggestions, not decisions, about how a dispute should be settled.

11. In arbitration, an impartial third party will render a binding decision in the labour dispute. A mediator can only make suggestions.

12. In the future, unions will focus on

    a. child and elder care

    b. worker retraining

    c. two-tiered wage plans

    d. employee empowerment

    e. integrity and honesty testing

When Unions and Management Disagree

1. a. i.   rotating strikes

      ii.   full-fledged strikes

      iii. boycotts

      iv. pickets

   b. i.   lockouts

      ii.   layoffs

      iii. shortened workweek

      iv. close or go bankrupt

2. Lists will vary, but will probably include hospital workers, utility workers, customs workers, prison guards, firefighters. These people provide "essential services," and segments of the public would be put at risk if they were out on strike.

3. A strike provides public focus on a labour dispute and at times causes operations in a company to slow down or totally shut down.

4. A primary boycott is when labour encourages its membership not to buy the product of a firm involved in a labour dispute. A secondary boycott is an attempt to convince others to stop doing business with a firm that is the subject of a primary boycott.

5. For unions to grow, they will have to adapt to a workforce that is increasingly culturally diverse, white

collar, female, foreign born and professional. Increased global competition, advanced technology, and the changing nature of work have altered and threatened the jobs of many workers.

6. There are three options available. The players union could have filed grievances against the owners before going on strike in an attempt to resolve their differences without putting an end to the season. Either side could have brought in a mediator, before or during the strike. The mediator's job is to make suggestions for resolving the dispute. Lastly, arbitration could have been used. In arbitration, the parties agree to bring in a third party to make a binding decision that both parties must accept. The arbitrator must be acceptable to both parties. An arbitrator was discussed between the players and the owners, but neither could agree on the choice of an arbitrator!

Strikes, Lockouts, and the Law

1. Picketing is the process of strikers carrying picket signs and walking back and forth across entrances to their places of employment. The aim is to publicize the strike and discourage or prevent people, vehicles, materials, and products from going in or out.

2. Unions call them scabs; management calls them replacement workers. Hiring of replacement workers is illegal in Quebec and British Columbia.

3. An injunction is a court order requiring strikers to limit or cease picketing or to stop some threatening activity. Such injunctions are sought by the employer.

Structure and Size of Trade Unions in Canada

1. Just under four million
2. a. Canadian Labour Congress
   b. Confederation of National Trade Unions
   c. Canadian Federation of Labour
   d. American Federation of Labour and Congress of Industrial Organizations
3. Answers will vary, but include: salary level, group insurance plans, flexible working hours, child care, limited overtime, retraining.
4. Union leadership is becoming aware of the need to be competitive with foreign companies. Concepts such as constant improvement and constant creative innovation require the cooperation of employees working as a team with management, and unions have begun to encourage this. Unions are taking a leadership role in securing retraining programs. In cooperation with management, some unions are improving job security and establishing profit-sharing arrangements.

Future of Labour-Management Relations

1. Job security is now the number one issue.
2. Top current issues include:
   a. wage discrimination against women
   b. pension benefits for same-sex couples
   c. workforce reductions
   d. affirmative action
   e. AIDS-related issues.

Executives as Employees of Companies

1. Answers will vary, but should include consideration of the senior executive's high level of responsibility.
2. Management consultant Peter Drucker suggests that CEOs should not earn much more than 20 times as much as the company's lowest-paid employee.

Caring for Children and Elders

1. The issue has become important because the number of households with at least one adult providing elder care increased dramatically and continues to rise rapidly.
2. Two questions surrounding child care are
   a. who should provide child-care services
   b. who should pay for them

CHAPTER CHECK ANSWERS

1. 300,000
2. A quasi-judicial body that administers labour codes in each jurisdiction, including the right to union certification and collective bargaining
3. Closed: all new hires must already be union members
   Union: all new hires must become union members within a short period
   Open: employees are free to choose whether or not to join the union
   Agency: employees are free to choose whether to join the union, but must pay union dues in any event
4. a. wages, salaries, and other forms of compensation
   b. working hours and time off
   c. seniority rights
   d. benefit programs
   e. grievances
   f. health and safety
   g. union activities
   h. hiring conditions
   i. discipline
5. Conciliation
6. Quebec and British Columbia
7. a. 34.1%
   b. 38%, 29%
   c. Newfoundland, Alberta
8. Massive layoffs and plant closings associated with the need to be cost competitive in global markets.
9. A generous settlement given to a CEO when his employment with a company is terminated.
10. Computers, the recession, employee empowerment, and global competition.

PRACTICE TEST

Multiple Choice		True/False	
1.	c	1.	T
2.	c	2.	F
3.	d	3.	T
4.	d	4.	T
5.	c	5.	T
6.	b	6.	T
7.	d	7.	F
8.	c	8.	T
9.	b	9.	F
10.	d	10.	F
		11.	T

CHAPTER 15

Marketing: Building Customer and Stakeholder Relationships

Learning Goals

After you have read and studied this chapter, you should be able to

1. Explain the marketing concept.
2. Give an example of how to use the four Ps of marketing.
3. Describe the marketing research process, and tell how marketers use environmental scanning to learn about the changing marketing environment.
4. Explain various ways of segmenting the consumer market.
5. List several ways in which the business-to-business market differs from the consumer market.
6. Show how the marketing concept has been adapted to fit today's modern markets.
7. Describe the latest marketing strategies, such as stakeholder marketing and customer relationship management.

Key Terms and Definitions

Listed here are important terms found in this chapter. Choose the correct term for each definition and write it in the space provided.

	Green product	Primary data
Benefit segmentation (behavioural segmentation)	Market	Product
Brand name	Market segmentation	Promotion
Business-to-business (B2B) market	Marketing	Psychographic segmentation
Census metropolitan area (CMA)	Marketing concept	Relationship marketing
Consumer market	Marketing management	Secondary data
Customer relationship management	Marketing mix	Segment marketing
Demographic segmentation	Marketing research	Stakeholder marketing
Environmental scanning	Mass marketing	Target marketing
Focus group	Niche marketing	Test marketing
Geographic segmentation	One-to-one (individual) marketing	

1. _____ The analysis of markets to determine opportunities and challenges, and to find the information needed to make good decisions.

2. _____ Marketing directed toward those groups (market segments) an organization decides it can serve profitably.

3. _____ The ingredients that go into a marketing program: product, price, promotion, and place.

4. _____ The process of determining the wants and needs of others and

then satisfying those wants and needs with quality goods and services.

5. _____ The process of planning and executing the conception, pricing, promotion, and distribution of ideas, goods, and services to create mutually beneficial exchanges.

6. _____ A three-part business philosophy: (1) a customer orientation, (2) a service orientation, and (3) a profit orientation.

7. _____ Establishing and maintaining mutually beneficial exchange relationships over time with all the stakeholders of the organization.

8. _____ Word, letter, or groups of words or letters that differentiates one seller's goods and services from those of competitors.

9. _____ Any physical good, service, or idea that satisfies a want or need.

10. _____ All the individuals and organizations that want goods and services to use in producing other goods and services or to rent, sell, or supply goods to others.

11. _____ All the individuals or households that want goods and services for personal consumption or use.

12. _____ All the techniques sellers use to motivate people to buy products or services.

13. _____ A small group of people who meet under the direction of a discussion leader to communicate their opinions about an organization, its products, or other given issues.

14. _____ A product whose production, use, and disposal don't damage the environment.

15. _____ Developing products and promotions that are designed to please large groups of people.

16. _____ The process of finding small but profitable market segments and designing custom-made products for them.

17. _____ Marketing whose goal is to keep individual customers over time by offering them products that exactly meet their requirements.

18. _____ A group of people with unsatisfied wants and needs, and who have the resources, willingness, and authority to buy products.

19. _____ Information that has been compiled by others, found in published newspapers, magazines, textbooks, online, etc.

20. _____ Facts and figures not previously published that you have gathered on your own.

21. _____ The process of dividing the total market into several groups whose members have similar characteristics.

22. _____ Developing a unique mix of goods and services for each individual customer.

23. _____ The process of testing products among potential users.

24. _____ The process of identifying the factors that can affect marketing success.

25. _____ Dividing the market by geographic area.

26. _____ Dividing the market by age, income, and education level.

27. _____ Dividing the market using the group's values, attitudes, and interests.

28. _____ Dividing the market by determining which benefits of the product to talk about.

29. _____ Learning as much as possible about your present customers and getting very close to them rather than constantly seeking new customers.

30. _____ The process of deciding which groups to serve and then developing products specially tailored to their needs.

31. _____ A geographic area that has a population of 100,000 or more.

A Brief History of Marketing

1. What is the popular slogan used to describe marketing?

   _____

2. What is the idea of *customer relationship management?*

   _____
   _____
   _____
   _____

3. What is the goal of the marketing process?

   _____
   _____
   _____
   _____

4. Marketing concepts are applied in nonprofit institutions as well as profit-making ones. This is a time of declining enrolments for many schools. How has your college adopted the marketing concept to avoid drastic drops in enrolment?

   _____
   _____
   _____
   _____

5. The focus of business in Canada has evolved from a production orientation to a sales orientation to the current consumer orientation, known as the marketing concept.

   Match the following statements to the correct orientation.

   a. _____ "Sales are down. We need to call in our sales force and give them a pep talk."

b. _____ "Let's find out what's causing this increase in consumer complaints."

c. _____ "As long as we make a good product, people are going to buy it."

d. _____ "Our research indicates that our customers want more options to choose from. Let's see if we can work with production to make those options available."

e. _____ "The competition is killing us. Let's put some more money into advertising."

f. _____ "The competition is killing us. Let's step up production and flood the market with our product."

Marketing Management and the Marketing Mix

1. What is mutually beneficial exchange?

   _____
   _____
   _____
   _____

2. What does a marketing manager do? What is marketing management?

   _____
   _____
   _____
   _____

3. What three elements are necessary for a market?
   a. _____
   b. _____
   c. _____

4. What are the eight steps in the marketing process?
   a. _____
   b. _____
   c. _____
   d. _____
   e. _____
   f. _____
   g. _____
   h. _____

5. What is meant by "concept testing"?

   _____
   _____
   _____
   _____

6. What are four promotion techniques?
   a. _____

b. _____

c. _____

d. _____

7. What are *prototypes?*

_____
_____
_____
_____

8. What are marketing intermediaries?

_____
_____
_____
_____

9. Todd Whitman was a full-time student at Mount Royal College. In addition to going to school Todd also worked for a company out of P.E.I. that made ice cream. As Todd tells it: "Alan Reed owns a potato farm in P.E.I. He was looking for another market for his potatoes when he realized that the chemical make-up of the potato was such that it could be used in making a tasty ice cream without using any sugar — i.e., a sugar-free ice cream. He figured there had to be a market for that kind of product, and so made a few batches and tried it on his friends, without telling them it was made of potatoes." He called the ice cream Al and Reed's. This is where Todd came in: While in Calgary, Todd's job was to attempt to get the product sold to Calgarians. His employers shipped him a few gallons (as much as he could hold in his home freezer). Todd started with a local grocery store chain, and ultimately got one of them to sell the ice cream on a trial basis. He also brought some samples to his business class, after persuading his teacher to allow a taste testing in class. The product went over pretty well, until the students found out it was made from potatoes!

Todd continued his promotional efforts with the grocery stores, calling on them whenever he could, leaving pamphlets explaining the concept and production of ice cream made from potatoes, and offering the stores discounts for volume buying.

a. Identify the steps in marketing which were taken by Todd and Alan Reed.

i. _____

ii. _____

iii. _____

iv. _____

v. _____

vi. _____

b. What potential problem might they confront with this product? How could Todd and Alan use the last step of the marketing process to overcome the problem?

_____
_____
_____
_____
_____

10. The marketing mix consists of four variables that are partly controlled by the marketing manager. The variables are

Product	A good or service designed to appeal to customers.
Price	What and how the customer pays for the product.
Promotion	The means of communicating product attributes to the customer, and of determining customer wants.
Place	Making goods and services available where and when customers need them.

Identify whether each statement below reflects an activity relating to product, price, promotion, or place.

a. _____ Procter & Gamble introduces a new version of an old product, a concentrated form of powdered laundry detergent, Tide.

b. _____ A furniture retailer makes a "90 days same as cash" offer i.e., no interest charges if you pay within 90 days.

c. _____ Colgate Palmolive offers toothpaste with a flip-top cap.

d. _____ Discovery Toys are distributed through "at home" parties.

e. _____ A grocery store buys its fresh produce from a local food broker.

f. _____ To encourage sales, sample-size boxes of new Froot Loops with new lime green flavours are mailed to homes in selected neighbourhoods.

g. _____ General Foods spends $450 million on advertising in one year.

h. _____ Sony offers a $1 rebate on its blank videotapes.

i. _____ Domino's pizza offers 12" and 16" pizzas with a choice of 12 different toppings.

j. _____ The student bookstore on a college campus offers a 10% discount to faculty and staff members.

Providing Marketers With Information

1. What are three things that marketing research helps to determine?

   a. _____

   b. _____

   c. _____

2. Who should market researchers pay attention to?

   _____

   _____

   _____

   _____

3. What are the four steps of the marketing research process?

   a. _____

b. _____
c. _____
d. _____

4. What is the difference between primary and secondary data?

_____
_____
_____

5. How does a database help in the marketing of products?

_____
_____
_____
_____

6. What are six general sources of secondary data?

a. _____ d. _____
b. _____ e. _____
c. _____ f. _____

7. What are five sources of primary data?

a. _____ d. _____
b. _____ e. _____
c. _____

8. What do marketers need to do in order to conduct effective marketing research?

_____
_____
_____

9. Why is the need for research even greater for international markets?

_____
_____
_____

10. What does it take to do effective marketing research?

_____
_____
_____
_____
_____

11. What is the benefit of secondary data?

_____
_____
_____
_____

12. What is the observation method of collecting data?

_____
_____
_____
_____

13. What are some of the most common types of surveys?

_____
_____
_____
_____

14. How have company web sites improved the market research process?

_____
_____
_____
_____

15. What is the most dramatic global change? Why?

_____
_____
_____
_____

16. What have been the most dramatic technological changes? Why?

_____
_____
_____
_____

17. What are some social trends that marketers must monitor?

_____
_____
_____
_____

18. How has the Internet affeted competition?

_____
_____
_____
_____

19. How would marketing change with a change in the economy?

_____
_____
_____

The Consumer Market and Market Segmentation

1. What are two major markets in marketing?

   _____

   _____

   _____

   _____

2. What determines if a product is a business-to-business product or a consumer product?

   _____

   _____

   _____

   _____

3. Why do companies use market segmentation?

   _____

   _____

   _____

   _____

4. What are five ways in which the consumer market can be segmented?

   a. _____

   b. _____

   c. _____

   d. _____

   e. _____

5. What kind of segmentation is being used when we:

   a. segment by what qualities a customer prefers?   _____

   b. segment by where people live?   _____

   c. segment by how much a customer uses?   _____

   d. segment by a group's values, attitudes, or interests?   _____

   e. segment by age, income, or education?   _____

6. Because many sellers offer products that don't have universal appeal, the seller divides the total market into groups whose members have similar characteristics. The segmentation variables are

] Geographic	] Benefits
] Demographic	] Volume
] Psychographic	

   Determine (a) which of these variables was used to segment the market in the following situation; and (b) where applicable, which specific variable was used.

   i. Secret brand deodorant is "made for a woman."   a.

                                                                                   b.

   ii. "Jolt" pop is available only in western Canada.   a.

iii.   Charlie perfume is aimed at women aspiring to shape their own lives and develop a career.

                                                        b.
                                                        a.

iv.   General Electric offers G.E. Spacemaker Appliances to mount under kitchen cabinets and reduce "counter clutter."

                                                        b.
                                                        a.

v.   Detergent manufacturers package their products in "king-size" packages for families who do a lot of laundry.

                                                        b.

7.   What are the steps in the consumer decision-making process?

  a. _____

  b. _____

  c. _____

  d. _____

  e. _____

8.   List the four types of influences on the consumer decision-making process.

  a. _____

  b. _____

  c. _____

  d. _____

9.   What is a "reference group"?

_____

_____

_____

_____

10. Before consumers make a purchase, they often go through a series of steps before making the final selection. Those steps are

☐ Problem recognition

☐ Information search

☐ Alternative evaluation

☐ Purchase decision

☐ Post-purchase evaluation (Cognitive dissonance)

Match the following statements to the correct decision-making stage.

a. _____ "There are three stereo systems in my price range, but this compact disc player has the best sound quality."

b. _____ "My old stereo system just blew a speaker. I'm ready for a new one."

c. _____ "How do you like that compact disc player you bought last month?"

d. _____ "I got a great deal on this system. I'm glad I bought it when I did."

e. _____ "I'm going to buy this system. It looks like the best value."

11. We have been "creating" a company, and its product, Music-stor, throughout several chapters. Now is the time to begin developing a marketing plan for our product. We will become more specific in the following chapters. Generally,

a. What need did Eric see when he came up with the idea of Music-stor?

_____

_____

_____

_____

b. Who/what do you think should be Music-stor's customers?

_____

_____

_____

_____

c. How could concept testing have helped Eric?

_____

_____

_____

_____

d. How do the various elements of the marketing environment affect Music-stor?

_____

_____

_____

_____

_____

e. Could Music-stor make use of "customized marketing"?

_____

_____

_____

_____

_____

_____

12. How does a mass marketer "operate"?

_____

_____

_____

_____

13. What is the goal of relationship marketing?

_____

_____

_____

_____

14. How is a "community of customers" established?

_____

_____

_____

15. What has made "niche marketing" possible?

_____

_____

_____

16. What is one-to-one marketing?

_____

_____

_____

_____

The Business-To-Business Market

1. How does industrial marketing (business-to-business marketing) differ from consumer marketing?

_____

_____

_____

_____

2. What are five factors that differentiate industrial marketing (business-to-business marketing) from consumer marketing?

   a. _____
   b. _____
   c. _____
   d. _____
   e. _____

3. "... the buyer's reason for buying and the end use of the product is what determines whether a product is considered a consumer product or an industrial product."
   Determine whether the following describe consumer or industrial products.

   a. _____ Monsanto Inc. buys apples to sell in its company cafeteria.
   b. _____ Jeff Walter buys a lawn mower for his lawn-mowing business.
   c. _____ Darlene Knott buys a lawn mower to mow her new lawn.
   d. _____ Marti Galganski buys apples for her daughter's lunch.

4. Although the basic principles of industrial marketing are similar to those used in consumer marketing, the marketing strategies are different, because industrial buyers are different. Show how industrial marketing is different from consumer marketing for the following marketing factors.

   a. Target market

_____

b. Product

_____

_____

c. Price

_____

_____

d. Promotion

_____

_____

e. Place

_____

_____

f. Influence on the purchase decision

_____

_____

5. How would you classify Music-stor's product? What characteristics of the business-to-business market will affect Music-stor's marketing efforts, and why?

_____

_____

_____

_____

_____

_____

_____

_____

Updating the Marketing Concept

1. What is a customer orientation?

_____

_____

_____

2. What is a service orientation?

_____

_____

_____

3. What is a profit orientation?

_____

4.	What is meant by "delighting customers"?

_____

_____

_____

5.	How is the implementation of the marketing concept integrated into a firm's decisions about its marketing mix variables?

_____

_____

_____

_____

_____

6.	Let's continue helping Music-stor develop a marketing plan:
	a.	Who would you choose as Music-stor's target market?

	_____

	_____

	_____

	_____

	b.	If you choose to target the consumer market, what are some variables that you would want to consider?

	_____

	_____

	_____

	_____

	c.	How would marketing your product to an industrial market differ from marketing the product to the consumer market?

	_____

	_____

	_____

	_____

	_____

	_____

Establishing Relationships With All Stakeholders

1.	How does the traditional marketing concept differ from modern marketing? What must be balanced?

_____

_____

_____

_____

2.　How have companies responded to the environmental movement? How does this demonstrate stakeholder marketing?

_____
_____
_____
_____

3.　What is the "80/20" rule?

_____
_____
_____
_____

4.　Why is customer relationship management so important?

_____
_____
_____
_____

CHAPTER CHECK

1.　Name three phases of business philosophy that Canadian firms have gone through.
   a.　_____
   b.　_____
   c.　_____

2.　What are the three basic elements of the marketing concept?
   a.　_____
   b.　_____
   c.　_____

3.　Describe the concept of a "societal orientation."

_____
_____
_____
_____

4.　List the four variables in the marketing mix — the four Ps.
   a.　_____　c.　_____
   b.　_____　d.　_____

5.　What are the four factors important in environmental scanning?
   a.　_____　c.　_____
   b.　_____　d.　_____

6.　What are the two major types of markets in marketing?
   a.　_____
   b.　_____

7. What two things determine the classification of a product as an industrial good or a consumer good?

   a. _____

   b. _____

8. There are five major variables used to segment the consumer market. They are

   a. _____   d. _____

   b. _____   e. _____

   c. _____

9. What are the four variables used to determine if a target market is worthwhile?

   a. _____

   b. _____

   c. _____

   d. _____

10. Describe (a) the consumer decision-making process, and (b) the outside influences on the process.

   a. _____

   _____

   _____

   _____

   _____

   _____

   b. _____

   _____

   _____

   _____

   _____

   _____

   _____

   _____

   _____

11. What are seven characteristics of industrial markets?

   a. _____

   b. _____

   c. _____

   d. _____

   e. _____

   f. _____

   g. _____

PRACTICE TEST

Multiple Choice: Circle the best answer.

1. If a "customer is king," then _____ must come first in business activities.

   a. production   c. marketing

   b. distribution   d. planning

2. The basis of marketing is to

   a. find a need and fill it.

   b. produce as many products as possible.

c. look for a market, then make a product.

d. find a good product and make it available at a reasonable price.

3. When McDonald's considered adding pizza to their menu, the company made pizza available in some of their markets to determine customer reactions. That process is called

   a. promotion   c. outsourcing

   b. test marketing   d. concept testing

4. Which of the following would NOT be included in a discussion of the marketing concept?

   a. a customer orientation

   b. training employees in customer service

   c. profit orientation

   d. establishing a market

5. When a firm is in the business of "delighting" the customer, what is it doing?

   a. charging the lowest possible price

   b. using advertising that is attractive and humorous

   c. providing products that exceed customer expectations

   d. making products available in unexpected places

6. Businesses have learned that employees won't provide first-class goods and services to customers unless they

   a. receive first-class treatment themselves

   b. are paid wages considerably above average

   c. are members of cross-functional, self-managed teams

   d. are given regular promotions

7. Balancing the wants and needs of all a firm's stakeholders, such as employees, suppliers, dealers, and the community, is known as

   a. a consumer orientation   c. mass marketing

   b. relationship marketing   d. forming a community of buyers

8. At one time, companies developed products and promotions to please large groups of people, and tried to sell as many products to as many people as possible. This is known as

   a. relationship marketing

   b. a consumer orientation

   c. forming a community of buyers

   d. mass marketing

9. A mutually beneficial exchange occurs when

   a. the company gets the price it wants

   b. the marketing mix has been satisfied

   c. both the company and its stakeholders believe they have received good value for their efforts

   d. a marketing manager has designed a marketing program that effectively combines the marketing mix variables

10. Which of the following is NOT considered one of the marketing mix variables?

   a. producing a want-satisfying product

   b. promoting the product

   c. simplifying the production process

   d. setting a price for the product

11. Alonzo Wilder has just been hired as the marketing manager for the L. Ingalls farming co-op. In his job as marketing manager, Alonzo's primary responsibility will be to

   a. make sure the product is priced reasonably

   b. manage the primary sales force

   c. monitor production and make sure the product is in the right place at the right time

d. manage the marketing mix variables to ensure an effective marketing program

12. Which of the following is NOT a requirement for a "market"?
   a. people with unsatisfied wants and needs
   b. people who have the authority to buy
   c. people who have the resources to buy
   d. people who have the willingness to buy

13. Marketing research helps determine all of the following EXCEPT
   a. how customer needs will change
   b. what customers have purchased in the past
   c. what changes have occurred to change what customers want
   d. what customers are likely to want in the future

14. What is the first step in the marketing research process?
   a. analyze data   c. define the problem
   b. collect data   d. develop potential solutions

15. Curious George went to the library to look up government statistics on the amount of bananas imported into Canada during the previous year. Curious was making use of
   a. primary data   c. the observation method
   b. secondary data   d. focused research

16. What must be done in order to conduct effective marketing research?
   a. Develop a good understanding of the mass market.
   b. Make sure that all research is up-to-date.
   c. Use as many secondary sources as possible to keep costs down.
   d. Get out of the office and close to customers to determine their needs.

True/False

1. The role of marketing is to make a good or service, and then make sure people want to buy it.

2. Marketing middlemen are organizations that traditionally are in the middle of a series of organizations that distribute goods from producers to consumers.

3. According to the text, most organizations have reached the goal of delighting customers.

4. Competitive benchmarking means that companies will only concentrate on those activities which they do best, and they will outsource those functions at which they do not excel.

5. Relationship marketing leads away from mass production toward more custom-made goods and services.

6. The four marketing mix variables are product, price, packaging, and promotion.

7. One goal of marketing research is to determine exactly what the consumers what and need.

8. To minimize costs, it is best to use secondary data first, when possible.

9. In determining the best solution in the marketing research process, companies should consider what's the right thing to do as well as the profitable thing to do.

10. The process of dividing the total market into several groups is called target marketing.

11. The reason for distinguishing between consumer markets and the business-to-business market is that strategies for reaching the market are different, because the buyers are different.

12. Industrial sales tend to be less direct than consumer sales, because industrial buyers use more middlemen.

ANSWERS

Key Terms and Definitions

1. marketing research
2. target marketing
3. marketing mix
4. Marketing
5. marketing management
6. marketing concept
7. stakeholder marketing
8. brand name
9. Product
10. business-to-business (B2B) market
11. consumer market
12. Promotion
13. Focus group
14. Green product
15. Mass marketing
16. niche marketing
17. Relationship marketing
18. Market
19. Secondary data
20. primary data
21. market segmentation
22. one-to-one (individual) marketing
23. test marketing
24. environmental scanning
25. geographic segmentation
26. demographic segmentation
27. psychographic segmentation
28. benefit (behavioural) segmentation
29. customer relationship management (CRM)
30. segment marketing
31. census metropolitan area (CMA)

A Brief History of Marketing

1. "Find a need and fill it."
2. The idea of customer relationship management is to get close to your customers and spend time with them, rather than to continually seek out new customers. It is important to learn as much as possible about customers and do everything you can to satisfy them or delight them with goods and services over time.
3. The goal of the marketing process is to find a need and fill it.
4. Schools can take a number of steps to implement the marketing concept: student forums to encourage students to express their needs; classes at times all students can take them; improved quality by hiring professors with good qualifications; enforced academic standards for admission and progression; as well as constantly following trends in business and other areas to keep updated.
5. a. Sales orientation
    b. Marketing concept
    c. Production orientation
    d. Marketing concept
    e. Sales orientation
    f. Production orientation

Marketing Management and the Marketing Mix

1. A mutually beneficial exchange means that both parties to the exchange believe they have received good value for their efforts.
2. A marketing manager designs a marketing program that effectively combines the ingredients of the marketing mix in order to please customers. Marketing management is the process of planning and executing the conception, pricing, promotion, and distribution of goods and services to create mutually beneficial exchanges.

3. A market must have
   a. people with unsatisfied wants and needs.
   b. people who have the resources to buy.
   c. people who have the willingness to buy.
4. a. Find a need
   b. Conduct research
   c. Design the product
   d. Do product testing
   e. Determine brand name, design package, set price
   f. Select distribution system
   g. Design promotional program
   h. Build relationship with customers
5. In concept testing, an accurate description of a product is developed, and then people are asked whether the concept appeals to them.
6. Promotion techniques include
   a. advertising
   b. personal selling
   c. publicity
   d. sales promotion
7. Prototypes are samples of the product that you take to consumers to test their reactions.
8. Marketing intermediaries or middlemen are organizations that specialize in distributing products. They are called middlemen because they are in the middle of a series of organizations that distribute goods from producers to consumers.
9. a. i. Alan Reed recognized the need for a sugar-free ice cream.
   ii. He tested the concept by making small batches (prototype) and testing the product with his friends.
   iii. The test marketing stage was combined with concept testing. You could also say that the product was tested in Calgary.
   iv. The brand name stems from the originator's name, Al and Reed.
   v. The marketing middleman is the grocery store that finally agreed to sell the product through the efforts of Todd Whitman.
   vi. Promotion was done primarily through pamphlets.
   b. Probably the biggest potential problem is the negative reaction to the product due to the fact that it's made from potatoes. Todd found this reaction in his class test. By talking with both the consumers and the grocery store managers, they may find ways to overcome the perception that ice cream made from potatoes must taste terrible!
10. a. Product
    b. Price
    c. Product
    d. Place
    e. Place
    f. Promotion
    g. Promotion
    h. Price
    i. Product
    j. Price

Providing Marketers With Information

1. Marketing research helps to determine
   a. what customers have purchased in the past.
   b. what situational changes have occurred to change what customers want.
   c. what they're likely to want in the future.

2. Market researchers should pay attention to what employees, shareholders, dealers, consumer advocates, media representatives, and other stakeholders have to say.

3. The steps of the marketing research process are as follows:
   a. Define the problem and determine the present situation.
   b. Collect data.
   c. Analyze the research data.
   d. Choose the best solutions.

4. Primary data are statistics and information not previously published that you gather on your own through observation, surveys, and personal interviews or focus groups. Secondary data are published reports and research from journals, trade associations, the government, information services, and others. Secondary data would be used before primary whenever possible.

5. The role of marketing is to determine exactly what the customers want and then to provide products that fill those needs. Because purchases are recorded in a database, knowing what customers want is much easier. Using the information in the database, stores can send out coupons and advertisements specifically designed to appeal to certain groups.

6. Sources of secondary data include the following:
   a. Government publications
   b. Commercial publications
   c. Magazines
   d. Newspapers
   e. Internal company sources
   f. Internet searches

7. Sources of primary data include the following:
   a. Observation
   b. Surveys
   c. Experiments
   d. Focus groups
   e. Questionnaires

8. Effective marketing research calls for getting out of the office and getting close to customers to find out what they want and need. Laboratory research and consumer panels can never replace going into people's homes, watching them use products, and asking them what improvements they would like.

9. In international markets, one must learn the culture of the people and talk with them directly. To find a need and fill it in the international market, marketers must adapt to all the customs and beliefs of the people with whom they are dealing.

10. To be effective in conducting market research, one must get out of the office and get close to consumers to find out what they want and need.

11. The benefit of secondary data is that it is less expensive to gather information that has already been researched by others.

12. In the observation method, data are collected by observing the actions of potential buyers.

13. The most common methods of gathering survey information are telephone surveys, online surveys, mail surveys, and personal interviews.

14. Company websites have improved the market research process because the company can now continuously interact with its customers and other consumers to improve products and services.

15. The most dramatic global change is the growth of the Internet. Now a company can reach many of the consumers in the world relatively easily, and can carry on a dialogue about what consumers want.

16. The most important technological changes also involve the Internet and the growth of consumer

databases. Using these, companies can develop products and services that more closely match the needs of consumers.

17. Marketers must monitor social trends such as population growth and changing demographics such as the growing population of older people and the shifting ethnic nature of the Canadian population.

18. Brick and mortar companies must be aware of new competition from the Internet. Consumers can now search literally all over the world for the best prices through the Internet.

19. If the economy slows or falls on hard economic times, marketers have to adapt by offering products that are less expensive or more tailored to a slow-growth economy.

The Consumer Market and Market Segmentation

1. The two major markets in marketing are the consumer market and the business-to-business market.

2. The buyer's reason for buying and the end use of the product determine whether a product is considered a consumer product or an industrial product.

3. Consumer groups differ in age, education level, income and taste, and a business usually cannot fill the needs of every group. So the company must decide what groups to serve, and develop products and services tailored to meet their needs.

4. a. geographic
   b. demographic
   c. psychographic
   d. benefit/behavioural
   e. volume

5. a. benefit/behavioural
   b. geographic
   c. volume
   d. psychographic
   e. demographic

6. i.   a. Demographic
        b. Gender
   ii. a. Geographic
        b. Region
   iii. a. Psychographic
        b. Lifestyle
   iv. a. Benefit
        b. Convenience
   v.   a. Volume
        b. Heavy users

7. The steps in the consumer decision-making process are as follows:
   a. Problem recognition
   b. Information research
   c. Alternative evaluation
   d. Purchase decision
   e. Post-purchase evaluation (Cognitive dissonance)

8. Types of influence on consumer decision-making include
   a. Marketing mix influences — product, price, promotion, place
   b. Sociocultural influences — reference groups, family, social class, culture, subculture
   c. Situational influences — type of purchase, social surroundings, physical surroundings, previous experience

d. Psychological influences — perception, attitudes. learning, motivation

9. A reference group is the group that an individual uses as a reference point in the formation of his beliefs, attitudes, values, or behaviour.

10. a. Alternative evaluation
    b. Problem recognition
    c. Information research
    d. Post-purchase evaluation (cognitive dissonance)
    e. Purchase decision

11. a. Eric may have seen that more people are listening to tapes and compact discs in their cars. Compact discs especially are growing in popularity. When people want to listen to their own music in the car, a convenient place to store several tapes or CDs would be a real benefit.

    b. We have discussed two types of customers, the automotive manufacturers, for installation as an option in new cars, and the after-market dealers, like auto supply stores, for people who want to install their own.

    c. Asking people if they need a product such as this would have given Eric a feel for what demand might have been. He would have to be sure to ask the right questions of the right people to get an accurate idea. He could have given prototypes to friends, or potential customers, for use, to "field test" or test market the product.

    d. The *social* environment consists of trends and population shifts, for example. The trend toward installing compact disc players in autos, for example, contributes to a positive outlook for Music-stor's product. As the population ages, more people may prefer to listen to music they bring along, rather than the radio. Since that type of equipment comes only in certain kinds of cars, *economic factors* such as disposable income and unemployment would affect demand for the cars, and thus for Music-stor's product. With a rapidly expanding *global* market, there may be possibilities outside the United States, as well as potential competition. *Technology* has affected Music-stor simply by virtue of the fact that CD players are a fact of life in cars today. Further, new high-tech production techniques will help Music-stor to produce more products with fewer people at a lower cost.

    f. Can Music-stor adopt customized marketing? Basically, the product must be made to suit many different models of car, with different interior shapes, different interior colours. The product is "custom made" for "customized marketing."

12. A mass marketer tries to sell products to as many people as possible, using mass media such as TV, radio, and newspapers. Many marketing managers will get so caught up with their products and competition that they become less responsive to the market.

13. Relationship marketing leads away from mass production toward more custom-made goods and services. The goal is to keep individual customers over time by offering them more products that exactly meet their requirements. It is more concerned with retaining old customers than creating new ones. This is done with special deals, fantastic service, loyalty programs, and maintaining databases that enable companies to custom-make products for customers.

14. A community of customers is established by creating a database so that every contact with customers results in more information about them. Over time, the seller knows more and more about consumers. Companies establish Web sites where customers can provide their input and talk to other customers. Some companies will have events where the manufacturer sends merchandise, staff, information, and giveaway items. Community bonding leads to a strong commitment to the company and its products.

15. New manufacturing techniques make it possible to develop specialized products for small market groups. This is called niche marketing.

16. One-to-one marketing means developing a unique mix of goods and services for each individual

customer. Travel agencies often develop such packages. This is easier to do in industrial markets where customers buy in large volume.

The Business-To-Business Market

1. The strategies differ between consumer marketing and industrial (business-to-business) marketing.
2. Factors that differentiate industrial (business-to-business) marketing from consumer marketing include the following:
   a. The number of customers in the industrial market is relatively few.
   b. The size of industrial customers is relatively large.
   c. Industrial markets tend to be geographically concentrated.
   d. Industrial buyers generally are more rational than individual consumers.
   e. Industrial sales tend to be direct.
3. a. Industrial   c. Consumer
   b. Industrial   d. Consumer
4. a. Target market is smaller, but individual customers make larger purchases. The customers are geographically concentrated.
   b. Demand for industrial products is derived from demand for consumer products. Product is used in making other goods and services, rather than by an end consumer.
   c. Price changes don't always significantly affect demand.
   d. Promotion is primarily performed through personal sales, with little advertising.
   e. Products are sold directly to the industrial buyer, rather than through wholesalers and retailers, as they would be for the consumer market.
   f. Industrial buyers are more rational in their purchases than consumers. There are fewer influences in the decision-making process.
5. Music-stor's product could be classified as both a consumer product and a product for the business-to-business market. If Eric sells the storage case through after-market auto equipment retailers, the product would be considered a consumer good. In attempting to reach automobile manufacturers, Eric is developing a business-to-business marketing relationship. The characteristics of the business-to-business market listed in your text will affect Music-stor in a number of ways. First, the primary market is the automotive industry, which has relatively few customers compared to the consumer market. The few car manufacturers are very large corporations, among the largest in the world, each with significant buying power. The domestic car market, at least, is concentrated in one geographic area. If Eric were to try to appeal to buyers for foreign manufacturers, he would have to do some more travelling. These buyers will consider Eric's product based on the "total product offer," including how much more marketable Music-stor will make *their* product, in addition to factors such as quality and price. If the customer is the auto industry, Eric won't need to use wholesalers or retailers, but will instead sell directly to the car companies. For the consumer market, he will have to use at least a retail distribution centre.

Updating the Marketing Concept

1. A customer orientation is to find out what customers want and provide it for them.
2. A service orientation involves training employees from all areas in customer service to ensure customer satisfaction.
3. In pursuing a profit orientation, a firm will market those goods and services that will earn the firm a profit and enable it to survive and expand to serve more customers.
4. The goal of some total quality firms is to delight customers by providing goods and services that exactly meet their requirements or exceed their expectations. The objective then is to make sure

that the response to customer wants and needs is so fast and courteous that customers are truly surprised and pleased by the experience.

5. The consumer is the focus of the decisions made about the marketing mix variables. A consumer orientation helps a firm to make better, more appropirate marketing mix decisions.

6. Keep in mind these are suggested answers, and you may come up with a totally different plan.

    a. We have often mentioned two target markets for Music-stor: the automotive equipment market, to be installed as cars are assembled; and a consumer market, through auto parts stores, for people who want to install the product later. You may have decided on another way to approach the market.

    b. If you chose the consumer market, many variables need to be considered. Demographic and geographic factors must be considered as well as other related variables. This is where research can really come in handy.

    c. To market to the industrial market, Music-stor must focus on personal selling in a very concentrated market. The automobile industry has few domestic producers, some foreign manufacturers with production facilities here in the United States. You would have to focus on quality, be able to meet the volume required to sell to the industrial market, and meet delivery requirements that may include dealing with a just-in-time inventory control system. This would require a sophisticated production and delivery system on the part of Music-stor.

7. Competitive benchmarking means that companies compare their processes and products with those of the best companies in the world to learn how to improve them.

8. In pursuing a profit orientation a firm must make sure that everyone in the organization understands that the purpose behind pleasing customers and uniting the organization is to ensure a profit for the firm. Using that profit, the organization can then satisfy other stakeholders of the firm.

Establishing Relationships With All Stakeholders

1. The traditional marketing concept emphasized giving customers what they want. Modern marketing goes further by recognizing the need to please other stakeholders as well. The firm must balance the needs and wants of all the firm's stakeholders, such as employees, customers, suppliers, dealers, stockholders, media representatives and the community.

2. Organizations have responded to the environmental movement when designing and marketing green products. Organizations that adopt stakeholder marketing keep the environmental community's needs in mind when designing these green products.

3. The 80/20 rule says that 80% of your business is likely to come from just 20% of your customers.

4. Customer relationship management is so important because it is far more expensive to get a new customer than to strengthen a relationship with an existing one.

CHAPTER CHECK ANSWERS

1. a. Production
    b. Sales
    c. Marketing concept
2. a. A consumer orientation
    b. Training all employees in customer service
    c. A profit orientation
3. A societal orientation includes a consumer orientation, but is broader to include programs designed to improve the community, reduce energy consumption, and other programs designed to respond to the broader needs of society and the environment. These goals are pursued without putting profit as a primary consideration, but often result in higher profits.

4. a. Product
   b. Price
   c. Place
   d. Promotion
5. a. Societal forces
   b. Economic realities and conditions
   c. Technological development
   d. Legal and regulatory
6. a. Consumer market
   b. Industrial market
7. a. The buyer's reason for buying
   b. End use
8. a. Geographic segmentation
   b. Demographic segmentation
   c. Psychographic segmentation
   d. Benefit segmentation
   e. Volume segmentation
9. a. Size and growth potential
   b. How reachable the segment is
   c. The nature of the market
   d. The nature of the company
10. a. Decision Process
    i. Problem recognition
    ii. Information search
    iii. Alternative evaluation
    iv. Purchase decision
    v. Post-purchase evaluation
   b. *Marketing Mix Variables*
    i. Product
    ii. Price
    iii. Promotion
    iv. Place
   Psychological Influences
    i. Perception
    ii. Attitudes
    iii. Learning
    iv. Motivation

   Situational Influence
    i. Type of purchase
    ii. Social surroundings
    iii. Physical surroundings
    iv. Previous experience
   Sociocultural Influence
    i. Reference group
    ii. Family
    iii. Social class
    iv. Culture
    v. Subculture

11. a. Derived demand
    b. Inelastic demand
    c. Few customers
    d. Customers are large
    e. Customers are geographically concentrated
    f. Rational decision making in the purchase process
    g. Direct sales — fewer middlemen

PRACTICE TEST

Multiple Choice
1. c
2. a
3. b

True/False
1. F
2. T
3. F

4.	d
5.	c
6.	a
7.	b
8.	d
9.	c
10.	c
11.	d
12.	b
13.	a
14.	c
15.	b
16.	d

4.	F
5.	T
6.	F
7.	T
8.	T
9.	T
10.	F
11.	T
12.	F

CHAPTER 16

Developing and Pricing Quality Products

Learning Goals

After you have read and studied this chapter, you should be able to
1. Explain the concept of a value package.
2. Describe the various kinds of consumer and industrial goods.
3. Give examples of a brand, a brand name, and a trademark, and explain the concepts of brand equity and loyalty.
4. List and describe the six functions of packaging.
5. Explain the role of brand managers and the six steps of the new-product development process.
6. Identify and describe the stages of the product life cycle, and describe marketing strategies at each stage.
7. Give examples of various pricing objectives and strategies.
8. Explain why non-pricing strategies are growing in importance.

Key Terms and Definitions

Listed here are important terms found in this chapter. Choose the correct term for each definition and write it in the space provided.

brand	generic goods	product screening
brand association	generic name	shopping goods and services
brand awareness	high-low pricing strategy	skimming price strategy
brand equity	industrial goods	specialty goods and services
brand loyalty	knockoff brands	target costing
brand manager	manufacturer's brand names	total fixed costs
break-even analysis	penetration price strategy	trademark
concept testing	price leadership	unsought goods and services
convenience goods and services	product analysis	Utility
commercialization	product differentiation	Value
dealer (private) brands	product life cycle	value package (total product offer)
everyday low pricing (EDLP)	product line	value pricing
fad products	product mix	variable costs
fashion products		

1. _____ Strategy in which a product is priced low to attract many customers and discourage competitors.

2. _____ The combination of product lines offered by a manufacturer.

3. _____ Taking a product idea to consumers to test their reactions.

4. _____ Everything that consumers evaluate when deciding whether or not to buy something.

5. _____ The degree to which customers are satisfied, like the brand, and are committed to further purchases.

6. _____ A theoretical model of what happens to sales and profits for a product class over time.

7. _____ Strategy in which a new product is priced high to make optimum profit while there is little competition.

8. _____ A brand that has been given exclusive legal protection for both the brand name and the pictorial design.

9. _____ The linking of a brand to other, favourable images.

10. _____ Products used in the production of other products.

11. _____ Illegal copies of national brand-name goods.

12. _____ When marketers provide consumers with brand-name goods and services at fair prices.

13. _____ A name, symbol, or design that identifies the goods or services of one seller or group of sellers and distinguishes them from the goods and services of competitors.

14. _____ A manager who has direct responsibility for one brand or one product line.

15. _____ Products that the consumer wants to purchase frequently and with a minimum of effort.

16. _____ The name of a product category.

17. _____ Products that do not carry the manufacturer's name, but carry a distributor or retailer's name instead.

18. _____ Products that have a special attraction to consumers who are willing to go out of their way to obtain them.

19. _____ How quickly a particular brand name comes to mind when a product category is mentioned.

20. _____ A group of products that are physically similar or are intended for a similar market.

21. _____ Non-branded products that usually sell at a sizable discount from national or private brands, have very basic packaging, and are backed with little or no advertising.

22. _____ The creation of real or perceived product differences.

23. _____ Products that consumers are unaware of, haven't necessarily thought of buying, or find that they need to solve an unexpected problem.

24. _____ Products that the consumer buys only after comparing value, quality, and price from a variety of sellers.

25. _____ A process designed to reduce the number of new-product ideas being worked on at any one time.

26. _____ A combination of factors such as awareness, loyalty, perceived quality, feelings, images, and any other emotion

313

people associate with a brand name.

27. _____ Good quality at a fair price; to calculate it, consumers look at the benefits and then subtract the cost to see if the benefits exceed the costs.

28. _____ The want-satisfying ability that is added to goods or services by organizations when the products are made more useful or accessible to consumers than before.

29. _____ The brand names of manufacturers that distribute products nationally.

30. _____ Making cost estimates and sales forecasts to get a feeling for profitability of new product ideas.

31. _____ Promoting a product to distributors and retailers to get wide distribution and developing strong advertising and sales campaigns to generate and maintain interest in the product among distributors and consumers.

32. _____ Products that go through the complete product life cycle and then return again some time later.

33. _____ Products that attract a limited number of consumers and experience a rapid rise and fall in their complete product life cycle.

34. _____ Designing a product so that it satisfies customers and meets the profit margins desired by the firm.

35. _____ The process used to determine profitability of various levels of sales.

36. _____ Costs that change according to the level of production.

37. _____ All the expenses that remain the same no matter how many products are sold.

38. _____ The procedure by which one or more dominant firms set the pricing practices that all competitors in an industry follow.

39. _____ Setting prices that are higher than EDLP stores, but having many special sales where the prices are lower than competitors.

40. _____ Setting prices lower than competitors and then not having any special sales.

Product Development and the Value Package

1. What must marketers do today to satisfy customers? What must managers do?

_____
_____
_____
_____
_____
_____

2. What are the factors that make up the "value package" of a product?

a. _____ g. _____
b. _____ h. _____
c. _____ i. _____
d. _____ j. _____
e. _____ k. _____
f. _____

3. How can businesses keep customers?

_____
_____
_____
_____

4. In chapter 15 you read about the importance of the marketing process. Explain the relationship of the marketing concept to the importance of developing new products, as it is described in the text.

_____
_____
_____
_____

5. What appears to be the most important factor of the new product development process?

_____
_____
_____
_____

6. When people buy a product, they evaluate several dimensions about the product before making a purchase.

For each product listed below, identify three specific dimensions that a customer would evaluate in his purchase decision.

Product		Dimensions to be Evaluated
Bicycle	i.	_____
	ii.	_____
	iii.	_____
Toothpaste	i.	_____
	ii.	_____
	iii.	_____
A new suit	i.	_____
	ii.	_____
	iii.	_____

7. Identify two different customer perceptions of the following products.

Product		Customer Perceptions
Bicycle	i.	_____
	ii.	_____
	iii.	_____

Toothpaste

    i. _____

    ii. _____

    iii. _____

A new suit

    i. _____

    ii. _____

    iii. _____

8. What is the difference between a product line and a product mix?

_____

_____

_____

_____

The Utilities Created by Marketers

1. What is *utility*, as defined in marketing?

_____

_____

_____

_____

2. What are the six types of utilities that can be added to goods or services? Give an example of each.

a. _____

_____

b. _____

_____

c. _____

_____

d. _____

_____

e. _____

_____

f. _____

_____

Product Differentiation

1. How does a marketer create product differentiation?

_____

_____

_____

_____

2. What are questions to ask when determining how to improve a customer's experience with your product?

a. _____

b. _____

c. _____

d. _____

3. What are three variables important to marketers of convenience goods?

a. _____

b. _____

c. _____

_____

4. What can marketers of shopping goods emphasize?

_____
_____
_____
_____

5. How are specialty goods marketed?

_____
_____
_____
_____

6. Where are unsought goods often displayed?

_____
_____
_____
_____

7. What's the best way to market convenience goods?

a. _____

_____

b. _____

_____

8. What are the best appeals for promoting shopping goods?

a. _____

b. _____

c. _____

9. What do makers of specialty goods rely on to appeal to their markets?

a. _____

b. _____

c. _____

10. What determines how a good is classified?

_____
_____
_____
_____

11. a. What distinguishes a consumer good from an industrial good?

_____

_____

_____

_____

b. Can a good be classified as both? How?

_____

_____

_____

_____

12. The two major product classifications are consumer goods and services and industrial goods and services.

Classify the following products according to the most common use:

a. Milk _____

b. Steel _____

c. Tickets to the Olympics _____

d. Dry cleaners _____

e. Diesel engines _____

f. Flashlight batteries _____

g. Auto repair _____

h. Heart surgeon _____

i. Management consultant _____

j. Winter coat _____

13. Product differentiation is used when differences between products are very small. Use your creative skills to differentiate the following:

a. A brand of soda crackers

_____

_____

b. White bread

_____

_____

c. Green beans

_____

_____

Packaging

1. How can packaging change a product?

_____

_____

_____

_____

2. How has the importance of packaging changed?

_____

_____

_____

_____

3. Packaging is being given an increasing role in the promotion variable of the marketing mix. The functions of packaging include the following
   - Attract the buyer's attention.
   - Describe contents and give information about contents.
   - Explain benefits of good inside.
   - Provide information on warranties, warnings.
   - Indicate price value and uses.
   - Protect goods through handling and storage, easy to open yet tamper-proof.

   a. Using items in the grocery store, evaluate the packaging of a specific brand in performing these four functions.

   Example:

   Children's Cereal   Froot Loops   ] Bright primary colors and pictures of cartoon characters attracts children's attention.
   ] Content information provided for parents, flavour information for children.
   ] Nutrition information provided.
   ] Convenient multiple-serving box.

Product	*Brand Name*	*Functions*
Shampoo		
Children's cereal		
Graham crackers		
Lunch meat		

   b. Using items found in the grocery store, find two recent consumer-goods packaging innovations. What function does the new packaging perform?

	Package	*Function*
i.	_____	_____
ii.	_____	_____

Branding and Brand Equity

1. How important is brand loyalty to a firm?

   _____
   _____
   _____
   _____

2. How can a company create brand associations?

   _____
   _____
   _____
   _____

3. How can a brand name become a generic brand?

   _____
   _____
   _____
   _____

4.. List the important elements of brand equity.

   a. _____
   b. _____
   c. _____
   d. _____
   e. _____

5. What is the difference between brand awareness and brand preference?

   _____
   _____
   _____
   _____

6. Why is perceived quality an important part of brand equity?

   _____
   _____
   _____
   _____

7. A brand name and a trademark serve to distinguish one company's products from those of all its competitors. When combined with other marketing mix variables, a brand can also create a certain image for a product.

   Identify four brand names, and describe their brand mark.

a. _____

b. _____

c. _____

d. _____

8. How does the brand name affect your perception of the product?

_____
_____
_____
_____

9. You are in conference with the marketing manger of Music-stor and are still in the process of developing a marketing plan. In evaluating the disc and tape storage product produced by Music-stor, you want to know

   a. What dimensions might customers consider in purchasing Music-stor from a retailer?

   _____
   _____
   _____
   _____

   b. What is the total product offer?

   _____
   _____
   _____
   _____

   c. How can we differentiate the product?

   _____
   _____
   _____
   _____

   d. How would Music-stor be classified?

   _____

   e. Will packaging be an important consideration for Music-stor?

   _____
   _____
   _____
   _____

Brand Management

1. What benefit does a brand name have for a buyer? For the seller?

_____
_____
_____
_____
_____
_____

2. What are the four most important sources of new product ideas for consumer products?

a. _____

b. _____

c. _____

d. _____

3. What are the four sources of new product ideas for industrial products?

a. _____

b. _____

c. _____

d. _____

4. What are four reasons for product failure?

a. _____

b. _____

c. _____

d. _____

5. What is product screening?

_____
_____
_____
_____

6. What are product concepts?

_____
_____
_____
_____

7. What is concept testing?

_____
_____
_____
_____

8. What are two important elements for commercialization?

a. _____

b. _____

9. What must Canadian firms do with the new product development process to compete internationally?

_____
_____
_____
_____

10. You and your friend Al stopped at the corner bar one night after work. Al mentioned an article he read about product management and said you might want to start to update your resume soon! You just got promoted to product manager for Fiberrific cereal. What did Al mean?

_____
_____
_____
_____
_____
_____

11. There are five steps in the new-product development process:
   ☐ Generating new product ideas
   ☐ Screening
   ☐ Development
   ☐ Testing
   ☐ Commercialization

Match the following statements to the correct stage of new-product development.

a. _____ Initially, AT&T introduced video phones to selected markets.

b. _____ Pillsbury conducts the Pillsbury Bake-off, a recipe contest to get new recipe ideas.

c. _____ Medtronic, a high-technology medical firm, used a weighted point system to determine the potential for new medical products.

d. _____ Well before the 1992 Winter Olympics, engineers at 3-M worked on a suspension system for the luge which would minimize bouncing on the luge course.

e. _____ National Starch & Chemical Company introduced N-Lite, a fat substitute designed to reduce fat in a variety of processed food products.

The Product Life Cycle

1. What's important about the product life cycle?

_____
_____
_____
_____

323

3. The product life cycle is a model of what happens to classes of products over time. It consists of four stages. Label the following illustration.

a. _____   d. _____

b. _____   e. _____

c. _____   f. _____

3. Complete the following chart.

	Product	Price	Promotion	Place
Introduction				
Growth				
Maturity				
Decline				

Competitive Pricing

1. Name two ways used to set prices.

_____

_____

_____

_____

2. What influences pricing objectives?

_____

_____

_____
_____

3. In the long run, who or what determines price?

_____
_____
_____
_____

4. What is the difference between cost-based pricing, price-led pricing, and value pricing?

_____
_____
_____
_____

5. How do service industries use the same pricing tactics as goods-producing firms?

_____
_____
_____
_____

6. Describe five pricing strategies for new products.

    a. _____   d. _____

    b. _____   e. _____

    c. _____

7. How does *target costing* work?

_____
_____
_____
_____

8. What is the best way to offer value prices and not go broke?

_____
_____
_____
_____

9. What is a *break-even point?*

_____
_____
_____
_____

10. What is the formula for determining a break-even point?

_____
_____

11. What are some of the expenses included in *fixed costs*? *Variable costs*?

Fixed: _____

_____

Variable: _____

_____

12. What happens when sales go above the break-even point?

_____

_____

_____

_____

13. At what level is price set in a *skimming strategy*? Why?

_____

_____

_____

_____

14. At what level are prices set in a *penetration strategy*? Why?

_____

_____

_____

_____

15. What is the idea behind *EDLP*?

_____

_____

_____

_____

16. What is the idea behind *high-low pricing?*

_____

_____

_____

_____

17. What is *demand-oriented pricing*?

_____

_____

_____

_____

18. What is *competition-oriented pricing*?

_____

_____
_____
_____
_____
_____

19. What will determine the price level in competition-oriented pricing?

_____
_____
_____
_____

20. What is likely to spur on non-price competition?

_____
_____
_____
_____

21. How do firms compete using something other than price?

_____
_____
_____
_____

22. How is the Internet affecting pricing?

_____
_____
_____
_____

23. Describe three strategies for avoiding price wars.

a. _____

_____

b. _____

_____

c. _____

_____

24. Among the objectives that firms use in setting prices are the following:

|] Achieve a target profit |] Achieve greater market share |
|] Build traffic |] Create an image |

Match the correct pricing objective to each of the following statements:

a. _____ Safeway advertises eggs at 10 cents a dozen.

b. _____ Ralston Purina charges a price which gives them a 25% profit on dog food, higher than they need, but consumers are willing to pay the high price for this particular pet food.

c. _____ "Crest," a cologne for men by Ralph Lauren, costs $40

327

for a small bottle.

d. _____ If you go to Midas Muffler with a bid from a competitor, Midas will meet that price in order to keep your business.

25. When you're in the grocery store, compare two products of the same type, but which are different in price. (Bottled water is an example.) How does price reflect the other marketing mix variables?

_____

_____

_____

_____

CHAPTER CHECK

1. Explain the difference between a product and a value package.

_____

_____

_____

2. List nine elements that determine a customer's perception of a total product.

a. _____   f. _____

b. _____   g. _____

c. _____   h. _____

d. _____   i. _____

e. _____

3. What are three classifications of consumer goods and services?

a. _____

b. _____

c. _____

4. What is the best way to market
    a. Convenience goods?

    _____

    b. Shopping goods?

    _____

    c. Specialty goods?

    _____

5. What are the two major classifications of industrial goods?

a. _____

b. _____

6. Name six functions of packaging.

a. _____

b. _____

c. _____

d. _____

e. _____

f. _____

7. What are four categories of brands?

a. _____

b. _____

c. _____

d. _____

8. Describe how the four categories of brands differ from each other.

_____

_____

_____

_____

9. List the stages of the new-product development process.

a. _____

b. _____

c. _____

d. _____

e. _____

f. _____

10. Name the top four sources for new-product ideas for consumer products and industrial products.

Consumer	*Industrial*
a. _____	e. _____
b. _____	f. _____
c. _____	g. _____
d. _____	h. _____

11. What are the four stages of the product life cycle?

a. _____

b. _____

c. _____

d. _____

12. What are two ways to extend the life of a product during the maturity stage of the PLC?

a. _____

b. _____

13. Identify four general pricing objectives.
    a. _____
    b. _____
    c. _____
    d. _____

14. Describe
    a. Gross profit _____
       _____

    b. Total cost _____
       _____

    c. Fixed cost _____
       _____

    d. Variable cost _____
       _____

15. What are two new-product pricing strategies?
    a. _____
    b. _____

16. Identify 13 pricing tactics.
    a. _____   h. _____
    b. _____   i. _____
    c. _____   j. _____
    d. _____   k. _____
    e. _____   l. _____
    f. _____   m. _____
    g. _____

PRACTICE TEST

Multiple Choice: Circle the best answer.

1. Which of the following would NOT be included in the overall value package of benefits consumers consider when they purchase a product?
   a. price
   b. image created by advertising
   c. brand name
   d. buyer's income

2. Ford Motor Company produces cars and trucks, provides financing, and has interest in a major bank. These products are part of Ford's
   a. product mix
   b. product depth
   c. product width
   d. product line

3. Which of the following is NOT included in a list of questions to ask when determining how a consumer's experience with a company can be improved?
   a. How do consumers become aware of a need?
   b. How do consumers find your product?
   c. How do consumers order your product?
   d. How do consumers feel about the economy?
4. Small businesses often have an advantage in product differentiation because
   a. they have fewer products, so they can spend more time working on them.
   b. they are more flexible in adapting customer wants and needs.
   c. larger businesses aren't as interested in getting close to the customer.
   d. larger businesses don't have to differentiate their products.
5. Which of the following is NOT one of the classifications of consumer products?
   a. convenience goods and services
   b. unsought goods and services
   c. shopping goods and services
   d. desired goods and services
6. Which of the following would be considered a shopping good?
   a. toothpaste
   b. funeral services
   c. washing machine
   d. bank
7. When a manufacturer buys a personal computer for use at work, the computer would be considered a(n)
   a. industrial good
   b. specialty good
   c. consumer good
   d. shopping good
8. The Jolly Green Giant would be an example of a
   a. brand name
   b. generic name
   c. trademark
   d. knockoff brand
9. Xerox is working to make sure that when people refer to photocopying, they don't use the name Xerox to refer to the process. Xerox is afraid that their brand name will become a
   a. generic name
   b. knockoff brand
   c. private brand
   d. trademark
10. Because products are often being sold in self-service outlets, rather than by salespersons,
    a. brand names have become less important.
    b. packaging has become more important as a way to promote the product.
    c. the popularity of generic products has declined.
    d. packaging has become less important, because consumers want to see what they are buying.
11. The first step in the product development process is
    a. development
    b. product screening
    c. commercialization
    d. idea generation

12. Which of the following is NOT an important criterion for screening products?
    a. how the product fits with current products
    b. profit potential
    c. personnel requirements
    d. ease of production
13. The process of taking a product idea to consumers to test their reactions is known as
    a. test marketing
    b. concept testing
    c. product screening
    d. business analysis
14. In order for Canada to remain competitive in the new-product development process
    a. managers must continually develop new ideas to test.
    b. companies must look at what foreign competitors are offering.
    c. managers must go out into the market and interact with dealers and customers.
    d. the new-product development process must be shortened.
15. Which of the following is NOT one of the stages of the product life cycle?
    a. Introduction
    b. Growth
    c. Maturity
    d. Saturation
16. The importance of the product life cycle is that
    a. different stages in the product life cycle call for different marketing strategies.
    b. most brands follow the same pattern in the product life cycle.
    c. all products go through the product life cycle in the same length of time.
    d. in the growth stage, marketers will differentiate their product from competitors.
17. During the _____ stage of the product life cycle, marketers will keep the product mix limited, adjust the price to meet competition, increase distribution, and do significant competitive advertising.
    a. introduction
    b. growth
    c. maturity
    d. decline
18. Which of the following is NOT included in a list of pricing objectives?
    a. increase sales
    b. increase market share
    c. create an image
    d. beat the competition

True/False

1. _____ In today's market, marketers must learn to listen to consumers and adapt to a constantly changing market.
2. _____ An organization can use low price to create an attractive value package.
3. _____ It is often easier for larger companies to establish a close relationship with customers because they have representatives in most parts of the country.
4. _____ An example of a convenience good would be a candy bar.
5. _____ The importance of packaging is declining in relation to the marketing mix variables.
6. _____ Brand loyalty means that your product comes to mind when a product category is mentioned.
7. _____ The Internet has become an important variable in the commercialization step of the new

product development process.

8. _____ Global marketers today are using cross-functional teams to develop new products.
9. _____ A firm may have several pricing strategies all at once.
10. _____ Pricing objectives generally will have no effect on the other marketing mix variables.
11. _____ When movie theatres charge lower rates for children, and companies give discounts to senior citizens, they are using demand-oriented pricing.
12. _____ Most pricing depends upon what the competition is charging.
13. _____ Marketers will often compete on product attributes other than price.

ANSWERS

Key Terms and Definitions

1. penetration price strategy
2. product mix
3. concept testing
4. value package
5. brand loyalty
6. product life cycle
7. skimming price strategy
8. trademark
9. brand association
10. industrial goods
11. knockoff brands
12. value pricing
13. brand
14. brand manager
15. convenience goods and services
16. generic name
17. dealer (private) brands
18. specialty goods and services
19. brand awareness
20. product line

21. Generic goods
22. Product differentiation
23. Unsought goods and services
24. Shopping goods and services
25. Product screening
26. Brand equity
27. Value
28. Utility
29. Manufacturers' brand names
30. Product analysis
31. Commercialization
32. Fashion products
33. fad products
34. Target costing
35. Break-even analysis

36. Variable costs
37. Total fixed costs
38. Price leadership

39. High-low pricing strategy
40. Everyday low pricing (EDLP)

Product Development and the Value Package

1. To satisfy consumers, marketers must learn to listen and to adapt constantly to changing market demands, and to price challenges from competitors. Products must be perceived to have the best value – high quality at a fair price.
   Manager must learn to manage change, in particular, new-product change.

2.
   a. Price
   b. Package
   c. Store surroundings
   d. Image created by advertising
   e. Guarantee
   f. Reputation of the producer
   g. Brand name
   h. Service
   i. Buyer's past experience
   j. Speed of delivery
   k. Accessibility of marketer (e.g., on the Net)

3. One way to keep customers is to establish a dialogue with them and keep the information they provide in a database. One of the easiest ways to do this is to establish a Web site where a consumer

can ask questions, get information, and chat with others.

4. Part of the marketing concept involves determining consumer needs and wants and making a product to fill those needs. Knowing consumer preferences is crucial in the new-product development process. Companies must constantly monitor the marketplace to determine customer preferences and how they are changing, if they want to meet and beat the competition.

5. Listening to the marketplace and adapting to changing needs seems to be a critical factor in the new-product development process.

6. *Suggested Answers*

Bicycle	i.	Reputation of producer
	ii.	Guarantee
	iii.	Service
Toothpaste	i.	Brand name
	ii.	Past experience
	iii.	Package
A new suit	i.	Image created by advertising
	ii.	Price
	iii.	Store surroundings

7. *Suggested Answers*

Bicycle	i.	A way to get around campus
	ii.	A way to get exercise
Toothpaste	i.	To prevent cavities
	ii.	To freshen breath
A new suit	i.	To create an image
	ii.	To wear to a formal occasion

8. A product mix is the combination of products that a company has available for sale. The product mix consists of a company's product lines. Product lines are groups of products that are similar or are intended for a similar market.

The Utilities Created By Marketers

1. Utility is the value or want-satisfying ability that is added to goods or services when products are made more useful and accessible to consumers.

2. Form utility
   Time utility
   Place utility
   Possession utility
   Information utility
   Service utility

   Examples will, of course, vary.

Product Differentiation

1. Marketers use a mix of pricing, advertising, and packaging to create a unique attractive image to differentiate their products.

2. a. How do customers become aware of a need for your product?
   b. How do customers find your product?
   c. How do customers order your product?
   d. How quickly do you deliver your product?

3. Variables important to marketers of convenience goods are

    a. location
    b. brand awareness
    c. image

4. Marketers of shopping goods can emphasize price differences, quality differences, or a combination of the two.
5. Specialty goods are often marketed through specialty magazines and through interactive Web sites.
6. Unsought goods are often displayed at the checkout counter in a store.
7. The best way to market convenience goods is to
    a. make them readily available
    b. create the proper image
8. The best appeal for promoting shopping goods is
    a. price
    b. quality
    c. service
9. Makers of specialty goods rely on
    a. advertising
    b. the Internet
    c. creative and highly visible displays
10. Whether a good or service falls into a particular class depends on the individual customer. For example, what is a shopping good for one customer could be a specialty good for another.
11. a. Consumer goods are purchased for personal consumption, while industrial goods are products used in the production of other products.
    b. A product can be classified as both a consumer good or an individual good depending upon the end use of the product.
12.

a.	Consumer		f.	Consumer
b.	Industrial		g.	Consumer
c.	Consumer		h.	Consumer
d.	Consumer		i.	Industrial
e.	Industrial		j.	Consumer

13. *Possible Answers*
    a. Crispier, better, more convenient packaging, stay fresh longer.
    b. Softer, higher fiber, more fun, makes sandwiches better.
    c. Fresher, better tasting, crispier, high quality.

Packaging

1. Packaging changes the product by changing its visibility, usefulness, or attractiveness.
2. Packaging is carrying more of the promotional burden than in the past. Many products that were once sold by sales persons are now being sold in self-service outlets, and the package has been given more sales responsibility.
3. a. and b. Answers will vary.

Branding and Brand Equity

1. A loyal group of consumers can represent substantial value to a firm.
2. Brand associations can be created by linking your brand to other product users, to a popular celebrity, to a particular geographic area, or to competitors.
3. A brand name can become generic when a name becomes so popular, so identified with the products that it loses its brand status and becomes the name of the product category. Examples include aspirin, nylon, escalator, and zipper.

4. The elements of brand equity are as follows:
   a. Brand loyalty
   b. Perceived quality
   c. Brand awareness
   d. Feelings and images
   e. Emotions people associate with a brand name
5. Brand awareness means that your product comes to mind when a product category is mentioned. Brand preference means that consumers prefer one brand to another because of perceptions determined by price, appearance, and reputation.
6. Perceived quality is an important part of brand equity because a product that is perceived as better quality than its competitors can be priced higher and thus improve profits.
7. Answers will vary.
8. Often we perceive nationally recognized brand names as being better quality, or able to fill our needs more effectively.
9. a. Customers may look at price, image, guarantee, and service. The retailer will be an important variable in this combination. Will the retailer install the case? Will the store take it back if it breaks?
   b. Total product offer is convenience, image, and the kind of store in which the product is sold, in addition to such product considerations as the size, colour, and fit of Music-stor.
   c. Music-stor could differentiate the product by giving it an image of not only convenience, but of the "ultimate" kind of auto accessory that everyone needs to have in today's cluttered world. You could create the perception that this product isn't merely a luxury, but a *necessity*. Advertising could be aimed at the end consumer, with the idea of people asking for the product when they go to the dealership to buy the car.
   The main consideration for an auto manufacturer will be price, how much it will add to the sticker price of the car, guarantee, and speed of delivery and reputation of Music-stor. The ease of installation at the factory will also be a factor—where does it fit into the car? Colour will also be a consideration.
   d. Music-stor would be classified as a consumer good, and could be marketed as either a shopping good or a specialty good. It is also an industrial good, when it is marketed to manufacturers for direct installation on the assembly line.
   e. Packaging could be an important variable for Music-stor for the consumer portion of the market. We may want to attract attention to our product on the shelf, give consumers an idea of what it is, and protect it from being scratched or broken. These decisions depend upon our perception of the product as a shopping good or as a specialty good. The package will be less important for the industrial market, the focus being primarily on protection during shipping and handling.

Brand Management

1. For the buyer, a brand name assures quality, reduces search time, and adds prestige to purchases. For the seller, brand names facilitate new product introductions, help promotional efforts, add to repeat purchases, and differentiate products so that pries can be set higher.
2. a. analysis of competition
   b. company sources other than research and development
   c. consumer research
   d. research and development
3. a. company sources other than research an development
   b. analysis of the competition
   c. research and development
   d. product users
4. Reasons for product failure include
   a. products don't deliver what they promise.
   b. poor positioning.

c. not enough differences from competitors.

d. poor packaging.

5. Product screening is designed to reduce the number of ideas being worked on at any one time. Criteria needed for screening include whether the product fits in well with present products, profit potential, marketability, and personnel requirements.

6. Product concepts are alternative product offerings based on the same product idea that have different meanings and values to different consumers.

7. Concept testing involves taking a product idea to consumers to test their reactions.

8. Two important elements for commercialization are

a. promoting the product to distributors and retailers to get wide distribution.

b. developing strong advertising and sales campaigns to generate and maintain interest.

9. To stay competitive in world markets, Canadian businesses must develop an entirely new product development process. Keeping products competitive requires continuous incremental improvements in function, cost, and quality. Attention must be given to developing products in cooperation with their user. Managers must go out into the market and interact closely with their dealers and their ultimate customers. Changes are made over time to make sure that the total product offer exactly meets customers' needs.

10. Al probably said that because many companies are challenging the value of product managers today. As customer brand loyalty declines, national brand names are becoming less important to retailers. Market segment managers, market teams, and similar consumer-oriented forms of management are taking the place of the product management concept. There is a shift from selling and advertising to a more consumer-oriented emphasis, and niche marketing and custom-made goods are taking over the mass merchandising idea.

11. a. Testing

b. Generating new product ideas

c. Screening

d. Development

e. Commercialization

The Product Life Cycle

1. The product life cycle is important because different stages in the product life cycle call for different strategies. It can provide some basis for anticipating future market developments and for planning marketing strategies.

2.
a.	Introduction	d.	Decline
b.	Growth	e.	Sales
c.	Maturity	f.	Industry profits

3.

	Product	Price	Promotion	Place
Introduction	Offer market-tested product	High price	Selective distribution	Primary advertising sales promotion
Growth	Improve product	Adjust to meet competition	Increase distribution	Competitive advertising
Maturity	Differentiate to satisfy different segments	Reduce price further	Intensify distribution	Emphasize brand name and product benefits and differences
Decline	Cut product mix, develop new	Consider increase	Drop some outlets	Reduce advertising

	products			

Competitive Pricing

1. Ways to set prices include
    a. cost-based pricing   b. value pricing
2. Pricing objectives should be influenced by other marketing mix variable decisions, such as product design, packaging, branding, distribution, and promotion.
3. In the end, the market determines what the price of a product will be.
4. Cost-based pricing bases the end selling price upon the cost of manufacturing the product plus some margin of profit. It does not take into consideration what the consumer believes is a fair price. Price-led costing, used by the Japanese, determines what the market is willing to pay for a product, and then designs a product which can be sold for that price. Value pricing means providing quality, name-brand goods at "value" prices.
5. Service industries can use the same pricing tactics as goods-producing firms by cutting costs as much as possible. Then they determine what services are most important to customers. Those services that aren't important are cut. An example is cutting meal service on airlines. The idea is to give the consumer value.
6. Pricing strategies for new products include the following:
    a. Skimming pricing, setting a high initial price.
    b. Penetration pricing, setting a low initial price.
    c. Demand-oriented pricing, reflecting consumer demand rather than cost or some other calculation.
    d. Price leadership, where all competitors follow similar pricing practices, usually those of a dominant firm in the industry.
    e. Competition-oriented pricing based upon all competitors.
7. Target costing makes cost an input to the development process. To use target costing, the firm will estimate the selling price people would be willing to pay for a product and subtract the desired profit margin. The result is the target cost of production.
8. The best way to offer value prices and not go broke is to redesign products from the bottom up and to cut costs wherever possible. The idea is to sell brand name items at low prices.
9. The break-even point is the point where revenues from sales equal all costs.
10. Break-even point = Fixed costs/(price per unit – variable cost per unit)
11. Expenses included in fixed costs: e.g., rent and insurance
    Expenses included in variable costs: e.g., materials and direct labour costs
12. When sales go above the break-even point, the firm makes a profit.
13. A skimming price strategy sets initial prices high to make optimum profit while there is little competition.
14. A penetration strategy sets prices low, which attracts more buyers and discourages other companies. This enables the firm to penetrate or capture a large share of the market quickly.
15. The idea of EDLP is to set prices lower than competitors and then not have any special sales. As a result, consumers will come to this stores whenever they want a bargain and not wait until there is a sale, as they often do with department stores.
16. When a firm uses high-low pricing, regular prices are higher than EDLP stores, but a store will have many special sales where the prices are lower than competitors'. The problem with this type of strategy is that it teaches consumers to wait for sales, and that can cut into profits.
17. Demand-oriented pricing is used when price is set on the basis of consumer demand rather than cost or some other calculation. An example is movie theatres with low rates for children or during certain times of the day.
18. Competition-oriented pricing is a strategy based on what all the other competitors are doing.
19. In competition pricing, the price will depend on customer loyalty, perceived differences, and the

competitive climate.

20. Non-price competition will rise as the level of price competition is affected by the availability of products on the Internet.
21. Firms using non-price competition will stress product images and consumer benefits such as comfort, style, convenience, and durability.
22. Customers can now compare prices of many goods and services on the Internet, and can get lower prices on items such as airline tickets. You can also buy used items online if you are unwilling to accept the prices of new goods. Price competition is going to heat up with the Internet, as more customers have access to price information from around the world.
23. a. add value
    b. educate consumers
    c. establish relationships
24. a. Build traffic
    b. Achieve a target profit
    c. Create an image
    d. Achieve a greater market share
25. If you were to look at bottled water as an example, you would probably see the higher-priced product with a unique brand name, packaged more expensively. There may be "flavours" which are more unique than with the inexpensive brand.

CHAPTER CHECK ANSWERS

1. A product is a physical good, service, or idea that meets a need. A value package consists of all the tangibles and intangibles that consumers evaluate when purchasing a product.
2. a. Price
   b. Package
   c. Store surroundings
   d. Image created by advertising
   e. Guarantee
   f. Reputation of the producer
   g. Brand name
   h. Service
   i. Buyer's past experience
3. a. Convenience goods and services
   b. Shopping goods and services
   c. Specialty goods and services
4. a. It is important to emphasize location, brand awareness, and image.
   b. Emphasize price differences, quality differences, or both.
   c. Specialty magazines, advertising.
5. a. Production goods
   b. Support goods
6. a. Attracts attention
   b. Gives information about contents
   c. Explains benefits
   d. Provides information about warranties or warnings
   e. Gives indication of price, value, and user
   f. Protects contents from damage, is tamper-proof but easy to open.
7. a. Private
   b. Generic
   c. Manufacturer's
   d. Knockoff
8. *Manufacturer's brands* are the brand names of manufacturers that distribute the product nationally. *Private brands* are products that do not carry the manufacturer's name, and carry the name of a distributor or retailer instead.
   Generic goods are nonbranded products that usually sell at a sizable discount from national or private brands, have very basic packaging, and are backed with little or no advertising.
   Knockoffs are illegal copies of manufacturers' brand-name goods.

9. a. Generating new product ideas
   b. Screening
   c. Development
   d. Testing
   e. Commercialization
10. *Consumer*
    a. Analysis of competition
    b. Company sources other than research and development
    c. Consumer research
    d. Research and development
    Industrial
    e. Company sources other than research and development
    f. Analysis of competition
    g. Research and development
    h. Product users
11. a. Introduction
    b. Growth
    c. Maturity
    d. Decline
12. a. Product modification
    b. Market modification
13. a. Achieve a target profit
    b. Build traffic
    c. Achieve greater market share
    d. Create an image
14. a. Money left after all costs are deducted and before taxes are paid.
    b. Total cost incurred in production. The sum of fixed costs plus variable costs.
    c. The sum of expenses that don't change with quantity of product produced.
    d. The sum of expenses that vary directly with the quantity of product produced.
15. a. Penetration pricing
    b. Skimming pricing
16. a. Market price
    b. Demand-oriented pricing
    c. Pricing leadership
    d. Competition-oriented pricing
    e. Value pricing
    f. Adaptive pricing
    g. Cost-oriented pricing
    h. Customary pricing
    i. Product-line pricing
    j. Target pricing
    k. Uniform pricing
    l. Odd pricing
    m. Price lining

PRACTICE TEST

Multiple Choice

1. d
2. a
3. d
4. b
5. d
6. c

True/False

1. T
2. T
3. F
4. T
5. F
6. F

7.	a
8.	c
9.	a
10.	b
11.	d
12.	d
13.	b
14.	c
15.	d
16.	a
17.	b
18.	d

7.	T
8.	T
9.	T
10.	F
11.	T
12.	F
13.	T

CHAPTER 17

Promoting and Distributing Products Efficiently And Interactively

Learning Goals

After you have read and studied this chapter, you should be able to

1. Define promotion and list the four traditional tools that make up the promotion mix.
2. Define advertising and describe the advantages and disadvantages of various advertising media, including the Internet.
3. Illustrate the seven steps of the selling process and discuss the role of a consultative salesperson.
4. Explain the importance of sales promotion and word of mouth as promotional tools.
5. Describe integrated marketing communication and the role of interactive communications within it.
6. Explain the concept of marketing channels and the value of marketing intermediaries.
7. Describe the various wholesale organizations in the distribution system.
8. Explain the ways in which retailers compete and the distribution strategies they use.
9. Explain the various kinds of non-store retailing.
10. Discuss how a manufacturer can get wholesalers and retailers in a channel system to cooperate by the formation of systems.

Key Terms and Definitions

Listed here are important terms found in this chapter. Choose the correct term for each definition and write it in the space provided.

administered distribution system	integrated marketing communication (IMC)	push strategy
advertising	intensive distribution	qualify
brokers	interactive marketing program	rack jobbers
cash-and-carry wholesalers	interactive promotion	retail sale
category killer stores	intermodal shipping	retailer
channel of distribution	limited-function wholesaler	sales promotion
closing techniques	marketing intermediaries	sampling
consultative salesperson	materials handling	selective distribution
contractual distribution system	merchant wholesalers	supply chain
corporate distribution system	personal selling	telemarketing
drop shippers	physical distribution (logistics)	trade show
electronic data interchange (EDI)	promotion	viral marketing
e-tailing	promotion mix	wholesale sale
	prospecting	wholesaler
exclusive distribution	prospects	word-of-mouth promotion
freight forwarder	public relations (PR)	
full-service wholesaler	publicity	

infomercial   pull strategy

1. _____ Selling goods and services to ultimate customers over the Internet.

2. _____ The promotional tool that stimulates consumer purchasing and dealer interest by means of short-term activities.

3. _____ Paid, nonpersonal communication through various media by organizations and individuals who are in some way identified in the advertising message.

4. _____ The management function that evaluates stakeholder attitudes, changes policies and procedures in response to stakeholder's requests, and executes a program of action and information to earn public understanding and acceptance.

5. _____ Promotional strategy in which heavy advertising and sales promotion efforts are directed toward consumers so that they will request the products from retailers.

6. _____ The combination of promotional tools an organization uses.

7. _____ Organizations that assist in moving goods and services from producer to industrial and consumer users.

8. _____ Wholesaler that performs only selected functions.

9. _____ A marketing intermediary that sells to other organizations.

10. _____ The movement of goods within a warehouse, factory, or store.

11. _____ Software that enables the computers of producers, wholesalers, and retailers to communicate with each other.

12. _____ Wholesaler that performs all distribution functions.

13. _____ The movement of goods and services from producers to industrial and consumer users.

14. _____ A technique that combines all the promotional tools into one comprehensive and unified promotional strategy.

15. _____ A whole set of marketing intermediaries, such as wholesalers and retailers, who join together to transport and store goods in their path from producers to consumers.

16. _____ An organization that sells to ultimate consumers.

17. _____ Researching potential buyers and choosing those most likely to buy.

18. _____ Any information about an individual, a product, or an organization that is distributed to the public through the media and that is not paid for, or controlled by, the seller.

19. _____ Use of promotional tools to convince wholesalers and retailers to stock and sell merchandise.

20. _____ A TV program devoted exclusively to promoting goods and services.

21. _____ Face-to-face presentation and promotion of products and services.

22. _____ Marketing intermediaries who bring buyers and sellers together and assist in negotiating an exchange but do not take title to the goods.

23. _____ A distribution system in which all of the organizations in the channel of distribution are owned by one firm.

24. _____ The sale of goods and services by telephone.

25. _____ A distribution system in which producers manage all of the marketing functions at the retail level.

26. _____ An organization that puts many small shipments together to create a single large shipment that can be transported cost-effectively to the final destination.

27. _____ An event where marketers set up displays and potential customers come to see the latest goods and services.

28. _____ An attempt by marketers to inform people about products and to persuade them to participate in an exchange.

29. _____ Everything from paying people to say positive things on the Internet to setting up multilevel selling schemes whereby consumers get commissions for directing friends to specific websites.

30. _____ Independently owned firms that take ownership of the goods they handle.

31. _____ Distribution that sends products to only one retail outlet in a given geographic area.

32. _____ People with the means to buy a product, the authority to buy, and the willingness to listen to a sales message.

33. _____ A promotional tool that involves people telling other people about products they have purchased.

34. _____ Wholesalers that furnish racks or shelves full of merchandise to retailers, display products, and sell on consignment.

35. _____ A system in which consumers can access company information on their own and supply information about themselves in an ongoing dialogue.

36. _____ Wholesalers that solicit orders from retailers and other wholesalers and have the merchandise shipped directly from a producer to a buyer.

37. _____ Distribution that sends products to only a preferred group of retailers in an area.

38. _____ Ways of concluding a sale including getting a series of small commitments and then asking for the order and showing the client where to sign.

39. _____ A promotional tool in which a company lets consumers have a small sample of a product for no charge.

40. _____ In the selling process, to make sure that people have a need for the product, the authority to buy, and the willingness to listen to a sales message.

41. _____ Distribution that puts products into as many retail outlets as possible.

42. _____ Wholesalers that serve mostly smaller retailers with a limited assortment of products.

43. _____ Large stores that offer wide selection at competitive prices.

44. _____ The sale of goods and services to consumers for their own use.

45. _____ The sale of goods and services to businesses and institutions for use in the business or to wholesalers or retailers for resale.

46. _____ A salesperson who begins by analyzing customer needs and then comes up with solutions to those needs.

47. _____ Changing the promotion process from a monologue, where sellers try to persuade buyers to buy things, to a dialogue in which buyers and sellers can work together to create mutually beneficial exchange relationships.

48. _____ A distribution system in which members are bound to cooperate through contractual agreements.

49. _____ The sequence of linked activities that must be performed by various organizations to move goods from the sources of raw materials to ultimate consumers.

The Importance of Promotion/The Promotion Mix

1. How much is spent on advertising in Canada each year?

    _____

2. List five types of promotional tools used by marketers.

    _____
    _____
    _____
    _____
    _____

3. According to the text, how is technology changing an organization's approach to working with customers?

    _____
    _____
    _____
    _____

4. a. A company uses several tools to communicate with its different markets. Those tools include

] Advertising	] Publicity
] Personal selling	] Sales promotion
] Public relations	] Word-of-mouth

    Identify two promotion mix variables a company selling large computer systems and personal computers can use to communicate with

    i.   Stockholder   a. _____
                               b. _____

    ii.   Business customers   a. _____
                               b. _____

    iii. Individual customers a. _____
                               b. _____

    iv.   Employees   a. _____
                               b. _____

    b. Identify which of the techniques is being illustrated in each example below:

    i.   _____ A course in Introduction to Business fills up on the first day of registration. In line, a student is heard to say, "I hear this prof is really good."

    ii.   _____ The makers of Oreo cookies sponsor a 75th birthday celebration sweepstakes.

    iii. _____ McDonnell-Douglas sponsors a program to match their employees with organizations asking for volunteer help.

    iv.   _____ The Ford Taurus wins Motor Trend's Car of the Year award.

    v.   _____ Target, a discount store, encloses a full-colour, multipage supplement in the Sunday papers.

vi. _____ Newly hired employees at IBM go through a nine-month training program before calling on customers.

Advertising: Persuasive Communications

1. How does the public benefit from advertising?

   _____

   _____

   _____

   _____

   _____

2. Determine what might be the most appropriate form of advertising media for the following. (There may be more than one answer for each.)

   a. A rock concert at an outdoor theatre _____

   b. Sales at the local mall_____

   c. Products aimed specifically at women _____

   d. A local news show _____

   e. Long distance telephone service _____

   f. Credit cards_____

   g. Computer software _____

   h. A storage case for CDs and tapes for the car _____

3. In today's marketplace, there are many alternatives to advertising in the traditional media such as print, television, and radio. Compare the benefits of advertising using infomercials, the Internet, and other forms of technology.

   _____

   _____

   _____

   _____

4. What are the benefits of infomercials?

   _____

   _____

   _____

   _____

5. How has technology changed advertising?

   _____

   _____

   _____

   _____

6. a. Seven different kinds of advertising are
   -] Retail advertising
   -] Trade advertising
   -] Product advertising
   -] Advocacy advertising

] Industrial advertising   ] Comparison advertising
] Institutional advertising

Match the correct form of advertising to the following:

i. _____ A supermarket distributes a weekly flyer which is included in the local newspaper.

ii. _____ A glove manufacturing company advertises its gloves in a trade journal to companies that employ labourers.

iii. _____ "Baseball fever —catch it" is an advertisement which attempts to build demand for the sport.

iv. _____ Procter & Gamble advertises in trade journals targeting grocery and convenience stores.

v. _____ When introducing their new fried chicken menu items, Hardees ran advertisements showing people saying they preferred Hardee's fried chicken over that of Kentucky Fried.

vi. _____ "I've actually squeezed my way into some of the finest restaurants in the world" is the slogan used in advertising by the National Honey Board. Seven recipes are included in the ad.

vii. _____ "Stop for good" is a slogan sponsored by the Canadian Medical Association to encourage smokers to quit.

b. What is the challenge of advertising products commonly used in Canada to overseas markets?

_____
_____
_____
_____

7. List some of the advantages and disadvantages of each form of advertising media below:

a. newspapers _____

_____
_____

b. television _____

_____
_____

c. radio _____

_____
_____

d. magazines _____

e. outdoor

f. direct mail

g. yellow pages

h. Internet

8. How do people react to ads on the Internet? What is the goal of advertising on the Internet?

9. How does Customer Relationship Management software work?

10. How will technology and the speed of the Internet affect Internet advertising and customer relationship management?

Personal Selling: Providing Personal Attention

1.   How do we define "effective selling"?

2.   In personal selling, what does it mean to qualify a customer?

_____

_____

_____

_____

3.   What activities take place in the preapproach?

_____

_____

_____

_____

4.   What is the objective of an initial sales call during the approach stage?

_____

_____

_____

_____

5.   What does the salesperson do during the presentation?

_____

_____

_____

_____

6.   What activities are involved in closing a sale?

_____

_____

_____

_____

7.   Identify the activities involved in the follow-up.

_____

_____

_____

_____

8.   How is technology aiding the salesperson of today?

_____

_____

_____

_____

9.   According to the text, what are the two goals of a salesperson?

_____

_____

_____

_____

10. How is technology changing the role of the B2B salesperson?

_____

_____

_____

_____

11. According to the text, the role of both B2B salespersons and consumer salespersons is to be a consultant. What does that mean, and why has that change occurred?

_____

_____

_____

_____

12. There are seven steps in the selling process:
- ☐ Prospect
- ☐ Preapproach
- ☐ Approach
- ☐ Make presentation
- ☐ Answer objections
- ☐ Close sale
- ☐ Follow up

Match the stage of the selling process to each of the following statements or situations:

a. _____ "If I can get delivery within the next two weeks, will you sign the order today?"

b. _____ "Hello, Mr. Jones, I'm John Brown. We met last week at the trade show in Burlington."

c. _____ "I'm calling you to see how you are doing with your new word processing system. Any problems I can help you with?"

d. _____ "I think you'll be able to see from a demonstration how this system will help you cut down on paperwork."

e. _____ "I can get back to you with the answer to that question by tomorrow afternoon."

f. _____ "I think I'll go to the trade show next month. There could be a lot of potential customers there."

g. _____ "I've got an appointment next week with the buyer at Acme. I've got a friend who works there; maybe he can tell me what system they're using now and how well they like it."

13. a. While we haven't yet decided on a promotion mix for Music-stor (that will come shortly), it will most likely include some form of personal selling. Using the seven steps in your text, prepare an outline for a sales presentation to your automotive manufacturing customers.

_____

_____
_____
_____
_____
_____
_____
_____
_____

b. How will the presentation differ for selling Music-stor to a retailer?

_____
_____
_____
_____
_____
_____
_____
_____

Public Relations: Building Relationships With All Publics

1.   Identify the three steps in creating a good public relations campaign.
       a.   _____
       b.   _____
       c.   _____

2.   What is the responsibility of a public relations department? Why?

       _____
       _____
       _____
       _____

3.   What are three benefits that publicity has over other promotion mix variables?
       a.   _____
       b.   _____
       c.   _____

4.   What are three drawbacks of publicity?
       a.   _____
       b.   _____
       c.   _____

Sales Promotion: Getting a Good Deal

1.   List five types of B2B sales promotions.
    a. _____
    b. _____
    c. _____
    d. _____
    e. _____

2. List the kinds of consumer sales promotion.

a. _____

b. _____

c. _____

d. _____

e. _____

f. _____

g. _____

h. _____

i. _____

j. _____

k. _____

l. _____

3. What are sales promotion programs designed to do?

_____

_____

_____

_____

4. Identify two targets of sales promotion.

_____

_____

5. Who are the targets of internal sales promotion and what is internal sales promotion designed to do?

_____

_____

_____

_____

6. What comes after internal sales promotion?

_____

_____

_____

_____

7. What is the benefit of sampling as a sales promotion tool?

_____

_____

_____

_____

8. What is a *virtual trade show*, and what is the benefit for customers?

_____

_____

_____
_____

9.   What is *event marketing?*
_____
_____
_____
_____

10.   What is the best way to generate good word-of-mouth?
   a. _____
   b. _____
   c. _____

11.   List three elements of effective word-of-mouth promotion.
   a. _____
   b. _____
   c. _____

12.   How do the other elements of the promotion mix affect word-of-mouth promotion?
   a.   Product _____
   b.   Sales promotion _____
   c.   Advertising _____
   d.   Publicity_____
   e.   Personal selling_____

13.   What is the trend regarding the use of the Internet in promotion, and how is that trend affecting traditional methods of promotion?
_____
_____
_____
_____

14.   How has promotion become interactive?
_____
_____
_____
_____

Managing The Promotion Mix: Putting It All Together

1.   What is the best way to reach
   a. large homogeneous groups?
_____
_____
_____

   b. large organizations?
_____

_____
_____

2. What is the idea of a push strategy?

_____
_____
_____

3. What is the idea of a pull strategy?

_____
_____
_____

4. What is a total systems approach to marketing?

_____
_____
_____
_____
_____
_____

5. What is interactive marketing?

_____
_____
_____

6. What is an interactive marketing communication system?

_____
_____
_____

7. What are the steps necessary to develop an interactive marketing communications system?
   a. _____
   b. _____
   c. _____

8. Why are smaller firms capturing markets from large firms?

_____
_____
_____
_____
_____
_____

9. What are the advantages of interactive marketing on the Internet?
   a. _____
   b. _____
   c. _____

d. _____

10. Why is marketing services more difficult on the Internet?

_____
_____
_____
_____

11. What elements are blended in integrated marketing communications?

_____
_____
_____
_____

12. What impact could new technologies have on TV and mass advertising?

_____
_____
_____
_____

13. What impact will the Internet have on traditional mall retailing?

_____
_____
_____
_____

14. a. Identify three groups that are the focus of sales promotion efforts, and a technique used to reach each group.

	Group		Technique
i.	_____	iv.	_____
ii.	_____	v.	_____
iii.	_____	vi.	_____

b. Identify six sales promotion techniques you've seen used recently (including specialty advertising).

i.	_____	iv.	_____
ii.	_____	v.	_____
iii.	_____	vi.	_____

15. Now that we have covered the promotion mix variables, you are an expert in designing an effective promotion campaign. What do you think would be the most effective promotion mix for Music-stor to use? Will it be more important to use a push or a pull strategy, a combination, or a "total systems" approach?

_____
_____
_____
_____
_____

The Importance of Channels of Distribution

1. What are the functions and activities that are included in physical distribution?

   a. _____   d. _____

   b. _____   e. _____

   c. _____   f. _____

2. What are two types of marketing intermediaries?

   a. _____

   b. _____

3. Why do we have marketing intermediaries?

   _____

   _____

   _____

   _____

4. How do marketing intermediaries add efficiency to the distribution system?

   _____

   _____

   _____

   _____

5. How has the Internet affected distribution?

   _____

   _____

   _____

   _____

6. Identify the relationship between the first two Ps in the marketing mix (Product and Price), and the third P (Place).

   _____

   _____

   _____

7. What activities *don't* brokers perform? What are some kinds of brokers?

   _____

   _____

   _____

   _____

8. Pick a product from each category, industrial and consumer, and attempt to identify the channel of distribution for each.

   _____

   _____

   _____

9. What is the value versus the cost of intermediaries?

_____
_____
_____
_____

10. What are three important points to remember about intermediaries?

a. _____
b. _____
c. _____
_____

11. It's pretty easy to go to the store to buy a can of soup or a tube of toothpaste. Identify five ways intermediaries add value to the products we buy.

a. _____
b. _____
c. _____
d. _____
e. _____

Wholesale Intermediaries

1. What is the difference between a "retail sale" and a "wholesale sale"?

_____
_____
_____
_____

2. Identify two types of merchant wholesalers.

a. _____
b. _____

3. What is the difference between the types of merchant wholesalers?

_____
_____
_____
_____

4. List three types of limited-function wholesalers.

a. _____
b. _____
c. _____

5. How does a rack jobber operate?

_____
_____
_____
_____

6. How does a cash-and-carry wholesaler function?

_____
_____
_____
_____

7. How does a drop shipper operate?

_____
_____
_____
_____

8. Who uses a freight forwarder, and what does a freight forwarder do?

_____
_____
_____
_____

9. How is a lot of B2B wholesaling being done?

_____
_____
_____
_____

Retail Intermediaries

1. What are five ways retailers compete?

    a. _____ d. _____
    b. _____ e. _____
    c. _____

2. How can smaller, independent retailers compete with discount stores and warehouse stores?

_____
_____
_____

3. What is involved in service competition?

_____
_____
_____

4. What is a category-killer store?

_____
_____
_____

5. How do smaller retailers compete with category killers?

_____
_____
_____
_____

6.   What is a total quality retailer?

_____
_____
_____
_____

7.   How is the Internet affecting price competition?

_____
_____
_____
_____

8.   How do brick and mortar stores offer entertainment competition?

_____
_____
_____
_____

9.   Name three retail distribution strategies.
      a.   _____
      b.   _____
      c.   _____

10.   What types of products are sold using each of the three types of distribution strategies?

_____
_____
_____
_____

11.   There are several different categories of retailing establishment. The categories include
      ]   Department stores   ]   Chain stores
      ]   Discount stores   ]   Convenience stores
      ]   Specialty stores   ]   Catalogue stores
      ]   Supermarkets   ]   General stores

      Match the correct category to each statement below:

      a.   _____ Wicks and Sticks carries a wide selection of candles and
                                    candleholders.

      b.   _____ At Consumers Distributing customers can order
                                    merchandise displayed in the store from an attached
                                    warehouse. Often, catalogues are sent to customers and
                                    are available to look at in the store.

c. _____ When Bill Barnes buys gas, he also purchases several grocery items at the food mart where he pays for the gas.

d. _____ The Bay has many departments in each of its stores to serve its customers.

e. _____ Bill's Store, in Mahone Bay, Nova Scotia, offers its customers a wide variety of merchandise, and still has a soda fountain section.

f. _____ At Superstore, a customer can purchase groceries, pay bills, send flowers, and choose from a wide variety of non-food items.

g. _____ Fairweather's, a women's fashion store, has locations nationwide.

h. _____ At Bi-Way, the customer selects his merchandise without sales help and pays at one general location. Prices at Bi-Way are often lower than those for similar items at the department store.

Nonstore Retailing

1. What are five types of non-store retailing?

   a. _____   d. _____

   b. _____   e. _____

   c. _____

2. What are the benefits of kiosks and carts?

   _____

   _____

   _____

   _____

3. What are the "battles," or challenges of e-tailing?

   _____

   _____

   _____

   _____

4. What are some of the customer service problems e-tailing sites have experienced?

   _____

   _____

   _____

   _____

5. What are the latest trends in e-commerce? What will be needed in the future?

   _____

   _____

   _____

6.   What is *direct selling?*

_____
_____
_____
_____

7.   How does *multilevel marketing* work?

_____
_____
_____
_____

8.   What are an *upliner* and a *downliner* in multilevel marketing?

_____
_____
_____
_____

9.   What are two attractions of multilevel marketing?

    a. _____
_____

    b. _____
_____

10.   What are four forms of *direct marketing?*

    a. _____
    b. _____
    c. _____
    d. _____

Building Cooperation in Channel Systems

1.   Idenify three types of distribution systems.

    a. _____
    b. _____
    c. _____

2.   What are three types of contractual distribution systems?

    a. _____
    b. _____
    c. _____

3.   Why do retailers cooperate with producers in an administered distribution system?

_____
_____
_____

4. What makes a value chain efficient?

_____
_____
_____

5. How does a supply chain compare to a channel of distribution?

_____
_____
_____
_____

6. Music-stor is looking at the distribution function. You and the marketing manager must make a proposal soon. In general, what kind of marketing intermediaries should we consider? How does the classification of Music-stor as either a convenience good, shopping good, or specialty good affect the answer to this question? What would the channel of distribution look like? Is there a need for a marketing intermediary if we target primarily the automotive manufacturers? What kind of utilities will our customers find most important?

_____
_____
_____
_____
_____
_____
_____
_____
_____
_____

7. A further look at Music-stor's distribution shows the need to consider the kind of cooperation necessary for us to create an efficient system.

In what kind of distribution system (corporate, contractual, or administered) will Music-stor take part?

_____
_____
_____

8. How does supply chain management relate to what we have learned earlier about technology and customer service?

_____
_____
_____
_____
_____

9. What poses the biggest problem for the new online retailers?

_____
_____

Choosing the Right Distribution Mode and Storage Units

1.   a.   Identify seven activities involved in physical distribution.

    i.   _____

    ii.   _____

    iii.   _____

    iv.   _____

    v.   _____

    vi.   _____

    vii.   _____

    b. What is the "basic idea" for a physical distribution manager?

_____

_____

_____

_____

2.   List five transportation modes used in physical distribution, in order of volume.

    a. _____

    b. _____

    c. _____

    d. _____

    e. _____

3.   What is a *mode* in the language of distribution?

_____

_____

_____

_____

4.   What does a logistics system involve?

_____

_____

_____

_____

5.   Name six criteria used to evaluate transportation modes.

    a. _____

    b. _____

    c. _____

    d. _____

    e. _____

    f. _____

6. What are the primary concerns for distribution managers regarding selecting a mode of transportation?

a. _____

b. _____

7. What is *intermodal shipping?*

_____
_____
_____
_____

8. What is meant by a *piggyback* system?

_____
_____
_____
_____

9. What are two kinds of warehouses?

a. _____

b. _____

10. What is the difference between the two kinds of warehouses?

_____
_____
_____
_____

11. How much of the cost of physical distribution comes from storage? What does the cost include?

_____
_____
_____
_____

CHAPTER CHECK

1. List five variables in the promotion mix.

a. _____   d. _____

b. _____   e. _____

c. _____

2. Explain the difference between advertising and the other promotion mix tools.

_____
_____
_____

3. Identify six media available to advertisers.

a. _____   d. _____

b. _____   e. _____
c. _____   f. _____

4. Which advertising media are the largest in terms of total dollars spent?

_____

_____

5. What are two major benefits the public receives from advertising?
   a. _____
   b. _____

6. The classes of advertising are
   a. _____   f. _____
   b. _____   g. _____
   c. _____   h. _____
   d. _____   i. _____
   e. _____

7. What are two important elements needed in developing international advertising?
   a. _____
   b. _____

8. Identify the seven steps of the personal selling process.
   a. _____   e. _____
   b. _____   f. _____
   c. _____   g. _____
   d. _____

9. Can you think of three important ways to generate positive word-of-mouth promotion?
   a. _____
   b. _____
   c. _____

10. List three steps in developing a marketing communication system.
    a. _____
    b. _____
    c. _____

11. Name two types of marketing intermediaries.
    a. _____
    b. _____

12. Identify the three major channels of distribution for consumer goods.
    a. _____
    b. _____
    c. _____

13. List three types of distribution systems.

a. _____

b. _____

c. _____

14. Identify three forms of contractual channel systems.

a. _____

b. _____

c. _____

15. What is meant by the term "logistics?"

_____

_____

16. List five modes of transportation available for the physical distribution of goods.

a. _____   d. _____

b. _____   e. _____

c. _____

17. Name two criteria for selecting a distribution system.

a. _____

b. _____

18. Describe the difference between a wholesaler and a retailer.

a. Wholesaler _____

_____

b. Retailer _____

_____

19. Name three types of limited-function wholesalers.

a. _____

b. _____

c. _____

20. List eight functions a full-service wholesaler performs.

a. _____   e. _____

b. _____   f. _____

c. _____   g. _____

d. _____   h. _____

21. List two major categories of retailing.

a. _____

b. _____

22. List three kinds of retail distribution strategy.

a. _____

b. _____

c. _____

PRACTICE TEST

Multiple Choice: Circle the best answer.

1. _____ allows customers to buy products by interacting with various advertising media without meeting a sales person face-to-face.
   - a. Target marketing
   - b. Market segmentation
   - c. Direct marketing
   - d. Promotion

2. Promotion is an attempt by marketers to
   - a. help retailers sell products.
   - b. inform and persuade people to buy.
   - c. segment markets to reach them more effectively.
   - d. search for new prospects.

3. In personal selling, the relationship must continue for a long time, as the salesperson responds to new requests for information from current customers. This is an important part of the _____ step in personal selling.
   - a. prospecting
   - b. closing
   - c. follow-up
   - d. presentation

4. Which of the following is true regarding personal selling today?
   - a. Technology has had a big impact on personal selling with the use of high-tech hardware and software.
   - b. The objective of an initial sales call is to make a sale immediately.
   - c. Big customers should always be treated with more care than small ones.
   - d. It is more difficult to find customers in the business-to-business market than in the consumer market.

5. Which of the following is NOT a part of developing a good public relations program?
   - a. Listen to the public.
   - b. Inform people of the fact you're being responsive.
   - c. Develop policies and procedures in the public interest.
   - d. Advertise in a way that promotes positive word-of-mouth.

6. Which of the following is NOT considered a benefit of publicity?
   - a. Publicity may reach people who wouldn't read an advertisement.
   - b. Publicity may be placed on the front page of a newspaper.
   - c. You can control when the publicity release will be used.
   - d. Publicity is more believable than other forms of promotion.

7. Which of the following is NOT true regarding sales promotion efforts?
   - a. Sales promotion efforts are aimed first at salespersons, then at the end consumer.
   - b. Sales promotion can be done both internally and externally.
   - c. Sales promotion programs are designed to supplement other promotion efforts.
   - d. Sales promotion efforts are designed to create long-term relationships.

8. Mama Barucci's Restaurant has had a big increase in business since Mama implemented an integrated marketing communications system. Mama has learned that much of the new business is coming from customers who have recommended the restaurant to their friends and associates. People seem to be hearing about Mama Barucci's and want to try it for themselves. Mama's is benefiting from
   - a. publicity
   - b. advertising
   - c. word-of-mouth
   - d. sales promotion

9. Which of the following is an advantage of Internet advertising over other media?
   - a. targets a specific audience
   - b. local market focus
   - c. no competition from other material
   - d. inexpensive global coverage

10. Which of the following would NOT be included in a discussion of the benefits of advertising using

infomercials?
a. They can show the product in great detail.
b. Infomercials are low in cost.
c. It is the equivalent of sending your best salesperson into the home.
d. Infomercials provide the opportunity to show the public how a product works.

11. Technology has
a. had little impact on the area of advertising.
b. affected other areas of business more than advertising.
c. had a tremendous impact on advertising.
d. decreased the need for personal selling.

12. Microsystems advertises in several software publications, as well as on the Internet. Their salespeople call on computer stores, and often leave brochures and other materials describing their products and customer service programs. The company has a Web site where the customers can purchase products on-line. These efforts are part of the company's
a. marketing mix
b. promotion mix
c. push strategy
d. corporate platform

13. Which of the following is NOT one of the basic steps of developing an interactive marketing communication system?
a. Make it possible for customers to access information they need to make a purchase.
b. Respond quickly to customer information by designing wanted products.
c Gather data about the groups affected by the organization.
d. Develop a promotion mix to satisfy the needs of interactive customers.

14. Which statement would NOT be included in a discussion of the advantages of interactive marketing on the Internet?
a. Customers can access information any time they want.
b. Large companies can reach the markets more effectively than smaller companies.
c. Buyers and sellers can engage in a dialogue.
d. Electronic ads and catalogues do not have to be printed, stored, or shipped.

15. What is likely to be the impact of technology on television and other forms of mass advertising?
a. The Internet has probably peaked as a form of advertising, and will not have a further impact on any other forms of advertising.
b. There will be a big drop-off in TV and other mass advertising.
c. Technology will be a complementary effort, but will not increase in use as a tool for advertising.
d. Infomercials will probably replace the Internet as the primary form of promotion.

16. Which of the following is an activity that would NOT be considered a physical distribution function?
a. storage
b. transportation
c. inventory
d. production

17. Minimizing inventory and moving goods more quickly, using computers and other technology is called
a. supply chain management
b. channels of distribution
c. electronic data interchange
d. quick response

18. Which of the following statements is accurate regarding marketing intermediaries?
a. Intermediaries add cost to products, but not value.
b. Intermediaries must adopt the latest technology to maintain their competitive position.
c. The functions performed by marketing intermediaries are easily eliminated.
d. Intermediaries have never performed their job efficiently; that's why they are being eliminated.

19. McDonald's, Baskin-Robbins, and other franchisors are examples of a(n)
a. corporate distribution system
b. contractual distribution system

    c. retail cooperative

    d. administered distribution system

20. A value chain is efficient because

    a. organizations within the chain are electronically linked so information flow is smooth.

    b. one organization is performing most of the activities, so things happen faster.

    c. the activities begin only after the products are made and shipped to the wholesaler.

    d. each organization signs a written contract, and has agreements with a union.

21. Because of improved, more customer-oriented logistics systems,

    a. wholesalers have become obsolete.

    b. businesses carry less inventory, and costs have decreased significantly.

    c. certain transportation modes have been eliminated.

    d. final customers are now able to go direct to the manufacturer, or to the wholesaler.

22. When Hans Kaupfmann bought his car while on a trip to Germany, he wasn't sure how it would be shipped. The dealer assured him that many people buy cars and have them shipped, and it's a smooth transition from land to sea and back to land, by trucking the car to the port, loading the entire truck trailer on to the ship, then trucking again to the destination. This process is known as

    a. piggyback   c. bimodal transportation

    b. fishyback   d. transatlantic transportation

23. A _____ gathers, then redistributes products.

    a. distribution warehouse   c. full-service wholesaler

    b. storage warehouse   d. drop shipper wholesaler

24. The major difference between wholesalers and retailers is that

    a. retailers sell only in certain parts of the country, while wholesalers are nationwide.

    b. wholesale organizations are generally more profitable than retail organizations.

    c. retailers sell only consumer goods, and wholesalers sell business-to-business goods.

    d. retailers sell to final consumers, while wholesalers sell to another member of the channel of distribution, not final consumers.

25. Discount stores such as Wal-Mart and Zellers are hard to compete against, because these stores are the best at

    a. selection competition   c. location competition

    b. price competition   d. total quality competition

True/False

1. ____ Most data indicate that personal selling is not a major force in our economy.

2. ____ It is said that 50% of a sales negotiation's outcome is determined before you meet a customer face-to-face.

3. ____ The idea of public relations is to establish a dialogue with stakeholders.

4. ____ One of the problems with publicity is that it is not believable.

5. ____ Sales promotion can be used as an attempt to keep salespeople enthusiastic about the company.

6. ____ The best way to generate positive word-of-mouth is to have a good product and provide good service.

7. ____ Word-of-mouth is really another form of advertising.

8. ____ Evidence supports the theory that promotional efforts specifically designed for individual countries are not any more successful than more general advertising.

9. ____ When using a pull strategy, advertising and sales promotion efforts are directed at consumers.

10. ____ Small firms are capturing markets from large firms because small firms tend to be better

listeners and more responsive to changes in the market.

11. ____ The promotion of services is often harder than for goods because the product is intangible.

12. ____ Disk-based advertising may take the place of infomercials in the future.

13. ____ A channel of distribution consists of marketing intermediaries who join together to store and transport goods in their path from producer to consumer.

14. ____ Companies are now able to carry lower levels of inventory because of supply-chain management.

15. ____ Generally, it is much less expensive and much faster when we can avoid the use of a marketing intermediary and go straight to the producer.

16. ____ In a corporate distribution system, a retailer signs a contract to cooperate with a manufacturer.

17. ____ The primary concern of a physical distribution manager is keeping costs down, regardless of anything else.

18. ____ Railroads could experience an increase in use if energy prices go up.

19. ____ Merchant wholesalers do not buy what they sell; they primarily match buyers with sellers.

20. ____ The Internet has made wholesalers obsolete.

21. ____ Consumers will often pay a bit more for goods and services if a retailer will offer outstanding service.

22. ____ Smaller retailers can compete with category-killer stores by offering lower prices and better store hours.

23. ____ Telemarketing is expected to be one of the fastest growing areas in marketing.

ANSWERS

Key Terms and Definitions

1. e-tailing
2. sales promotion
3. advertising
4. public relations (PR)
5. pull strategy
6. promotion mix
7. marketing intermediary
8. limited-function wholesaler

9. wholesaler
10. materials handling

11. electronic data interchange (EDI)
12. full service wholesaler
13. physical distribution (logistics)
14. integrated marketing communication (IMC)
15. channel of distribution
16. retailer
17. prospecting

26. freight forwarder
27. trade show
28. promotion
29. viral marketing
30. merchant wholesalers
31. exclusive distribution
32. prospects
33. word-of-mouth promotion
34. rack jobbers
35. interactive marketing program
36. drop shippers

37. selective distribution
38. closing techniques

39. sampling

40. qualify
41. intensive distribution
42. cash-and-carry

	wholesalers
18. publicity	43. category killer stores
19. push strategy	44. retail sale
20. infomercial	45. wholesale sale
21. personal selling	46. consultative salesperson
22. brokers	47. interactive promotion
23. corporate distribution system	48. contractual distribution system
24. telemarketing	49. supply chain
25. administered distribution system	

The Importance of Promotion/The Promotion Mix

1.   Marketers spend more than $13 billion yearly on advertising.
2.   a. Personal selling   d. Public relations
     b. Sales promotion   e. Publicity
     c. Advertising
3.   The Internet is changing the whole approach to working with customers. The latest trend is to build relationships with customers over time. That means carefully listening to what customers want, tracking their purchases, providing them with better service, and giving them access to more information.
4.   a. *Suggested Answers*
        i.   a.   Public relations
              b.   Publicity

        ii.   a.   Personal selling
              b.   Advertising
        iii. a.   Advertising
              b.   Sales promotion
        iv.   a.   Word-of-mouth
              b.   A good product
     b.   i.   Word-of-mouth   iv. Publicity
         ii. Sales promotion   v.   Advertising
         iii. Public relations   vi. Personal selling

Advertising: Persuasive Communication

1.   The public benefits from advertising because ads are informative. It provides us with free TV and radio because advertisers pay for the production costs. Advertising also covers the major costs of producing newspapers and magazines.
2.   a. Radio, newspaper
     b. Newspaper, radio
     c. Magazines, direct mail
     d. Outdoor, local TV, radio
     e. TV, direct mail
     f. Direct mail
     g. Magazines, direct mail
     h. Newspapers, TV, direct mail

3.   Technology has changed advertising in terms of the way the message can be delivered to the customer. Interactive TV allows promoters to carry on a dialogue with customers. CD-ROM allows promoters to follow up with even more information using the latest in multimedia. Hand-held computers can be used to place orders, and to help customers design custom-made products. Information can be received over e-mail, and can reach service people using cellular telephones and pagers.

Further, companies are making use of such on-line services as Prodigy, America Online, and CompuServe to provide information. Potential customers can go on-line with sellers and get information immediately.

Infomercials allow producers to provide more in-depth information about their products and offer testimonials, demonstrations, and more.

4.   Infomercials allow the seller to show the product in detail, which helps the product to sell itself. They allow for testimonials and for showing the customer how the product actually works, and allow for the use of drama, demonstration, graphics, and other advertising tools.

5.   Technology is having a major impact on advertising. Promoters are using interactive TV to carry on a dialogue with customers, and using CD-ROM technology to provide more information. Salespeople are using hand-held computers to place orders and to help consumers design custom-made products. Customers can request information via e-mail or fax and can reach service people from almost any location.

6.   a. i.   Retail
         ii.   Trade
         iii. Institutional
         iv.   Industrial
         v.   Comparison
         vi.   Product
         vii. Advocacy

      b. Products used in Canada may be used differently overseas as in the example of Corn Flakes in Brazil. It is important to research the culture as well as the wants and needs of a specific country, then design appropriate advertising.

7.   a. Newspapers
          Advantages: good local coverage; ads place quickly; high acceptance; ad can be clipped and saved
          Disadvantages: ads compete with other features; poor colour; ads get thrown away

      b. Television
          Advantages: sight, sound, motion; reaches all audiences; high attention with no competition
          Disadvantages: high cost; short exposure time; takes time to prepare ads

      c. Radio
          Advantages: low cost; can target specific audiences; flexible; good for local market
          Disadvantages: people may not listen; short exposure time; audience can't keep ad

      d. Magazines
          Advantages: target specific audiences; good use of colour; long life; ad can be clipped and saved
          Disadvantages: inflexible; ads must be placed weeks before publication; cost is relatively high

      e. Outdoor
          Advantages: high visibility and repeat exposures; low cost; local market focus
          Disadvantages: limited message; low selectivity of audience

      f. Direct mail

      Advantages: best for targeting specific markets; very flexible; ad can be saved
      Disadvantages: high cost; consumer rejection as junk mail; must conform to postal
      regulations

  g. Yellow pages
      Advantages: great coverage of local markets; widely used by consumers; available at point
      of purchase
      Disadvantages: competition with other ads; cost may be too high for very small businesses

  h. Internet
      Advantages: inexpensive global coverage; available at any time; interactive
      Disadvantages: relatively low readership

8. Most ads today on the Internet are ignored. Companies continue to use the Internet to advertise because ultimately the goal is to send customers and potential customers over to a website where they can learn more about the company, and vice versa.

9. Customer relationship software makes it possible to track customer's purchases and answer their questions online.

10. New technology will greatly improve the speed and potential of Internet dialogues. Companies will be able to provide better online videos, online chat rooms, and other services that will take customers to a virtual store where they will be able to talk to other customers, talk to sales people, examine goods and services and buy products.

Personal Selling: Providing Personal Attention

1. Effective selling is a matter of persuading others to buy and helping others to satisfy their wants and needs.

2. To "qualify customers" means to make sure that they have a need for the product, the authority to buy, and the willingness to listen to a sales message. People who meet these criteria are called prospects.

3. Before making a sales call, the sales representative must do further research, which is done during the preapproach. As much as possible should be learned about customers' wants and needs.

4. The objective of an initial sales call is to give an impression of professionalism, create rapport, and build credibility.

5. During the sales presentation, the sales representative matches the benefits of his or her value package to the client's needs. The presentation will be tailored to the customer's needs, and will be relatively easy to present because the sales representative has done the homework of getting to know the customer.

6. Closing techniques include getting a series of small commitments and then asking for the order and showing the client where to sign.

7. The follow-up includes handling customer complaints, making sure that the customer's questions are answered, and supplying what the customer wants.

8. Salespeople can use the Internet, portable computers, pagers, and other technology to help customers search the Net, design custom-made products, look over prices, and generally do everything it takes to complete the order.

9. The goals of a salesperson are to help the buyer buy, and to make sure the buyer is satisfied after the sale.

10. With current technology, a salesperson has data about the customer, competitors, where products are in the supply chain, pricing and more. B2B salespeople will have new roles to play as more customers buy over the Internet. Sales personnel will have to add value to the product and become a consultative salesperson.

11. A consultative salesperson begins by analyzing customer needs and then comes up with solutions

to those needs. Often customers have already searched the Internet for information and will already know what they want. So the role of the salesperson is to be a consultant, to provide enough helpful assistance that it will be worth dealing with the salesperson. The salesperson will have to be computer proficient, and be able to walk the customer through the exchange process quickly and easily.

12. a. Close sale   e. Answer objections
    b. Approach   f.Prospect
    c. Follow up   g. Preapproach
    c. Make presentation

13. a. A sales presentation for Music-stor will have to begin with prospecting. Which car makers are you going to target? Are you going to go after just one car maker, or several? Initially, you will probably be wise to begin with just one. The question then becomes which maker to go after. After research, you may be able to make that decision more easily. Then, the preapproach will call for learning as much as possible about the products your customer sells. Which models will be the best suited for Music-stor? Which of the models could be most easily adapted? What's the production volume on those models? What's the competition doing? How could Music-stor benefit your customer? Making the approach will involve making an appointment with the *right person*, the decision-maker. You will need to look professional, have a prototype of the product with you. Come prepared with questions geared to help you find out what they may be looking for. During the presentation, you will have to show the car maker how

Music-stor will make their cars better than the competition. You could discuss the benefits of convenience, luxury, and have something the competition doesn't have. You could come prepared with visuals demonstrating how easily Music-stor would fit into the interior of the car (with the magic of computer graphics). You will also want to know something about who your customer's customers are, in order to be able to demonstrate how Music-stor will fit into existing models, perhaps by driving a car (one of their models, of course) with Music-stor installed, and taking the customer for a ride to show them Music-stor convenience. You could show them how easily the interior could be adapted for Music-stor by using your computer graphics presentation. Eventually you will have to close the sale, perhaps by asking to make Music-stor an available option, or asking your customer to put Music-stor in some of their cars. Finally, always be available for questions, "hand-holding," and problems that may arise. Keep in mind that this process will take a lot of time, and won't be accomplished in one sales call.

    b. In order to convince retailers to sell the product, you will need to convince them that the shelf space you are asking for will pay off. You will still need to determine which type of retailer will be most appropriate (prospecting and qualifying), and research retailers in terms of who their customers are, the needs of the retailer, and exactly what they want from the products they carry. During the presentation, you will need to convince the retailer that this is a product consumers will want, why they will want it (convenience and the ability to store more tapes and CDs), and how carrying the product will benefit the retailer. You will need to have a sample of Music-stor with you and show the retailer how it works easily with most interiors and how easily it can be taken out of the car if necessary.

Public Relations: Building Relationships with All Publics

    1. Steps in creating a public relations campaign are as follows:
        a. Focus on customer satisfaction and quality.
        b. Deliver on promises.
        c. Target opinion leaders.

2. It is the responsibility of the public relations department to maintain close relationships with the media, community leaders, government officials, and other corporate stakeholders. The idea is to establish and maintain a dialogue with those stakeholders so that the company can respond to questions, complaints, and suggestions quickly.
3. The benefits of publicity are as follows:
   a. It's free, if the material is interesting or newsworthy.
   b. It may reach people who would not read an advertisement.
   c. It's believable.
4. The drawbacks of publicity are as follows:
   a. No control over how or when the media will use the story.
   b. The story may be altered, and could end up not as positive as the original.
   d. Once a story has run, it won't be repeated.

Sales Promotion: Getting a Good Deal

1. a.   trade shows
   b.   portfolios for salespeople
   c.   deals (price reductions)
   d.   catalogues
   e.   conventions
2. a.   coupons
   b.   cents-off promotions
   c.   sampling
   d.   premiums
   e.   sweepstakes
   f.   contests
   g.   bonuses (buy one, get one free)
   h.   catalogues
   i.   demonstrations
   j.   special events
   k.   lotteries
   l.   exhibits
3. Sales promotion programs are designed to supplement the other promotion mix variables by creating enthusiasm for the overall promotional program.
4. Sales promotion targets can be both internal, within the company, and external, outside the company.
5. Internal sales promotion efforts are directed at salespeople and other customer contact people. It is an attempt to keep salespeople enthusiastic about the company through sales training and the development of sales aids, and participation in trade shows where salespeople can get leads.
6. After the company's employees have been motivated, the next step is to promote to final consumers using samples, coupons, cents-off deals, displays, store demonstrations, premiums, and other incentives such as contests, trading stamps, and rebates.
7. Sampling is a quick, effective way of demonstrating a product's superiority at the time when consumers are making a purchase decision.
8. A virtual trade show is a trade show on the Internet. This allows customers to see many products without leaving the office, and the information is available 24 hours a day.
9. Event marketing means sponsoring events such as rock concerts or going to various events to promote products.
10. The best way to generate word-of-mouth is to
    a. have a good product
    b. provide good services
    c. keep customers happy
11. The elements of an effective word-of-mouth promotion are
    a. focusing on customer satisfaction and quality

b. delivering on promises
   c. targeting opinion leaders
12.   a. *Product* — A good product will generate positive word-of-mouth because customers will be happy with the product and pass the word along.
   b. *Sales promotion* — Techniques such as special events and contests often create positive word-of-mouth promotion.
   c. *Advertising* — When an advertisement is easily remembered or funny, it will often create positive word-of-mouth. A good technique is to advertise to people who already use your product.
   d. *Publicity* — A news story can create word-of-mouth by stimulating the public's interest in the product.
   d. *Personal selling* — A good salesperson can help the customer to develop a positive image of the product, thus creating positive word-of-mouth.
13.   As people purchase goods and services on the Internet, companies keep track of these purchases and gather other kinds of information about consumers. Over time, the company learns who buys what, when and how often. Because of the availability of so much information, companies are tending to use traditional promotional tools less and are putting more money into direct mail and other forms of direct marketing, including catalogues and the Internet.
14.   Promotion has become interactive because you can search the Internet on your own and find the information about products when you want it. If you can't find the information you want, you can request it and get it immediately.

Managing the Promotion Mix: Putting it All Together

1.   a. Large homogeneous groups of consumers are usually most efficiently reached through advertising.
   b. Large organizations are best reached through personal selling.
2.   In a push strategy, the producer uses promotion tools to convince wholesalers and retailers to stock and sell merchandise. If it works, consumers will walk into the store, see the product, and buy it. The idea is to push the product through the distribution system to the stores.
3.   In a pull strategy, heavy advertising and sales promotion efforts are directed toward consumers so they'll request the products from retailers. If it works, consumers will go to the store and order the products. Seeing demand, the store owner will then order them from the wholesaler. The wholesaler in turn will order from the producer. The idea is to pull products down through the distribution system.
4.   A total systems approach to marketing is when promotion is a part of supply-chain management. In such cases retailers would work with producers and distributors to make the supply chain as efficient as possible. Then a promotional plan would be developed for the whole system. The idea would be to develop a value package that would appeal to everyone.
5.   Interactive marketing is the use of new information technologies such as fax on demand, 900 telephone service, the Internet, databases, e-mail, and CD-ROMs. Marketers are now able to establish and maintain a dialogue with customers over time. Control over promotional messages is being shifted from the seller to the buyer.
6.   An interactive marketing communication system is one in which consumers can access company information on their own and supply information about themselves in an ongoing dialogue.
7.   Steps to develop an interactive marketing communications systems are as follows:
   a. Gather data constantly about the groups affected by the organization and keep the information in a database. Make it available to everyone.
   b. Respond quickly to information by adjusting company policies and practices and by designing

wanted products and services for target markets.

   c. Make it possible for customers and potential customers to access information that they may need to make a purchase.

8. Small firms are capturing markets from large firms because small firms tend to be better listeners, to have fewer layers of management in which information gets lost, and to be more responsive to changes in the market.

9. Advantages of interactive marketing on the Internet are as follows:

   a. Customers can access information 24 hours a day. A company can reach markets anywhere in the world.

   b. Electronic ads and catalogues don't have to be printed, stored, or shipped, and can be easily updated, continuously.

   c. Small companies have an equal or better chance to reach consumers.

   d. Buyers and sellers can engage in a dialogue over time, so both feel they are getting the best deal.

10. Marketing services on the Internet is more difficult than marketing goods because the product is intangible and customers can't visualize all the benefits they may receive.

11. Integrated marketing communication blends with interactive communications when phones, faxes, e-mail, television, and radio are all combined in one promotion.

12. The net result of the new technology is that companies will have to totally rethink how marketing and promotion will be done in the future. There is likely to be a big drop-off in TV and other mass advertising. There will be a huge increase in the use of the Internet as a promotional and marketing tool. The same is true of e-mail, fax, and other communication tools.

13. Soon there may be as many Internet malls as there are regional malls. Shoppers will be able to request information from multiple firms, compare prices, and make purchases from their homes.

14. a. *Suggested Answers*

Group	Technique
i. Salespeople	Sales training, conventions, trade shows
ii. Dealers	Catalogues, special events, price reduction
iii. Customers	Coupons, sweepstakes, displays, samples

   b. Answers will vary.

15. Your response to this question will really depend upon whom you have selected as your primary target market. If you have decided to go after the automotive manufacturers as your primary market, then most likely your promotion mix will include lots of personal selling, and some advertising in the form of brochures aimed at the car dealerships who will be selling the cars with your product installed. If your research has been done, and a need for this kind of product has been established, you could design a public relations campaign for the auto manufacturer, indicating that the company listened to your need for a product like Music-stor, then made the product in response.

     If your primary market is the retail market, then you must design a campaign aimed at encouraging the retailers to carry the product. Some kind of sales promotion will be appropriate such as price deals, incentives for the retailers selling the most product, and so on. You could participate in trade shows featuring the latest car models, which are held all over the United States and are attended by thousands of consumers. You could use some advertising, after the retailers have been convinced to carry Music-stor. Any form of publicity could be useful, as will the word-of-mouth generated by satisfied customers.

     You may have your own Web site, with attractive graphics and interactive sales techniques. You may be able to advertise on-line, on Web sites that appeal to a younger market, for example, which may be more likely to purchase your product for their car. You may also consider direct marketing, such as order forms in music magazines.

Most likely you will use a combination of push and pull strategies for the product. You will be using primarily a push strategy if you are aiming at the automotive manufacturers. A combination will be most effective if you are aiming at the consumer market. Probably the best approach, once you are an established company, will be to work with your customers and retailers and develop a value package that will appeal to everyone — the manufacturers, retailers, and consumers.

The Importance of Channels of Distribution

1. a. Transportation
   b. Storage
   c. Purchasing goods
   d. Receiving goods
   e. Moving goods through the plant
   f. Inventorying goods
2. The types of marketing intermediaries are
   a. wholesalers
   b. retailers
3. We have marketing intermediaries because it is usually faster and cheaper to use intermediaries to perform certain marketing functions, such as transportation, storage, selling, and advertising. The intermediaries can perform these functions more effectively and efficiently than manufacturers could.
4. Marketing intermediaries add efficiency to the distribution system by reducing the number of transactions necessary to get products from the producer to the consumer.
5. Technology has made it possible for manufacturers to reach consumers more efficiently. Some manufacturers, such as Dell Computer, reach consumers directly on the Internet. Retailers, too, are so closely linked to manufacturers that they can get delivery as often as once or twice a day. All this means that there is often no need for a wholesaler to perform functions such as storage and delivery. Wholesalers are not yet obsolete, but they need to change their functions to remain viable in today's rapidly changing distribution systems.
6. The type of product will determine which mode of transportation to use and what kinds of store it should be sold in. The price will be determined in part by the mode of transportation (if it's fast it's more expensive) and in part by the kind of store — e.g., the image of the store, pricing policies.
7. Brokers don't take title to, or own, the goods they deal with. They don't carry inventory, provide credit or assume risk. Some kinds of brokers are insurance brokers, real estate brokers, and stockbrokers.
8. Answers will vary.
9. Some people believe that if they could get rid of the intermediary they could reduce the cost of what they buy. However, if we got rid of a retailer, for example, we may be able to buy a product for a little less, but we would still have to drive further and spend more time looking for the product. The value of intermediaries is that they make products available to us at times and places that are convenient for us. That often outweighs the cost they add to the product.
10. a. marketing intermediaries can be eliminated, but their activities cannot.
    b. intermediaries have survived because they have performed functions more effectively and efficiently than others. They must adopt the latest technology to remain competitive.
    c. Intermediaries add cost, but the cost is usually offset by the value they create.
11. *Suggested Answer*
    a. Storage
    b. Transportation
    c. Convenient time and place to shop

 e. Lower prices through convenience added

 f. Information

Wholesale Intermediaries

1. A retail sale is a sale of goods and services to *consumers* for their own use. A wholesale sale is the sale of goods and services to *businesses and institutions* for use in the business or for resale.
2. Two types of merchant wholesalers are
   a. full-service
   b. limited-function
3. Full-service wholesalers perform all distribution functions, such as transportation, storage, risk bearing, credit, market information, grading, buying, and selling. Limited-function wholesalers perform only selected functions.
4. Three types of limited-function wholesalers are
   a. cash and carry
   b. drop shippers
   d. rack jobbers

5. Rack jobbers furnish racks or shelves full of merchandise to retailers, display products and sell on consignment. They sell magazines, snack foods, etc.
6. A cash-and-carry wholesaler serves mostly smaller retailers with a limited assortment of products. Retailers go to them, pay cash, and carry the goods home.
7. A drop shipper solicits orders from retailers and other wholesalers and has the merchandise shipped directly from a producer to a buyer. They own the merchandise but don't handle, stock, or deliver it.
8. Smaller manufacturers that don't make large shipments use freight forwarders. The freight forwarder puts many small shipments together to create a single large shipment that can be transported cost-effectively to a final destination. Some will offer additional services, such as warehousing and customs assistance, along with pick-up and delivery.
9. Much B2B wholesaling is being done over the Internet through sites like E-Bay's Business Exchange and Yahoo's Business-to-Business Marketplace.

Retail Intermediaries

1. Retailers compete by
   a. price
   b. service
   c. location
   d. selection
   e. total quality
2. Smaller independent retailers have to offer truly outstanding service and selection to compete with giant retailers such as Office Depot.
3. Retail service involves putting the customer first. This requires that all front-line people be courteous and accommodating to customers. It also means follow-up service such as on-time delivery, guarantees, and fast installation. Customers are frequently willing to pay a little more for goods and services if the retailers offer outstanding service.
4. Category-killer stores offer a wide selection of a certain category of products at competitive prices. Examples are Toys 'R' Us and Borders Books.
5. Smaller retailers compete with category killers by offering more selection within a smaller category of items. You may have successful smaller stores selling nothing but coffee or party products.

Smaller retailers also compete with more personalized service.
6. A total quality retailer offers low price, good service, wide selection, and total quality management.
7. Price competition is getting fiercer as Internet firms help consumers find the best prices on various items.
8. Brick and mortar stores, in an effort to overcome the convenience of Internet shopping, have begun to make their stores more fun places to shop. The stores are becoming entertainment destinations with features like live music, giant aquariums, video games and skate parks.
9. Retail distribution strategies include
   a. intensive distribution
   b. selective distribution
   m. exclusive distribution
10. Intensive distribution puts products into as many outlets as possible and is used to sell products like cigarettes, gum and magazines.
    Selective distribution is the use of only a selected group of retailers in a given area and is used to sell appliances, furniture, and clothing.
    Exclusive distribution is the use of only one retail outlet in a given geographic area and is used by automobile manufacturers and for specialty goods.
11. a. Specialty
    b. Catalogue store
    c. Convenience store
    d. Department store
    e. General store
    f. Supermarket
    g. Chain store
    h. Discount market

Nonstore Retailing

1. Types of non-store retailing include
   a. telemarketing
   b. vending machines, kiosks, and carts
   c. direct personal selling
   d. network marketing
   e. selling by catalogue
2. Kiosks and carts have lower costs than stores. Therefore they can offer lower prices on items such as T-shirts and umbrellas. Mall owners often like them because they are colourful and create a market atmosphere. Customers enjoy interactive kiosks because they dispense coupons and provide information when buying products.
3. The major challenges, or battles, of e-tailing are getting customers and delivering the goods, providing helpful service, and keeping your customers.
4. E-tailers have had problems with handling complaints, taking back goods that customers don't like and providing online personal help.
5. The latest trend in e-tailing is for traditional retailers to go online. Further, online marketers are building "brick and mortar" stores, so that now customers can pick and choose which shopping form they prefer. Companies that want to compete in the future will probably need both a store presence and an online presence to provide consumers with all the options they want.
6. Direct selling involves selling to consumers in their homes or where they work.
7. Multilevel marketing salespeople work as independent contractors. They earn commissions on their own sales and create commissions for the upliners who recruited them.

8.   In multilevel marketing, an upliner is an individual who has recruited others to sell for them. The downliners are the people who have been recruited to sell.

9.   The main attractions of multilevel marketing are
   a. great potential for making money
   b. low cost of entry

10.   Direct retail marketing includes:
   a. direct mail
   b. catalogue sales
   c. telemarketing
   d. online shopping

Building Cooperation in Channel Systems

1. The three types of distribution systems are
   a. corporate systems
   b. contractual systems
   c. administered systems

2. The three types of contractual distribution systems are
   a. franchise systems
   b. wholesaler-sponsored chains
   c. retail cooperatives

3. Retailers cooperate with producers in an administered distribution system because they get so much help for free.

4. A value chain is efficient because the various organizations are linked electronically so that information flows among firms are as smooth as information flows were within a single firm.

5. A supply chain is longer than a channel of distribution because it includes suppliers to manufacturers whereas the channel of distribution begins with manufacturers. Channels of distribution are part of the supply chain.

6. Initially we may use some kind of wholesaler, who will then sell to a retailer. If we primarily target the auto industry, we will not necessarily need a wholesale middleman, unless we use a broker in lieu of employing our own sales force. The channel of distribution will look like this:

Music-stor	Music-stor
wholesaler	auto manufacturers
retailer	
consumer	

   The most important utility for the end consumer may be information utility, as the consumer may need to know more about the product. Place utility is important, but is affected by our classification of Music-stor as either a shopping good or specialty good. This affects the kind of store we will choose, as shopping goods may be found in several kinds of stores and specialty goods will be found in fewer, different kinds of stores.
   For the auto manufacturers, time and place utility will be important, as they will need the product delivered when they need it, where they need it.

7. Music-stor will most likely be a part of an administered distribution system when we are using retailers. As a new company, we can't afford to own our own retail stores right away, which cuts out a corporate distribution system. Moreover, for this type of product, a corporate distribution system would not be practical. A franchise system is not appropriate without many more product lines. Wholesaler-sponsored chains and retail cooperatives don't fit either.

8. Supply chain management is the process of minimizing inventory and moving goods through the

channel faster by using computers. This allows members of the channel to save money and serve customers much faster. A way to minimize inventory, for example, is just-in-time inventory control. Inventory control is also the point of electronic data interchange, which makes it possible for retailers to be directly linked to their supplier. Faster service at less cost allows firms to better serve customers, which has been the focus of the changes we are observing in today's corporations.

9. The biggest problem for the new online retailers has been outbound logistics.

Choosing the Right Distribution Mode and Storage Units

1. a. i. Shipping raw materials
      ii. Purchasing goods
      iii. Receiving goods
      iv. Moving goods through the plant
      v. Inventorying goods
      vi. Storing goods
      vii. Shipping finished goods

   c. The physical distribution manager is responsible for coordinating and integrating all movement of materials, including transportation, materials handling, and warehousing. The idea of a physical distribution manager's job is to keep distribution costs low for the whole system as well as for each individual organization in the channel.

2. a. railroad
   b. motor vehicles
   c. pipeline
   d. water transportation
   e. air

3. A mode refers to the various means used to transport goods, such as trucks, trains, planes, ships, and airplanes.

4. A logistics system involves activities such as processing orders and inventorying products, as well as transporting products. It is whatever it takes to see that the right products are sent to the right place quickly and efficiently.

5. Criteria used to evaluate transportation modes include
   a. cost
   b. speed
   c. on-time dependability
   d. flexibility in handling products
   e. frequency of shipments
   f. reach

6. The primary concern for distribution managers is selecting a transportation mode that will
   a. minimize costs
   b. ensure a certain level of service

7. Intermodal shipping uses multiple modes of transportation, including highway, air, water, and rail to complete a single long-distance movement of freight. Services that specialize in intermodal shipping are known as intermodal marketing companies.

8. A piggyback system means that a truck trailer is detached from the cab, loaded onto a railroad flatcar, and taken to a destination where is offloaded, attached to a truck, and driven to customers' plants.

9. The two kinds of warehouses are
   a. storage warehouses
   b. distribution warehouses
10. A storage warehouse stores products for a relatively long time, such as what is needed for seasonal goods. Distribution warehouses are facilities used to gather and redistribute products.
11. About 25% to 30% of the total cost of physical distribution is for storage. This includes the cost of the warehouse and its operation plus movement of goods within the warehouse.

CHAPTER CHECK ANSWERS

1. a. Advertising   d. Publicity
   b. Personal selling   e. Sales promotion
   c. Public relations
2. Advertising is paid, nonpersonal communication through various media. It is different from each of the other forms of promotion either because it is paid for, it is nonpersonal (unlike personal selling), or it goes through some form of media (unlike sales promotion).
3. a. Newspapers   d. Magazines
   b. Television   e. Outdoor
   c. Radio   f. Direct mail
4. The top media in terms of dollars are newspapers, television, and direct mail, in that order.
5. a. Advertising is informative.
   b. It allows us to have free TV and radio programs because advertisers pay for production costs.
6. a. Retail advertising   f. Advocacy advertising
   b. Trade advertising   g. Comparison advertising
   c. Industrial advertising   h. Interactive advertising
   d. Product advertising   i. On-line advertising
   e. Institutional advertising
7. a. Do research into the needs, wants, and culture of specific countries.
   b. Develop a promotional campaign specifically designed for individual countries.
8. a. Prospect
   b. Preapproach
   c. Approach
   d. Make presentation
   e. Answer objections
   f. Close sale
   g. Follow up
9. a. Focusing on customer satisfaction and quality
   b. Delivery on promises
   c. Targeting opinion leaders
10. a. Listening
    b. Responding
    c. Letting stakeholders know
11. a. Wholesalers
    b. Retailers
12. a. Manufacturer – consumer
    b. Manufacturer – retailer – consumer
    c. Manufacturer – wholesaler – retailer – consumer
13. a. Contractual
    b. Corporate

   c. Administered
14. a. Franchising
   b. Wholesaler sponsored
   c. Retail cooperative
15. "Logistics" is a comprehensive term that refers to distribution, storage, and all other functions having to do with the movement of goods.
16. a. Railroad
   b. Motor vehicles
   c. Water
   d. Pipeline
   e. Air
17. a. Customer service
   b. Cost
18. a. Wholesalers sell products to businesses and institutions for use in business, or to wholesalers, retailers, or individuals for resale.
   b. Retailers sell to the final consumer.
19. a. Drop shippers
   b. Truck jobbers
   c. Cash and carry
20. a. Transportation
   b. Storage
   c. Risk bearing
   d. Credit
   e. Market information
   f. Grading
   g. Buying
   h. Selling
21. a. Store
   b. Out-of-store
22. a. Intensive distribution
   b. Selective distribution
   c. Exclusive distribution

PRACTICE TEST

Multiple Choice		True/False	
1.	c	1.	F
2.	b	2.	T
3.	c	3.	T
4.	a	4.	F
5.	d	5.	T
6.	c	6.	T
7.	d	7.	F
8.	c	8.	F
9.	d	9.	T
10.	b	10.	T
11.	c	11.	T
12.	b	12.	T

13.	d
14.	b
15.	b
16.	d
17.	a
18.	b
19.	b
20.	a
21.	b
22.	b
23.	a
24.	d
25.	b

13.	T
14.	T
15.	F
16.	F
17.	F
18.	T
19.	F
20.	F
21.	T
22.	F
23.	T

CHAPTER 18

Accounting Fundamentals

Learning Goals

After you have read and studied this chapter, you should be able to

1. Define accounting and explain the differences between (a) managerial accounting and financial accounting, and (b) private and public accountants.
2. Compare accounting and bookkeeping.
3. Identify and describe the major accounts used to prepare financial statements.
4. Understand simple income statements and balance sheets, and explain their functions.
5. Describe the role of computers in accounting.
6. Explain the concept of cash flow.
7. Explain how a business can be making profits and still be short of cash.
8. Understand the new concerns of accounting.

Key Terms and Definitions

Listed here are important terms found in this chapter. Choose the correct term for each definition and write it in the space provided.

accounting	financial accounting	managerial accounting
accounting system	financial statements	net income
amortization (depreciation)	fixed or capital assets	operating expenses
assets	fundamental accounting equation	other assets
balance sheet	gross margin (profit)	owner's equity
bookkeeping	income statement	private accountants
cash flow	independent audit	public accountants
cost of goods sold	liabilities	ratio analysis
current assets	liquid	retained earnings

1. _____ Providing information and analyses to managers within the organization to assist them in decision making.

2. _____ Reports the financial position of a firm at the end of a specified period of time.

3. _____ The recording of transactions.

4. _____ Accumulated profits less dividends to shareholders.

5. _____ How quickly an asset can be turned into cash.

6. _____ Independent firms that provide accounting, auditing, and other professional services for clients on a fee basis.

7. _____ Assets that are not current or fixed.

8. _____ Net sales minus cost of goods sold before expenses are deducted.

9. _____ Examination of a company's books by public accountants to

give the public, governments, and shareholders an outside opinion of the fairness of financial statements.

10. _____ Various expenses of a business incurred in the course of earning revenue.

11. _____ Things of value owned by a business.

12. _____ Items that are acquired to produce services or products for a business. They are not bought to be sold.

13. _____ The recording, classifying, summarizing, and interpreting of financial transactions to provide management and other interested parties with the information they need.

14. _____ Employees who carry out managerial and financial accounting functions for their employers.

15. _____ A particular type of expense measured by the total cost of merchandise sold, including costs associated with the acquisition, storage, transportation, and packaging of goods.

16. _____ A way to analyze financial statements by comparing results with the previous year's, the budget, and competing firm's results.

17. _____ Cash and assets that are normally converted into cash within one year.

18. _____ The preparation of financial statements for people inside and outside of the firm.

19. _____ Since assets such as machinery lose value over time, part of their cost is calculated as an expense each year over their useful life.

20. _____ Reports revenues, expenses, and profit or loss during a specific period of time.

21. _____ The difference between cash receipts and cash disbursements.

22. _____ The methods used to record and summarize accounting data.

23. _____ Assets = liabilities + owner's equity.

24. _____ Revenue minus costs and expenses.

25. _____ Amounts owed by the organization to others.

26. _____ Report the operations and position (condition) of a firm; they include the income statement and the balance sheet.

27. _____ Owners' investments in the company plus all net accumulated profits.

What Is Accounting?

1. What are the three parts of the accounting system?

    a. _____

b. _____

c. _____

2. What are two purposes of accounting?

   a. _____

   b. _____

3. Why is accounting different from other business functions such as marketing, management, and human resources management?

   _____

   _____

   _____

   _____

4. What are the inputs to the accounting system?

   _____

   _____

   _____

   _____

5. What are the outputs from the accounting system?

   _____

   _____

   _____

   _____

6. Identify the areas with which managerial accounting is concerned.

   _____

   _____

   _____

   _____

7. How does financial accounting differ from managerial accounting?

   _____

   _____

   _____

   _____

8. Who receives financial accounting information?

   _____

   _____

   _____

   _____

9. Where can you find the information derived from financial accounting?

   _____

   _____

   _____

10. What is the difference between a public accountant and a private accountant?

_____

_____

_____

_____

11. What are some of the things a public accountant might do?

_____

_____

_____

_____

12. Why are audits performed? Who performs audits?

_____

_____

_____

_____

Accounting and Bookkeeping

1. Distinguish between accounting and bookkeeping.

_____

_____

_____

_____

2. What is the first task of a bookkeeper?

_____

_____

_____

_____

3. What do accountants do with data provided by bookkeepers?

_____

_____

_____

_____

_____

_____

4. Music-stor is doing very well! They need a bookkeeper to help them with their paperwork, and an **accountant. You have been given the task of writing a brief job description for each job. How would you write the job description for each?**
    Bookkeeper —

_____

_____
_____
_____
_____
_____

Accountant —
_____
_____
_____
_____
_____

The Accounts of Accounting

1. There are six major categories of accounts used to prepare financial statements:
   - ☐ Assets (current, fixed, intangible)
   - ☐ Liabilities
   - ☐ Owner's equity
   - ☐ Revenues
   - ☐ Cost of goods sold
   - ☐ Expenses

   a. Match the type of account to each of the following (if an asset, indicate current, fixed, or intangible):

i.	_____	Cash
ii.	_____	Retained earnings
iii.	_____	Accounts payable
iv.	_____	Interest
v.	_____	Rent
vi.	_____	Land
vii.	_____	Commission revenue
viii.	_____	Gross sales
ix.	_____	Capital stock
x.	_____	Copyright
xi.	_____	Notes payable
xii.	_____	Accounts receivable
xiii.	_____	Equipment
xiv.	_____	Advertising
xv.	_____	Wages
xvi.	_____	Retained earnings
xvii.	_____	Accrued expenses
xviii.	_____	Cost of finished goods for sale
xix.	_____	Inventories
xx.	_____	Investments

   b. List the liquid assets from the list above in order of liquidity.
   - i. _____
   - ii. _____
   - iii. _____
   - iv. _____

Financial Statements

1. For each of the preceding 20 accounts listed in question 1(a) above, indicate whether you would find them on a balance sheet, or an income statement.

   i. _____   xi. _____
   ii. _____   xii. _____
   iii. _____   xiii. _____
   iv. _____   xiv. _____
   v. _____   xv. _____
   vi. _____   xvi. _____
   Vii. _____   xvii. _____
   Viii _____   xviii. _____
   .
   ix. _____   xix. _____
   x. _____   xx. _____

2. List the three major types of accounts on a balance sheet.

   a. _____
   b. _____
   c. _____

3. What kinds of things are considered assets?

   _____
   _____
   _____
   _____

4. List the three categories of assets on a balance sheet.

   a. _____
   b. _____
   c. _____
   _____

5. In what order are assets listed on the balance sheet?

   a. _____
   b. _____
   c. _____
   _____

6. a. What is the difference between current liabilities and long-term liabilities?

   _____
   _____
   _____
   _____

   b. What are
      i. accounts payable?

   _____
   _____

ii. notes payable?

_____

_____

iii. bonds payable?

_____

_____

7.   What is "equity"? Shareholder's equity?

_____

_____

_____

_____

8.   What is the formula for owner's equity?

_____

_____

_____

_____

9.   How does owner's equity in sole proprietorships and partnerships differ from that in a corporation?

_____

_____

_____

_____

10. What is the fundamental accounting equation, or the formula for a balance sheet?

_____

_____

_____

_____

11. What is the formula for developing an income statement?
     a. _____
     b. _____
     c. _____

12. How does one arrange an income statement according to accepted accounting principles?

_____

_____

_____

_____

_____

_____

_____

13. What is the difference between revenue and sales?

_____

_____
_____
_____
_____

14.   What is the difference in gross margin between a service firm and a manufacturing firm?

_____
_____
_____
_____

15.   What are some kinds of operating expenses? What are two categories of expenses?

_____
_____
_____
_____

16.   What is the *bottom line?*

_____
_____
_____
_____

17.   What is a poor, or negative, cash flow? How does poor cash flow cause problems?

_____
_____
_____
_____

18.   List the three major activities for which cash receipts and disbursements are reported on a statement of cash flows.

_____
_____
_____
_____

19.   Two methods of determining the value of inventory, and therefore the cost of goods sold, are
        ☐ LIFO, last in, first out
        ☐ FIFO, first in, first out
       The method chosen will directly affect the "bottom line," or profits.

       The basic formula for cost of goods sold is as follows:
            Beginning inventory + purchases = Cost of goods sold
            Cost of goods available – ending inventory = Cost of goods sold

A. Determine the cost of goods sold, using FIFO and LIFO with the following information:

FIFO

Beginning inventory	20,000	units @ $10	$200,000
+ Purchases	7,000	units @ $12	84,000
= Cost of goods available	27,000	units	$284,000
– Ending inventory	5,000	units	

LIFO

Beginning inventory	20,000	units @ $10	$200,000
+ Purchases	7,000	units @ $12	84,000
= Cost of goods available	27,000	units	$284,000
– Ending inventory	5,000	units	

Cost of goods sold   FIFO _____ LIFO_____

B. What is gross margin on revenues of $450,000 using FIFO? LIFO?

FIFO_____LIFO _____

20. Jim Van Fleet runs his own small business painting houses. Right now Jim is concerned about paying his bills. He has several jobs lined up for this spring when the weather breaks, but his creditors are asking for their money now! The jobs he bid were based on paint prices he could get when he bid them. In addition, the manager of the paint store said prices were going up next week and Jim would like to buy the paint now. What is Jim's problem and what can he do?

_____
_____
_____
_____
_____

21. a. The income statement reports revenue and expenses for a specific period of time. The basic formula is as follows:

Revenue minus cost of goods sold = gross profit
Gross profit minus operating expenses = profit before taxes
Profit before taxes minus taxes = net profit

Construct an accurate income statement using the list of accounts shown below. Be careful! Not all the accounts listed will be used on an income statement.

MERAMEC MUNCHIES, INC.
List of Accounts

Notes Receivable	$ 9,300
Accounts Payable	6,400
Marketable Securities	7,400
Net Sales	77,800
Accounts Receivable	15,400
Depreciation Expense	3,200
Inventories	16,100
Advertising	8,600
Sales Salaries	19,400
Notes Payable (Current)	6,000
Rental Revenue	3,700
Cost of Goods Sold	33,300
Buildings	32,500
Cash	8,400
Retained Earnings	26,200
Long-Term Debt	20,000
Accrued Salaries	2,300
Common Stock	33,200
Interest Expense	3,100
Insurance	4,300
Land	5,000

MERAMEC MUNCHIES, INC.
INCOME STATEMENT*
Year ending December 31, 20__

* For purposes of determining net income after taxes, assume a tax rate of 25%.

b.   The balance sheet reports the financial position of a firm on a specific date. The basic formula for a balance sheet is as follows:

Assets = Liabilities + Owner's Equity

Total Assets consists of current, fixed, and intangible assets.

Total Liabilities consists of current and long-term liabilities.

Owner's equity consists of common stock and retained earnings.

Construct an accurate balance sheet using the list of accounts shown in section a. Be careful! Not all of the accounts listed will be used.

MERAMEC MUNCHIES, INC.
BALANCE SHEET
December 31, 20__

22. Using the following list of accounts, construct an accurate balance sheet for Music-stor, Inc. Be careful! Not all of the accounts listed will be used for the balance sheet.

MUSIC-STOR, INC.

List of accounts

Accounts payable	$25,000
Net sales	$60,000
Accounts receivable	$110,000
Depreciation expense	$4,000
Inventories	$62,000
Advertising	$28,000
Wages and salaries	$125,000
Notes payable (current)	$15,000
Rental revenue	$3,000
Cost of goods sold	$313,000
Property, plant, equipment	$204,000
Cash	$18,000
Retained earnings	$165,000
Accrued taxes	$40,000
Long-term debt	$60,000
Common stock	$130,000
Utilities	$12,000
Supplies	$3,700
Investments	$45,000
Rent	$35,000

23. Using the previous list of accounts, construct an accurate income statement for Music-stor. Again, look at each account carefully! For purposes of illustration, assume a 28% tax rate on income.

Accounting Complexity

1. What does it mean when financial reports are prepared in accordance with GAAP?

_____

_____

_____

_____

2. How can depreciation affect a firm's net income?

_____

_____

_____

_____

Cash-Flow Problems

1. The number one financial cause of small-business failure today is inadequate cash flow. Cash flow is the difference between cash receipts and cash disbursements. Cash-flow problems arise when a firm has debt obligations that must be met before cash for sales is received.

    a. Prepare a personal cash-flow forecast for two months. Include all projected income and all projected cash disbursements (payments). Do you have a cash-flow problem?

	Month One	Month Two	Month Three
Projected Income	_____	_____	_____
Projected Cash Disbursements	_____	_____	_____
	_____	_____	_____
	_____	_____	_____
Surplus (deficit)	_____	_____	_____

    b. How can small businesses avoid cash-flow problems?

    _____

    _____

    _____

    _____

2. Identify and describe at least one of the new areas of concern that is creating major issues for accountants because of the difficulty of evaluating intangibles in accounting terms.

    _____

    _____

    _____

    _____

Ratio Analysis (Appendix/Website)

1. What are the four financial issues dealt with using ratio analysis?

    _____

    _____

    _____

    _____

2. What are the two primary indicators of a company's liquidity?

    a. _____

    b. _____

3. What is the formula for inventory turnover? What does it measure?

    _____

    _____

    _____

    _____

4. What does it indicate if you have inventory turnover ratios which are lower than or higher than average?

_____
_____
_____
_____

5.   What is the formula for return on sales? What does it measure?

_____
_____
_____
_____

6.   What is the formula for determining basic earnings per share?

_____
_____
_____
_____

7.   What is the formula for debt to equity ratio?

_____
_____
_____
_____

8.   What does it mean if a firm has a debt to equity ratio above 1?

_____
_____
_____
_____

9.   What is the formula for the current ratio?

_____
_____
_____
_____

10.   To what is the current ratio compared?

_____
_____
_____
_____

11.   Identify the formula for the quick ratio or acid test ratio. What does this ratio measure?

_____
_____
_____
_____

CHAPTER CHECK

1. What are the two major categories of accounting?

   a. _____

   b. _____

2. Identify four areas of concern in managerial accounting.

   a. _____

   b. _____

   c. _____

   d. _____

3. What is the difference between managerial accounting and financial accounting?

   _____

   _____

   _____

   _____

4. Who are the potential users of financial accounting information?

   _____

   _____

   _____

   _____

5. What are six "original transaction" documents used by bookkeepers?

   a. _____

   b. _____

   c. _____

   d. _____

   e. _____

   f. _____

6. List the six major categories of accounts.

   a. _____ d. _____

   b. _____ e. _____

   c. _____ f. _____

7. Identify the two most important financial statements.

   a. _____

   b. _____

8. Name three categories of assets.

   a. _____

   b. _____

   c. _____

9. What are three kinds of liabilities?

   a. _____

   b. _____

   c. _____

10. What is the formula for owner's equity?

_____

11. What is the fundamental accounting equation used as the basis for a balance sheet?

_____

12. What is the set of three basic formulas for determining net income after taxes?

a. _____

b. _____

c. _____

13. What are two choices companies have for using profits?

a. _____

b. _____

14. What is cash flow?

_____

_____

15. What are the three types of degrees or "designations" held by accountants in Canada?

a. _____

b. _____

c. _____

16. List seven types of financial ratios.

a. _____

b. _____

c. _____

d. _____

e. _____

f. _____

g. _____

17. What is depreciation? How is depreciation related to net income?

_____

_____

_____

_____

18. What functions can computers perform in accounting?

_____

_____

_____

_____

PRACTICE TEST

Multiple Choice: Circle the best answer.

1. The purpose of accounting is to
   a. allow for government tracking of business activities.
   b. make sure a business is paying its taxes.
   c. help managers evaluate the financial condition of the firm.
   d. provide a method of spending money wisely.

2. Which of the following is NOT one of the activities associated with accounting?
   a. recording
   b. summarizing
   c. classifying
   d. promoting

3. The type of accounting that is concerned with providing information and analyses to managers within the organization is called
   a. financial accounting
   b. managerial accounting
   c. auditing
   d. tax accounting

4. Jim Hopson is an accountant who works for a number of businesses as a "consultant." He has helped to design an accounting system, provides accounting services, and has analyzed the financial strength of many of his clients. Jim is working as a
   a. private accountant
   b. certified management accountant
   c. certified internal auditor
   d. public accountant

5. If you were a bookkeeper, the first thing you would do is
   a. record transactions into a ledger.
   b. develop a trial balance sheet.
   c. prepare an income statement.
   d. divide transactions into meaningful categories.

6. The _____ reports the firm's financial condition on a specific day.
   a. income statement
   b. cash flow statement
   c. statement of stockholder's equity
   d. balance sheet

7. Which of the following would be considered a current asset?
   a. accounts payable
   b. accounts receivable
   c. copyrights
   d. buildings

   Use the information below to answer questions 8 and 9:

Net sales	30,000
Total Assets	16,000
Taxes	2,300
Cost of goods sold	12,500
Total Liabilities	8,000
Operating expenses	3,200

402

8. Net income is
   a. 14,000
   b. 17,500
   c. 14,300
   d. 12,000
9. Stockholder's equity is
   a. 16,000
   b. 24,000
   c. 8,000
   d. can't determine from information given
10. Which of the following would NOT be shown on a statement of cash flows?
    a. cash from operations
    b. cash paid for long-term debt obligations
    c. cash raised from new debt or equity
    d cash paid in donations
11. Financial ratios
    a. are used to calculate profits from one year to the next.
    b. are a poor indicator of a company's financial condition.
    c. are only used by independent auditors.
    d. are helpful to use in analyzing the actual performance of a company.
12. Which kind of ratio is used to determine the ability of a firm to pay its short-term debts?
    a. activity ratios   c.   debt
    b. profitability   d.   liquidity
13. A debt-to-equity ratio of over 1 would mean
    a. the company has more debt than equity.
    b. the company has more equity than debt.
    c. by comparison with other firms, the company is probably in good shape.
    d. the company is in too much debt, and should restructure.
14. Earnings per share, return on sales, and return on equity are all
    a. activity ratios   c.   liquidity ratios
    b. profitability ratios   d.   debt ratios
15. Which of the following is NOT considered a part of the basis for the budgeting process?
    a. ratio analysis statements   c.   balance sheets
    b. income statements   d.   statement of cash flows
16. Which of the following is NOT true of the use of computers in accounting?
    a. Most big and small companies use computers to simplify the task of accounting.
    b. Computers can provide continuous financial information for the business.
    c. Computers can make accounting work less monotonous.
    d. Computers have been programmed to make financial decisions on their own.

True/False

1.   You must know something about accounting if you want to understand business.
2.   A major purpose of accounting is to report financial information to people outside the firm.
3.   Financial accounting is used to provide information and analyses to managers within the firm to assist in decision making.
4.   A private accountant is an individual who works for a private firm that provides accounting services to individuals or businesses on a fee basis.
5.   The fundamental accounting equation is assets = liabilities + owner's equity.

6. The "bottom line" is shown in the balance sheet.
7. Cash flow is generally not a problem for companies that are growing quickly.
8. Depreciation will most often not have any effect on net income.
9. The four types of financial ratios include liquidity, debt, profitability, and activity ratios.
10. The higher the risk involved in an industry, the lower the return investors expect on their investment.
11. Often the accounting needs of a small business are significantly different from the needs of larger companies.

ANSWERS

Key Terms and Definitions

1.	managerial accounting	15.	cost of goods sold
2.	balance sheet	16.	ratio analysis
3.	bookkeeping	17.	current assets
4.	retained earnings	18.	financial accounting
5.	liquid	19.	amortization (depreciation)
6.	public accountants	20.	income statement
7.	other assets	21.	cash flow
8.	gross margin (profit)	22.	accounting system
9.	independent audit	23.	fundamental accounting equation
10.	operating expenses	24.	net income
11.	assets	25.	liabilities
12.	fixed or capital assets	26.	financial statements
13.	accounting	27.	owner's equity
14.	private accountants		

What Is Accounting?

1. a. Inputs — accounting documents such as sales documents, purchasing documents, payroll records, and others
    b. Processing — recording, classifying, and summarizing
    c. Outputs — financial statements such as balance sheets and income statements
2. a. To help managers evaluate the financial condition and the operating performance of the firm so they make better decisions.
    b. To report financial information to people outside the firm such as owners, creditors, suppliers, employees, and the government.
3. Accounting is different from other business functions because most of us have limited understanding of accounting principles. As consumers, we have had some experience with marketing, and as workers or students we probably have some understanding of management. But most of us have little experience with accounting.
4. Inputs to accounting include sales documents, purchasing documents, shipping documents, payroll records, bank records, travel records, and entertainment records.
5. Outputs consist of financial statements – income statements, balance sheets, and other outside reports.
6. Managerial accounting is concerned with measuring and reporting costs of production, marketing, and other functions, preparing budgets, checking whether or not units are staying within their budgets, and designing strategies to minimize taxes.
7. Financial accounting differs from managerial accounting because the information and analysis are

for people outside the organization. This information goes to owners and prospective owners, creditors, lenders, employee unions, customers, suppliers, governmental units, and the public. These external users are interested in the organization's profit, its ability to pay its bills, and other financial information.

8. As indicated in the answer to question 7, financial accounting information goes to *external* users.

9. Much of the information derived from financial accounting is contained in the company's annual report.

10. A private accountant works for a single firm, government agency or nonprofit organization as an employee. A public accountant provides his or her services to individuals or businesses on a fee basis.

11. A public accountant can assist a business by designing an accounting system for a firm, helping select the correct computer and software to run the system, and analyzing the financial strength of an organization.

12. Internal audits are performed by private accountants to ensure that proper accounting procedures and financial reporting are being performed within the company. Public accountants will also conduct independent audits of accounting records. Financial auditors examine the financial health of an organization and additionally look into operational efficiencies and effectiveness.

Accounting and Bookkeeping

1. Accounting includes bookkeeping. Bookkeeping involves only the recording of transactions, but accounting also includes classifying, summarizing, reporting, analyzing, and interpreting the data.

2. The first task a bookkeeper performs is to divide all of the firm's transactions into meaningful categories such as sales documents, purchasing receipts, and shipping documents.

3. Accountants classify and summarize the data provided by bookkeepers. They interpret the data and report them to management.

4. BOOKKEEPER JOB DESCRIPTION – The bookkeeper for Music-stor will be responsible for collecting all original transaction documents, and dividing them into meaningful categories (sales, purchasing, shipping, and so on). The information will be recorded on a daily basis, using the double-entry method. The bookkeeper must be familiar with computer accounting applications.

ACCOUNTANT JOB DESCRIPTION – The accountant for Music-stor will be responsible for classifying and summarizing the data provided by the bookkeeper. He/she will interpret the data, report to management, and suggest strategies for improving the financial condition and progress of the firm. Must be able to suggest tax strategies and be skilled in financial analysis.

The Accounts of Accounting

1. a.

i.	Current assets	xi.	Liabilities	
ii.	Owner's equity	xii.	Current assets	
iii.	Liability	xiii.	Fixed assets	
iv.	Expenses	xiv.	Expenses	
v.	Expenses	xv.	Expenses	
vi.	Fixed asset	xvi.	Owner's equity	
vii.	Revenue	xvii.	Expenses	
viii.	Revenue	xviii.	Expenses	
ix.	Owner's equity	xix.	Current assets	
x.	Intangible asset	xx.	Current assets	

b. i.   Cash
    ii.   Investments
    iii. Accounts receivable
    iv.   Inventories

Financial Statements

1.						
	i.	Balance sheet		xi.	Balance sheet
	ii.	Balance sheet		xii.	Balance sheet
	iii.	Balance sheet		xiii.	Balance sheet
	iv.	Income statement		xiv.	Income statement
	v.	Income statement		xv.	Income statement
	vi.	Balance sheet		xvi	Balance sheet
	vii.	Income statement		xvii.	Balance sheet
	viii.	Income statement		xviii.	Income statement
	ix.	Balance sheet		xix.	Balance sheet
	x.	Balance sheet		xx.	Balance sheet

2. a. Assets
    b. Liabilities
    c. Owner's equity

3. Assets include productive, tangible items such as equipment, building, land, furniture, fixtures, and motor vehicles that help generate income, as well as intangibles of value such as patents or copyrights.

4. a. current assets
    b. fixed assets
    c. intangible assets

5. Assets on a balance sheet are listed in order of their liquidity, which refers to how fast an asset can be converted into cash. The three broad categories are presented: current assets first followed by fixed assets and intangible assets.

6. a. Liabilities are what the business owes to others. Current liabilities are payments due in one year of less; long-term liabilities are payments not due for one year or longer.
    b. i.   Accounts payable is money owed to others for merchandise and/or services purchased on credit but not yet paid. If you have a bill you haven't paid, you have an account payable.
        ii.   Notes payable is short-term or long-term loans that have a promise for future payment.
        iii. Bonds payable is money loaned to the firm that it must pay back.

7. The value of things you own, assets, minus the amount of money you owe others, liabilities, is called equity. The value of what stockholders own in a firm minus liabilities is called stockholder's equity.

8. Owner's equity is assets minus liabilities.

9. For businesses that are not incorporated, like proprietorships and partnerships, owner's equity means the value of everything owned by the business minus any liabilities of the owners. For a corporation, owner's equity represents the owner's claims to funds they have invested in the firm, such as capital stock, plus earnings kept in the business, which are called retained earnings.

10. Assets = Liabilities + Owner's equity

11. a. Revenue – Cost of goods sold = Gross profit
     b. Gross profit – Expenses = Net income (loss) before taxes
     d. Net income before taxes – taxes = Net income (loss)

12. Revenue
    −   Cost of goods sold
            Gross margin
    −   Operating expenses
            Net income before taxes
    −   Taxes
            Net income (or loss)

13. Revenue is the value of what is received for goods sold, services rendered, and other financial sources. Most revenue comes from sales, but there could be other sources of revenue such as rents received, money paid to the firm for use of its patents, interest earned, and so forth.

14. It's possible in a service firm that there may be no cost of goods sold; therefore, net revenue could equal gross margin. In a manufacturing firm, it is necessary to estimate the cost of goods manufactured.

15. Obvious expenses include rent, salaries, supplies, utilities, insurance, even depreciation on equipment. Two categories of expenses are selling and general expenses.

16. The bottom line is the net income the firm earned from operations.

17. A poor, or negative, cash flow, indicates that more money is going out of the business than is coming in from sales or other sources of revenue.
    In order to meet the demands of customers, more and more goods are bought on credit. Similarly, more and more goods are sold on credit. This can go on until the firm uses up all the credit it has with banks that lend it money. When the firm requests money from the bank to pay a crucial bill the bank refuses the loan because the credit limit has been reached. All other credit sources may refuse a loan as well. The company needs to pay its bills or else it s creditors could force it into bankruptcy.

18. a. operations – cash transactions associated with running the business
    b. investments – cash used in or provided by the firm's investment activities
    c. financing – cash raised from new debt or new equity capital, or cash used to pay expenses, debts, or dividends

19. A. **FIFO**

Beginning inventory	20,000	@ $10	$200,000
+ Purchases	7,000	@ $12	84,000
= Cost of goods available	27,000	units	$284,000
– Ending inventory	5,000	@$12	60,000
Cost of goods sold			$224,000

LIFO

Beginning inventory	20,000	@ $10	$200,000
+ Purchases	7,000	@ $12	84,000
= Cost of goods available	27,000	units	$284,000
– Ending inventory	5,000	@ $10	50,000
Cost of goods sold			$234,000

B. Gross margin for

	FIFO	LIFO
Revenues	$450,000	$450,000
COGS	224,000	234,000
Gross margin	$226,000	$216,000

In going from FIFO to LIFO the effect is to reduce gross profit. This will have the effect of reducing operating income and tax liabilities.

20. Jim's problem stems from cash flow. He has the potential for profits from future jobs but has problems paying his bills right now. One thing Jim could do is look into borrowing money from his bank to pay the bills and buy the paint. He could repay the loan with the money he will earn from future painting jobs.

21. a.

MERAMEC MUNCHIES, INC.
INCOME STATEMENT
Year ending December 31, 20___

Net Sales	77,800		
Rental Revenue	3,700		
Total Sales		81,500	
Cost of Goods Sold		3,300	
Gross Profit			48,200
Operating Expenses			
Sales Salaries	19,400		
Advertising	8,600		
		28,000	
General Expenses			
Interest Expense	3,100		
Insurance	4,300		
Depreciation Expenses	3,200		
		10,600	
Total Operating Expenses			$38,600
Net Income Before Taxes			$9,600
Less Income Tax Expense			2,400
Net Income			$7,200

b.

MERAMEC MUNCHIES, INC.
BALANCE SHEET
December 31, 20___

Assets

Current Assets

Cash	$ 8,400		
Marketable Securities	7,400		
Accounts Receivable	15,400		
Notes Receivable	9,600		
Inventories	16,100		
Total Current Assets		$ 56,900	
Fixed Assets			
Building	32,500		
Land	5,000		
Total Fixed Assets		37,500	
Total Assets			**$ 94,400**

Liabilities

Current Liabilities

Accounts Payable	6,700		
Notes Payable (current)	6,000		
Accrued Salaries	2,300		
Total Current Liabilities		$ 15,000	
Long-Term Liabilities			
Long-term debt		20,000	
Total Liabilities			$35,000

Owner's Equity

Common Stock	33,200		
Retained Earnings	26,200		
Total Owner's Equity			$ 59,400
Total Liabilities and Owner's Equity			**$ 94,400**

22.

MUSIC STOR, INC.
BALANCE SHEET
Year ending December 31, 20___

Assets

Current Assets

Cash	$ 18,000	
Investments	45,000	
Accounts Receivable	110,000	
Inventory	62,000	
Total Current Assets		$235,000
Property, plant, and equipment		
Less: accumulated depreciation		200,000
Total Assets		$435,000

Liabilities and stockholder's equity

Liabilities

Current Liabilities		
Accounts Payable	$ 25,000	
Notes Payable (current)	15,000	
Accrued Taxes	40,000	
Total Current Liabilities		$ 80,000
Long-term debt		60,000
Total Liabilities		$140,000
Stockholder's Equity		
Common Stock	$130,000	
Retained Earnings	165,000	
Total Stockholder's Equity		$295,000
Total Liabilities and Stockholder's Equity		$435,000

23.

MUSIC STOR, INC.
INCOME STATEMENT
Year ending December 31, 20___

Revenues

Net Sales	$600,000	
Rental Revenue	3,000	
Total Revenues		$603,000
Cost of Goods Sold		313,000
Gross Profit		$290,000
Operating Expenses		
Wages and Salaries	$125,000	
Rent	35,000	
Advertising	28,000	
Depreciation	4,000	
Utilities	12,000	
Supplies	3,700	
Total Operating Expenses		$207,700
Net Income Before Taxes		$82,300
Less Income Taxes		23,044

Accounting Complexity

1. The independent accounting professional bodies, notably the CICA, define what are generally accepted accounting principles that accountants must follow. If financial reports are prepared "in accordance with GAAP" users know the information is reported according to the standards agreed upon by accounting professionals.

2. A firm may use one of several different methods to calculate depreciation. Each method will result in a different depreciation amount, and thus a different expense to be taken from gross profit. This will then result in a different bottom line.

Cash-Flow Problems

1.   a. Answers will vary.
        b. Small businesses can avoid cash-flow problems by developing a good relationship with their bankers, keeping track of inventory levels, and creating good collection procedures for collecting due bills.

12. Answers will vary, but might include the dollar valuation of brain power, skills, and abilities, or the evaluation of potential liabilities to various parties with regard to toxic or polluted material, land, or buildings.

Ratio Analysis (Appendix/Website)

1. Ratio analysis provide insights in important financial issues such as liquidity, debt, profitability, and activity.

2.   a. Current ratio
        b. Acid-test ratio

13. (Cost of goods sold)/(Average inventory) = Inventory turnover
The inventory turnover measures the speed of inventory moving through a firm and its conversion into sales. Inventory sitting idly by in a business costs money.

14. A lower than average inventory turnover ratio often indicates obsolete merchandise on hand or poor buying practices. A higher than average ratio may signal lost sales because of inadequate stock. An acceptable turnover ratio is generally determined on an industry-by-industry basis.

15. (Net Income)/(Net sales) = Return on sales
Firms use this ratio to see if they are doing as well as the companies they compete against in generating income on sales they achieve.

16. (Net income)/(Number of common shares outstanding) = basic earnings per share

17. (Total liabilities)/(Owners' equity) = debt equity ratio

18. A debt-to-equity ratio of above 1 would show that a firm actually has more debt than equity. It is possible that this firm could be perceived as a risk to both lenders and investors. It is always important to compare ratios to other firms in the same industry because debt financing is more acceptable in some industries.

19. (Current assets)/(current liabilities) = current ratio

20. The current ratio is compared to competing firms within the industry to measure how the company sizes up against its main competitors. It is also important that the firm evaluate its ratio from the previous year to note any significant changes.

21. (Cash + marketable securities + receivables)/current liabilities = acid test ratio

This ratio measures the cash, marketable securities and receivables of a firm. This ratio is important to firms with difficulty converting inventory into quick cash.

CHAPTER CHECK ANSWERS

1. a. Managerial accounting
    b. Financial accounting
2. a. Cost accounting
    b. Preparing budgets
    c. Checking to be sure units are within budget
    d. Designing strategies to minimize taxes
3. Managerial accounting is used to provide information and analyses to managers within the organization to assist them in decision making. Financial accounting is used to provide information and analyses to people outside the organization.
4. Financial accounting information goes to owners, prospective owners, creditors and lenders, employee unions, customers, suppliers, governmental units, and the public.
5. a. Sales documents
    b. Purchasing documents
    c. Shipping documents
    d. Payroll records
    e. Bank documents
    f. Various expense documents
6. a. Assets
    b. Liabilities
    c. Owner's Equity
    d. Revenues
    e. Expenses
    f. Cost of goods sold
7. a. Income statement
    b. Balance sheet
8. a. Current assets
    b. Fixed assets
    c. Intangible assets
9. a. Accounts payable
    b. Notes payable
    c. Bonds payable
10. Assets minus liabilities
11. Assets = Liabilities + Owner's Equity
12. a. Net sales – Cost of Goods Sold = Gross Profit
    b. Gross Profit - Operating Expenses = Net Profit before Income Taxes
    c. Net Profit before Taxes - Taxes = Net Income after Taxes
13. a. Distribute to shareholders in the form of dividends
    b. Keep in the firm as retained earnings
14. Cash flow is the difference between cash receipts and cash disbursements. (In other words, the difference between what you bring in and what you pay out.)
15. a. CA
    b. CMA
    c. CGA
16. a. Average Collection Period of Receivables
    b. Return on Sales
    c. Return on Investment (ROI)

    d. Inventory Turnover
    e. Debt to Equity Ratio
    f. Current Ratio
    g. Quick Ratio

17. Depreciation is the systematic write-off of the value of an asset. Companies are allowed to use depreciation as an expense of business operations.

18. Computers can record and analyze data and print out financial reports. Even small companies are learning that data processing is usually done best by computer.

PRACTICE TEST

Multiple Choice		True/False	
1.	c	1.	T
2.	d	2.	T
3.	b	3.	F
4.	d	4.	F
5.	d	5.	T
6.	d	6.	F
7.	b	7.	F
8.	d	8.	F
9.	c	9.	T
10.	d	10.	F
11.	d	11.	T
12.	d		
13.	a		
14.	b		
15.	a		
16.	d		

CHAPTER 19

Managing Financial Resources

Learning Goals

After you have read and studied this chapter, you should be able to

1. Explain the role and importance of finance and the responsibilities of financial managers.
2. Outline the steps in financial planning by explaining how to forecast financial needs, develop budgets, and establish financial controls.
3. Recognize the financial needs that must be met with available funds.
4. Distinguish between short-term and long-term financing and between debt capital and equity capital.
5. Identify and describe several sources of short-term capital.
6. Identify and describe several sources of long-term capital.
7. Compare the advantages and disadvantages of issuing bonds and identify the classes and features of bonds.
8. Compare the advantages and disadvantages of issuing stock, and outline the differences between common and preferred stock.

Key Terms and Definitions

Listed here are important terms found in this chapter. Choose the correct term for each definition and write it in the space provided.

blue chip stocks	debt capital	Pledging
bond	dividends	preferred stock
buying on margin	equity capital	principal
capital budget	factoring	secured bonds
cash budget	finance	secured loan
cash-flow forecast	line of credit	short-term forecast
commercial paper	long-term forecast	stock certificate
common stock	maturity date	stock exchange
convertible bond	mutual fund	trade credit
cumulative preferred stock	operating budget	unsecured bonds

1. _____ The practice of buying goods now and paying for them in the future.

2. _____ The face amount of a bond.

3. _____ Stock that gives owners preference over common shareholders in the payment of dividends and in a claim on assets if the business is liquidated; it does not include voting rights.

4. _____ Tangible evidence of stock ownership.

5. _____ The spending plan for the acquisition of capital assets that involve large sums of money.

6. _____ A fund that buys a variety of securities and then sells units of

ownership in the fund to the public.

7. _____ The date on which a borrower must legally repay the bond principal to the bondholder.

8. _____ Loan backed by something valuable, such as property.

9. _____ The business function that is responsible for the efficient acquisition and disbursement of funds.

10. _____ A contract of indebtedness issued by a corporation or government unit that promises payments of a principal amount at a specified future time plus annual or semi-annual interest at a specified or variable rate.

11. _____ Bonds that are not backed by any collateral.

12. _____ Funds raised by borrowing that must be repaid.

13. _____ Market where the securities of public companies are traded.

14. _____ Selling accounts receivable for cash.

15. _____ The plan of the various costs and expenses needed to operate the business, based on the short-term forecast.

16. _____ Purchasing securities by borrowing some of the cost from the broker.

17. _____ Using accounts receivable, inventory, or other assets as security for a loan.

18. _____ Preferred stock that accumulates unpaid dividends.

19. _____ The maximum amount a bank will agree to lend a borrower.

20. _____ Bonds backed by some tangible asset that is pledged to the bondholder to guarantee repayment of principal and interest.

21. _____ Stocks of high-quality companies.

22. _____ A projection of expected cash inflows and outflows in the coming year.

23. _____ A prediction of revenues, costs, and expenses for more than one year, sometimes as long as 5 or 10 years into the future.

24. _____ Represents ownership of a firm and the rights to vote and receive the firm's profits (after preferred shareholders are paid), in the form of dividends declared by the board of directors.

25. _____ Part of the firm's profits that are distributed to shareholders.

26. _____ A bond that can be converted into shares of common stock.

27. _____ The projected use of cash during a given period.

28. _____ Funds raised from selling shares in the firm.

29. _____ A short-term corporate equivalent of an IOU that is sold in the marketplace by a firm. It matures in 270 days or less.

30. _____ A prediction of revenues, costs, and expenses, usually for a

period of one year.

The Role of Finance

1. What is the difference between an accountant and a financial manager?

   _____

   _____

   _____

   _____

2. What are three of the most common ways for any firm to fail financially?

   a. _____

   b. _____

   c. _____

3. To whom is an understanding of finance important?

   _____

   _____

   _____

   _____

4. What is financial management?

   _____

   _____

   _____

   _____

5. Among the functions a finance manager performs are

] Planning	] Collecting funds
] Budgeting	] Auditing
] Obtaining funds	] Managing taxes
] Controlling funds	] Advising top management

   Match the correct function to each statement below.

   a. _____ Before Debbie Breeze sends out the quarterly financial statements for her firm, she determines that no mistakes were made in posting journal entries into the general ledger.

   b. _____ Joe Saumby determined that his firm's accounts receivable were too high, and developed a more effective collection system.

   c. _____ Ann Bizer decided to include money for a new microcomputer in the operating budget in her department.

   d. _____ In an effort to generate capital, managers of a closely held corporation decided to sell their stock to the public.

   e. _____ A major automotive company developed a long-range objective of automating its production facilities, which would cost millions of dollars.

f. _____ In order to monitor expense accounts, many companies require employees to submit a receipt for any expenditure over $25.00.

g. _____ In a report to top management, Joe Kelly outlined the effect of newly proposed pollution control requirements on the company's long-range forecasts.

6. Why is the collection of payments and overdue accounts particularly critical to small businesses?

_____

_____

_____

_____

7. Why does tax management fall under the area of finance?

_____

_____

_____

_____

8. What is the role of the internal auditor?

_____

_____

_____

_____

Financial Planning

1. What is financial planning? What is the objective of financial planning?

_____

_____

_____

_____

2. What are the three steps involved in financial planning?
   a. _____
   b. _____
   c. _____

3. What is used as a basis for forecasting company budgets>

_____

_____

_____

_____

4. What is the difference between a short-term forecast and a long-term forecast?

_____

_____

_____

_____

5. Identify three types of budgets.

a. _____

b. _____

c. _____

6. What is a cash-flow forecast based upon?

_____

_____

_____

_____

7. What is determined in an operating budget?

_____

_____

_____

_____

8. What is the primary concern in a capital budget?

_____

_____

_____

_____

9. What information does a cash budget provide?

_____

_____

_____

_____

10. When is a cash budget prepared?

_____

_____

_____

_____

The Need to Have Funds Available

1. What is the financial challenge of managing daily business operations?

_____

_____

_____

_____

2. Why is it better to take money today, rather than wait until later?

_____

_____

_____
_____

3. What do financial managers try to do with cash expenditures?

_____
_____
_____
_____

4. Why do financial managers want to make credit available?

_____
_____
_____
_____

5. What is a problem with offering credit?

_____
_____
_____
_____

6. What is a way to decrease the time and expense of collecting accounts?

_____
_____
_____
_____

7. What does inventory control have to do with finance?

_____
_____
_____
_____

8. What job does a financial manager have with regard to capital expenditures?

_____
_____
_____
_____

9. A firm has four basic financing needs:
   ☐ Financing daily operations
   ☐ Financing accounts receivable
   ☐ Financing the purchase of inventory
   ☐ Financing major capital expenditures

   Match the activity to each example below:
   a. _____ Mark Hunter is a finance manager for Wescan industries.

Each Wednesday he reviews the cash balance the firm carries, the interest-bearing accounts the firm has, and the schedule for bill payments.

b. _____ Cal Brady is in the process of determining the need to invest in a mainframe computer system for his company, Riverside Enterprises.

c. _____ Diana Gallagher has just finished revising her company's credit collection procedure.

d. _____ At MEMC, Inc., a just-in-time inventory control process has been in place and successful in controlling costs for several months.

10. Eric is upset! He has just stormed into Music-stor's finance manager's office. "What's going on? I just looked at our inventory levels, and they're lower than what I think we ought to see. Don't we have the money to buy inventory? How are we going to make our orders? And what's the idea of all these credit sales? Visa? MasterCard? And another thing! Why are we always paying our bills at the last minute? Are we that short of cash?" "Hold on," said Bill Whittier, the new finance manager. "Things look pretty good to me. We're actually in great shape!" "What? I don't understand," replied Eric. "You know, I want to look into building a new plant within the next two years. Sales are going to continue to go way up. I need to know whether or not we're going to be able to afford it. Right now, it looks as if we are too short of cash." Explain what Bill is saying.

_____
_____
_____
_____

Alternative Sources of Funds

1. What is the difference between long-term and short-term financing?

_____
_____
_____
_____

2. Describe the difference between debt capital and equity capital.

_____
_____
_____
_____

Short-Term Financing

1. Why do firms need to borrow short-term funds?

_____
_____
_____
_____

2. Describe the invoice terms of 2/10 net 30.

    _____
    _____
    _____
    _____

3. When would a supplier require a promissory note?

    _____
    _____
    _____
    _____

4. What steps are recommended when borrowing from family or friends?
    a. _____
    b. _____
    c. _____

5. Why is it important for a businessperson to keep a close relationship with a banker?

    _____
    _____
    _____
    _____

6. Identify five types of bank loans.
    a. _____   d. _____
    b. _____   e. _____
    c. _____

7. Three kinds of banks loans are
    ☐ Unsecured loans
    ☐ Secured loans (including pledging)
    ☐ Line of credit

    Match the type of loan to the following examples:
    a. _____ A company is having some short-term cash problems, but they
                                         have substantial accounts receivable which could be used as
                                         collateral for a loan.

    b. _____ When a company that had been in business for a fairly long
                                         time and had a great financial record needed money, they
                                         went to their banker and received the loan, without needing to
                                         put up the collateral.

    c. _____ Because they often have a need for short-term funds with
                                         short notice, Binny and Jones Mfg. applied to their bank for a
                                         sort of "continual" unsecured loan. The bank lends Binney a
                                         given amount without Binney having to re-apply each time.
                                         While not a guaranteed loan, the funds will be available if
                                         Binny's credit limit is not exceeded.

8. What is meant by the term *collateral*?

_____

_____

_____

_____

9. What kind of bank customer is most likely to get an *unsecured* loan? Why?

_____

_____

_____

_____

10. What is the primary purpose of a *line of credit*?

_____

_____

_____

_____

11. How do the interest rates of commercial lending companies compare to those of banks? Why?

_____

_____

_____

_____

12. How does *factoring* work?

_____

_____

_____

_____

13. Why do many small companies make use of factoring?

_____

_____

_____

_____

14. How can small businesses make factoring less expensive?

_____

_____

_____

_____

15. What kinds of companies sell *commercial paper*?

_____

_____

_____

_____

16. What are the benefits of commercial paper?

_____

_____

_____

_____

Long-Term Financing

1. What is long-term capital used for?

_____

_____

_____

_____

2. What is the advantage of a long-term loan?

_____

_____

_____

_____

3. What are some drawbacks to a long-term loan?

_____

_____

_____

_____

4. What is a simple explanation of a bond?

_____

_____

_____

_____

5. What does a potential investor evaluate in the purchase of a bond?

_____

_____

_____

_____

6. What are two forms of equity financing?

_____

_____

_____

_____

7. What legal obligation does a firm have when using debt financing?

_____

8. What is the *risk/return tradeoff*?

_____

_____

_____

_____

9. What is a *debenture*?

_____

_____

_____

_____

10. Who are the *owners* of a corporation?

_____

_____

_____

_____

11. What is the most favoured source of *long-term capital*? Why?

_____

_____

_____

_____

12. What is *venture capital*?

_____

_____

_____

_____

13. What are some considerations to remember when exploring venture capital?

_____

_____

_____

_____

14. What are the key jobs of the *finance manager*, or CFO?

_____

_____

_____

_____

15. How can a firm use *leverage* to get a higher rate of return, compared to equity financing?

_____
_____
_____
_____
_____

16. Long-term funds are obtained from owners and from lenders who do not expect repayment within one year. These initial sources of long-term capital are
    ☐ Equity capital
    ☐ Debt capital
    ☐ Surplus cash

    Match the correct source of long-term capital to each of the following statements:

    a. _____ The most favoured source of long-term capital.

    b. _____ Enables just about anyone to become an owner in the firm.

    c. _____ For this, a business must sign a term-loan agreement because of the long repayment period.

    d. _____ Obtained by selling ownership in the firm.

    e. _____ Most of this type of financing requires some form of collateral such as machinery, real estate, or equipment.

    f. _____ A major source of funds for a firm, this is income earned from its operations.

17. Eric and his finance manager, Joel, are in disagreement over how to finance the future growth of Music-stor. "I just want to stay out of debt if I can," says Eric, "so I think the best idea is to sell stock, go public." "Well, I understand your perspective, Eric, but I'm not sure you have thought of all the consequences of selling stock. Do you like being your own boss?" asks Joel. "Yeah, sure!" replies Eric, "but what the heck does that have to do with wanting to sell stock in the company?" What does Joel mean, and what are the other arguments for and against each type of funding?

    _____
    _____
    _____
    _____

18. If leverage means raising money through debt, what do you suppose is meant by a "leveraged buyout"?

    _____
    _____
    _____
    _____

Securities Markets

1. What are two major functions of securities markets?

    _____
    _____
    _____

2. How do businesses benefit from the securities markets?

_____
_____
_____
_____

3. How do individuals benefit from the securities markets?

_____
_____
_____
_____

4. Explain the difference between the primary and the secondary markets.

_____
_____
_____
_____

5. How would companies prefer to meet their long-term financial needs?

_____
_____
_____
_____

6. What does an *investment banker* do for companies?

_____
_____
_____
_____

7. What are some examples of *institutional investors*?

_____
_____
_____
_____

Debt Financing Through Selling Bonds

1. What is the legal obligation of a company when selling bonds?

_____
_____
_____
_____

2. What is meant by the term "coupon rate" with regard to bonds?

_____
_____
_____
_____
_____

3. If a $1,000 bond has an interest rate of 10% and a maturity date of 2020, what does that mean to a bondholder?

_____
_____
_____
_____

4. What affects the interest rate of a bond?

_____
_____
_____
_____

5. Why are sinking funds attractive to firms and investors?
   a. _____
   b. _____
   c. _____

6. Describe the two classes of corporate bonds.

_____
_____
_____
_____

7. What is the benefit to a company of a *callable bond*?

_____
_____
_____
_____

8. Why would an investor convert a bond to common stock?

_____
_____
_____
_____
_____

9. The financial manager of Music-stor has convinced the management that a bond issue is needed to raise capital for future growth. He wants to avoid the difficulty of looking for and marketing to potential investors himself, and prefers to let "experts" perform those functions. How should he go about selling this new bond issue?

_____

_____
_____
_____
_____

10. Firms often call on alternative debt financing through the issuance of corporate bonds. In discussing bonds, there are several terms with which you need to be familiar:

] Bond   ] Call provision
] Interest   ] Unsecured bonds
] Principal   ] Secured bonds
] Maturity date   ] Convertible bonds

Match the correct term to each of the following descriptions or situations:

a. _____ Gerry Hoffman will receive this on the date her bond comes due in 2010.

b. _____ Beth Galganski will be paid $1,000 on this date, 2010.

c. _____ IBM has an excellent credit rating, and so may issue this type of bond.

d. _____ Bonnie Anderson has a bond that pays her $100 a year.

e. _____ Mobil Oil issued an unsecured one at 14.4%, due in 2004.

f. _____ TNC Enterprises issued their debentures with this provision because they forecasted the decline in interest rates in 1991–92.

g. _____ Caldwell Industries used real estate holdings to ensure their bonds.

h. _____ Katie Barnes bought this type of bond because she anticipated exchanging it for common stock in that firm at some future date.

Equity Financing Through Issuing Stock

1. What is the difference between the interest on a bond and a dividend paid on a share of stock?

_____
_____
_____
_____

2. How is preferred stock like a bond?

_____
_____
_____
_____

3. How do preferred stock and bonds differ?

_____
_____
_____
_____

4. What are some special features of preferred stock?

_____
_____
_____
_____
_____

5. What are two privileges of owing common stock?

_____
_____
_____
_____

6. There are several types of stocks. Some of them are
    ☐ Common
    ☐ Convertible preferred
    ☐ Cumulative preferred

    a. Match the correct type of stock to the statements:
        i.   _____   Has no voting rights, and can be exchanged for shares of common stock at a predetermined exchange rate.

        ii. _____   Pays a dividend every year.

        iii. _____   Has voting rights and may receive dividends.

        iv. _____   Has no voting rights, and if the dividend isn't paid the amount owed accumulates.

        v.   _____   Dividends on this must be paid before common stockholders receive any dividends.

    b. How does an investor benefit from cumulative preferred over non-cumulative preferred?

    _____
    _____
    _____
    _____

7. What information is contained in a *stock certificate?*

_____
_____
_____
_____

Trading in Bonds and Stocks

1. What does a 50% margin rate mean?

_____
_____
_____
_____

2. What is a margin call?

_____
_____
_____
_____

3. What is the investment with the least possible risk? Why?

_____
_____
_____
_____

4. What does the market price of a stock depend upon?

_____
_____
_____
_____

5. What is the benefit of a mutual fund for an investor?

_____
_____
_____
_____

6. In discussing stocks and bonds, there are several terms with which you need to be familiar:
   ] Stock certificate   ] Buying on margin
   ] Stock broker   ] Common stock
   ] Dividends   ] Preferred stock
   ] Blue chip stocks

   Match the correct term to each of the following descriptions or situations.

   a. _____ The most common form of ownership; holders have the first right to purchase any new issues.

   b. _____ A paper showing the name of the company, the number of shares it represents, and the type of stock.

   c. _____ Periodic payments to stockholders.

   d. _____ The dividend rate is higher than other forms of stock, but the owners lose voting rights.

   e. _____ Ownership in a company.

   f. _____ Stocks of high quality companies.

   g. _____ Joe Continue works for Nesbitt Thomson Deacon, selling stocks for his clients.

   h. _____ Dextor Liholt wanted to buy 500 shares of Ford at $50, but he only had $10,000, so he borrowed $15,000 from the brokerage firm.

7. There are several types of stocks and bonds available in the market. Some of them are
   ☐ Collateral trust
   ☐ Convertible
   ☐ Coupon
   ☐ Debenture
   ☐ Equipment trust
   ☐ Mortgage bond
   ☐ Zero-coupon bond

Match the correct type of stock or bond to each of the following statements:

a. _____ Backed by the stock the company owns, and that is held in trust by a commercial bank.

b. _____ Pays no interest before maturity; the return comes from the difference between the purchase price and face value.

c. _____ Secured only by the good credit of the issuer.

d. _____ Secured by real property, such as a building.

e. _____ Can be exchanged for common stock.

f. _____ The holder submits coupons for interest payment.

g. _____ Backed by equipment the company owns that is widely used in industry.

Cycles in the Stock Market and Interest Rates

1. What happened to the stock markets in October of 1987, October of 1997, and April of 2000?

    _____
    _____
    _____
    _____

2. What is speculated to be the reason for the drop in 1987?

    _____
    _____
    _____
    _____

3. What lessons can be learned from the stock market crashes of the past?

    _____
    _____
    _____
    _____

CHAPTER CHECK

1. What are three common reasons for a firm's financial failure?

   a. _____

   b. _____

   c. _____

2. List eight functions of a financial manager.

   a. _____   e. _____

   b. _____   f. _____

   c. _____   g. _____

   d. _____   h. _____

3. What are three steps involved in financial planning?

   a. _____

   b. _____

   c. _____

4. List three kinds of budgets.

   a. _____   c. _____

   b. _____

5. What are four financial needs that affect the operations of business enterprises?

   a. _____

   b. _____

   c. _____

   d. _____

6. Distinguish between

   a. Short-term and long-term financing

   _____

   _____

   _____

   b. Debt capital and equity capital

   _____

   _____

   _____

   _____

7. Name six sources of short-term funds.

   a. _____   d. _____

   b. _____   e. _____

   c. _____   f. _____

   _____

8. What determines how much and for how long a business will borrow money?

   _____

   _____

   _____

   _____

9. What are three ways to borrow from a bank?
   a. _____
   b. _____
   c. _____

10. What are three questions a firm will consider in setting long-term financing objectives?
    a. _____
    b. _____
    c. _____

11. List two sources of long-term debt capital.
    a. _____
    b. _____

12. Identify four sources of equity capital.
    a. _____
    b. _____
    c. _____
    d. _____

13. What are the two types of securities traded in securities markets?
    a. _____
    b. _____

14. List the advantages and disadvantages to a corporation of selling bonds.
    a. Advantages
       i. _____
       ii. _____
       iii. _____

    b. Disadvantages
       i. _____
       ii. _____
       iii. _____

15. What are four types of secured bonds?
    a. _____
    b. _____
    c. _____
    d. _____

16. Identify six types of bonds.
    a. _____ d. _____
    b. _____ e. _____
    c. _____ f. _____

17. List the advantages and disadvantages to raising funds by selling stock.
    a. *Advantages*

    i. _____
    ii. _____
    iii. _____

  b. *Disadvantages*
    i. _____
    ii. _____
    iii. _____

18. Name the two basic types of stock.
  a. _____
  b. _____

19. Describe the difference between preferred dividends and common stock dividends.

  _____
  _____
  _____
  _____

20. List three investment criteria to use in selecting investments.
  a. _____
  b. _____
  c. _____

21. What is the benefit of investing in a mutual fund?

  _____
  _____
  _____
  _____

22. What five Canadian cities have stock exchanges?
  a. _____
  b. _____
  c. _____
  d. _____
  e. _____

PRACTICE TEST

Multiple Choice: Circle the best answer.
1. Which of the following is NOT included in a list of reasons why businesses fail financially?
   a. Inadequate expense control
   b. Poor control over cash flow
   c. Undercapitalization
   d. Stock is undervalued
2. Jackie Jones is a finance manager for Pokey Poseys, a wholesale florist. As finance manager, which of the following would NOT be one of Jackie's responsibilities?
   a. Preparing financial statements
   b. Preparing budgets

c. Doing cash flow analysis

d. Planning for spending funds on long-term assets, such as plant and equipment

3. The process of analyzing short-term and long-term money flows to and from the firm is known as _____.

a. internal auditing
c. financial planning
b. forecasting
d. financial controls

4. Ima Midas is currently in the process of projecting how much his firm will have to spend on supplies, travel, rent, advertising, and salaries for the coming financial year. Ima is working on the _____.

a. operating budget
c. cash budget
b. capital budget
d. master budget

5. Which of the following is NOT one of the steps involved in financial planning?

a. Forecasting short-term and long-term financial needs

b. Developing budgets to meet those needs

c. Establishing financial controls to keep the company focused on financial plans

d. Developing financial statements for outside investors

6. What is the major problem with selling on credit?

a. Too much of a firm's assets could be tied up in accounts receivable.

b. You can't control when customers will pay their bills.

c. It makes production scheduling more difficult.

d. Customers who aren't allowed to buy on credit become unhappy.

7. Companies must maintain a sizable investment in inventories in order to

a. be able to accept credit cards.

b. keep customers happy.

c. increase demand for their products.

d. reduce the need for long-term funds.

8. The time value of money means that

a. the value of money will fall over time.

b. it is better to make purchases now, rather than wait until later.

c. a monetary system will devalue its money over time.

d. it is better to have money now, rather than later.

9. Which of the following is NOT a source of short-term funds?

a. The sale of bonds

b. The use of trade credit

c. Promissory notes

d. The use of inventory financing

10. The credit terms 2/10 net 30 means the following:

a. The full amount of a bill is due within 2–10 days.

b. Customers will receive a 10% discount if they pay in 30 days.

c. A 2% discount will be given if customers pay within 30 days.

d. Customers will receive a 2% discount if they pay within 10 days.

11. When accounts receivable or some other asset is used as collateral for a loan, the process is called

a. a line of credit
c. trade credit
b. a promissory note
d. pledging

12. Commercial finance companies accept more risk than do banks, and the interest rates they charge are usually _____ than commercial banks.

a. higher
c. lower
b. about the same as
d. more variable

13. Dave Sinclair Ford usually obtains its short-term financing by offering the cars they are selling as

collateral for a loan. This form of financing is called

a. factoring   c. a revolving credit agreement

b. inventory financing   d. a line of credit

14. Raising debt capital includes using _____ as a source of funds.

a. the sale of bonds   c. the sale of inventory

b. the sale of stock   d. the sale of accounts receivable

15. One of the benefits of selling bonds over selling stock, as a source of long-term funds, is that

a. bonds don't have to be paid back.

b. the company isn't required to pay interest.

c. bondholders do not have a say in running the business.

d. interest is paid after taxes are paid.

16. The most favoured source of meeting long-term capital needs is

a. selling stock   c. selling bonds

b. venture capital   d. retained earnings

17. When starting his new software business, Bob Campbell considered using venture capital as a source of initial funding. One of the drawbacks of venture capital is that

a. venture capitalists generally want a stake in the ownership of the business.

b. venture capitalists charge a very high rate of interest.

c. venture capital is very difficult to find.

d. venture capital firms generally don't provide additional financing later on.

18. The benefit of the securities market for investors is

a. a guaranteed high return.

b. a convenient place to build financial future with investments.

c. a safe alternative to putting money in a bank.

d. a good place to look for long-term sources of funds.

19. Which of the following is NOT considered an advantage of selling bonds?

a. The debt is eventually eliminated when the bonds are paid off.

b. Interest on the bonds is not a legal obligation.

c. Bondholders have no say in running the firm.

d. Interest is tax deductible.

20. A _____ permits a bond issuer to pay off the bond's principal prior to its maturity date.

a. sinking fund bond   c. callable bond

b. convertible bond   d. collateral trust bond

True/False

1. Financial understanding is important primarily for anyone wanting to major in accounting, but not necessary for others involved in business.

2. Financial managers are responsible for collecting overdue payments and making sure the company doesn't lose too much money to bad debts.

3. The cash budget is often the first budget that is prepared.

4. Financial control means that the actual revenues, costs, and expenses are reviewed and compared with projections.

5. One way to decrease the expense of collecting accounts receivable is to accept bank credit cards.

6. Equity capital is money raised primarily through the sale of bonds.

7. Firms often need to borrow short-term funds to be able to pay unexpected bills.

8. One benefit of borrowing from friends or family is that you don't have to draw up formal papers as you do with a bank loan.

9. It is important for a business person to keep close relations with a banker because the banker

may be able to spot cash flow problems early and point out problems.
10. A line of credit guarantees a business a given amount of unsecured short-term funds.
11. Long-term capital is generally used to pay for supplies, rent, and travel.
12. Potential investors in bonds compare the risk involved in purchasing a bond with the return the bond promises to pay.
13. In the securities markets, the primary markets handle the sale of new securities.
14. An institutional investor is a large investor who buys the entire bond or stock issues a company wants to sell.
15. A company is legally bound to pay the interest on a bond, but not the principal amount.
16. A sinking fund is a provision allowing for a company to pay off a bond prior to its maturity date.
17. Dividends may be distributed as cash payments or additional shares of stock.
18. One of the advantages of raising capital through selling stock is that the stockholder's investment never has to be repaid.
19. Common stock normally does not include voting rights.
20. A stockbroker is a registered representative who acts as an intermediary to buy and sell stocks for clients.
21. A young person saving for retirement can afford to invest in higher risk stocks than a person who is nearing retirement age.
22. One of the disadvantages of a corporate bond is that if you buy it, you must hold it to the maturity date.
23. Mutual funds are probably the best way for smaller investors to get started.
24. Buying on margin allows an investor to borrow money from a brokerage firm.

ANSWERS

Key Terms and Definitions

1.	trade credit	16.	buying on margin
2.	principal	17.	Pledging
3.	preferred stock	18.	Cumulative preferred stock
4.	stock certificate	19.	line of credit
5.	capital budget	20.	secured bonds
6.	mutual fund	21.	blue chip stocks
7.	maturity date	22.	cash flow forecast
8.	secured loan	23.	long-term forecast
9.	finance	24.	common stock
10.	bond	25.	dividends
11.	unsecured bonds	26.	convertible bond
12.	debt capital	27.	cash budget
13.	stock exchange	28.	equity capital
14.	factoring	29.	commercial paper
15.	operating budget	30.	short-term forecast

The Role of Finance

1. Financial managers use the data prepared by accountants and make recommendations to top management regarding strategies for improving the health of the firm.
2. a. Undercapitalization—not enough funds to start with.
   b. Poor control over cash flow.
   c. Inadequate expense control.
3. Financial understanding is important to anyone who wants to start a small business, invest in stocks

and bonds, or plan a retirement fund.

4. Financial management is the job of managing a firm's resources so it can meet its goals and objectives.

5. a. Auditing   e. Planning
   b. Collecting funds   f. Controlling funds
   c. Budgeting   g. Advising top management
   d. Obtaining funds

6. Collection of accounts receivable and overdue accounts is critical to all types of businesses. However, small businesses typically have smaller cash or credit cushions than large corporations.

7. Tax payments represent an outflow of cash from the business, and therefore fall under finance. As tax laws and tax liabilities have changed, finance specialists have become increasingly involved in tax management by analyzing the tax implications of various managerial decisions, in an attempt to minimize taxes paid by the business.

8. The internal auditor checks on the journals, ledgers, and financial statements prepared by the accounting department to make sure that all transactions have been treated in accordance with established accounting rules and procedures. Without such audits, accounting statements would be less reliable.

Financial Planning

1. Financial planning involves analyzing short-term and long-term money flows to and from the firm. The overall objective of financial planning is to optimize the firm's profitability and make the best use of its money.

2. a. Forecasting both short-term and long-term financial needs
   b. Developing budgets to meet those needs
   c. Establishing financial controls

3. The basis for forecasting company budgets is historical cost and revenue information derived from past financial statements.

4. A short-term forecast predicts revenues, costs, and expenses for a period of one year or less. A long-term forecast predicts revenues, costs, and expenses for a period of longer than one year, sometimes as far as 5 or 10 years into the future.

5. a. operating (master) budgets
   b. capital budgets
   c. cash budgets

6. A cash flow forecast projects the expected cash inflows and outflows in future periods. This is based on expected sales revenues and on various costs and expenses incurred and when they'll come due.

7. How much the firm will spend on supplies, travel, rent, advertising, salaries, and so forth is determined in the operating budget.

8. The capital budget primarily concerns itself with the purchase of such assets as property, buildings, and equipment.

9. Cash budgets are important guidelines that assist managers in anticipating borrowing, repaying debt, cash needed for operations and expenses, and short-term investment expectations. Cash budgets assist the firm in planning for cash shortages or surpluses.

10. The cash budget is often the last budget that is prepared.

11. Many companies hold monthly financial reviews as a way to ensure financial control. This helps managers identify deviations and take corrective action if necessary. These controls provide feedback to help identify which accounts, departments and people are varying from the financial plan.

The Need to Have Funds Available

1. The challenge of sound financial management is to see that funds are available to meet daily cash

needs without compromising the firm's investment potential.

2. Money has a time value. If someone offered to give you money today or one year from today, you would benefit by taking the money today. You could start collecting interest or invest the money you receive today, and over time your money would grow.

3. Financial managers often try to keep cash expenditures at a minimum, to free funds for investment in interest-bearing accounts. It is not unusual for finance managers to suggest the firm pay bills as late as possible and collect what is owed as fast as possible.

4. Financial managers know that making credit available helps to keep current customers happy and attracts new customers. In today's highly competitive environment, many businesses would have trouble surviving without making credit available to customers.

5. The major problem with selling on credit is that as much as 25% or more of the business's assets could be tied up in its accounts receivable.

6. One way to decrease the time, and therefore expense, of collecting accounts receivable is to accept bank credit cards.

7. To satisfy customers, businesses must maintain inventories that often involve a sizable expenditure of funds. A carefully constructed inventory policy assists in managing the use of the firm's available funds and maximizing profitability.

8. Financial managers and analysts evaluate the appropriateness of capital purchases. It is critical that companies weigh all the possible options before committing what may be a large portion of their available resources.

9. a. Financing daily operations
   b. Financing major capital expenditures
   c. Financing the firm's credit services
   d. Financing purchase of inventory

10. Eric doesn't understand some basic ideas about financial management. Bill needs to explain the financial needs of all businesses: managing daily operations, managing accounts receivable, obtaining needed inventory (including inventory management) and major capital expenditures, and how a finance manager deals with each area.

One of the first things a finance manager will do is to see that funds are available to meet daily cash needs, without using too much cash to take advantage of other investments. So, bills are paid at the latest date possible to allow the firm to take advantage of interest-bearing accounts. Music-stor allows for credit purchases because it helps to keep their customers happy and helps to attract new customers. With effective collection procedures, selling on credit can be a benefit to the firm. It's important to keep inventories at a level necessary to fill orders, but too high an inventory level will tie up funds that could be used elsewhere for investment. Programs like just-in-time inventory help to reduce the amount of funds a firm must tie up in inventory.

There is no way to tell if the firm can afford to build a new plant in two years, but the finance manager will be able to evaluate the various alternatives, such as buying a facility, expanding on a current facility, or building their own building.

Alternative Sources of Funds

1. Short-term financing comes from funds used to finance current operations, which will be repaid in less than one year. Long-term financing refers to capital needed for major purchases, which will be repaid over a period longer than one year.

2. Debt capital is raised through borrowing that must be repaid. Equity capital is raised from selling stock or raised from within the company.

Short-Term Financing

1. Firms need to borrow short-term funds for purchasing additional inventory or for meeting bills that come due unexpectedly. A business sometimes needs to obtain short-term funds when the firm's money is low.
2. Terms of 2/10 net 30 means that the buyer can take a 2% discount for paying within 10 days. The total bill is due (net) in 30 days if the purchaser does not take advantage of the discount.
3. Some suppliers hesitate to give trade credit to organizations with a poor credit rating, no credit history, or a history of slow payment. In such cases, the supplier may insist that the customer sign a promissory note as a condition for obtaining credit.
4. a. Agree on terms at the beginning
   b. Write an agreement
   c. Pay them back the same way you would pay a bank loan
5. It is important for a businessperson to keep friendly and close relations with a banker, because the banker may spot cash flow problems early and point out danger areas. Additionally, the banker may be more willing to lend money in a crisis if the businessperson has established a strong, friendly relationship built on openness and trust.
6. a. Unsecured loans   d. Line of credit
   b. Secured loans   e. Revolving credit agreement
   c. Inventory financing
7. a. Secured loan
   b. Unsecured loan
   c. Line of credit
8. Collateral is something valuable, such as property, that is used to back a secured loan.
9. An unsecured loan doesn't require a borrower to offer the lender any collateral to obtain the loan. Normally, only highly regarded customers, long-standing customers or customers considered financially stable, will receive an unsecured loan.
10. The primary purpose of a line of credit is to speed the borrowing process so that a firm doesn't have to go through the hassle of applying for a new loan every time it needs funds.
11. Commercial credit companies charge higher interest rates than commercial banks, because they are willing to accept higher degrees of risk than commercial banks.
12. In the process of factoring, a firm sells many of its products on credit to consumers and businesses, creating accounts receivable. Some of these buyers may be slow in paying their bills, causing the company to have a large amount of money due in accounts receivable. A factor is a market intermediary that agrees to buy the accounts receivable from the firm at a discount, for cash.
13. Small companies often cannot qualify for a loan, so they make use of factoring, or the sale of their accounts receivable, to raise needed cash.
14. Factoring can be less expensive if the small business selling its accounts receivable agrees to reimburse the factor for slow paying accounts. Factoring charges are even lower if the company assumes the risk of not collecting at all on some accounts.
15. Commercial paper is unsecured and is sold at public sales, so only financially stable firms, mainly large corporations, are able to sell it.
16. Commercial paper is a way to get short-term funds quickly and for less than bank interest rates. It is also an investment opportunity for buyers who can afford to put up cash for short periods to earn some interest.

Long-Term Financing

1. In business, long-term capital is used to buy fixed assets such as plant and equipment, and to finance expansion of the organization.

2. A major advantage of debt financing is that the interest paid on a long-term debt is tax deductible.
3. Long-term loans are often more expensive to the firm that short-term loans, because larger amounts of capital are borrowed. In addition, since the repayment period could be as long as 20 years, the lenders are not assured their capital will be repaid in full. Therefore, most long-term loans require some form of collateral.
4. To put it simply, a bond is like a company IOU with a promise to repay on a certain date. It is a binding contract through which an organization agrees to specific terms with investors, in return for investors lending money to the company.
5. Potential investors in bonds measure the risk involved in purchasing a bond with the return the bond promises to pay.
6. Two forms of equity financing are selling ownership in the firm in the form of stock, or using retained earnings the firm has reinvested in the business.
7. If a company uses debt financing, it has a legal obligation to repay the amount it has borrowed!
8. The risk/return tradeoff is the idea that the greater the risk a lender takes in granting a loan, the higher the rate of interest it requires.
9. A debenture is an unsecured bond, backed only by the reputation of the issuer.
10. The purchasers of stock become owners of the corporation – the shareholders are the owners.
11. Retained earnings are usually the most favoured source of meeting long-term capital needs, since the company saves interest payments, dividends, and any possible underwriting fees. There is also no dilution of ownership in the firm, which occurs with selling additional stock.
12. Venture capital is money that is invested in new companies with great profit potential.
13. The venture capital firm generally wants a stake in the ownership of the business. Venture capitalists also expect a very high return on their investment. It is also important that the venture capital firm be able to come up with and be willing to provide more financing if the firm needs it.
14. A key job of the finance manager or CFO is to forecast the need for and to manage borrowed funds.
15. If a firm's earnings are larger than the interest payments on the borrowed funds, then the business owners are realizing a higher rate of return than if they used equity financing.
16. a. Surplus cash
    b. Equity capital
    c. Debt capital
    d. Equity capital
    e. Debt capital
    f. Surplus cash
17. Joel's point to Eric is that when you sell stock to the public, the common stockholders get voting rights, and management must answer to the stockholders. Creditors, such as lending institutions or bondholders, generally have no say in running the business. The plus side of the equity financing is that there is no repayment obligation, as there is with debt financing, and the firm is not legally liable to pay dividends to the stockholders. Interest on debt is a legal obligation. However, the interest is tax deductible, whereas dividends are paid out of after-tax profits, and so are not deductible.
18. Leveraged buyouts occur when one firm purchases the assets of another using funds that were borrowed, either through selling bonds or obtaining loans, or a combination of both.

Securities Markets

1. Two major functions of securities markets are to help businesses find long-term funding and to give investors a place to buy and sell investments such as stocks and bonds.
2. Business benefit from securities markets by obtaining the capital they need to finance operations, expand their businesses, or buy goods and services.
3. Individuals benefit from the securities markets by having a convenient place to build their financial

future by buying and selling stocks, bonds, mutual funds, and other investments.

4. The primary market handles the sale of new securities. After the corporation has made their money on the sale of the securities, the secondary market handles the trading of securities between investors.

5. Companies normally prefer to meet long-term financial needs by using retained earnings, or by borrowing from a lending institution.

6. Investment bankers are specialists who assist in the issue and sale of new securities. They underwrite new issues, or in other words, the investment banker will buy the entire bond or stock issue a company wants to sell at an agreed upon discount and then sells the issue to private or institutional investors at full price.

7. Institutional investors are mutual funds, pension funds, insurance companies and banks. Because they have such large buying power, they are a powerful force in the securities markets.

Debt Financing Through Selling Bonds

1. By issuing bonds, a company has a legal obligation to pay regular interest payments to investors and repay the entire bond principal amount at a prescribed time, called the maturity date.

2. The interest rate paid on bonds is also called the bond's coupon rate.

3. A 10% bond with a maturity date of 2020 means that the bondholder will receive $100 in interest per year until the year 2020, when the full principal must be repaid.

4. The interest rate paid on a bond varies according to factors such as the state of the economy, the reputation of the company issuing the bond, and the going interest rate for government bonds or bonds of similar companies.

5. a. They provide for an orderly retirement of a bond issue.
   b. They reduce the risk of not being repaid, and so make the bond more attractive as an investment.
   d. They can support the market price of a bond because of reduced risk.

6. Unsecured bonds, called debentures, are not supported by any collateral. Generally, only firms with excellent credit ratings can issue debentures. The other class of bonds, secured bonds, are backed by some tangible asset, or collateral, that is pledged to the bondholder if bond interest isn't paid.

7. Callable bonds give companies some direction in long-term forecasting. The callable bond permits the bond issuer to pay off the bond's principal before its maturity date. The company can benefit if it can call in a bond issue that pays a high rate of interest, and reissue new bonds at a lower rate of interest.

8. If the firm's common stock grew in value over time, bondholders can compare the value of the bond's interest with the possibility of a sizable profit by converting to a specified number of common shares.

9. The finance manager of Music-stor has the opportunity to avoid the difficulties of a new issue by making use of specialists in the securities markets such as investment bankers. These companies will underwrite the new issue by purchasing the entire bond issue for a discount. The investment banker will then sell the issue on the open market to either private or institutional investors, such as pension funds, mutual funds, insurance companies, or banks.

10. a. Principal   e. Bond
    b. Maturity date   f. Call provision
    c. Unsecured bond   g. Secured bond
    d. Interest   h. Convertible bond

Equity Financing Through Issuing Stock

1. Interest on bonds is a legal obligation that the company must pay. It is a tax-deductible expense for the firm. Dividends are a part of a firm's profits that *may* be distributed to shareholders. Unlike bond interest, companies are not required to pay dividends.

2. Both preferred stock and bonds have a face (or par) value, and both have a fixed rate of return. Preferred stocks are rated by Standard & Poor's and Moody's Investment Service, just like bonds.

3. As debt, companies are legally bound to pay bond interest and must repay the face value of the bond on its maturity date. Even though preferred stock dividends are generally fixed, they do not legally have to be paid, and stock never has to be repurchased. Though both bonds and stock can increase in market value, the price of stock generally increases at a higher percentage than a bond.

4. Like bonds, preferred stock can be callable. This means a company could require preferred stockholders to sell back their shares. Preferred stock can also be convertible to common stock. An important feature of preferred stock is that it is often cumulative. If one or more dividends are not paid when due, the missed dividends of cumulative preferred stock will accumulate and be paid later.

5. The privileges of common stock include the right to vote for the board of directors and important issues affecting the company, and to share in the firm's profits through dividends declared by the board of directors.

6. a. i. Convertible preferred
      ii. Cumulative preferred
      iii. Common
      iv. Cumulative preferred
      v. Cumulative preferred

   b. The investor is guaranteed to receive dividends with cumulative preferred stock. If the company is unable to pay a dividend for one year, the dividend will carry over to the following year. This is not the case with non-cumulative preferred.

7. A stock certificate specifies the name of the company, the number of shares it represents, and the type of stock being issued. They will sometimes also indicate a par value.

Trading in Bonds and Stocks

1. If a margin rate is 50%, an investor may borrow 50% of the stock's purchase price from a broker.

2. If an investor's account goes down in market value, the broker will issue a margin call, requiring the investor to come up with more money to cover the losses the stock has suffered. If the investor is unable to make the margin call, the broker can legally sell shares of the investor's stock to reduce the broker's chance of loss.

3. Government bonds have the least possible risk, because they are a secure investment backed by the full faith and credit of the government.

4. According to investment analysts, the market price of a common stock is dependent upon the overall performance of the corporation in meeting its business objectives. If a company reaches its stated objectives, there are opportunities for capital gains.

5. The benefit of a mutual fund to an investor is that they can buy shares of the mutual fund and share in the ownership of many different companies they could not afford to invest in individually. Thus mutual funds help investors diversify, and provide professional investment management.

6. a. Common stock
   b. Stock certificate
   c. Dividends
   d. Preferred stock
   e. Stock
   f. Blue chip stocks
   g. Stock broker
   h. Buying on margin

7. a. Collateral trust bond
   b. Zero-coupon bond
   c. Debenture
   d. Mortgage bond
   e. Convertible bond
   f. Coupon bonds
   g. Equipment trust bond

Cycles in the Stock Market and Interest Rates

1. On October 19, 1987, the stock market suffered the largest one-day drop in its history, up to that time. The Dow Jones Industrial Average fell 508 points. In October of 1997, and April of 2000,

the Dow fell again, by even larger amounts. The market continued to drop in 2000, and in 2001.
2. Many analysts believe that program trading was a big cause of the stock market drop in 1987. In program trading, investors give computers instructions to automatically sell if the price of their stock dips to a certain price, to avoid potential losses.
3. Lessons to be learned are the importance of diversifying your investments and understanding the risks of investing with borrowed money that may have to be repaid quickly when prices fall. It is also wise to take a long-term perspective.

CHAPTER CHECK ANSWERS

1. a. Poor cash flow
    b. Undercapitalization
    c. Inadequate expense control
2. a. Planning   e. Collecting funds
    b. Budgeting   f. Auditing
    c. Obtaining funds   g. Managing taxes
    d. Controlling funds   h. Advising top management
3. a. Forecasting financial needs, long and short term
    b. Developing budgets to meet those needs
    c. Establish financial control
4. a. Operating budget
    b. Cash budget
    c. Capital budget
5. a. Financing daily operations
    b. Financing firm's credit services
    c. Financing the purchase of inventory
    d. Financing the purchase of major assets
6. a. Short-term financing comes from funds used to finance current operations which will be repaid in less than one year. Long-term financing comes from owners and lenders who will be repaid over a time period longer than one year.
    b. Debt capital is raised through borrowing. Equity capital is raised within the company or from selling
        stock.
7. a. Trade credit   d. Factoring   g. Government programs
    b. Family and friends   e. Commercial paper
    c. Commercial banks   f. Internal sources
8. How much a business borrows and for how long depends on the kind of business it is and how quickly the merchandise purchased with a bank loan can be resold or used to generate funds.
9. a. Get an unsecured loan
    b. Get a secured loan
    c. Apply for a line of credit
10. a. What are the long-term goals and objectives of the organization?
    b. What are the financial requirements needed to achieve those long-term goals and objectives?
    c. What sources of long-term capital are available and which will best fit our needs?
11. a. Sale of bonds
    b. Long-term loans from financial institutions
12. a. Sale of stock to existing owners
    b. Sale of stock to public
    c. Venture capital companies

d. Business Development Bank of Canada
13. a. Stocks
    b. Bonds
14. a. Advantages to the corporation
       i. Bondholders have no vote
       ii. Interest paid on bonds is tax deductible
       iii. The debt is temporary. Bonds are repaid and debt eliminated.
    b. Disadvantages to the corporation
       i. Increase in debt
       ii. Legal obligation to pay interest
       iii. Principal (face value) must be paid
15. a. First mortgage bonds
    b. Collateral trust bonds
    c. Equipment trust bonds
    d. Zero-coupon bonds
16. a. Collateral trust   d. Debenture
    b. Convertible bond   e. Mortgage bond
    c. Coupon bond   f. Zero-coupon bond
17. a. Advantages
       i. Investment doesn't have to be repaid
       ii. No obligation to pay dividends
       iii. Improves the condition of the balance sheet
    b. Disadvantages
       i. Loss of some control due to stockholder voting
       ii. Paying dividends is more costly than paying interest
       iii. Decisions must be made to keep stockholders happy
18. a. common stock
    b. preferred stock
19. Preferred stock is issued generally with a par value. The par value becomes the basis for the pre-
    ferred dividend. Preferred dividends are generally fixed, and must be paid in full before any common
    stock dividends can be distributed. As a result of the preferred treatment, preferred stockholders
    normally lose their voting rights. Common stock dividends are declared by the board of directors.
20. a. income
    b. security
    c. growth
21. Mutual funds offer smaller investors and beginning investors a way to diversify the risk of investing in
    stocks and bonds.
22. a. Toronto
    b. Montreal
    c. Vancouver
    d. Calgary
    e. Winnipeg

PRACTICE TEST

Multiple Choice		True/False	
1.	d	1.	F
2.	a	2.	T
3.	c	3.	F
4.	a	4.	T
5.	d	5.	T
6.	a	6.	F
7.	b	7.	T
8.	d	8.	F
9.	a	9.	T
10.	d	10.	T
11.	d	11.	F
12.	a	12.	T
13.	b	13.	T
14.	a	14.	F
15.	c	15.	F
16.	d	16.	F
17.	a	17.	T
18.	b	18.	T
19.	b	19.	F
20.	c	20.	T
		21.	T
		22.	F
		23.	T
		24.	T

Getting Ready for Prime Time

Never cruised the World Wide Web? What to learn some basic tips? The purpose of this Appendix is to help ease novices toward the on-ramp to the information superhighway. If you are an experienced Internet user, you may just want to skim this material for features you haven't used yet. The material is arranged in a question-and-answer format so that you can easily jump to a topic you would like to know more about. Don't worry if you have never so much as pressed an Enter key—we won't get too technical for you. You don't have to understand the technical complexities of the Internet to travel on the information superhighway. But, as in learning to drive, it's usually a good idea to learn which end of the car to put the gas in.

Technology changes so quickly that writing about how to use the Internet is like washing the windows of a skyscraper—as soon as you're finished it's time to start over again. For this reason we've tried to keep the discussion as general as possible and not give too many specific steps that may be out of date by the time you read this. The important thing to remember is that you can't break anything on the information superhighway, so just jump right in, explore the online world, and have fun!

What Is the Internet?

The Internet is a network of networks. It involves tens of thousands of interconnected computer networks that include millions of host computers. The Internet is certainly not new. The U.S. Pentagon began the network in 1969 when the world feared that a nuclear war would paralyze communications. The computer network was developed to reach far-flung terminals even if some connections were broken. The system took on a life of its own, however, and grew as scientists and other academics used it to share data and electronic mail. No one owns the Internet. There is no central computer; each message you send from your computer has an address code that lets any other computer in the Internet forward it to its destination. There is no Internet manager. The closest thing to a governing body is the Internet Society in Reston, Virginia. This is a volunteer organization of individuals and corporate members who promote Internet use and oversee development of new communication software.

What Is the World Wide Web, and How Is It Different from the Internet?

The World Wide Web (WWW, or the Web) is a means of accessing, organizing, and moving through the information in the Internet. Therefore, the Web is part of the Internet. Think of the Internet as a gigantic library and the Web as the Dewey Decimal System. Until the creation of the World Wide Web in 1993, it was as though that gigantic library simply threw all of its books and other materials into mountainous piles. If you wanted to find something on the Internet, you needed to type in a complex code representing the exact address of the site you wanted.

The basic difficulty of navigating the Internet without the Web is twofold: (1) the traffic signs on the Internet are written in Unix, and (2) there is no defined structure for organizing information. Unix is an operating system that was designed long before anyone thought of the term *user-friendly*. And since the Internet does not require a prescribed structure for entering information, even experienced users have difficulty retrieving information without a tool like the Web.

When the Web evolved, the game changed. Not only did the Web add graphics and sound, which breathed life into the dreary text-only Internet, but it also made navigating parts of the Internet easy even for beginners. Now Web cruisers don't need to know Unix in order to travel the Net. You can go from place to place on the Web simply by clicking on a word or a picture called *hypertext*. Hypertext allows any part of the document to be linked to any other document, no matter where it is, allowing you to jump around from place to place with a click of the mouse. Hypertext links are usually shown in a contrasting color on the computer screen. *Cruising* or *surfing* means following hypertext links from page to page on the Web.

What Do I Need to Be Able to Get on the Web?

The first thing you need in order to cruise the information superhighway is a computer with a modem (a device that connects your computer with other computers via phone lines) and a Web browser. There are other ways to connect to the Internet, but until they become more widely available, more economical, and/or more user-friendly, most of us will use modems and standard phone lines to access the Net. Many schools offer students Internet service, so check out what is available at your school. You may have already paid computer-service fees that include Internet connection, so get your money's worth and get on-line now. If you can't connect through your school, you can connect to the Net by signing up with an Internet service provider (ISP). Your ISP will give you the phone number and a set of directions for connecting your computer to the Net. At this time most ISPs provide unlimited access to the Internet for a flat monthly fee.

What Is a Web Browser?

A Web browser is a program or application that provides you with a way to access the World Wide Web. The first graphical Web browser that allowed pointing and clicking was Mosaic, developed by Eric Bina and Marc Andreessen at the National Center for Supercomputing Applications. Andreessen, an undergraduate at the time, later went on to fame and fortune as the developer of Netscape Navigator. Mosaic was based on a code written by Tim Berners-Lee of CERN, the European laboratory for particle physics.

Which Is the Best Browser?

Currently, the two most popular Web browsers are Netscape Navigator and Microsoft Internet Explorer. At the time of this writing, the best browser is the one you have access to—in other words, neither has a clear advantage over the other. The case may be different by the time you read this. If we had to predict the future, we would have to say that both Netscape and Microsoft will continue to improve their browsers to compete with each other and that Web users will benefit from the competition as the browsers become more powerful and easier to use.

Why Would I Want to Cruise the Internet?

You can use the Internet to do the following:
] *Communicate online.* You can communicate with others through the following:
News groups. These are special-interest groups through which you can get advice or just share thoughts with people.
Electronic mail (e-mail). E-mail lets you stay in touch with friends, trade files, and do business, all from the comfort of your computer desktop.
Internet relay chat (IRC). IRCs allow you to chat with other people all over the world in real time (that is, talk with someone else while you are both on the line rather than send messages that are read later). Live and uncensored, IRC can sometimes sound like a junior high school boys' locker room, so choose your chats wisely.
] *Gather information.* Internet users can tap into such diverse institutions as Statistics Canada and the International Monetary Fund. Some Web sites offer news headlines, stock market information, access to encyclopedias, and other databases. Search engines can help you find the sites that

have the information you need. There are special Web sites that offer push technology that makes gathering information automatic: after you tell it what you are interested in, the program searches the Web periodically and then pushes the information to you without your having to ask for it.

] *Shop*. Forgot you mom's birthday? No problem. Get on-line and order roses to be delivered to her door before she disinherits you. Or, if things get too bad, book a flight out of town with a few mouse clicks and a credit card number. Note, however, that credit card security is a concern that is getting lots of attention as more and more businesses open their doors to customers on the Internet.

] *Play games (after you finish studying, of course)*. You can play games against another person or against the computer while you're online.

Can You Tell Me How to Cruise the Web Without Turning Me into a Computer Major?

There are only four simple things you need to know about to navigate the Web: (1) Web addresses, (2) directories and search engines, (3) links, and (4) the Back Page button.

What are Web Addresses?

Every Web site has an address called a uniform resource locator (URL). To get to any Web site, you just type its address in the space for the URL entry in your Web browser. This means, of course, that you know the exact URL. It is important to know that the Web is constantly evolving and therefore URLs often change as new sites are added and old ones dropped. Sometimes a new URL is supplied when you visit an old site, but often it is not, in which case you reach a dead end.

What If I Don't Know Which Site I Need, Much Less its URL?

To find topics that interest you, you can use one of several Web directories or search engines. Once you are at a search engine's home page, all you have to do is enter the key words for the topic you want and you will quickly receive a list of links to sites related to your request. Some of the most popular directories and search engines are Yahoo! (*www.yahoo.com*), Infoseek (*www.infoseek.com*), Lycos (*www.lycos.com*), Alta Vista (*www.altavista.com*), Excite (*www.excite.com*), and Web Crawler (*www.webcrawler.com*).

What Do I Need to Know about Links?

Once you're at a site, the two main ways to cruise around are by clicking on an icon button link or on a text link. One way to tell if something is a link is to place your cursor over the graphic icon or text. If it changes into a hand, then you know it is a live link. When you click on a link, you will be sent to another Web site or to another page on the current Web site.

What If I Want to Get Back to Someplace I've Been?

If you want to go back to a site you have left recently, you can just click on the Back Page button in your browser. This will lead you back through the exact same page route you travelled before. Or you can enter the desired site's URL. If you are on the same Web site, you can choose the home page link or one of the section icons to take you back to the home page or another section.

Where Do I Go When I Click on Something?

When you're navigating the Net, you can go from a Web page in Paris to one in Peru. What happens? When you click on a link, your computer sends out a request for information to another server. That

server, which may be next door or across the planet, interprets your request, finds the information (text, graphics, or entire Web pages), and then breaks it up into packets. The server sends the packets to your computer,
where your browser puts them back together and you see the Web page, all in the blink of an eye (or an eternity—they don't call it the World Wide Wait for nothing).

Why Does It Take So Long to Move from One Place to Another on the Web?

The speed with which you reach other Internet sites depends not only on the speed and size of your phone line and computer but also on the speed and size of phone lines and computers at the other site. You won't get to class any faster in a Ferrari than in a bus if you're locked in a traffic jam. The same is true on the information superhighway. Sometimes your computer will seem to take forever to get to a site or to open an image. If this happens, you can click the Stop button on your menu bar and try again later when the Internet may be less busy.

How Can I Communicate with Others Online?

You can reach out and touch your fellow Internet surfers via newsgroups, e-mail, or an IRC.

What are Newsgroups?

The Usenet is a global network of discussion groups known as newsgroups. Newsgroups are collections of messages from people all over the world on any subject you can imagine (and some you'd rather not imagine). Newsgroups are divided into categories indicated by the first letters of their name. There are many different category prefixes, but the main ones you will see are comp (computer), sci (science), rec (recreation), soc (society), and alt (alternative). Under these headings are thousands of subcategories from alt.alien.visitors to za.humour.

How Do I Join a Newsgroup?

Web browsers have built-in newsreading capabilities. You first need to go to the Mail and News options menu and enter your server information, which is usually something like "news.myserver.com" (contact your Internet service provider to find out exactly what it is). There are also options for organizing how you read your messages. Some people like their messages "threaded" (meaning all postings on a particular topic are grouped together), while others prefer to sort their messages by date.

When you find a group you like, don't jump into the conversation right away. Take time to read the Frequently Asked Questions (FAQ) list for that group first. The FAQ list includes the questions that most newcomers ask. After you read the FAQs, you should read at least a week's worth of postings to get a feel for the group and what kinds of discussions its members have. Remember, you may be joining discussions that have been going on for a year or more, so you may feel like the new kid on the block for a while. Most newsgroups are quite friendly if you follow these few basic rules.

How Do I Sent E-mail?

As with "snail mail" delivered by the Canadian postal system, e-mail is delivered to its recipient by an address. An Internet e-mail address has two parts: the user name and the name of the computer on which that user has an account. For example, Professor Ulysses R. Smart's e-mail address at Brant University may be ursmart@brant.ca. The symbol "@" is pronounced "at." The suffix "ca" indicates that the address is in Canada.

There are several e-mail software packages available. Netscape and Internet Explorer include e-mail capabilities. To compose a message, click on the Mail button. Enter the e-mail address of the person to whom you are writing in the To field. Enter the subject of your message in the Subject field. If you want others to receive the message, enter their e-mail address in the CC field and separate each e-mail address with a comma. Next, enter the body of the message in the large space. When you have completed your message, click on the Send button. To check for new messages received, simply click on the Get Mail button. If you have received new mail, the subject and sender will be displayed in a window. Click on a message to display its contents.

You can also send files with your e-mail. To send files from a graphics program or word processor, simply choose Attach File and navigate your hard drive to find the file you want to send.

One of the more interesting ways to take advantage of e-mail is to join one or more mailing lists (or listservs, to use the technical term).

What are Listservs?

Listservs, or mailing lists, are similar to Usenet newsgroups. Unlike newsgroups, though, listserv discussions are delivered to your in-box as e-mail, and responding is as easy as punching your Reply button (which sends the message to everyone on the mailing list). To find a mailing list that piques your interest, try the mailing list directory Listz at *www.listz.com*. Be careful, though, mailing lists can quickly jam your in-box.

What is IRC?

Internet relay chat (IRC) is an Internet protocol that allows you to have real-time conversations with other people around the world. As with newsgroups, it's best at first to observe, or "lurk," and see how the others on the IRC channel interact. To use an IRC channel you must have a chat "client" or program. The two most popular freeware chat clients are PIRCH for Windows and Ircle for the Mac.

The first step is to connect to a server. Then choose a nickname, join a room (or "channel"), and start lurking away. All IRC channels start with a # sign, and most servers have a channel called #newbie where you can ease into the swing of things.

There are Web sites devoted to some of the more popular IRC networks such as DalNet, AnotherNet, and the UnderNet. All of them have extensive information on IRC and how to use it. Not all IRC is idle chat. Many people have discovered ways to use IRC to help one another by developing virtual support groups on-line. Talk City is one example of an on-line community that uses IRC as a vehicle for people to draw support in a safe and friendly environment.

IRC is one of the most popular uses for the Internet, but could easily be replaced by Internet phones, or more advanced Web chat, like America Online's Virtual Places (VP). VP's attraction is that you create an on-screen avatar, or 3-D representation of yourself. Then you can go to designated Web pages and chat with other people who have VP.

How Do You Use Search Engines?

You'll always get better results from a search engine if you define what you're searching for as specifically as possible. The two easiest ways to narrow your search are by adding and subtracting terms from your search string. Let's say you want to read more about the death of Princess Diana. If you search Yahoo! for Princess Di, you may get back 78 (or more) site matches. However, you can focus the search a little more by adding another search word. Just typing in the word itself isn't good enough, though. In order to receive only sites that contain both Princess Di and the other word, you have to use the word *and* to link them. If you search for "and death," you get four matches—all memorials to the princess.

If adding search items doesn't narrow the field enough, try subtracting them—tell the search engine what *not* to look for. Say you're looking for business opportunities. You search for *business and opportunity* and get overwhelmed by more than 2,500 site matches, most of which are Amway-type, multilevel marketing operations (commonly known as MLMs). You can narrow your search by asking for these items to be excluded. For example, use the word *not* instead of *and*. This time you search for *business and opportunity not mlm* and get just seven items back.

A third way to define your search more closely is to put your search term in quotes. That tells the search engine that you're looking for exactly those words in exactly that order.

Don't worry about remembering all these surfing tips. Most search engines have an Advanced Options menu that lists ways to search using a form. Also, many search engines offer specific instructions on how to make the most of your search on their site.

If you try different search engines to look for the same topic, you'll get different results. That's because the search engines are different. Each search engine uses its own program (called a bot or crawler) to search the Web. Not only do these programs use different methods of searching and indexing, but they start from different points on the Web. You probably will also get different results if you search on a directory rather than a search engine, again because of the different approach to indexing sites.

Do I Have to Be Online to Surf the Web?

Why watch and wait for your favourite sites to download when you can browse while you sleep? You can do this using a program like Freeloader, Pointcast, Webwacker, or After Dark Online. These programs allow you to set a time and a list of Web sites, and the program goes to work, downloading page after page, graphic after graphic, and leaving them neatly on your desktop, to be surfed at your leisure.

Where Can I Go to Learn More About the Web?

The best way to learn how to do something is by doing it, so the best place to learn about the Web is on the Web. it's time for you to put the pedal to the metal and get yourself onto the information superhighway. The following Web sites can help you learn more about the Web:

Newbie-U (New User University): *www.newbie-u.com*
How Do I Explore the Web?: *www.squareonetech.com/hdiesplor.html*
Cyberspace Companion: *www.w3aces.uiuc.edu/AIM/scale*
Learn the Net: *www.learnthenet.com*
Exploring the World Wide Web: *www.gactruga.edu/exploring*

What Is the Internet?

1. What is the Internet?

_____

_____

_____

_____

2. What is the World Wide Web?

_____

_____

_____

_____

3. What are two basic difficulties in navigating the Internet without the Web?

a. _____

b. _____

4. What did the Web add to the Internet?

_____

_____

_____

_____

5. What does hypertext allow for?

_____

_____

_____

_____

What Do I Need to Be Able to Get on the Web?

6. What two devices do you need to cruise the information highway?

_____

_____

_____

_____

7. What are some ways that you can have access to the Net?

_____

_____

_____

_____

8. Describe a Web browser.

_____

_____

_____

_____

9. What were the two most popular Web browsers at the time the text was written?

_____

_____

_____

_____

Why Would I Want to Cruise the Internet?

10. What are six uses for the Internet?

a. _____   d. _____

b. _____   e. _____

c. _____   f. _____

How Do I Cruise the Web?

11. What are the four things you need to know about to navigate the Web?

a. _____

b. _____

c. _____

d. _____

12. What does URL stand for, and what is a URL?

_____
_____
_____
_____

13. What are the most popular search engines?

_____
_____
_____
_____

14. How do you move around a site?

_____
_____
_____
_____

15. How do you get back to a previous site after having left?

_____
_____
_____
_____

16. What determines the speed with which you reach Internet sites?

_____
_____
_____
_____

17. What are newsgroups?

_____
_____
_____
_____

18. What are some things you should do before joining a newsgroup?

_____
_____
_____
_____

19. What are the two parts of an e-mail address?

_____

_____

_____

_____

20. List the steps to compose an e-mail message.

   a. _____   d. _____

   b. _____   e. _____

   c. _____   f. _____

21. How do you check for new e-mail messages?

_____

_____

_____

_____

22. What are listservs?

_____

_____

_____

_____

23. How do you join a chat room (i.e., have a real-time conversation with other people)?

   a. _____

   b. _____

   c. _____

24. What are the best ways to use a search engine?

   a. _____

   b. _____

   c. _____

25. Describe the development of the Internet.

_____

_____

_____

_____

26. What impact do you think the Internet has had, or will have, on the global marketplace?

_____

_____

_____

_____

PRACTICE TEST

Multiple Choice: Circle the best answer.

1. Workers at the Acquatech Corp. send and receive hundreds of e-mail messages every day. They collaborate with scientists at labs around the world, and keep abreast of the latest developments in their field by accessing various news and discussion groups. This is possible because Acquatech's workers have access to millions of interconnected networks known as the
   a. Compunet
   b. Electronic Village
   c. World Wide Web
   d. Internet

2. _____ owns the Internet.
   a. The government
   b. A consortium of multinational corporations
   c. A group of researchers and scientists
   d. No one

3. One of the basic difficulties of navigating the Internet is
   a. there are too many computers on it.
   b. it is difficult to retrieve information without some kind of tool.
   c. there isn't enough information on the Internet to make it worth the effort at this point.
   d. there are no addresses.

4. The _____ is a means of accessing, organizing, and moving through the information on the Internet.
   a. modem
   b. search engine Excite
   c. World Wide Web
   d. Internet manager

5. The earliest users of the Internet were
   a. researchers and scientists.
   b. corporations as a way of selling and advertising.
   c. computer manufacturers.
   d. members of the media.

6. Which of the following would NOT be considered a use of the Internet?
   a. Communicate on-line
   b. Electronic mail
   c. Shopping
   d. Word processing

7. A URL is
   a. a type of software need to cruise the Net.
   b. an Internet address.
   c. a piece of hardware needed to access the Net.
   d. a Web browser.

8. The speed with which you reach an Internet site depends upon
   a. the type of Web browser you are using.
   b. the speed and size of your phone line and computer.
   c. the area of the country in which you are located.
   d. which Internet you are using.

9. Which of the following is NOT a step in sending e-mail?
   a. Enter the e-mail address of the person to whom you are writing.
   b. Type in the message.
   c. Alert the person to whom you are sending a message that a message is coming in.
   d. Click on the Send button.
10. Which of the following is NOT included in suggestions on using a search engine more effectively?
   a. adding more terms from your search string
   b. subtracting terms from the search string
   c. putting the search term in quotes
   d. deleting spaces between words to make the string shorter

True/False

1. The Internet is relatively new, and has only been around since the early 1990s.
2. There is a central computer which controls all the activities on the Internet.
3. The World Wide Web is a way of navigating the Internet.
4. The first thing you need in order to cruise the information highway is a computer with a modem.
5. Once you are on a Web site, you have to go to a home page before going to another site.
6. Credit card security is not a major concern for shoppers on the Internet.
7. Before you can join a newsgroup, you need to fill out an application.
8. One way to narrow a search is by inserting "and" between the words you are using to search.

ANSWERS

What Is the Internet?

1. The Internet is a network of networks. It involves thousands of interconnected computer networks that include millions of host computers.
2. The World Wide Web is a means of accessing, organizing, and moving through the information in the Internet. Therefore, the Web is part of the Internet.
3. a. The traffic signs on the Internet are written in Unix.
   b. There is no defined structure for organizing information.
4. The Web added graphics and sound to the Internet. It also made navigating parts of the Internet easier.
5. Hypertext allows any part of any document to be linked to any other document, no matter where it is. This allows you to jump around from place to place on the Internet with only a click of the mouse.

What Do I Need to Be Able to Get on the Web?

6. In order to cruise the information superhighway, you need a computer with a modem and a Web browser.
7. You can access the Net through schools, or with an Internet service provider.
8. A Web browser is a program or application that provides you with a way to access the World Wide Web.
9. The two most popular Web browsers are (were) Netscape Navigator and Microsoft Internet Explorer.

Why Would I Want to Cruise the Internet?

10. a. Communicate on-line
    b. Newsgroups
    c. Electronic mail (e-mail)
    d. Internet relay chat (IRC)
    e. Shop
    f. Play games

How Do I Cruise the Web?

11. a. Web addresses
    b. directories and search engines
    c. links
    d. Back Page button
12. URL stands for *uniform resource locator.* It is the address for a Web site.
13. The most popular search engines are Yahoo!, Infoseek, Lycos, Alta Vista, Excite, and WebCrawler.
14. Once you're at a site, the two main ways to cruise around are by clicking on an icon button link or on a text link.
15. If you want to go back to a site you have recently left, you can just click on the Back Page button in your browser, or you can enter the desired site's URL.
16. The speed with which you reach other Internet sites depends not only on the speed and size of your phone line and computer but also on the speed and size of phone lines and computers at the other site.
17. Newsgroups are collections of messages from people all over the world on any subject you can imagine. Newsgroups are divided into categories indicated by the first letters of their name.
18. Before joining a newsgroup, you should take time to read the Frequently Asked Questions list for that group. After you read the FAQs, you should read at least a week's worth of postings to get a feel for the group and what kinds of discussions its members have.
19. The two parts of an e-mail address are the user name and the name of the computer on which that user has an account.
20. To compose an e-mail message, do the following:
    a. Click on the Mail button.
    b. Enter the e-mail address of the person to whom you are writing.
    c. Enter the subject of your message in the subject field.
    d. Enter the addresses of others whom you want to receive the message in the CC field.
    e. Enter the body of the message.
    f. When you have completed the message, click on the Send button.
21. To check for new e-mail messages, click on the Get Mail button.
22. Listservs are mailing lists that are similar to Usenet newsgroups. However, listserv discussions are delivered to your In-box as e-mail.
23. To join a chat room or IRC you need to
    a. connect to a server.
    b. choose a nickname.
    c. join a room (or channel).
24. To use a search engine effectively, do the following:
    a. Add words appropriate to what you are searching for linked with an "and."
    b. Subtract words from your search by using "not."
    c. Put your search terms in quotes.

25. The U.S. Pentagon began a network in 1969 when the world feared that a nuclear war would paralyze communications. The computer network was developed to reach far-flung terminals even if some connections were broken. The search began to change as scientists and academics used it to share data and electronic mail. No one owns the Internet, and there is no central computer. There is no Internet manager.

26. The Internet allows for a fast, economical, and efficient method of communicating. Companies around the world can keep track of operations and keep in touch with employees anywhere with the ease of a mouse click. The Internet also enables companies to reach customers around the world through advertising and sales.

PRACTICE TEST

Multiple Choice		True/False	
1.	d	1.	F
2.	d	2.	F
3.	b	3.	T
4.	c	4.	T
5.	a	5.	F
6.	d	6.	F
7.	b	7.	F
8.	b	8.	T
9.	c		
10.	d		